Albertus C. Van Raalte

Dutch Leader and American Patriot

JEANNE M. JACOBSON

ELTON J. BRUINS

LARRY J. WAGENAAR

HOPE COLLEGE   HOLLAND, MICHIGAN

Albertus C. Van Raalte: Dutch Leader and American Patriot
Jeanne M. Jacobson, Elton J. Bruins, Larry J. Wagenaar

© 1996 by Hope College
ISBN: 0-9634061-1-6

Hope College
Holland, Michigan 49423

Copies may be purchased through
Hope-Geneva Bookstore
Hope College
Holland, Michigan 49422-9000

Library of Congress Cataloging-in-Publication Data: ISBN: 0-9634061-1-6

printed in the United States of America

to

Peter H. Huizenga

Hope College, 1960

Benefactor

*who, in honoring his heritage,
benefits posterity*

Contents

*** Citations, sources, and comments on information in the text
are provided chapter by chapter, in the Endnotes section.**

Had he been placed by by Providence at the head of a nation, he would have made a wise and powerful ruler.

He was a short man. All the records and reminiscences agree on that point. When he was in his twenties, an official document summarized his appearance: *small stature, healthy color, blue eyes, round face, brown hair, brown beard.* Some thirty years later, another document also recorded a formal description: Age: *54 years.* Stature: *5 feet 3 inches. English.* Forehead: *high and broad.* Eyes: *blue.* Nose: *prominent.* Mouth: *medium.* Chin: *small.* Hair: *brown.* Complexion: *light.* Face: *medium.*

In 1866 the short man with a medium face carried a United States passport for himself and his wife — "to all to whom these Presents shall come Greeting" — stamped with the signature of William Seward, Secretary of State. They were sailing to visit the Netherlands, where, in the small city of Zwolle, in the northern province of Overijssel, the earlier of these two descriptions of Albertus Christiaan Van Raalte is recorded, in the registers of the city jail.

The distance between two Hollands — a small country in Europe and a small city in America — is over five thousand miles. With each technological advance in transportation, that distance, in terms of time and trouble required to travel it, grows less; but one hundred and fifty years ago a transatlantic voyage, which Albertus and Christina Van Raalte took three times, was long and arduous. The distance between a jail cell and an honored place in history cannot be measured in miles, and few people travel that course. This book tells the story of such a journey.

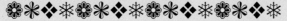

REV. ALBERTUS C VAN RAALTE, D.D.

No name is more widely known and respected in Ottawa County than that of the father of the Dutch settlements. He has imprinted himself on its history, and a hundred years hence his name will stand out in still bolder relief that it does to-day; for as the fruition of his life becomes more apparent his fame will increase.

Portrait and Biographical Record of Muskegon and Ottawa Counties Michigan, **1893**

1

One of the many scholars who has written about Albertus Van Raalte has pointed out a surprising fact: he was "born a Frenchman, grew up a Dutchman, and died as an American." Every history of Europe explains this oddity, often at length, but the situation was most neatly summarized by Hendrik Willem Van Loon, in *Van Loon's Geography: The Story of the World.*

> *Napoleon, who knew only as much geography as he needed to win his battles, claimed that since the Low Countries were merely a delta formed by three French rivers, the Rhine, the Meuse and the Scheldt, the country belonged by right of geographical descent to the empire of the French. A large N scrawled at the bottom of a piece of paper undid the work of three entire centuries. Holland disappeared from the map and became a French province.*

The years immediately before and after the turn of the nineteenth century were stormy times. In France the Revolution of 1789 escalated into the Reign of Terror in 1793. In the following year the French invaded the Netherlands and in 1795 Willem V, stadtholder of Holland, escaped with his family to England. French revolutionaries were enthusiastic re-namers, and they imposed a new name on the occupied country: the Batavian Republic. Centuries before, the Batavi were a small tribe with primitive ways and weapons, living in lowland territory near the northeastern coast of the European continent. They had no written language, so it is impossible to know how long the Batavi had lived in their isolated and somewhat damp homeland before the Romans took over in the first century A.D. The French decided that the Dutch ought to be called *les Bataves.*

In the same year that France invaded the Netherlands, Napoleon Bonaparte began his rise to power. In 1804, the charismatic, megalomaniac young general — like Albertus Van Raalte, a notably short man — was proclaimed emperor by the Senate and Tribunate of France. At his magnificent coronation ceremony, when Pope Pius VII reached out to place the crown on his head, Napoleon took it from the pope, and crowned himself. He continued to march triumphantly at the head of his armies, conquering country after country. As he did so, he made his brothers kings. Louis Bonaparte was awarded the Kingdom of Holland in 1806.

Louis was married to his brother's step-daughter, Henrietta Beauharnais, a marriage unwillingly entered into by both parties. A biographer has written that "while his actions in private life were hardly those of a sane man, as a sovereign he was beyond reproach and soon gained the affection of his people." The same excellent biographer contradicts himself within the same paragraph, quoting the reproach Napoleon sent to his brother in 1807: "I advise you to cultivate in private life that paternal and pliant character you display in government and to apply to public business the severity you show in your household." Louis did not change his ways in private or in public — the latter were of greater concern to Napoleon — and he continued in his actions as sovereign to favor the interests of his new country, rather than those of France. Two years later, Napoleon gave his brother an ultimatum: unless all Dutch ports were immediately closed to English ships, Holland would be annexed to France. French troops advanced and occupied Dutch territory; Louis abdicated, fled the country and "did not halt in his flight until he had reached the baths of Teplitz in Bohemia." Holland then went out of existence for a time, and became a province of France, its former provinces downgraded to *départements.* What had once been the province of Overijssel became, in 1810, *le Département des Bouches de l'Issel,* and there, in 1811, Albertus Christiaan Van Raalte II was born, in the town of Wanneperveen, where his father was minister of the Hervormde Kerk.

As is often the case with people who become famous through their own efforts rather then because of their family position, information about young Van Raalte's early life is scanty. He was the eleventh of the seventeen children of Albertus Christiaan and Catharina Christina

Harking Van Raalte, and many of his siblings died young. An early school certificate, printed in Latin, announces that "the excellent youth Albertus Christiaan van Raalte studied with us in the gymnasium for two years, applying himself chiefly to Latin and Greek, but also to mathematics, geography, and history, both modern and ancient. He was industrious, and a young man of excellent morals." One biographer reports that as a child little Albertus raised rabbits and that he — and the rabbits — were so successful that they undermined the parsonage in which the Van Raalte family lived. Such a peaceful picture of childhood and youth contrasts with the tumultuous period of history in the old world he was born into, and the new world to which he would come.

In that new world, as the nineteenth century opened, the United States consisted of sixteen states (Vermont, Kentucky and Tennessee had joined the original thirteen) and territories extending westward to the Mississippi River. By the terms of the Northwest Ordinance, passed by Congress in 1787, a system of government for the Northwest Territory had been established, providing for administration by five Congressional appointees: governor, secretary, and three judges. Progress toward statehood would occur as population increased, with population being defined as the number of adult white males. Ohio became a state in 1803; the remainder of the area became the Indiana territory out of which the Michigan territory was created in 1805.

> *Although the inhabitants of the Michigan Territory did not participate in national elections at this period, they did not suffer from a lack of political activity. ...President Jefferson appointed William Hull, Yale graduate and Massachusetts officer in the Revolution, governor, Stanley Griswold, secretary and Augustus B. Woodward, Frederick Bates and John Griffin, judges. None of these men, excepting Judge Bates, had lived in the west. They were confronted with the dual task of rebuilding Detroit, which had been completely destroyed by fire on June 11, 1805, and establishing the new government. A code of laws was prepared, the tangle of land claims taken up, and a bank chartered.*

The qualifications needed by administrators in a chaotic situation — vast stretches of wilderness and a capital city razed by fire — do not seem to have been considered by Jefferson in making his first appointments. Hull was an egotistical autocrat; in creating a militia he named himself major general, designed elaborate uniforms, and had some citizens of Detroit who did not purchase them arrested and flogged. (Officers were to wear cocked hats with black plumes tipped with red, long blue coats trimmed with red and white, red sashes, and silver epaulettes; riflemen were to wear short green coats and tan capes, green feathers in their caps, and white pantaloons when it was warm, green and tan pantaloons when it was cold.)

Secretary Griswold was a minister whose parishioners disapproved of his ideas, which they believed to be atheistic; Judge Bates resigned in 1806 to become secretary of the Louisiana Territory. Until 1808, there were often four, rather than five, territorial officials, and they tended to separate into pairs and quarrel if they were not quarreling individually. Augustus Elias Brevoort Woodward, variously described as "brilliant and erratic" and "cantankerous and crafty," served longest: from 1805 to 1824. With a flair reminiscent of Hull's attention to militia uniforms, though exercised in a better cause, he designed a statewide system of public education, the "Catholepistemiad or University of Michigania," where thirteen didactors would represent every branch of learning. (In his early years as territorial judge, Woodward wrote *A System of Universal Science*, arranging all human knowledge into thirteen classifications.) Lewis Cass, when he became governor, called Woodward's brainchild "Cathole-what's-it's-name," and simplified human knowledge further by appointing only two didactors, but he and his successors did advance the cause of education, and one of the first laws passed after Michigan became a state established the University of Michigan, with free tuition for state residents, but a $10 admission fee.

While the sophisticated administrators in the eastern part of the territory dealt with lofty issues, the "tangle of land claims" remained troublesome. Native Americans had a different conception of land ownership from European-American settlers, and the Indian nations living around Lake Michigan had no written language. They did not think in terms of state and national boundaries, and did not claim the land on the basis of documents. On the eastern shore of Lake Michigan the Ottawa and Potawatomi nations lived; the Pokagons were a part of the Potawatomi tribe. For a time after the arrival of the first Europeans in the seventeenth century — explorers and missionaries and fur traders — land ownership was not controversial. French explorers reached the territory and planted the flag of France and claimed the land in the name of their king. People who were already there were regarded as primitive savages, as souls in need of conversion, or as invaluable scouts, trackers and suppliers of beaver pelts. In return, the Europeans were seen as strange pale men with impressive weapons. The Ottawas did not call them *mitchenawbe,* as they called male members of their own tribe; they named them *chemokomon,* or big knives, because many of the first Europeans they saw had knives — the word for knife was *komon* — far larger than any they had seen before: these men were soldiers, who carried swords. French words became part of their language. "In their dispositions the Indians of the lakes are peaceable, and they will meet you in the forest with the French words of salutation, *Bon Jour.*" As the European presence in North America grew, France and England carried on their wars on both sides of the Atlantic, and both welcomed Indian nations as allies.

The United States had won its independence in the Revolutionary War; now war clouds gathered again. In the middle of the next century, America's imminent involvement in another war was uppermost in the mind of a historian preparing an introduction for a small volume of documents written during the years preceding and during the War of 1812.

> *We pen these lines in mid-May, 1940; before they meet the reader's eye they will have passed into history. Through our open window may be seen the prodigal bloom of the lovely magnolias, the fresh hues of new-leaved maples and elms, green-carpeted lawns, jewelled with beds of yellow daffodils and flaming tulips. Bare-headed college youths stroll past, an old man, feeble and bent with age, a young mother leading a child, in the street a steady procession of vehicles, richer than King Midas ever knew. The entire scene is charged with eager, radiant life. So it might have been in the town of Detroit in May, 1812. No motor cars or cement-paved streets then met the eye, of course, but children and mothers, youths and old men went their accustomed ways; then, as now, the majestic river slipped past the town, hurrying to its union with the ocean in the distant Gulf of St. Lawrence. Then, as now, the mid-May sun shed its brilliance over the peaceful land, maples and elms donned anew their robes of summer verdure, while peach and apple and cherry were prodigal of their fragrant bloom.*
>
> *But over the peaceful scene a terrible menace impended. Across the sea, even as in 1940, a world-shaking conflict was going on. Although America desired to have no part in it, our national rights and our peaceful commerce were assailed with fine impartiality by both warring nations. President Jefferson, the greatest exponent of pacifism in our history, strove earnestly to promote the rule of sweet reason in a world where brute force alone was respected, and toward the end longed only to terminate his administration before the deluge arrived. Thus it was reserved for his political heir, President Madison, to pilot the country through a three-year war. With the cheerful*

unconcern which habitually characterizes America in her international relations, with
no real military machine and with practically no effort to provide one, we declared war
in 1812 upon the greatest military power in the world.

In Europe, French conquests led other nations to combine to oppose France. In 1803, Napoleon, acting with typically impetuous decisiveness, suddenly offered the whole of the Louisiana territory he had just gained from Spain to a surprised America emissary who had been sent to negotiate U.S. rights to use New Orleans as a port and the Mississippi River as a shipping route. "By this increase in territory," Napoleon declared, "the power of the United States will be consolidated forever, and I have just given England a seafaring rival which, sooner or later will humble her pride." The British could not fully grasp that their former colonies were now independent, just as twenty-five years earlier they could not understand — even when a few of their own leaders warned them — that America had a significant future.

...there is America, which at this day serves for little more than to amuse you with stories of savage men and uncouth manners, yet shall, before you taste of death, show itself equal to the whole of that commerce which now attracts the envy of the world.

Edmund Burke, Second speech on conciliation with America, March 22, 1775

By 1812, America was already a seafaring nation. "The core of the American navy consisted of seven of the best frigates in the world. ...The other nine United States naval vessels fit for the high seas were brigs, sloops, and corvettes... [and the country] had around 200 gunboats." The London *Times*, however, described the United States Navy as a "few fir built frigates with strips of bunting, manned by [illegitimates] and outlaws."

The War of 1812 originated on the sea. Just as plantation owners in the American south came to believe that slavery was essential to their way of life, the British viewed impressment — the "pressing" of unwilling men into service in the navy — as necessary for the national good. Sailors deserted from the harsh life at the rate of 2,500 a year. Press gangs roamed English seaside towns, and British ships stopped vessels from other countries and removed sailors they alleged were deserters. By 1812 American trade with other nations had been substantially reduced, and several thousand sailors had been taken from United States merchant ships by British captains. In June of that year, after efforts to stop harassment of American ships had failed, the United States declared war against Great Britain. The war lasted two and half years, and was fought on the ocean, on the Great Lakes, in the eastern states, in the Michigan territory, in Canada, and at the mouth of the Mississippi. General William Hull, territorial governor of Michigan, surrendered Detroit to British troops without a fight, and was court-martialed and sentenced to be shot, though the sentence was not carried out.

In entering into this capitulation, the general took counsel from his own feelings only. Not an officer was consulted. Not one anticipated a surrender, till he saw the white flag displayed. Even the women were indignant, at so shameful a degradation of the American character. To see the whole of our men flushed with the hope of victory, eagerly awaiting the approaching contest, to see them afterwards dispirited, hopeless and desponding, at least 500 shedding tears because they were not allowed to meet their country's foe and to fight their country's battles, excited sensations which no American has ever before had cause to feel, and which I trust in God will never again be felt, while one man remains to defend the standard of the union.

Lewis Cass to William Eustis, U.S. Secretary of War, September 10, 1812

The Star-Spangled Banner

by Francis Scott Key

O say, can you see, by the dawn's early light,
What so proudly we hailed at the twilight's last gleaming?
Whose broad stripes and bright stars, through the perilous fight,
O'er the ramparts we watched were so gallantly streaming?
And the rockets' red glare, the bombs bursting in air
Gave proof through the night that our flag was still there.
O say, does that star-spangled banner yet wave
O'er the land of the free and the home of the brave?

On that shore, dimly seen through the mists of the deep,
Where the foe's haughty host in dread silence reposes,
What is that which the breeze, o'er the towering steep,
As it fitfully blows, now conceals, now discloses?
Now it catches the gleam of the morning's first beam,
In full glory reflected, now shines on the stream;
'Tis the star-spangled banner! O, long may it wave
O'er the land of the free and the home of the brave!

And where is that band who so vauntingly swore
That the havoc of war and the battle's confusion
A home and a country should leave us no more?
Their blood has washed out their foul footsteps' pollution.
No refuge could save the hireling and slave
From the terror of flight or the gloom of the grave;
And the star-spangled banner in triumph doth wave
O'er the land of the free and the home of the brave!

O, thus be it ever when free men shall stand
Between their loved homes and the war's desolation!
Blest with victory and peace, may the heaven-rescued land
Praise the Power that hath made and preserved us a nation.
Then conquer we must, when our cause it is just,
And this be our motto, "In God is our trust";
And the star-spangled banner in triumph shall wave
O'er the land of the free and the home of the brave!

In August 1814 British troops captured Washington and burned the Capitol, the treasury, the buildings housing the state department and the war department, and the White House. James and Dolly Madison escaped as the British entered the city; when American forces recaptured Washington the Madisons lived temporarily in a handsome hexagonal building named the Octagon House.

When the British occupied Washington and besieged Baltimore, among the prisoners they took was an elderly doctor. President Madison sent two men under a flag of truce to attempt to obtain his release; one of the emissaries was Francis Scott Key. Because the British were planning an attack on Fort Henry in Baltimore harbor, the British commander detained Key and his companion on board his ship. During the bombardment of the fort, Key watched, as explosions lit the night sky, to see whether the American flag would be hauled down and the British flag raised in its stead. In the morning, when Key saw that the stars and stripes still flew over the fort, he drafted the verses to the song which became our national anthem; released by the British, he completed them on the following day. The words, with the title "Defense of Fort McHenry," were printed on a handbill and greeted with great enthusiasm. They were then set to the tune of a stirring drinking song, "To Anacreon in Heaven," and first publicly performed at the Baltimore Theatre on October 19, 1814.

British and American negotiators met in Belgium, and on December 24, 1814, signed the Treaty of Ghent (also known as the Peace of Christmas Eve), which ended the war by returning everything to the *status quo ante bellum* — the conditions which existed before the war. As the American negotiators sailed across the Atlantic with the treaty of peace, British troops were advancing on New Orleans. They offered a pardon, three thousand dollars, and a captaincy in the British navy to Jean Laffite, leader of the pirates of Barataria Bay, if he and his men would join them. The governor of Louisiana had offered $500 for Laffite's capture (and Laffite then offered $1,500 for the governor's head) but he refused the British and offered the pirates' services to General Andrew Jackson. On January 8, 1815, more than two weeks after the peace treaty was signed, and after a week of skirmishing and battling, the Battle of New Orleans was fought. It lasted half an hour.

> *Bounded by a cypress swamp on the left and a river levee on the right, the main British force launched a direct attack on the Americans sheltered behind an early wall. … at battle's end 500 redcoats who had saved themselves by feigning death rose from the fields like ghosts to surrender.*

The British lost over 2,000 men, the Americans about 70. A British officer who surrendered said, "These d____d Yankee riflemen can pick a squirrel's eye out as far as they can see it." Most of the British soldiers who died were buried in common graves, "hurled in as fast as we could bring them," an officer reported. Their general, killed before the battle, was sent home. "Our lamented General's remains were put in a cask of spirits and taken home by his Military Secretary." The ship carrying the peace treaty docked in New York City on February 11, and the news was rushed to Washington and major cities. An express rider sped to Boston, setting a record time of thirty-two hours. Despite the terms of the treaty, which favored neither side, America declared the war a glorious triumph, while the British expressed disdain for "this species of milito-nautico-guerrilla-plundering warfare."

One result of the war was to create interest in the Northwest Territory. Henry Rowe Schoolcraft, a New York glass manufacturer who had studied languages at college and was also deeply interested in mineralogy, traveled west to study the area. He became a student of Indian languages, customs and myths. His investigations were different from those of missionaries or traders because his interest was not in learning Indian languages in order to preach and translate the Bible, nor in acquiring just enough of Indian speech in order to barter. Schoolcraft wished to transliterate the spoken language of the tribes into written English with a translation of the meaning, and to record storytellers' tales and legends.

> *After the War of 1812, the soldiers who returned from the west had brought back marvelous tales of the prairie-country, and a new wave of emigrants moved out... but little was known about these regions. ...Schoolcraft went west himself on a mineralogical ramble, in 1817... and he drew up the first report on the mines and mineralogy of the country beyond the Alleghenies. Returning to New York, he exhibited the specimens that first revealed the wealth of the Mississippi valley, and President Monroe appointed him agent for Indian affairs on the northwest frontier. ...He found it intolerable to talk with the traders who used the native language without any knowledge of mood, person or tense; and thrown as he was with the Indians all day long, he had soon written a Chippewa lexicon and grammar.*

By the terms of the Treaty of Ghent, both sides agreed to make peace with the Indian tribes and restore to them "all the possessions, rights, and privileges which they may have enjoyed, or been entitled to, in one thousand eight hundred and eleven." However, the war cost the Indians a heavy price. In the northwest, farmers were secure from threat of war, and as they cleared the land, the animals and the fur traders moved into other wildernesses and Indians who remained lost this economic opportunity. The Native American people of Michigan needed freedom to roam over a wide territory. Also, like the Dutch settlers who bought Indian lands, they needed a place "where they would have room, ...and not be limited or enclosed by settlers of other nationalities, but keep their unity and principles."

> *For the Indians [the results of the War of 1812] had devastating consequences. Up to this time they had been regarded as a highly important element in the population because of the military role they played in time of war and the vital economic role they played in the fur trade. As the possibility of war in the area lessened after 1815, and the economy shifted away from the fur trade, the Indians of the area came to be regarded as a people whose well-being was of no great concern to those who were now in firm control.*

During the war, in order to raise and maintain an army, the government had paid a bounty to men who enlisted, and also promised them 320 acres of public land in the northwest territories. The western part of the Michigan Territory was largely unmapped wilderness, and the government sent in a team of surveyors, who gave a discouraging report. Veterans were therefore given lands in Illinois and Missouri, and Michigan became the subject of a derogatory jingle.

> The surveyors have been obliged to suspend their operations until the country shall be sufficiently froze so as to bear man and beast. ...The whole of the two million acres appropriated into the Territory of Michigan will not contain anything like one hundred part of that quantity that is worth the expense of surveying it. ...The country is, with some few exceptions, low, wet land, with a very heavy growth of underbrush, intermixed with very bad marshes... swampy beyond description, and it is with difficulty that a place can be found over which horses can be conveyed. ...On approaching the eastern part of the military lands the country does not contain so many swamps and lakes, but the extreme sterility and barrenness of the soil continues the same. Taking the country altogether so far as has been explored, and with the information received that the balance is as bad, there would be not more than one acre in a hundred, if there were one out of a thousand, that would in any case admit of cultivation.

Stevens T Mason

Nevertheless, under the leadership of Lewis Cass, who succeeded General Hull as territorial governor, Michigan's population began to grow. Cass served from 1813 to 1831, when President Andrew Jackson made him secretary of war. He negotiated treaties with Indian nations, saw to the building of roads, and encouraged settlement. In the last year of Cass' governorship, Jackson named John T. Mason territorial secretary, and he became acting governor when Cass was called to Washington. Mason appointed his son to replace him as secretary, and soon afterwards left the state. Stevens Thomas Mason, nineteen years old, then became acting governor; wisely, he carried on as much business as possible by letter, to avoid startling people by his youth. Michigan continued to grow; in 1835 a state constitution was drawn up and Michigan sought statehood. The first election for governor was conducted, under the terms of the state constitution, and Mason, then twenty-four, was elected.

Michigan, however, was not yet a state. Qualifications for statehood had been met; the constitution was approved. Following the custom established by the Missouri Compromise of admitting free states and slave states in pairs, Arkansas entered the Union as the twenty-fifth state on June 15, 1836. What delayed Michigan's entry was a border dispute.

In the years since Albertus Van Raalte founded his colony, people have come to Holland from around the world. A little less than a hundred years after Van Raalte left the Netherlands, a young man from Europe entered Hope College, and left again — as so many young men left at that time — to join the United States army and serve in World War II. He returned to graduate from Hope and to become an illustrious and beloved citizen of Holland. As a college senior, he gave a prize-winning speech.

> I was born in Germany. My father was a journalist. In 1933 he was sent to a concentration camp. I was in Austria when Hitler occupied that country and I landed in prison at that time. Later I escaped to Czechoslovakia. My family was still there when the war broke out. Where they are now, I don't know.
>
> Christmas 1939 I landed in the United States. For the first time in years I enjoyed peace and freedom from fear. For a while Ohio was my home, later Michigan. It occurred to me that neither of these two states, each about the size of an average European country, had any intention of attacking the other. Then I wondered how long it would take the world to learn from America that Poles and Czechs, Swedes and Germans, Italians and Russians could live together peacefully.
>
> Paul Fried, "The Price of Peace," Michigan Intercollegiate Speech League, 1946.

Paul Fried's speech is a moving reminder of the blessings of peace. "For a while Ohio was my home, later Michigan. It occurred to me that neither of these two states, each about the size of an average European country, had any intention of attacking the other." Perfectly true — and how fortunate twentieth century Americans are, to be cheerfully unconcerned about interstate aggression. The idea of a war between Michigan and Ohio is laughable. But Michigan and Ohio did get into a fight once.

The border between Michigan and Ohio was not unmapped; it was overly mapped. There was the Mitchell Map of 1755, the Harris Line of 1817, and the Fulton Line of 1818. The dividing line between the Michigan territory to the north, and the Indiana territory and the state of Ohio to the south, was supposed to run straight, west to east, from the southern tip of Lake Michigan to Lake Erie, and the Fulton Line did so. The border shown on the Mitchell map was a straight line, but Lake Michigan was inaccurately mapped, ending too far to the north. The Harris line was drawn, under dispute, following the orders of the U. S. Surveyor-General, a former Ohio governor (who was responsible for the report dismissing the whole of the Michigan territory as not "worth the expense of surveying it"). The eastern end of the Harris line was farther north than the western end. According to the Fulton Line, the mouth of the Maumee River and the fine port of Toledo were in Michigan; according to the others, they were in Ohio.

> *Come, all ye Michiganians, and lend a hearing ear;*
> *Remember, for Toledo we once took up sword and spear.*
> *And now, to give that struggle o'er and trade away that land,*
> *I think it's not becoming of valiant-hearted men.*
>
> *In eighteen hundred thirty-five there was a dreadful strife*
> *Betwixt Ohio and this State; they talked of taking life.*
> *Ohio claimed Toledo and so did Michigan;*
> *They both declared they'd have it, with its adjoining land.*
>
> *Old Lucas gave his order for all to hold a court;*
> *And Stevens Thomas Mason, he thought he'd have some sport.*
> *He called upon the Wolverines and asked them for to go*
> *To meet this rebel Lucas, his court to overthrow.*
>
> *We held a general muster; we trained till past sundown.*
> *At the head of the Wolverines marched Mason and old Brown,*
> *A valiant-hearted general, a governor likewise,*
> *A set of jovial Wolverines to bung Ohio's eyes.*

Congressional debate on the border issue was one-sided. Representatives of the state of Ohio could, and did, speak. Elected representatives of the territory of Michigan attended Congress, but were not allowed to speak. John Quincy Adams of Massachusetts, who served in the House of Representatives after being President of the United States, said, "Never in the course of my life have I known a controversy of which all the right was so clearly on one side and all the power so overwhelmingly on the other." Michigan claimed the territory and laid out towns; residents voted in the Michigan election. Ohio claimed the land and made it into a new county, named after their governor. The Ohio legislature appropriated $300,000 to defend its land; Michigan voted $315,000 to defend its land. Stevens Thomas Mason, "the boy governor," marched into the Toledo strip at the head of a troop of Michigan militia, and threatened to arrest any Ohio officials who didn't leave immediately. There was a single casualty: a Michigan sheriff was stabbed with a penknife by an ardent Ohioan named Two Stickney. (His father had two sons and gave them unusual but straightforward names: Two was the younger.)

On January 26, 1837, Michigan was admitted to the Union as the twenty-sixth state, having reluctantly ceded Toledo in return for the Upper Peninsula. The beauty of the Toledo War is that almost no one remembers it (and those that do find it funny). Paul Fried, in his speech in 1946, imagined a time when the world would learn from America that countries, like states, could live together peacefully. One step to such peaceful relationships among neighbors is to let old bitternesses fade or to regard them as a bygone tale — not to cherish vengefully the grievances and the grief of the past.

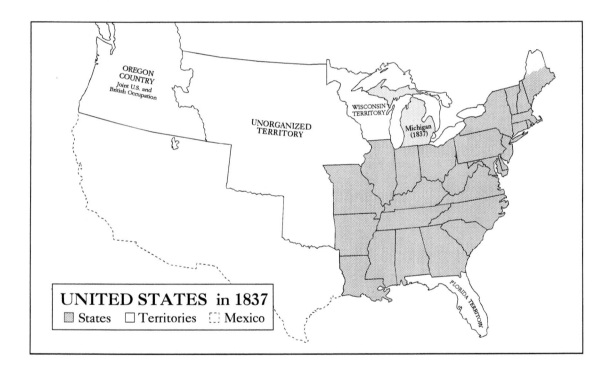

When Michigan joined the Union — taking as its motto, "If you seek a pleasant peninsula, look around you" — Albertus and Christina Van Raalte had been married almost a year. They looked forward to their life together in the Netherlands, not foreseeing a jail cell in Zwolle, an ocean voyage, or a new life in a new country; but only twelve years later, they and their five children crossed the Atlantic and made their way to Michigan. Albertus Van Raalte had been placed by Providence not at the head of a nation, but at the head of a group of immigrants. He looked around him, settled a colony on the shores of the Black River, and together he and his people helped to make the peninsula an even more pleasant place to live.

Portrait of Albertus Christiaan Van Raalte in his youth

The idea of emigration swept over the land like a breath of God.

Albertus Christiaan Van Raalte II did not plan to follow in his father's footsteps as a minister of the Hervormde Kerk. When he enrolled in the theological school of the University of Leiden in 1829, he did so primarily to please his father. He was attracted to the study of medicine, a field which interested him all his life. The event which caused him to experience a call to the ministry, and so altered his life and that of his descendants, and changed the map of a piece of America then unknown to him, was a deadly plague which "walked among the people as a secret angel of death from God." The plague was cholera.

> ...an affliction that killed rapidly, remorselessly and with symptoms that could not be seen as anything other than degrading. Half of all victims died from the disease. A period as short as twelve hours could elapse between the onset of symptoms and death, giving the victims no chance to make preparations or reconcile themselves to their fate. And cholera seemed to affect healthy adults just as much, or even more than, it affected the young and old, the sickly and weak. All this made it into an object of peculiar terror and revulsion to the contemporary imagination...

Albertus and Christina Van Raalte were born in the second decade of the nineteenth century, and died during its eighth decade. They and their agemates were among the last of the vast multitude of human beings who lived their entire lives before the nature of disease was well understood. A physician and medical historian, writing in 1987, referred to the years between 1887 and 1987 as "the health century" — a period when medical scientists at last discovered the causes, and in many cases the cures, for diseases which doctors had previously only been able to identify and to prescribe for on the basis of custom and hypothesis.

Eruptions of contagious diseases fall into three categories: endemic, epidemic, and pandemic — those which are (according to the derivation of the words) *in the people,* breaking out periodically in a particular population and place; those which are *on the people,* spreading rapidly over a large area; and those which attack *pan demos: all the people.* Before the invention of rapid modes of transportation, and the coming of the British army, cholera was an endemic disease confined to the continent of India. In 1817 it burst forth into Asia and Africa, and from that time until its cause was discovered in 1886 — and when the cause was known the disease became preventable — cholera was pandemic. The second of six worldwide outbreaks of cholera raged from 1826-1837, sweeping across Europe and North Africa and over the Atlantic to the eastern seaboard of North America.

Cholera is horrific. Some diseases such as tuberculosis, though deadly, do not transform their victims into objects of abhorrence, but cholera's symptoms are dreadful to look upon as well as

13

dreadful to endure. There is "massive vomiting and diarrhoea, in which a quarter of the body's fluids along with essential body salts may be lost within a few hours, reducing the victim to a comatose, apathetic state, with sunken eyes and blue-grey skin."

In 1832, cholera reached the Netherlands, and its rapid spread awakened religious fervor: "The Lord sent a striking angel with Cholera in his hand into our land." People were humbled by their own powerlessness, and trembled before God. Some who had ceased to take their religious beliefs seriously returned to their faith. Among these was a man in his early thirties, happily married, with two young children. He intended to become a contractor in the construction of dikes. "The death of his two only children, both on the same day, led him to conversion." The man was Cornelius Vander Meulen, who became first a follower of Van Raalte and his fellow pastors, then a preacher, then a pastor himself. When Van Raalte left for America, Vander Meulen soon followed, and the colonies of Holland and Zeeland in Michigan grew side by side.

Albertus Van Raalte was younger, not yet married, and he and his parents were spared, but he was deeply moved by the terrible sufferings around him. The cholera epidemic created a heartfelt need to worship, and to spread the word of God. "I desired nothing so much as to spend my life preaching," he wrote later. "That is when I understood the meaning of life. A fire burned inside me from which my first and serious prayer to God welled: 'O God spare my life, so that I can preach to my poor fellow human beings that You are, that You care about us, and that You invite us as the fallen ones to find justice and the eternal life in Jesus.'" His decision was a great joy to his parents, because their son, descended from ministers over many generations, would be extending a family tradition.

Van Raalte's experience at the University of Leiden was an extreme version of what happens to many college and university students: he was influenced by professors and by fellow students, and the two influences diverged. A dominant religious view within the school of theology, held by the professors and accepted by the majority of students, was that there is a historical inevitability to human progress. This position was not in accord with the belief that human salvation depends solely upon God's grace granted to His elect, and thus it conflicted with church doctrine.

A religious movement called the *Réveil* — the awakening, or revival — had spread from Switzerland into the Netherlands. The principles of the Réveil were based on a serious, devout return to church doctrines which had come to be ignored or glossed over by leaders in the established church. J. Henri Merle d'Aubigne, a renowned Swiss minister, who came to the Netherlands as Court Preacher for King Willem I, introduced the themes of the Réveil, and the movement attracted other religious leaders, among them inspiring preachers and writers such as Isaac DaCosta and Abraham Capadose, Jews by heritage who had become Christians. Influential leaders such as the writer Willem Bilderdijk and the political leader Guillaume Groen Van Prinsterer, who had been a student of Bilderdijk's, were also deeply involved in the Réveil.

Prolific and egotistical, romantic and reactionary, Bilderdijk was best known for his poetry, which was wide-ranging in style and subject matter. One lengthy poem, *De Ziekte der Geleerden* — "The Illness of the Scholars" — consisted of six cantos detailing symptoms and cures of physical and mental illnesses. He also wrote *Kort Verhaal van eene Aenmerklijke Luchtreis en Nieuwe Planeetontdekking* — "Brief Account of a Remarkable Air Voyage and Discovery of a New Planet" — a science fiction novel predating Jules Verne's work. (One dreadful feature of the mysterious planet, for a writer, was that paper was unavailable there.) The British poet laureate

Robert Southey was acquainted with Bilderdijk and praised him as one whose fame would have spread worldwide, "had not the curse that came from Babel clipt the wings of poetry."

Groen Van Prinsterer was an able and influential political leader; he has been described as the most famous of nineteenth century Dutch statesmen. He originated the Anti-Revolutionary party of Parliament in opposition to the ideas of the French Revolution, and promoted the founding of state supported religious schools. In the later 1840s, when Van Raalte and Antonie Brummelkamp began to advocate emigration, Groen Van Prinsterer opposed the idea, but he later wrote that their pamphlet, *Holland in Amerika*, was an example of firm liberal Netherlander belief in freedom. Eventually he gave public support to Van Raalte, who wrote to thank him before leaving the Netherlands, addressing him as *Welgeborn heer en geliefde broeder* — "Noble sir and beloved brother." In this letter Van Raalte wrote with great sadness of the schisms in the churches: "Oh, that the people were one!" and spoke of his dream for the new settlement as a place where this would be so. Years afterwards, in America, Van Raalte remembered him with gratitude: "And may God reward the noble Groen van Prinsterer, by whom I found brotherly acceptance and support in his public observations."

> *Under God's blessing at some place in America we soon shall grow to become a community or a village... There we hope to serve the brethren in this work of charity. God grant that through these means the world may be led to acknowledge that we love each other.*

As these influential leaders in the church and in the political realm were caught up in a desire to return the church and the nation to the orthodoxy of Calvinist beliefs, a small but impassioned group of university students, led by Hendrik Scholte, also became absorbed in the ideas of the Réveil. Scholte was twenty-four when he entered the university, older than most of his fellow students. He was a bold and vigorous young man with a hefty ego — one of his friends spoke of his "natural arrogance" — and he was not averse to displaying disrespect for his professors.

When Louis Bähler, a member of what came to be called "The Scholte Club," cautioned him about his failure to attend classes, Scholte replied, "De profs hoeven mij geen liegen meer te leren. Dat kan ik zelf wel" (No need for the profs to teach me how to lie. I can lie perfectly well myself.) Scholte's group was a small one; his followers were George Frans Gezelle Meerburg, Simon Van Velzen, Louis Bähler, Huibertus Jacobus Budding, and Antonie Brummelkamp.

Hendrik Scholte, in his university days

Van Raalte, who was introduced into the group by Van Velzen, was the most junior member of the group, and therefore the others graduated before him. This had unforeseeable and dramatic consequences.

Along with the drift away from Calvinist doctrine, examination of candidates for the ministry had become somewhat routine — as had, apparently, any requirements about class attendance at the university. In 1832 Scholte graduated, was ordained a minister of the Hervormde Kerk, married, and accepted a call to a pastorate in the province of North Brabant. In the next two years the other members of the Scholte club also graduated, were ordained, and became pastors of congregations. Albertus Van Raalte graduated in 1835, but in the few years which intervened between Scholte's graduation and his own there had been an upheaval in the Hervormde Kerk.

Some ministers — among them Scholte and Hendrik De Cock, a graduate of the University of Groningen — protested against church practices which they believed were not biblically and doctrinally sound, and many people flocked to hear these powerful new pastors preach. One source of controversy was that the leaders of the established church proposed to incorporate hymns in church services; pastors were supplied with *Evangelische Gezangen*, a collection of songs to supplement, but not supplant, the psalms. Hendrik De Cock wrote a violent denunciation, calling the hymns "one hundred ninety-two siren songs, designed to draw the members of the Hervormde Kerk from their Savior and to carry them into the false doctrine of lies."

Dominie Hendrik De Cock

At that time, in order for parents to have a child baptized, they had to acknowledge publicly their belief that the true and complete doctrine of salvation was taught in the Hervormde Kerk. In 1834, young parents asked to have their child baptized by Dominie De Cock, whose teachings they believed in, and he agreed to do so. Church membership was determined by the location of one's home, and the pastor who technically had the right to perform the baptism complained to church authorities. The ensuing dispute led to De Cock's separation from the Hervormde Kerk, and his congregation followed him. Scholte and his congregation were next to secede, followed by Brummelkamp, Van Velzen and others.

Albertus Van Raalte was known to be an associate of these men, and when it came time for him to be examined as a candidate for the ministry, the professors decided that here was where they would draw the line. That decision was unwise. Had the professors thought carefully, instead of acting out of irritation, they would have realized that the Scholte Club was done with. It had been a group based on personality, gathered around one dominant student who had graduated several years before. All his associates were gone except Van Raalte, who had made no attempt to keep the club going. To alter the usual examination process to exclude him was a petty form of revenge, applied to the wrong person. He passed the examinations without difficulty; then the examiners asked him whether he agreed with the laws of church government. To be examined on church regulations — which were voluminous — was unusual.

Van Raalte replied that like all other students he did not know all these laws, but that he would, like the others, bind himself to obey all those which did not violate the Confession of Faith, and would retain the privilege of protesting in case he found anything in the laws of which he could not approve. In case of such disapproval, he promised to give up his office if the matter could not be made right.

One of the examiners asked him "if he too wished to push himself into the church as Dominie Scholte had done, and, then as soon as he was in, to stir up a commotion." Van Raalte was dismissed, but told that he could return at any time, to be examined on the church laws. This decision of the examiners was upheld by church leaders, and so Albertus Van Raalte settled down to study ecclesiastical law. During this time, his father died, which was a great grief to him. When he returned to the examiners, he was able to give a knowledgeable answer to their earlier question —— *Do you agree with all church laws?* Although he could support most regulations of the church, he said, there was at least one which he did not agree with: "There is for example a law that no one may take charge of catechism who is over thirty years of age. I should disobey that law if any one above thirty, having sufficient information and being a Christian, came to me with a desire to teach." The examiners then declared he was unfit for the ministry — thinking, perhaps, that they had made an end of this upstart and insubordinate candidate.

Albertus Van Raalte was thus driven into secession from the Hervormde Kerk if he wished to fulfill his life's goal of being a minister. The *Afscheiding* — the separation or secession from the established church — had already begun, and his closest friends from the University were a part of it. The first Afgescheiding Synod was held in 1836, and there, after an examination conducted by Hendrik Scholte, Van Raalte was ordained a minister in the new church, which then called itself the Church of Christ under the Cross in the Netherlands. His strongest link to the Hervormde Kerk had been his love and devotion for his father, but Albertus Christiaan Van Raalte, senior, was dead, and could no longer be troubled by his son's departure from the established church. And within the group of Leiden citizens who shared Van Raalte's devout religious views, there was the family of the young woman with whom he had fallen in love.

A romantic story of "the girl in the purple cloak" appears in several accounts of Van Raalte's life. According to the tale, one Sunday in Leiden Albertus Van Raalte and some of his friends from the university saw three pretty girls in church, and although they knew what family they belonged to and where the family lived, they were not acquainted with the young women. Van Raalte boldly went to the house and asked to see "the girl who wears a purple cloak." She was the middle sister of three: Christina Johanna De Moen, and she was willing to talk with the unconventional young man, and later, to marry him. The only author who gives a source for the information cites a "story told the writer by a member of the family," and so, at least, we know that this was a pleasant part of the Van Raalte family history, passed along from generation to generation.

Other sources describe the meeting and marriage of Christina and Albertus more sedately. Christina De Moen was one of five children. Her father, Benjamin De Moen, had died while she was still a young girl. Her mother, Johanna Maria Wilhelmina Menzel De Moen, was his third wife; in the 1830s she was a well-to-do widow. Christina's brother, Johannes Benjamin De Moen, was a city councilor in Leiden; another brother, Carel Godefroi De Moen, later became a pastor in the Afgescheiding church. She had an older and a younger sister, Maria and Johanna. George Frans Gezelle Meerburg introduced his friends from the University to the

De Moen family, who welcomed the earnest and dedicated young students, and were persuaded by the pious ideas of the Réveil. The three sisters all married members of this group: Maria and Johanna wed Antonie Brummelkamp and Simon Van Velzen on the same day, in the summer of 1834. Albertus Van Raalte and Christina De Moen were married in Leiden on March 15, 1836, in a civil ceremony in the morning, and a church ceremony in the evening. He was 24, and she was 21.

In the meanwhile, opposition of the established clergy to the Afgescheidenen pastors had solidified. At a meeting of the Synod of the Hervormde Kerk held in 1835, a request signed by the president and the secretary of the Synod was sent to the government to request that three of the articles of the code of laws established by Napoleon during his reign over the Netherlands be reactivated and enforced as a way of combating the seceders. This was an ingenious strategy: the regulations, intended to prevent uprisings against the French occupation, strictly limited the formation of new groups and the number of people who could meet together. On July 5, 1836, the king issued a royal decree, denouncing the seceding pastors as *scheurmakers, onruststokers en geheime opruijers* — schismatics, fomenters of unrest and secret agitators — and declaring that their organization was illegal, but that individual seceding churches might apply, separately, to the king for recognition. This became the basis for a persecution which lasted for ten years.

ARTICLES 291, 292 AND 294 OF THE NAPOLEONIC CODE

Article 291. No association of more than twenty persons whose object is to meet daily or on special days appointed for the observance of religious, literary, political, or other purposes, shall organize themselves without the consent of the government or otherwise than under the conditions which it may please the public authorities to impose upon the society.

In the number of people indicated by the present article are not included those resident in the house where the society meets.

Article 292. Every association of the nature described above which is formed without authorization, or which having obtained it shall violate the conditions imposed upon it, shall be dissolved. The leaders, directors, or administrators of the association shall in addition be punished with a fine of from sixteen francs to two hundred francs.

Article 294. Any person who without the consent of the municipal authority shall grant or consent to the use of his house or of his apartment in whole or in part for the meeting of members of an association, even if that association be permitted, or for the celebration of a cult, shall be punished by a fine of from sixteen francs to two hundred francs.

Unfortunately, ...the Dutch government did not understand the signs of the time. Born in 1772, King William I was one of those few "very old people" who remembered the French Revolution only too well. The Seceders of 1834 were the first victims of this long memory. Firmly determined to maintain the authority of the state in church matters, the king started an active persecution of these Seceders when the latter rejected the terms upon which he had declared himself willing to recognize their organization. Meetings were broken up, ministers were fined and imprisoned, and soldiers were quartered upon members of the rebellious congregations. To give an appearance of legality to these inflictions, the government invoked articles 291 and 294 of the penal code which the Kingdom of the Netherlands had inherited from Napoleon.

These articles forbade the formation of groups of more than twenty persons for religious, literary, or political purposes without previous authorization by the government. The clause in the constitution which granted freedom of worship to all existing religious denominations did not apply to the Seceders — thus the government reasoned — because they were a new organization. Of course the persecutions failed to bring the Seceders back to the fold. On the other hand the fines proved an especially hard burden for the majority, who were people of only small means.

The regulations were intended to hamper, or eliminate, the new church. In fact, they strengthened it, though at the cost of much suffering. The king's ruling did succeed, however, in its obvious purpose of being divisive. In less than four years, Scholte, without consulting his colleagues, sought royal recognition of his church and received it. (One cannot divide and conquer, without first dividing. Scholte's ministry became acceptable, while the pastorates of Brummelkamp, Van Raalte and others were not. Some other churches applied for recognition, which was in some cases granted and in others denied.)

With many people turning to the new church, the shortage of pastors was acute. Van Raalte's first call was to serve congregations in the towns of Mastenbroek and Genemuiden in the province of Overijssel, where the Zuider Zee joins *Zwarte Meer* and *Zwartewater* — Black Lake and Black River. The pastor of the Hervormde Kerk at Mastenbroek, seeing the membership of his church declining, protested to the mayor.

> *1 juni 1836*
>
> *Eene zekere Van Raalte, zich noemende predikant voor Genemuiden en Mastenbroek, die zich aan het hoofd geplaatst heeft van eene dweepzieke menigte en voornamelijk en vooral des zondags in deze gemeente godsdienstoefeningen houdt, doorgaans aan de Zeedijk bij Albert Roetman of op de Riete voor Haaselt bij Jacob de Jong voor eene schare menschen, die eenige honderden tegelijk bedragen, waardoor de grootste wanorde in deze gemeente wordt aangerigt en waarvan de gevolgen in het godsdienstige en burgerlijke leven allernoodlottigst moeten zijn.*

> *June 1, 1836*
>
> *A certain Van Raalte, claiming to be pastor for Genemuiden and Mastenbroek and placing himself at the head of a fanatical crowd, preaches, especially on Sundays, by the home of Albert Roetman or on the Riete before Hasselt by the home of Jacob de Jong, for a crowd amounting to several hundred people, which creates much disorder in this congregation and is harmful to religious and community life.*

When the mayors of towns where seceding pastors had congregations were urged to quell these "fanatics," they appealed to the provincial governor for assistance, requesting that soldiers be quartered in these areas. The practice of making private homes into places where soldiers sleep and eat — that is, have their "quarters" — is a punitive process which the British used against rebellious American colonists at the end of the eighteenth century. In that time, quartering was well known and heartily disliked, and the framers of the Constitution prohibited it as part of the Bill of Rights.

Bill of Rights of the Constitution of the United States: Article III

No Soldier shall, in time of peace be quartered in any house, without the consent of the Owner, nor in time of war, but in a manner to be prescribed by law.

Quarterings occurred where many of the Afgescheiding ministers had congregations; at first the soldiers were assigned randomly within the towns, but the citizens who remained members of the Hervormde Kerk protested hotly, and thereafter soldiers were only quartered in the homes of Afgescheiding ministers and the leading members of their congregations. Thus at their home in Genemuiden, and later in Ommen, Christina and Albertus Van Raalte were forced to have soldiers living with them at various times. The hardship was heaviest for *Juffrouw* Van Raalte, who, in the ten years before the family emigrated, gave birth to six children, five of whom survived, and their care surely was her responsibility since her husband was so often away from home. While they lived at Genemuiden, he founded nine new congregations.

> *Before Van Raalte moved to the more centrally located Ommen in 1839, he made long journeys from Genemuiden through the province of Overijssel. He was a good horseman, which later was very useful in the woods of Michigan. He also traveled often with a buggy or chaise. At times he was gone from home for weeks. Then he wrote many letters to his wife.*

> *The horse is fresh and frisky, though sometimes he coughs. I am happy I brought along the riding cushion because the water of the Vecht is so high in this area that I have to do all by horseback.*

> *Van Raalte was very busy. The provincial pastor needed to be in perfect health, a good horseman, zealously ambitious and of great faith. On his trips to the churches, where he sometimes stayed for a week at a time, he met the congregations and always preached a sermon. ...Between December 11, 1837 and January 6, 1838, he traveled from Genemuiden and preached in Hellendoorn, Rijssen, Enter, again in Rijssen, Almelo, Hellendoorn, Ommen, Arriën, Stegeren (for a Classis meeting), Ommen, den Ham, Heemse and Dedemsvaart, and then returned to Genemuiden.*

Van Raalte and his fellow pastors attempted to follow regulations — or to evade them — while still serving the needs of parishioners who were eager to hear them preach. Many families permitted their farms or barns to be used, even though they risked heavy fines. When he held services outdoors, Van Raalte often met his congregation in places where they could quickly cross over into another town out of the jurisdiction of local officers sent to break up the meeting. Other pastors sometimes preached on board boats, while their congregation listened to them from smaller boats nearby. At indoor meetings, the pastors would carefully see to it that only 19 people were inside, while others listened outside the house. Nevertheless, official harassment continued, resulting in fines and sometimes imprisonment. Van Raalte was jailed in Zwolle between February 27 and March 7 in 1837, and his wife and his brother-in-law Antonie Brummelkamp visited him there.

20

Along with fines, soldiers quartered in their homes, and sometimes imprisonment, the seceding ministers — and their families — suffered in yet another way. Gangs of ruffians realized that they were easy targets for abuse, because the officials responsible for enforcing order often refused to intervene when the seceders were attacked. Hoodlums surrounded their homes, broke windows, shouted and hammered on the door ceaselessly, and sometimes threw stones that smashed furniture, and chased and stoned people who ran from the house.

Early in 1839, the Van Raalte family moved to a spacious, pleasant parsonage in Ommen. Little Albertus was two, and Johanna Maria Wilhelmina — Mina — was only a few months old. Although eventually they came to love this home — Van Raalte wrote later that Ommen was a place where his wife "found friends and peace" — at the beginning life was still very difficult. Van Raalte described his feelings as being like those of a partridge hunted in the mountains. The biblical image is more apt than he knew at the time, for the words were spoken by David as he hid from the wrath of King Saul — and yet it was the youthful David, though threatened by a mighty king, who would triumph and be remembered forever as a great leader of his people.

> And Saul knew David's voice, and said, Is this thy voice, my son David? And David said, It is my voice, my lord, O king.
>
> And he said, Wherefore doth my lord thus pursue after his servant? for what have I done? or what evil is in mine hand? Now therefore, I pray thee, let my lord the king hear the words of his servant. If the Lord hath stirred thee up against me, let him accept an offering: but if they be the children of men, cursed be they before the Lord; for they have driven me out this day from abiding in the inheritance of the Lord, saying, Go, serve other gods.
>
> Now therefore, let not my blood fall to the earth before the face of the Lord: for the king of Israel is come out to seek a flea, as when one doth hunt a partridge in the mountains.
>
> I Samuel 26:17-20, KJV

Official oppression was often, but not always, severe; sometimes the Afscheiding pastors were officially ignored. Unfortunately for Albertus Van Raalte, a brave but peace-loving man, when problems from outside their group waned, the other ministers quarreled among themselves. Contentiousness rose to such a peak that their synod meeting held in Amsterdam in 1840 became known as *de Rovers' Synode*, or the thieves' synod. A *rover* is a robber or brigand; the word is related to the familiar words *bereaved* and *bereavement*. What was stolen from the new church at that time was its internal unity and harmony. Scholte was expelled, and the brothers-in-law Van Velzen and Brummelkamp became estranged. Brummelkamp and Van Raalte, however, remained close colleagues, and in 1844, at Brummelkamp's urging, Van Raalte moved to Arnhem to work with the theological school which his brother had established. Neither he nor any one else could have foreseen the economic catastrophe that was about to fall on the countries of middle-northern Europe.

In the nineteenth century, potatoes were a staple crop in many European countries, and the main item of food for the poorer people. In bad seasons, when there was too much or too little rain, crops were sparse, but generally potatoes were not only easily grown but hardy, and they could be stored for use in winter. Potato Fairs, an annual celebration in many villages, were evidence of the importance of potatoes to the economy of the Netherlands in the 1840s. Such fairs must have been exciting and even joyous occasions — as long as the crops were good. But to have one's livelihood for a full year be dependent upon the previous year's harvest was a terrible risk — not simply to individuals, but to the economic health of the nation.

> *Every other night accounts are settled. Then all outstanding debts are paid. He who has paid, again has credit with the storekeeper and the landlord, and for an entire year receives all he needs on the security of next year's harvests. The potato crop straightens out everything. So it had been for years on the lowlands. Then came the potato disease. From that moment on the system of cultivation changed. The owner now sows the lands himself, and the laborer is out of work and does no longer know what to do. Village after village now has too many people and among them are a great number of reputable persons who know their jobs.*

The blight which appeared in the mid 1840s was unlike anything that had been seen before. "It struck down the growing plants like frost in summer. It spread faster than the cholera amongst men." Some people looked at the rotting potatoes and thought of the human body's disintegration when it was struck by cholera; superstitiously, they feared that contact with the potatoes would cause that dread disease. There was an underlying grain of truth in this idea. What was to be feared was too tiny to be seen — a germ — and it was germs which spread cholera in people, anthrax in animals, and blight in plants.

Murrain, derived from a Latin word meaning *death*, has as one meaning a deadly pestilence among humans. It also refers to highly lethal and infectious diseases of animals, such as anthrax, or of plants, such as the potato blight. In the summer of 1845, a British journal, *The Gardeners' Chronicle*, noted the first appearance of the disease in England, on the Isle of Wight. In the following issue, the editor described the blight, and castigated those who wrote to ask for the remedy.

> *...the disease consists in a gradual decay of leaves and stem, which become a putrid mass, and the tubers are affected by degrees in a similar way. The first obvious sign is the appearance on the edge of the leaf of a black spot which gradually spreads; the gangrene then attacks the haulms [i.e., stems], and in a few days the latter are decayed, emitting a peculiar and rather offensive odour. When the attack is severe, the tubers also decay.*
>
> *...As to cure for this distemper there is none. One of our correspondents is already angry with us for not telling the public how to stop it; but he ought to consider that Man has no power to arrest the dispensations of Providence. We are visited by a great calamity which we must bear.*

In September, the journal carried a "stop press" paragraph: "We stop the Press, with very great regret, to announce that the Potato Murrain has unequivocally declared itself in Ireland." For the Irish, the failure of the potato crop was catastrophic, leading to famine, and literal decimation of the population — worse than decimation since more than one in every ten of the people died, and nearly a million emigrated. There was virtually no potato harvest in 1846, only enough saved to provide some seed potatoes in the following year. During the summer of 1847 the potato crop thrived until the end of July. An excerpt from the diary of an Irish priest records the swiftness with which the blight descended and destroyed. "On July 27th," he wrote, "I passed from Cork to Dublin and this doomed plant bloomed in all the luxuriance of an abundant harvest. Returning on August 3rd I beheld with sorrow one wide waste of putrefying vegetation." Potatoes rotted in the ground, and rotted even faster if they were dug up and stored.

As *The Gardeners' Chronicle* continued its coverage of the potato blight, there was ongoing concern with its cause, despite the editor's early decision that it was best considered as an act of God. The suggestion that electricity might be causing the disease had popular appeal. "Someone had seen a lambent phosphorescent light playing over potato fields at night, somewhere in Ireland, where the disease was very bad." One of the *Chronicle's* more self-assured correspondents was able to assert unhesitatingly that the disease was caused "by simple eremacousis or excolation in consequence of a deficiency of vital energy in the plant," and helpfully defined "simple eramacousis" as "the burning or internal combustion of the weakened plant owing to the oxygen in the air having become too strong for it." A lively debate arose and continued between the editor of *The Gardeners' Chronicle*, John Lindley, and the Rev. M. J. Berkeley, a clergyman who subscribed to the journal. For modern readers it is startling to find the minister proposing the idea that the fungus which appeared on the leaves of the plants was the cause of the disease, while the journal editor pooh-poohed the idea as ridiculous.

> *The issue was the establishment or the rejection of a new conception of the nature of Disease, not only in plants, but ultimately in all living things. A grand philosophical controversy was beginning, in which nearly every scientist or natural philosopher in the world would soon be taking sides. In advancing the hypothesis that a living parasitic organism on the potato foliage was the cause and not the consequence of the Potato Disease, the Rev. M. J. Berkeley was anticipating the germ theory of Pasteur by nearly a quarter of a century.*

The potato crop was devastated in two consecutive years — 1845 and 1846 — and like other crises, was seen as the working of the hand of God. The first issue of Hendrik Scholte's *De Reformatie* featured an article on "The Potato Disease in Connection with the Signs of the Times."

In an early biography of Albertus Van Raalte, the information that the potato blight ruined the Netherlands' entire harvest of potatoes two years in a row is followed by a summary of the action, taken in July, 1846, by the Church Council in Arnhem, which, in gently formal dismissal of its second minister, stated the decision that "Dominie Van Raalte is given the freedom to look elsewhere." The two events are connected. An immediate and longlasting economic decline caused by the potato murrain affected whole populations, and within those populations it affected individuals — such as a young minister who was reluctantly dismissed from the parish he had been serving.

Increasingly, the poor and the middle class in the Netherlands considered emigration — the first group because the heads of households could no longer find work and saw their families sinking into abject poverty, the middle class because they were burdened with taxation to support the growing underclass and saw their own lot as increasingly troubled. At the same time, advances in transportation made transatlantic travel not only possible, but cheaper than it had ever been before.

> *Two factors help to explain why so many found the answer to [their] vexing problems in emigration to the United States. The first was the singularly good reputation which the North American republic enjoyed among the oppressed classes of Europe; the other, the abundance of cheap transportation available in western European ports during this period.*

Dominie Antonie Brummelkamp
husband of Christina Van Raalte's sister Maria

Western Seminary Collection of the Joint Archives

Brummelkamp and Van Raalte formed a society to consider and then to encourage emigration. They first thought of settling a colony on the Dutch-controlled island of Java, but rejected this idea when the government not only refused to provide support, but also made it clear that religious restrictions would be applied to groups who settled there. Meanwhile leaders of the American Dutch Reformed Church saw the advantages of encouraging emigration to America — where new lands in the west (Michigan, Wisconsin, Iowa) were being settled. In 1846, the Reverend Thomas De Witt of New York City traveled to the Netherlands, and when he returned he reported at a synod meeting that "when in Holland, I received information of a rising spirit of emigration to America, and especially among the seceders from the established church." In Albany the Reverend Isaac Wyckoff founded The Protestant Evangelical Holland Emigrant Society, whose aim was "to assist the pious poor in taking the necessary steps to obtain a settlement here."

At first, Albertus Van Raalte thought only of finding ways to support families from the Afgescheiding congregations who needed and wished to emigrate. But in 1846, during a serious illness — typhus — he became convinced that his presence was needed if an emigration movement was to succeed in establishing a colony of the faithful in America. Brummelkamp tried to dissuade him, but he was earnest in his intention to go, and as soon as he regained his health, everything moved swiftly.

Though they see more and more in this country the necessity of emigration, yet the nobility are mightily opposed to it, on account of the general loss which they expect from it, at least in case the way does not lead to one of the Dutch-owned colonies, of which colonies our Christian people are sorely afraid, as much in consequence of the unhealthy climate, as on account of the oppressive course of the Dutch government, in relation to religious liberty.

For all these reasons we have turned our eyes towards the United States of North America. Our heart's desire and prayer to God is, that on one of those uninhabited regions there may be a spot where our people, by the culture of the ground (for it is this quiet mode of life we prefer above all, and the greatest part of the emigrants are either husbandmen or industrious mechanics), may find their temporal subsistence secured, and be able also to save their families from the miseries of a declining state of community.

Excerpt from *Appeal to the Faithful in the United States of North America*, May, 1846

Petitions for divine guidance heartened them with faith, and, one by one, family by family, they felt that the call to "go with Van Raalte" was the call of the Lord. The Reverend Albertus Van Raalte had made his decision in the summer of 1846, and it was in September of that year that he and his family with fifty-three followers set sail from Rotterdam on the brig Southerner. This was the vanguard, the Mayflower of the emigration, and like its famous predecessor it too was given godspeed in psalm and prayer.

With sadness we see these people leave. They leave their birthland thoughtlessly, without reckoning whether they can better their lot in a strange country.

from a newspaper in the town of Heemse, September 18, 1846

Provisions for voyage to America: 160 pounds *per person* (160 lb. moet men hebben voor ieder persoon.)

Ten pounds of pork fairly thick for baking pancakes; ten pounds of ham to eat on bread; ten pounds of beef; twenty pounds of rice; twenty pounds of flour or meal; fifteen pounds of potatoes; twenty pounds of blue peas; twenty pounds of grey peas; thirty pounds of the best bread, sliced and dried; five pounds of ordinary rusk or biscuit. Besides this it is good to have headcheese, butter, cheese, sugar, lump sugar, prunes and everything that one can eat without cooking, sweet cake, several drinks. — wine, brandy, Rhine wine, gin, vinegar, salt, mustard, pepper, coffee, tea, as well as various medicines, for American ships have no doctors. The utensils necessary are a tea kettle, copper or iron, tin saucers and plates, tin water cans.

Hendrik Barendregt: letter of advice to those emigrating

The Ocean Voyage of Dr. A. C. Van Raalte
(on which I, the undersigned, was a companion)

We started on September 24, 1846, from Rotterdam. Professor Brummelkamp and Dominie Scholte came to Rotterdam and bade us God-speed on our ship. On that occasion I learned to love Dominie Brummelkamp so much that I could have carried him on my back to take him along — such an impression his hearty address had on me! From Rotterdam we sailed to Hellevoetsluis, and in good order. But at Hellevoetsluis we had a fire on board. It started in the cook's galley and from there a hole burned into the upper deck, but very soon this was repaired. We remained from Saturday to Saturday — a week, therefore — at Hellevoetsluis.

Dominie Van Raalte preached in a Reformed Church in Hellevoetsluis. The church was full, and so many people were standing crowded together that they could not have fallen down even if they had tried. It was so quiet that one could have heard a pin drop. That sermon did me so much good that I looked forward to the sea with courage.

From Hellevoetsluis over the North Sea, everything was in splendid order. With all the sails of the ship unfurled, and an eastern wind, we sailed through the English Channel.

On the ocean — I think it was the second day — the wind began to blow and grew into a storm. Every part of the ship was closed against the waves. Both the crew and the passengers were seasick, all except for Harm Kok, who was another passenger, and myself. The storm lasted for seven or eight days. The waves rolled over the deck from one side to the other. When the storm subsided, we were told for the first time about what had been happening. The man at the rudder of the ship was the ship's cook; he died soon after we landed in America.

When the storm was over, Dominie Van Raalte looked as if he had suffered severely. He had been thrown from one side of his cabin to the other, and his head and hands were injured. We did not see much of him on the voyage.

Model of the Southerner

But at New York he was ready. We all trusted him and submitted to his care. He made arrangements with all the offices, so our expenses were modest. I traveled with him to Buffalo New York; there I, with several others, remained behind. We had very little money, but Dominie Van Raalte recommended us to the care of a minister of the Reformed Church. For me, Dominie Van Raalte was, and remained until the day of his death, a much loved brother in Christ.

Hendrik De Kruif, Sr.

Captain Crosby was a good and a godly man, and the *Southerner's* passengers were fortunate to be traveling with him. Some of the Dutch captains were not in sympathy with people who had chosen to leave the homeland. During one voyage a ship was hailed by the captain of a passing vessel who asked what cargo the ship carried. The emigrants remembered their captain's reply: *"Valsche munt, die in Nederland niet meer gangbaar is!"* — referring to them as "false money" — counterfeit, no longer good currency in the Netherlands.

> *Our ship of three masts, the Southerner, to us looked large enough to plough through the waves with ease. But we soon discovered this belief was ill founded.*
>
> Recollections of Henry Cook

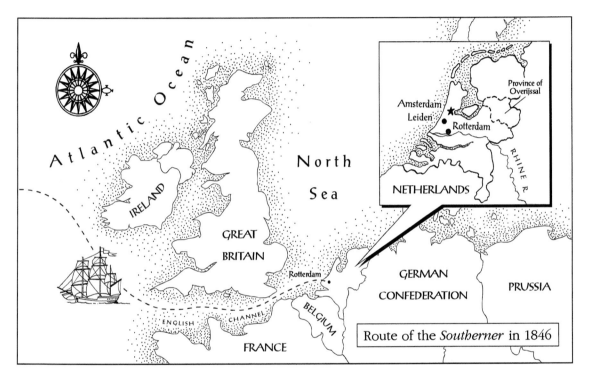

Route of the *Southerner* in 1846

There was a major storm during the *Southerner's* voyage, and during the seven weeks on the ocean there were three deaths, including the young wife of one of the passengers and a two year old child. Families and neighbors watched and wept and prayed as the bodies were cast into the sea. "And how sad a funeral is on the ocean! The truth of God consoled us: *'And the sea gave back the dead that were in her.'*" In the cold month of November, Dr. Thomas De Witt and elder James Forrester came to the dock, to welcome the new arrivals.

> *A new body of Pilgrims has reached our shores from Holland, the land of our fathers, and the shelter in ages gone by to outcasts from persecution, ...at an unpropitious season. We will extend to them the hand of fellowship and friendship.*
>
> Dr. Thomas De Witt, letter to the *Christian Intelligencer*, March 3, 1847

En ik zal de blinden leiden door den weg, dien zij niet geweten en hebben, ik zal ze doen treden door de paden, dien zij nicht geweten hebben. Ik zal de duisternisse voor hun aangezicht ten licht maken en het kromme tot recht: deze dingen zal ik hun doen en ik zal zo niet verlaten.

Jes. 42:16

And I will bring the blind by a way that they knew not; I will lead them in paths that they have not known: I will make darkness light before them, and crooked things straight. These things will I do unto them, and not forsake them.

Isaiah 42:16, KJV

Ik wist geen beter naam dan: HOLLAND.

The travelers had now ceased to be emigrants. They were no longer people leaving, migrating out of the Netherlands; they were people who had arrived: immigrants, moving into America. From New York City, Van Raalte and his people traveled up the Hudson River by steamer to Albany. There they were welcomed by the Reverend Isaac Wyckoff, pastor of the Second Dutch Reformed Church. For the weary, bewildered travelers, their brief stay in Albany must have been both awe-inspiring and soothing. Their national heritage in the city was evident in its buildings. First Dutch Reformed Church in Albany had been built by Dutch colonists in America in 1653, and was thus older, by more than a hundred years, than the United States itself. A more direct contribution to the comfort of the immigrants was that the minister of Second Church spoke Dutch, and was a man "well known, because of his kindliness toward Dutch immigrants and because of his learning."

> In Albany it was Wyckoff who most aided the Hollanders. He solicited and distributed funds for them. They came to his house on reaching the city, and, leaving their wooden shoes in the hall, they went into the sitting room where he listened to their story. He found lodging, helped with their luggage, provided them with means for obtaining food and work, and wrote of them, "There are among them the most lovely and noble Christians I have ever seen. They remind me of the fathers — their faith is like Abraham's."

Other groups of immigrants soon followed. Aleida Pieters, in a chapter titled "The Great Adventure" described their journey across the ocean, the wintry wait in the east while the lakes were frozen, and their sure knowledge of their destination.

> The emigrants came with high hopes, but no destination save that they were "going to Van Raalte." Their faith in him and their trust that the Lord was leading them into the promised land gave them courage and strength to endure the long journey and the rigors of a New York winter.

In those days, Michigan, along with Ohio, Indiana, Illinois, Iowa and Wisconsin, were "the west" — which is why the term "middle west" is still used to describe an area of the country that is, geographically, in the eastern half of the United States. Hendrik Van Eyck, who emigrated in 1848, noted in his diary that "letters received from the west" decided him to go to Michigan. He and his party left New York on the steamboat *North America*, were welcomed and assisted in Albany by Isaac Wyckoff, and reached Buffalo by way of the Erie Canal on the steam packet *General Harrison*.

The Erie Canal was a wonder. It was the project of Governor de Witt Clinton, and was derided, before it was completed and applauded as a triumph, as "Clinton's ditch." New York state paid the entire cost — over seven million dollars — because the federal government, in which the dominant influence was that of Virginia and other southern states, refused its support. Part of the money was raised by lotteries, and the rest by tolls and a tax of a dollar levied on everyone who traveled a hundred miles or more by steamboat. The canal opened in 1825 with an impressive ceremony of "The Wedding of the Waters," in which Governor Clinton poured five gallons of lake water into the Atlantic Ocean, declaring "May the God of the heavens and the earth smile propitiously on this work and render it subservient to the best interests of the human race." The canal put New York in the forefront of economic development and made it "The Empire State," spurred westward expansion, and inspired lively songs — one of which stressed the dangers of canal travel with its cautionary chorus: "Low bridge! Everybody down!"

The Erie Canal

I've got a mule, her name is Sal — fifteen miles on the Erie Canal —
she's a good old worker and a good old pal — fifteen miles on the Erie Canal.
We've hauled some barges in our day, filled with lumber, coal and hay,
and we know every inch of the way from Al-ban-y to Buff-a-lo.
Low bridge, everybody down! Low bridge, for we're comin' to a town!
And you'll always know your neighbor, you'll always know your pal,
if you've ever navigated on the Erie Canal.

The E-RI-E

We were forty miles from Albany, forget it I never shall,
what a terrible storm we had one night on the E-ri-e Canal...
The cook she was a kind old soul, she had a ragged dress;
we heisted her upon a pole as a signal of distress...
Oh the E-ri-e was a-risin' and the gin was a-gettin' low, and I scarcely think
we'll get a drink till we get to Buff-a-lo-o-o, till we get to Buffalo.

This canal shows that America need not blush when compared in initiative and accomplishment with any other people in the world. The canal at many points has been dug through great rocks, through small and low lying rivers which makes the canal look like a great trough. At one point the canal was 180 feet above low ground, which gave the appearance that we were passing through the air. Various villages are beginning to develop along the river.

from Hendrik Van Eyck's diary

In those days the travel to the west went up the Hudson River to Albany, then across the state by way of the Erie Canal. The canal trip lasted three weeks. On reaching Buffalo late in the fall, [Jan Kolvoord and his party] found that lake navigation for the season had closed. The immigrants were therefore compelled to winter in and around Buffalo, quite a number of them around Rochester.

In the meantime a letter was received from Dr. Van Raalte saying that if there were any young men or unmarried men that wished to come ahead, they might do so and start clearing the locality where now the city is located. The men who responded to this call ...started out afoot across Canada, crossing the Niagara River on ice by way of Grand Island, and walked all the distance with the exception of one day's travel by sleigh.

Reaching Detroit, they found Dr. Van Raalte waiting for them and traveled with him via the Michigan Central Railroad, whose terminus then was Kalamazoo. Thence they walked afoot via Allegan to the present site of Holland, and started to clear the forest for the future city.

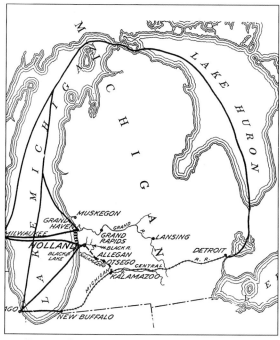

Routes the immigrants traveled to reach the Holland settlement

The Van Raalte group had traveled from Buffalo to Cleveland and then to Detroit, by which time winter weather made travel difficult. There Albertus Van Raalte found places for the families to stay, obtained work for the men in a shipyard, and rented a small apartment to accommodate his wife and children — Albertus, Mina, Ben, Dirk and the nine-month-old baby, Christina — and Bernardus and Janna Grootenhuis and their two children, one five years old, the other a ten month old baby. Van Raalte needed a friend and co-worker to be his second-in-command, and Bernardus Grootenhuis fulfilled that role admirably. He worked for and with Van Raalte tirelessly in the early days of the colony — on occasion, for Grootenhuis was a much larger man, carrying him through the snow. He and his wife were older than the Van Raaltes but survived them, and in later years he wrote a short history of the colony, which he prefaced with an impassioned defense of his leader and friend.

In Detroit, Van Raalte met several times with prominent citizens who encouraged him to settle in Michigan, and traveled to other areas to investigate possible locations, exploring lands bordering on the Kalamazoo, Rabbit, Black and Grand Rivers. A group of state leaders met while Van Raalte was traveling, to hear a report from the Rev. Ova P. Hoyt of Kalamazoo, the Rev. A. B. Taylor of Grand Rapids, and Theodore Romeyn, a lawyer and church leader from Detroit. Romeyn presented a "statement of the origin of the present movement in Holland, and of its probable importance." (The "Holland" he referred to was the Netherlands, Holland in Michigan not yet having received its name.)

...The interference of the government [of the Netherlands] with the exercise of religion and exclusive control of education, accompanied by inhibitions to teach or worship, except according to certain arbitrary ordinances, conjoined with the intolerable taxation and other civil oppression has led to such a state of feeling among a nation like the Dutch, always attached to their religion, and distinguished for their opposition to arbitrary power, that now large masses of the people are ready and anxious to leave. This emigration proceeding from such motives, and embracing men of various and diversified pursuits, would bring a most valuable class among us, if they selected our State as their resting place.

Michigan has been much misrepresented abroad, and the agent of these colonists has come here prepossessed against us, and inclined to go elsewhere. But he has met with sympathy, countenance and aid, and is disposed to commence his colonization here. By so doing, he is entitled to our cooperation; and a little sacrifice by individuals, a little advice and attention to the emigrants, might be of inestimable advantage. Several hundreds of them are already in the United States, and many more will soon arrive.

Romeyn's strong statement led to a later meeting, held on January 22, 1847, at which Van Raalte was present, and which was attended by civic and religious leaders from around the state. Those present included Judge Shubael Conant and the Hon. N. A. Balch of the Michigan Senate, who served, respectively, as chair and secretary of the meeting. Resolutions were presented and passed unanimously, and a committee from Detroit was appointed to support the immigrants. "Mr. Van Raalte having suggested the expediency of committees at the places hereinafter designated, and gentlemen being present from those parts of the country," committees were also appointed from Allegan, Grand Haven, Grand Rapids, Kalamazoo, Marshall and Saugatuck. Albertus Van Raalte, "in a most touching and impressive manner," then responded to the group with thanks.

THEODORE ROMEYN

It being understood that there was a probability of a large emigration from Holland in the course of this year and thereafter, and the agent of the first emigrants being in this city, after having explored the western part of this State with a view to the settlement in it, a meeting was convened at the Session-room of the Presbyterian Church, on the evening of Friday, the 22 inst., at which were present a number of citizens of Detroit, and of other portions of the State...

Resolved, That this meeting have heard with much interest of a large prospective emigration of Holland to this country, proceeding from a love of civil and religious liberty, and stimulated by the oppressive interference of that government with education and the exercise of religion, it commends itself to our admiration and sympathy. We pledge ourselves to co-operate, as far as we can, with those who elsewhere may aid and sustain this movement: and, if these emigrants make their abiding place in Michigan we will extend to them the hand of fellowship and friendship. We admire the past history and character of the people of the Netherlands. For their faith and independence they struggled for more than thirty years against the powers of Spain and Germany. They stood side by side with our English ancestors in arduous conflicts for freedom and civil and religious matters. They gave an asylum to the persecuted Puritans. They aided in the settlement of our most important State. In their industry, their enterprise, their frugality, their integrity, their love of country, their devotedness to their faith and to freedom in their civil institutions, we recognize those qualities which entitle their descendants to our respect and welcome.

Resolved, That a committee of seven be appointed, who may associate with them such others as they deem expedient, and whose duty it shall be to aid, in every practicable way, the emigrants who may reach our limits, and to correspond with such other associations or committees as may be found elsewhere, and in other ways, to invite, encourage and direct the settlement of these emigrants within our State.

Resolved, That we recommend the appointment of committees and associations for a similar purpose, at such other points as may be deemed desirable by the Rev. A. C. Van Raalte, the agent and pioneer of this movement, and whom we cheerfully recommend as a gentleman of energy, talent, piety and disinterested zeal.

…It was further resolved, that the proceedings of this meeting be published in the papers of this city, and that the country papers generally be requested to publish them.

Rev. Van Raalte, in a most touching and impressive manner, expressed his gratitude for the sympathy and aid proffered to his countrymen, and his gratification at having advanced thus far in the preparatory steps for the settlement in a land where labor would meet with its reward, and civil and religious freedom be secure.

After an interesting and appropriate reply from Hon. John Ball, the meeting adjourned.

S. Conant, chairman
N. A. Balch, secretary

Twenty-five years later, Albertus Van Raalte addressed the crowds gathered for a great celebration of the founding of the Holland colony. His wisdom shines forth from his words. He did not offer an ingenious interpretation of history based on hindsight, because he did not need to. When he summarized his reasons for choosing where *de Kolonie* would be placed, many in his audience could remember the early days, and everyone who was there could see that what he planned had been fulfilled.

The kind of life I saw in American pioneer homes, the credit which poor folk acquired by husbanding their earnings, their joyful labor to improve their condition in life and not merely to gain their daily bread, their civilized manner of life, their obvious educational development and their love for school and Sabbath influenced me strongly. On the other hand the decay of pioneer settlements which, I heard, frequently happened impressed upon me the necessity of securing good market prices, means of transportation and employment for our poor. Our workmen were my first care and also a source of strength. Some acquaintance with the Grand and Kalamazoo Rivers and the splendid future they offered as well as an inexhaustible opportunity for working men led me to choose a spot for settlement on Lake Michigan between these two rivers, provided a personal investigation should show that we had not been misled by maps or by Land Office representations.

Albertus C. Van Raalte's speech at the Ebenezer Celebration in 1872

The Dominie envisioned people working, working hard and with satisfaction. In his dream for the colony, he sought a place where people's work would not be a dragging, draining struggle for subsistence, but, instead, "joyful labor to improve their condition in life." He saw people living well, learning and worshipping, making their community a place of contentment and opportunity. And in his planning, he saw clearly that there were threats to this dream — the site for the colony must be chosen wisely, with an eye to present safety and future development, and only after cautious examination, to "show that we had not been misled by maps or by Land Office representations." It was necessary to be active and wide awake. As he wrote later, about establishing a settlement in a new place, "it is a difficult thing… it does not take place, sleeping!"

Three needs guided his choice of site: forest, river, and isolation. Because he was a true leader, he did not simply see a gleaming city and wish for it. Probably only he, and his Christina with whom he shared his dreams, understood clearly that roughly-built houses and a log church in the forest, by a river, away from other communities, were the seed and the roots of what would flower in years to come. He found his forest and his waterway — and in choosing to settle on the Black River, he achieved the third thing he needed. His people needed to be "where they would have room, … and not be limited or enclosed by settlers of other nationalities, but keep their unity and principles." The settlement would be isolated.

When Albertus Van Raalte chose the name for his colony, he marked his intention to plant the best of the Dutch heritage in a new world. "People have asked me what name I wish to give to our township," he wrote to his brother-in-law Antonie Brummelkamp. "Some wanted to call it after a member of the Association, but I could think of no better name than Holland. The petition for that I have already sent to the officials in question."

> *Men vroeg mij welken naam ik dat Townschip wilde geven. Sommigen wilden het noemen naar een der Heeren van de Associatiën; doch ik wist geen beter naam dan: HOLLAND: de petitié daaromtrent heb ik reeds aan de wetgevende vergadering opgezonden.*

With Judge John Kellogg of Allegan, who lent him a horse and traveled with him, Albertus Van Raalte explored the area near Black Lake — now Lake Macatawa. (Both names have the same meaning, since *Macatawa* is probably derived from an Ottawa word meaning *black earth*. When the lake was surrounded by thick pine forests, streams which ran through the forest carried deposits of dark soil as they flowed into the lake.) The black water was familiar to Van Raalte, a reminder of the *Zwarte Meer* and *Zwartewater* in his first pastorate at Genemuiden.

> *I now refer to January 1st 1847, when Dominie Van Raalte with John R. Kellogg gave me a call, and with the missionary George N. Smith waded through the snow which was then about 2 feet deep, from the mission to Black Lake, when the site for the Holland Colony was selected.*
>
> Isaac Fairbanks' description of Holland's founding and early days

Van Raalte met Isaac and Ann Fairbanks, and the Reverend George Smith and his wife Arvilla. Both of the men were employed by the federal government: Fairbanks as government agent for the Indians to assist them with farming and to serve as an interpreter; and Smith as a missionary. (The Indians wanted, and petitioned for, a Catholic priest — a "black gown" — but received a Congregationalist.) Isaac Fairbanks was seven years younger than Albertus Van Raalte; he and his wife had come to Michigan in 1844. When George Smith was appointed missionary to the Indians, Fairbanks built a home for him and Mrs. Smith, which became known as Old Wing Mission.

The lives of George Smith and Albertus Van Raalte had many common elements. One unusual shared accomplishment is that both were responsible for naming cities, and here, for once, Smith outranks Van Raalte, in that the city he named is larger, better known, and generally considered more elegant than Holland, Michigan. Larry and Priscilla Massie tell how this happened. A group from Iowa moved to southern California in 1875, and there "they formed a committee to name their settlement. One of the committee members wrote to Reverend Smith asking him to translate into Chippewa the phrase 'crown of the valley.' Smith sent four variants, all ending in *pa-sa-de-na* and despite the fact that neither Smith nor the Chippewa tribe had ever roamed within two thousand miles of the site, the committee voted 17 to 4 for the melodious new appellation."

Early in February, Van Raalte brought his family and other settlers as far as Allegan. Here Christina Van Raalte and her children, and most of the other women, stayed with friendly families. Mrs. Van Raalte and the children were guests of Judge Kellogg and his family. Lydia Ely, wife of Judge Ely, had family who had come from the Netherlands, and she could speak some Dutch, which was a great comfort to the immigrant families. Van Raalte returned to the place where he had determined the settlement would be built, with eight of the colonists: Egbert Frederiks, Bernardus and Janna Grootenhuis, Hermanus Lankheet, Willem Notting and his wife, and Evert Zagers.

Hon. John R. Kellogg

These first settlers arrived in the dead of winter. As Dr. Thomas De Witt wrote, this new band of Pilgrims had reached America "at an unpropitious season." While the men built the first shelters, the colonists lived with Mr. and Mrs. Fairbanks. "As I had a large fireplace I kept a fire burning day and night for several weeks," Fairbanks recalled. "The Rev. G. N. Smith furnished them a room in which they prepared their food. Bernardus Grootenhuis and his wife attended to the cooking." Grootenhuis' recollections give a picture of the colonists' bravery amid the hardships of that first winter.

> *As soon as we commenced living as colonists troubles were daily encountered. The first party, who arrived here in the month of February, 1847, thus in the heart of winter, landed at the cabin of Mr. Fairbanks. …They, with the help of four Americans who were hired in Allegan, had to make a road for the oxen, wagons, and sleds. As they started to do this work it began to rain a little, forming a crust on top of the snow a half inch thick and their clothing was covered with ice from head to foot, like a glazed pot. It often happened that when they stepped on the crust with their boots, they made a hole the size of a boot and since the snow was more than two feet deep, they sank in the snow to their knees, and could not go forward or backward without first breaking the crust around the hole with their fist.*
>
> *…The following day the weather was somewhat better and the oxen were made ready to clear away the trunks of the trees, but alas, what happened to them also happened to the poor animals; their legs became fast in the ice crust and that was enough to stop them. Then the men, as many as there were, had to proceed, one next to the other,*

and break the ice crust for more than two miles so as to allow the oxen, following them, to reach the destination. I think this was the proceeding for two or three days.

On another exploration trip, Dominie Van Raalte became so exhausted by walking through deep snow and overfallen tree trunks in the dense woods that he could go no further. Then an Indian, their guide, allowed him to stand on his great snow shoes and in that way carried him along and overcame a severe danger.

Beyond Fairbanks' small clearing we beheld surrounding us on all sides a virgin forest teeming with wild life as yet wholly undisturbed. We viewed with astonishment the mighty giant trees which perhaps were two centuries old, some of them a hundred feet tall and six feet in diameter, all growing on a rolling terrain of various kinds of soil; and the dense underbrush cut up by streams and creeks fed by springs and bubbling waters, a desert wild, fit only as a home for the timid creatures of the forest. Nevertheless this was the place, declared Dominie Van Raalte, where a city and a number of villages should rise, where an extensive Dutch Kolonie should be planted, where we and our children would enjoy an untrammeled existence, serve our God freely and without restraint, and thank Him for His gracious kindness.

Egbert Frederiks' Reminiscences

The place to which Van Raalte came was government land, ceded more than a decade earlier by the chiefs of the Ottawa and Pokagon nations by the Treaty of Chicago. Van Raalte was able to purchase land from the government for $1.25 an acre. Land which had been bought up by speculators, which included areas ceded by the Indian tribes, was purchased at $2.32 an acre. Although the treaty was peacefully obtained, to give up land was a great sadness. Native Americans — who at this time called themselves Indians — continued to live in the area. They were peaceful and helpful to the Dutch, but neither group found the other congenial.

With the exception of Dominie Smith and Mr. Fairbanks and their families, our neighbors were Indians. Some of them had built log houses and had made a little clearing where they raised a few things, but most of the Indians lived in tents made of slanting sticks stuck into the ground and covered with mats made of reeds. In the center of these tents were fireplaces. At a distance of from two to two and a half miles from Dominie Smith's was the Indian Village, as we called the collection of such tents, situated on the south shore of Black Lake. The Indians lived by hunting and fishing and made maple sugar, something they understood very well, and sold their product at Allegan and Saugatuck. They never did us any harm, but nevertheless did not trust us and appeared to fear us. Sometimes we visited them in their tents and saw them eat with wooden spoons of their own making. The women always carried their children on their backs. In church they often were not respectful, since the fact that the women then carried their children with them did not make for quiet.

Egbert Frederiks' Reminiscences

Many years after the founding of Holland, Gerrit Van Schelven collected oral histories from people who remembered those times. "The Indians looked upon the Hollanders as a very strange people," Chief Blackbird of the Ottawa nation recalled, "so much different from the American white people." Hoyt Post, Henry Post's brother, also said that the Indians recognized that the Dutch settlers were different from other groups — "rather inferior to the American white people they had met — a new class and race," who did not know how to live in the new territory. "The religious observances of the Hollanders tended to give them, on the other hand, a sort of respect for the Hollanders."

> *Isaac Fairbanks... helped us build our log house. Mrs. Fairbanks was hospitable. Mr. Fairbanks was popular with the people. They called him the "old squire."*
>
> *I went to school with the young Indians, of whom at that time there were a great many. ...Most of them were Catholics and they had a small Catholic church at what was long known as the Indian Village. The priest was a goodlooking man and was very popular with them.*
>
> *...The Dutch and the Indians got along fairly well together; but of course, their relations at times became somewhat complicated by the characteristic differences in aim between tillers of the soil and hunters. The Dutch settlers put up fences, which the Indians did not like, and their pigs, which roamed about in the woods, got into the Indians' corn.*
>
> Edward J. Harrington's Recollections

> *Of the character of the Indians I can say that they were kind and law abiding, and in their manner of life their wants were provided for. They would cheerfully feed the hungry with the best they had without money or price. Their greatest enemy was intoxicating liquor.*
>
> Isaac Fairbanks' description of Holland's founding and early days

Eventually the Smiths moved with many of the Indians in the Holland area to Grand Traverse Bay, for the reason that "the Hollanders were good men, but that they would clear up the land and conditions would be unfavorable for the Indians and their mode of life, [and therefore] that they would better take it good naturedly and find another place, for the Hollanders had come to stay." The Reverend George Smith died in April 1881; his wife survived him by many years and toward the end of her life she dictated her memoirs, which were published in the *Grand Traverse Herald*.

The Reverend George N. Smith

Arvilla A. Powers Smith

In 1848 Mr. Smith and some mission Indians visited Grand Traverse bay, selecting a location near the present village of Northport, on the land lying between the bay and Lake Michigan, now Lelanau county. In the meantime the government gave orders to James McLaughlin, Indian farmer, to move to Grand Traverse bay. Leaving the mouth of the Kalamazoo river May 27, 1849 in his schooner, the H. Merrill, McLaughlin stopped where Holland now is and got Mr. Smith and others. With fifteen persons on board a stormy passage was had, lasting two weeks and June 11 they rounded Cat Head point and entered Grand Traverse bay. The men, armed with axes, went ashore and began cutting logs for a house… and with the help of every man, woman and child who could pull on the ropes, the logs were gotten into place… [and] made a shelter for the beds until the Merrill could go for lumber.

…After building a shelter, the 4th of July was at hand. They resolved to celebrate but had no flag. A sailor who came with them on the schooner produced a red flannel shirt which he combined with a sheet, producing very gratifying results. They spent the day picknicking on what is now Marian Island.

About fifty families of Indians soon followed, and a village was laid out called Wakazooville, in honor of a noted Indian chief. …In the center of the village was the log schoolhouse built by Mr. Smith.

In 1893, a "Columbian Fair" was held in Chicago, and Simon Pokagon was invited to be a guest of honor. His grandfather, Potawatomi Chief Leopold Pokagon, had been the last chief to sign the treaty of Chicago, weeping as he did so. Pokagon declined the invitation to be a guest of honor, but attended the fair, bringing a small book which he had written: "The Red Man's Rebuke."

Chief Simon Pokagon

In behalf of my people, the American Indians, I hereby declare to you, the pale-faced race that has usurped our lands and homes, that we have no spirit to celebrate with you the great Columbian Fair now being held in this Chicago city, the wonder of the world. …[N]o sooner had the news reached the Old World that a new continent had been found, peopled with another race of men, than, locust-like, they swarmed on all our coasts. The cyclone of civilization spread westward; the forests of untold centuries were swept away; streams dried up; lakes fell back from their ancient bounds; and all our fathers once loved to gaze upon was destroyed, defaced, or marred, except the sun, moon and starry skies above, which the Great Spirit in his wisdom hung beyond their reach.

The Dutch-Indian experience, in gentler form, resembles other interactions between Europeans who came to North America and Native Americans, "settlers" and "settled," those who came to make a home and change their lives for the better and those who had been here for as near to always as made no difference. The newcomers changed the traditional world.

For the Hollanders, the forest provided homes, and later, industry. At first, however, it was dark and ominous. Forty years after the colony's founding, Henry Dosker wrote a commemorative poem with many stanzas about the somber place — *O somber oord* — and his words create an image of the thick forest and treacherous swamps, even for those who do not speak Dutch.

O somber oord, waar dof de echos galmen
En smoren in het woud of stillen waterplas.
Hier zweven nog de doodelijke dwalmen
Op 't groene slijm van 't slibberig moeras.

The colonists began immediately to fell trees in order to clear parts of the forest for homes and farms. This was arduous, dangerous work. The axes the Hollanders had brought with them were small, which made chopping the huge trees difficult, and their method, until the native tribesmen of the district and Americans who lived nearby showed them a better way, was to chop near the ground, all around the tree in a circle, chipping away until "the huge tree stood and swayed on a small spindle." Many colonists suffered injuries from a mis-stroke of an ax, or by being struck by a falling tree, and a few were killed. American settlers gave them a rule to follow: "Small notches and large chips; strike the axe each time in the place from which it came; make the cut as far from the ground as half the length of a man's body."

> *Notwithstanding all such difficulties, many colonists cleared four or five acres of land in the colony's first year. After pushing aside the stumps, the process of tilling the soil and sowing of grain began.*
>
> *The original colonists were fortunate to receive assistance from the Indians, earlier white settlers and occasional passers-by. They learned quickly how to fell trees in such a way that a whole row of trees would fall when the last tree in line was chopped down.*
>
> *Initially the Dutch could topple only one tree a day. Erelong they became so adept at it that they did twenty to thirty a day. Instead of chopping near to the ground they attacked the tree about four feet above the ground. The stumps were later removed by oxen after the roots had decayed somewhat. Some people tried to remove stumps by digging around them and building fires around them. Others dug a deep trench and then having cut the roots, pulled the stump into the trench. Both methods proved very costly and so were discontinued rather soon.*

Colonists undertook their work in the wilderness without knowing how best to do it — if they had not made a beginning immediately, they would not have survived. As they did with chopping trees and removing tree stumps, so they did in building houses and constructing roofs: they tried one thing and then another, and they also learned from others who helped them.

The size of the trees continued to amaze them. Once when a group of colonists had succeeded in felling a huge tree one of the woodsmen lay down across the stump to get a rough measure of the tree's size. Lying in this way, it could be seen that the tree's width was greater than his height — neither his head nor his feet reached as far as the outer bark on the stump. Their knowledge of the scriptures gave them a metaphor to use in talking about the trees, and also a joke to amuse themselves as they labored. The trees were giants, and so the colonists called them "sons of Anak." In the early days before they knew how to chop in a way that would enable them to determine the direction in which a tree would be toppled, they said to one another, "I wonder where this son of Anak will fall."

> **There were giants in the earth in those days... And there we saw the giants, the sons of Anak, which come of the giants: and we were in our own sight as grasshoppers, and so we were in their sight.**
>
> Genesis 6:4; Numbers, 13:33, KJV

One result of settling in a richly-forested area was that it was easy to get lost. The trees blocked out the sky, so travelers could not look to the position of sun or stars for direction. Marshes and swamps made it impossible to walk in a straight line. Little light penetrated the heavy foliage, so that during the day it was difficult, and at night it was impossible, to see the markings cut into trees to blaze a trail. Members of *de Kolonie*, however, devised strategies to help themselves and each other. Staying home after four o'clock in the afternoon was a sensible policy; when this was not possible, travelers usually carried a lighted stick of pinewood as a torch. Those who waited at home blew horns or rang bells as signals to guide family members home, or those at home and those on the trail called back and forth to one another, a method one early historian called "antiphonal shouting." Many times travelers were guided by the sound of psalm singing.

Domestic animals were often more skilled than humans in finding their way home. "In late afternoon [a colonist's] safest course was to follow a cow which wore a bell because the animal usually went to its own home. Whenever the cow led the way to another person's home, the wanderer received either a night's lodging there or proper directions to his own home." The colonists were able to find the humor in this bewildering situation. One joke was told about a young man who went out one evening, carrying no torch, to visit a neighbor who lived about a half mile away. After wandering around for some time, he found a house and went in, and was very surprised to see his own family there. "Waor bin je ewest?" said his mother. "Ik bin van huus ekommen," said her puzzled son. "Wel," she told him, "je bint tehuus." (Translation: "Where have you been?" "I came from home." "Well, you are home.")

Isolation was a means of keeping the colony intact in its early days. It was not easy to get in; once families reached the settlement, it was not easy to get out. Moreover, the isolated setting meant that the young colony stayed *intact* in the literal sense of the word's derivation: *not touched*. Van Raalte was establishing *Holland in Amerika*, and *de Kolonie* would stay Dutch while it was developing into a solid community. The immigrants were not surrounded by Americans, and so there would be neither absorption into the good aspects of American culture, nor contamination by what was bad. Nevertheless, once achieved, isolation had to be overcome. The first thing the colonists needed was food.

Many families — especially those which had followed the guidelines of bringing 160 pounds of food per person for the voyage — still had food left over when they arrived in the colony, but this little amount was soon gone. During the first winter, when the colony numbered forty people, there was a time when their only food was bran which had been brought for the oxen. The cooks prepared a kind of bread from bran and water, without shortening or leavening, but it crumbled and was almost inedible: "no matter how zealous the cooks were, ...in this they were not fortunate... and one piece fell here, another there, and crumbled away entirely."

> *So long as it was possible to come to the settlement by sleigh we had bran from which we made pancakes and bread and also had shelled corn, but when the snow thawed our supplies gave out. ...Our needs and the scarcity of supplies forced us to be saving, made us inventive, and we did everything we could think of in our determination to persevere. To this end the Lord gave us keen desire and courage, no matter how difficult our trials.*
>
> Recollections of Evert Zagers

People living in other settlements were helpful and generous. "Though we could not always be reached from the outer world," Bernardus Grootenhuis wrote, "we were not forgotten and the people from outside would not allow us to suffer the want of anything. ...In our utmost need God in His providence helped us and sent, late in the evening about 10 o'clock, a wagoner (a Quaker in religion) from Otsego, twelve miles south of Allegan, with a full wagon-load of living necessities of all kinds." Despite help from others, the colonists often had to travel on foot, through the forest, returning with whatever provisions they could afford, and could carry over a long distance and difficult terrain. Ingeniously, a colony store was planned, and Grootenhuis was sent east, with a large sum, to purchase provisions and other goods. Henry Post became the storekeeper, and his detailed records of purchases provide interesting glimpses of life in the colony: along with necessities of life, there were purchases of cloth and clothing, and little elegances such as antimacassars.

Besides food and shelter, families needed funds to sustain themselves until farms could become productive and industries be developed. Young people and unattached men left the colony to find work, in order to bring money back.

> *Meal and potatoes, meat or fat were not be had. Wheat, bran, and corn constituted our only food; and coffee -roasted corn was used in its place. ...We did not know how to prepare the corn until the Indians taught us - first softening it in wood ashes and water placed above the fire and finally, after washing it in clean water, cooking it.*
>
> *Those completely without financial means experienced much hardship in the beginning, but necessity is a hard teacher and concern for wife and children teaches a person how to endure privation patiently. Many a settler went far away from home to look for work among the English and returned with a bit of money or a load of flour and pork; and there were some who returned leading a cow or a calf. Thus Evert Zagers and I and two other persons went away from home in the month of May of 1847 and returned after having earned some money.*
>
> Egbert Frederiks' Reminiscences

The world the Van Raaltes lived in was radically different from our world today — much more like its past than its future. One facet of that differentness is that it was a world in which there were servants. It is tempting to write that "most people" had servants, without noticing that such a phrase is an obvious untruth. There were many families, in Europe and in America, too poor to have servants, but, more significantly, it was a matter of course that respectable households would have a number of people who were the "hired help." Thus there must have been more servants than employers. Servants were needed to help with the house work and the farm work; they had to be there, just as horses had to be there to provide transportation. People didn't write much about their horses, or their wells and pumps, or their plows; neither did they write much about their servants. A shadowy group in their own time, today we have almost forgotten they existed. A dramatically worded prediction, made toward the end of the nineteenth century by the British dramatist and poet Oscar Wilde, has come true.

> *The fact is, that civilization requires slaves. The Greeks were quite right there. Unless there are slaves to do the ugly, horrible, uninteresting work, culture and contemplation become almost impossible. Human slavery is wrong, insecure, and demoralizing. On mechanical slavery, on the slavery of the machine, the future of the world depends.*

Many of the colonists expected to have servants. The log of the Southerner listed the Van Raalte group as numbers 103 to 110 among the passengers, and the last of these was "Jennigje Lasker, servant." In her diary entries about the earliest days of the colony, when houses were log huts and food was scarce, Geesje Visscher recorded another deprivation: "Now we had four children but only one maid." The widow of missionary George Smith, who described a life which was often one of grinding poverty, recalled "Mrs. Van Raalta" and her kindness. "She gave up [to me] one of her servants that she had had in her family fifteen years." And Van Raalte's letters show that on occasion he himself was allotted a servant's role. "Often I have little Albertus with me and Annatje …to be assistant nursemaid. …Lena is writing, and therefore uses me as a nursemaid for the children."

To have servants was expected in that time, and in many groups — including the Dutch — to be a servant was not demeaning. Letters a servant girl in Detroit wrote to her sister describe hard work: washing, ironing, cooking, waiting at table, and "the upstairs work" as well. The letters are cheerful. "I like these people very well but I have got lots of work to do, but it is not every poor little girl in Detroit that gets $3 a week. …I often think of what I once read about two angels, if one came to this world to sweep a street and another to rule the city they would both try to do their work well." The life was not always a good one, however. Speaking of her life as a household servant in another setting, a woman who was interviewed gave this insightful comment, "There is no place where one is more lonely than to be alone *with people*, and that is what working in a house means to so many, though not all." This was rarely the case in Dutch homes, where servants were a respected and often beloved part of the family.

Allegan in 1840, from an old etching

Young people from the colony were better able to become wage-earners than their parents. They did not yet have families of their own and so they could leave for long periods of time, and they were quicker — and more willing — to learn English. One of the ways they could help their families was to become servants. "If the youths had not helped by taking service with Americans living in Allegan, Grand Haven, Kalamazoo, Grand Rapids, and with farmers around the colony, and then returning with money, living necessities, saws, oxen, and other much needed things," Bernardus Grootenhuis wrote, "I do not know how a number of families could have survived. These young sons and daughters deserve praise for their parent love and obedience."

> *We had to get busy to earn some money; but what were we to undertake here in the forest? To earn a penny among our people was out of the question, for they were poor and themselves had to look for work and besides the work first in order was much too heavy for boys of fourteen or eighteen. Cutting down trees, sawing up logs, splitting wood, working among logs, and moving them with cant hooks was out of the question. A few of our young people boys as well as girls, had already left for Kalamazoo and parts nearby to find work among the Americans. Three weeks after our arrival a group of six of us, four boys and two girls from fourteen to eighteen, followed their example. I was sixteen but small for my age. One of the boys had already worked among strangers. We packed our clothing and clean underwear in pillow cases or in bundles hung by a stick over our shoulders or wrapped in a cloth and carried under our arms, and so we went on our journey. The first day we had to travel 25 miles afoot before we thought it worth while to ask for work.*
>
> Rieks Bouws' Reminiscences

> *Then came a farmer, living five miles from Kalamazoo, to Allegan to get a yoke of oxen. From him Mrs. Ely learned that he could make use of at least two Hollanders. Having been recommended, we decided to accompany him. The next morning, we were told what do, but we could not understand a word of what was said. One of our host's three sons had to show us by example what was expected of us. The sons relieved each other every hour.*
>
> Recollections of Evert Zagers

In the spring, Albertus Van Raalte brought his family to the settlement, even though the house which was being built for them was still only partially completed. Christina Van Raalte rejoiced to be with her husband, and sang as she worked to make the house into a proper home. "I thank God," Van Raalte said, in a speech made after her death, "that my wife without hesitation, and with the singing of psalms, occupied our unfinished house." By this time new families were arriving continually.

> *There were fifty Hollanders on the ship — many pious people with their children. At first we prayed and read together a great deal but it was a long trip and when we struck stormy weather it was soon every family for itself. Food was prepared whenever facilities were available. Many children became ill and our children were sick too. The oldest recovered rather quickly but the youngest remained ill, but, to our great joy, God spared his life. Nine children and an old man died during the trip and they were thrown into the sea. We had never seen anything like this. We had left the fourth of October and arrived in Baltimore on the eighteenth of December [1847].*

> *...Now we received a letter from Van Raalte saying that he had established a colony in Michigan and that the people were to come there. ...[A]n Indian canoe took us to the Indian village. By day my husband and the other men went out to look for land to buy and then to work on it while we stayed with the Indians in their village. They were friendly and helpful and sold us fish, flour and sugar which they themselves had made. We were anxious to get a place of our own since three families had moved in with us. ...We had lived with the Indians for five weeks and they had never done us any harm although I always felt a little afraid.*
>
> *The other Hollanders also built small log houses... but it was all woods so we couldn't see anything of each other. On Sundays we all met with Dominie Van Raalte. His preaching and prayers were so excellent that it gave us renewed courage. Many people came together and all were happy that God had brought them to free and big America [where] they could worship God as they pleased, each according to the dictates of his own conscience.*
>
> *...At this time there was much singing and praising God but many were also ill. Many could not adjust themselves to the change in climate nor to the different food. Neither was the housing adequate or of the best. In some families there was much distress. So many people came to the colony that there was not enough food. The roads were bad and everything had to be hauled in from other places.*
>
> from the diary of Grace - Geesje - Van der Haar Visscher

As homes were being built and land cleared for planting, there was a pressing need for roads. In the colony, streets were laid out, and a bridge built over Black River to provide access to Grand Haven. Routes between Holland and other communities would require state aid. The support that brought Van Raalte to Michigan did not cease once he came. Each in his own style, friends of the colony petitioned government officials or addressed a wide audience through letters to newspapers. When the food shortage was acute, the Reverend A. B. Taylor sent out a call, through the *Christian Intelligencer,* to friends in the eastern churches.

> *Messrs. Editors:*
>
> *Hoping that there are some yet among our denomination who would gladly aid the Hollanders, whom a kind Providence has cast on our shores, permit me, through the medium of your columns, to say, that there is now a most pressing need of the exercise of their benevolence. There is now, and has been for some time, a most painful state of want among these devoted brethren. Their provisions have failed them, and some have been subsisting on bran. If this state of things continues, they will be scattered over the land, and become the prey of every rogue in whose hands they may chance to fall, or if they remain, Black River must afford them only a resting place for their bones. The sufferings which they, and especially their self-denying leader, have already endured, in erecting their temporary dwellings on the ground chosen as their new home, have been exceedingly great. ...The settlers in the neighboring region have acted a generous part toward them, and many are still willing to do for them; but owing to the difficulty of access to them, and their destitution of means of conveyance, a great portion of the generous aid offered to them is of no avail. They must buy at their nearest village, which is some twenty miles distant and then be conveyed to their settlement, in the midst of a forest.*
>
> *A B Taylor, written at Grand Rapids, April 26, 1847*
> *Donations may be left with Rev. Dr. De Witt, of New York, or at the office of The Christian Intelligencer.*

44

Later in the first year of the settlement, the Reverend George Duffield urged Michigan's newly elected governor to extend his care to the estimable new settlement, where "they are much in need of state roads."

To His Excellency
E. Ransom   *Detroit Nov. 12, 1847*
Dear Sir,

Allow me to congratulate you on your election. Although in general coinciding with other views than those of the dominant party, on certain great questions of political and public importance, yet I feel happy, along with my fellow citizens whose suffrages have placed you in the gubernatorial chair, that we shall have one whose legal acumen and other qualifications fit him so well for the station. I am not in the habit of troubling myself about party politics if we can have good and patriotic and well-qualified men to guide our affairs. Partizans I regard but little. Nor do I ever feel myself called, or even emboldened to intermeddle at all in political matters by the delivering or expression of a public opinion - much less by communicating with the powers that be.

My object in this letter is wholly disinterested. The interests of our state seem to render it proper, that the attention of authorities as well as of the public, should be turned to a very interesting and valuable foreign population arriving among us, and planting themselves in a county north of yours. They cannot have escaped your notice. I may say, that I was particularly instrumental in directing and determining their choice to settle in Michigan, and may therefore be excused for manifesting some solicitude on their behalf. But I am not alone. Many of our citizens begin to feel the importance of doing, what can be consistently done, to render their conditions comfortable, as speedily as possible, and thus counteract false representations abroad, and secure an increased tide of emigrants to our unsettled lands. They ask not, and need not charity; but the peculiarity of their situation will render some legislation in the position desirable, if not indispensably necessary. They are in Ottawa county, spreading out into the thickly timbered land north and northeast of Black River Lake. They are Hollanders who speak the low Dutch tongue, a frugal, industrious and moral lot of people. Remote from the seats of justice that may extend jurisdiction over them, and ignorant of the vernacular tongue, and few in this State being capable of acting as interpreters of the language, they are liable to make mistakes and to peril their possessions by not acting agreeably to prescribed forms in the purchase and sale of real estate.

They number now 2000 souls, all arrived within a year. Their leader is a minister of the Free Church of Holland and his people of the same communion. They are not a community like many of the Fourierites and different citizens' organizations that have consorted for the prosecution of one common trading interest. They have come in quest of liberty of conscience, where religion and the state are not in alliance but all are free to worship God after their own way. Mr. Van Raalte their minister has been under the necessity of assuming responsibilities, in the purchase of lands for conveyance to others, which makes him anxious in what way to guard against the contingency of his death and the distraction that might thence arise. They have no government among them but the restraints of religion and the rules of their church, but all are not church members. Some facility for organizing a township, with its officers among them is greatly needed until the disqualifications for citizenship shall have ceased. They are not anxious for *anything further than to promote order in the development of our own system of state government and have no idea of setting up or making separate community interests. They are also much in need of state roads to be opened, one from Michigan city to the Lake another from their settlement to the mouth of Grand River and another to that of Kalamazoo. Roads opened through this timber land would expedite the sale and settlement of lands in that region belonging to the state. I understand that the state of New York has passed a law founded on a similar state of things, recently developed among German immigrants in some new counties. You will excuse me for stating these things. I feel that it is but necessary to turn your attention to the subject, and that you will be prompt to give it whatever consideration it merits. You may obtain in your own vicinity information as to the amount of money which they have already circulated, and the prospect of benefit that the successful prosecution of their settlements will secure to our state. If anything can be suggested by you that will guard against the attempts made abroad to turn the tide of these emigrants away from our state, and to promote their more speedy diffusion over this region into which they have entered, you will confer not only benefit on our state but lasting good to the interests of humanity. It is probable that in some five years hence the number may reach 40,000 if the efforts made from Wisconsin, Illinois and Tennessee to divert the immigration should be rendered nugatory by some act showing the fostering care of our legislature.*

I have the honor to be very respectfully your excellency's most obedient servant,

George Duffield

This lengthy letter is rich with historical nuggets. The writer, a Presbyterian minister, was among the group of civic and church leaders who welcomed Van Raalte in Detroit in January, 1847, and thus, as he points out, influential in persuading him to settle in Michigan. (He is best remembered, however, as the author of the hymn, "Stand up, stand up for Jesus!"). Duffield addressed his letter to E. Ransom, thus saving himself some time in writing — the given name of the newly-elected governor was Epaphroditus. The first Michigan governor to be inaugurated in Lansing, Ransom was a Democrat, and thus we can infer that Duffield was, in general, a Republican. Ransom's home was in Kalamazoo, which Duffield refers to when he describes the Hollanders as "planting themselves in a county north of yours." His comments on the need to "counteract false representations abroad" and to "render nugatory" the efforts of other states to divert these worthy immigrants from settling in Michigan demonstrate the competitive relationships among states which were typical of the time, as well as the high value placed on immigrants with the qualities and characteristics of the Hollanders.

Epaphroditus Ransom

Duffield summarizes, first, the reasons why the Hollanders deserve support, and then reasons why such support is necessary. First, they have settled in an isolated area, at a distance from well-settled parts of the state where government agencies are established. Second, they do not speak English and there are few people in the state who can serve as their interpreters. There is a risk, therefore, that although they are eager to abide by national and state laws and regulations, they may inadvertently fail to do so, especially in the purchase of land. Duffield then returns to the topic of the worthiness of the Dutch immigrants, assuring the governor that they have not come solely to make money, nor are they members of a cult.

The phrase "a community like many of the Fourierites," which is obscure today, would have been familiar both to the minister who wrote the letter and to the state official who received it. At the beginning of the nineteenth century, François Marie Charles Fourier was a French clerk, working for an American wholesale house in Paris. Like a multitude of observers of the human condition, then and now, he saw and was troubled by human misery; like many others, he proposed a solution. Fourier believed that passions caused strife, unhappiness and criminality. Rather than repressing the passions, he wished to reorganize society in such a way that all human passions could be exercised in safety and harmony. His mathematical and analytical talents led him to determine that there were 12 passions, manifested in a total of 810 types, and therefore ideal communities — which he called phalansteries — would have a population of 1,620: one man and one woman for each type of passion, and he published a book setting forth his ideas in 1808, which was greeted with enthusiasm by American enthusiasts, among them Horace Greeley, and Louisa May Alcott's feckless father Bronson Alcott, whose phalanstery at Brook Farm was destroyed in a fire in 1848.

> *Fourier was magnificent. Not satisfied with creating a new type of communal life, he imagined a world-state, with its capital at Constantinople, and an entirely new cosmogony. He foresaw the time when the earth would bask in perpetual spring and when the salt waters of the sea would turn into an ocean of lemonade, with whales and dolphins acting as beasts of burden. His influence on American communities was great... and dozens of phalansteries were founded.*

Sober citizens — in the church and in government — were not eager to have phalansteries springing up in their territory, and Duffield was ready to assure the governor that Van Raalte had no plans to establish one. This was a certainty; a phalanstery is not a concept that would have appealed to the Dutch settlers.

The governor must have been an efficient soul, at least in terms of his own use of time. Duffield wrote to him in November, 1847, and in January 1848 the new governor addressed the legislature, incorporating chunks of the letter.

I cannot permit the present occasion to pass without directing your attention, for a moment, towards an interesting, and, I think, valuable class of foreigners, that, for the last five months, have been arriving in our state. They are a colony of Hollanders, settled in the County of Ottawa, near Lake Michigan, remote from the inhabited parts of the country. Their language is the low Dutch, they are ignorant of our vernacular tongue and few persons in our state can act as interpreters of theirs.

They are a hardy, industrious, frugal, moral, and religious people, of what is denominated the Free Church of Holland, and like the pilgrims of 1620, came to this country to escape the intolerance of their own, and in quest of liberty of conscience, where no alliance exists between the Church and the State, and where they may be permitted to worship God in their own way.

The Colony now numbers about two thousand souls, and it is believed will be increased annually by many thousands of their country men, should they receive the fostering care of our government and tokens of welcome and encouragement from our people.

Governor Ransom's message to the legislature, January 1848, quoted in Jenks, p. 74

As the colony prospered, Judge John Kellogg made sure that people were aware of the colony's excellent progress. He was delighted with the colony's success, and he expressed his pleasure in a way to catch readers' attention: "I was disappointed, *and most happily disappointed.*" Any faults or failings were due to the lack of good roads, and a harbor.

July 22, 1850, to Messrs. Hawks and Bassett, Grand River Eagle,

I returned on Saturday last, from a four day's visit to the Holland Colony. I went through the settlements in the county generally — visited the city on Black Lake and Dom. Van Raalte and his wife accompanied me and my wife to Zeeland and thence in company with Dom. Van de Muler [Vander Meulen], we made an excursion on foot to examine improvements, view the crops, see the people and make all manner of inquiries as to health, and other things of interest pertaining to this interesting and most valuable acquisition to Western Michigan. And although before I went I expected to be highly gratified with their progress, yet I was disappointed, and most happily disappointed. The quality of their land I know to be good, but the amount of clearing, the number of good comfortable habitations, the extent of good fencing, the amount of crops on the ground, and the extraordinary richness and burden of those crops - all these, considering the short time since the first blow was struck (3 years), the dense forest they had to clear, their utter inexperience in such an undertaking, the disadvantages of being so far in the woods, no roads, and a host of other obstacles to encounter — all these are truly astonishing. I have in my life time, seen much of improvement in new countries, but taking all the circumstances into consideration, I have never seen the equal of this Colony.

I was disappointed in not seeing more done in the city, but Dominie Van Raalte explained that. — They soon saw that so long as there remained the obstruction to their harbor, it would not do to congregate in towns or villages; they must spread out and improve their lands on a larger scale. This was a most wise and fortunate conclusion, and they are now satisfied of it. Now all that is needed is the removal of the obstruction at the entrance of this otherwise perfect harbor. The want of this improvement is preventing thousands in Old Holland from coming at once to this country and this location. If Congress but knew all the facts as they exist, they would, I am sure, make the necessary appropriation, and make it at once. For here it is not as it is at the mouths of our principal rivers, where there is a natural channel sufficient to admit of a certain extent of commercial intercourse, and consequently, business to a certain extent can be carried on, though the appropriations are expended from year to year. Here it will be necessary to do the whole work before it can be of any practical benefit.

...To me they addressed themselves in the following language "You people of Allegan do not know how much — how much you do lose by not making a good road from Allegan to the Colony." And I am sure if all our citizens would go and see for themselves, they would also feel its importance. I am fully convinced this county alone, loses enough every year to complete the work. And let any of our citizens go and thoroughly inform themselves of the facts, and they will so report. Why is flour now retailing there at $9 and upwards a barrel, when here it can be bought for $5.75 only 23 miles away? It is the state of the roads and nothing else.

Yours in haste, J. R. Kellogg

County Offices, Allegan Michigan

The greatest difficulty the colonists faced, after their first hard winter, was disease. In the middle of the nineteenth century, the great advances in science and medicine were still to come. Some years after the colony's founding, a young woman wrote to Albertus Van Raalte to tell him of her father's death, making a revealing comment on the state of medical knowledge in that day: "We cannot blame the doctor; he could not see the work of death within."

Fever, malaria and dysentery were common. Smallpox was brought in by incoming groups. There were not enough doctors and the sick suffered not only from lack of medicine but quite as much from the scarcity and quality of the food. Dominie Van Raalte succeeded in getting another physician whom he accompanied in his visits to the sick. Indeed, Van Raalte seemed more indispensable than ever, Besides bearing upon his shoulders the success of the settlement, and the necessity for giving the encouraging message on Sunday, he now became in a deeper sense the friend and comforter of his people. Each morning he held office hours in his house, during which time he doled out medicine - quinine, rhubarb, calomel or blue pills - to those who came. He was ready at all hours to go to the house of suffering and death, to comfort and aid in the preparation for the burial and conduct funeral services.

During that summer when sickness and death seemed to be in every hut and cabin, as in Plymouth more than two centuries before, there were not enough well ones to care for the sick or give proper burial for the dead.

The great mortality of that season [1847-48] among the colonists, had left them with many orphans on their hands, who were promptly taken in by other families and cared for. Their constant increase, however, led to the building of the orphan house, a project in perfect keeping with the spirit in which they had started out. One Sunday morning, a few months after the partial completion and occupation of the log church, Dominie Van Raalte suggested to his people the necessity that something of this kind should be done, and that forthwith. He urged it with all the power and force of language at his command. The result was, not only the opening of a subscription list, and the pledging of money, labor and material, but with a commendable devotion, the jewelry of the wives of the colonists was freely contributed towards this object.

The building was begun in May, 1848. ...It was not completed until the year following [and] it has never been occupied for the purposes for which it was built. It was afterwards used for a parochial school, town-house, and Holland Academy, and ...as De Hope's printing office.

Our trials rose to the highest point during the latter part of that first summer when the entire settlement became a sickbed, and although physicians had been called in at the common expense, many succumbed, especially through lack of suitable houses and properly prepared and adequate food. This heart breaking and discouraging situation produced a sharp conflict between painful necessity and human sentiment. Never had I been so near collapse as when in those crowded log houses in which each family had to manage to live in a few square feet of space I saw how all sorts of family activities - housekeeping, being sick, dying and the care of the dead - had to be discharged. Small wonder that in that hour of trial there appeared traces of despair and indifference. But God granted a change! The sufferers recovered, the autumn was most beautiful, and the winter that followed was unusually mild so that everybody could continue building and while at work even enjoy his meals under the open sky. Most of our settlers went to work on their land; those that were sick and in need of care remained at the landing place by the Lake.

After the first year, the colonists had made Holland a healthier place to live. There were houses, snug and sound against the weather; there was enough good food. Sunless swamps — where mosquitoes thrived — gave way to tilled fields, and though the connection between mosquitoes and malaria was yet unknown, the sunniness itself was an improvement. Under Van Raalte's leadership and care, health precautions were as good as they could be in a time when disease itself remained a mystery.

Precautions against Cholera

1. *Sleep* in well ventilated apartments, and comfortably warm: having all bed clothing aired daily.
2. Avoid all excitement or fatigue of mind or body, and overcome all fear if possible.
3. As to *Clothing* - keep comfortable and change as the weather changes. Woolen is the best fabric to come in contact with the body - Have fires in cool, damp weather.
4. Baths as usual, if a good recreation follows with or without friction.
5. Take care to remove all nuisances undergoing putrefaction.
6. *Food* must be plain, well cooked, nutritious and easy of digestion. May take beef, mutton, corned beef, tongue, boiled ham, salt codfish, salt pork, good potatoes, rice, hominy, maccaroni, stale bread and fresh butter.
   Avoid shell fish, stale and unripe fruits, stale and uncooked vegetables and salads, radishes, etc.
7. *Drinks* - Water, milk, tea, coffee, chocolate as usual
   Avoid all acid drinks - soda water, and use ice water sparingly.
   Make no sudden changes in usual habits, and eat and drink nothing between the regular periods of taking food.
   Do not eat late in the evening, and never overextend the stomach.
   Avoid all preventive medicines - alcoholic and vinous drinks are not preventives, and will tend to produce the disease in those persons who are not accustomed to their use.
   In case of any derangement of the bowels, seek medical aid without delay.

Grand River Eagle, July 6, 1849

In the 1840s and 1850s, the third cholera pandemic swept across the continents. There would be three more such worldwide catastrophes before an understanding of its causes became a protection against the dreadful disease. In 1884 Robert Koch — a young country physician in Germany whose wife had made him a present of a microscope — discovered the bacillus which caused cholera and showed how it was transmitted by drinking water, and therefore how it might be prevented. In Albertus Van Raalte's lifetime, cholera was a plague to be endured.

The third summer we were here we got a letter from the old country that there was a cholera epidemic there. A little later we got a letter that two of my uncles had died of it. …The cholera epidemic spread over many lands, and also in America, particularly in the big cities. Everyone lived in dread.

from the diary of Grace - Geesje - Van der Haar Visscher

During the 1850s, the small country of Panama became one of the most disease-ridden places in the world. Before the Panama Canal, there was a Panama railroad, built under appallingly difficult conditions, and with an enormous loss of life. It was started in 1850, and the impetus for it was the California Gold Rush. To travel to California from Europe or the east coast of the United States by water would be easier and faster than to travel by land — if the isthmus of Panama could be crossed. Therefore a railroad was begun, and travel along it was brisk even before the line was complete. Workers came from all over the world, and hordes died there. "The climate stood like a dragon in the way."

> *The worst year was 1852. Cholera swept along the line shortly after the arrival from a boat from New Orleans. …Among those making the crossing in July was Captain Ulysses S. Grant, who, with several hundred soldiers and their wives and children, was on his way to California for garrison duty. Grant saw more than 150 of his party die at Panama — men, women, and children — and all miserably. In later years he would talk more of the horrors he had seen in Panama than of any battles he had known.*

Advances in travel and communication preceded advances in medical knowledge, and in the case of cholera, caused the spread of the highly infectious disease. Nevertheless communication and connections were necessary and welcome. In the colony's earliest days, the nearest post office was twelve miles to the south, in Manlius. Willem Notting and his wife, who lived three miles south in Graafschaap, were the mail carriers: he walked to and from Manlius to collect the mail; then she carried it to Holland and returned home. Early in 1848, Van Raalte corresponded with Congressman Charles E. Stuart to obtain congressional approval for a post office in the colony. At the time there was another post office in Michigan called Holland, so this was called Black River Post Office; Henry Post, who held many positions in the colony, was postmaster. The mail continued to be delivered to Manlius and carried by the Nottings for some time. Delivery was once a week, and Anna Post reported that she often assisted her husband in opening the mail bags and making packets for delivery.

Holland Historical Trust Collection of the Joint Archives

In the Netherlands, one of the well-to-do *burgers* who paid some of Van Raalte's fines was Peter Pfanstiehl. He and his wife Helena emigrated in 1847. On April 14, 1854 Peter Pfanstiehl became a citizen of the United States, abjuring allegiance to every foreign prince, potentate, state, or sovereignty, particularly William, King of Holland. Early photographs of them, staring soberly at the camera, were handed down in their family. The tattered treasures are annotated on the reverse sides: "Peter Frederick Pfanstiehl, early colonist who paid fines for Rev. Van Raalte when he was arrested in the Netherlands." "Mrs. Helena Muelenbroek, wife of Peter Frederick Pfanstiehl, early colonists in 1847, Holland Mich." In Michigan, Peter Pfanstiehl found work which made the other colonists look forward to seeing him.

> *The isolation of the community was still further decreased by the coming of the stage... a large, light covered wagon drawn by two horses. It carried passengers, freight, and express. The bugle call of the driver must have been a welcome sound. ...P. F. Pfanstiehl and his son Peter had charge of the Grand Haven-Kalamazoo stage line, passing through Holland.*

Besides his role in ministering to the spiritual and also to the physical needs of his people, Albertus Van Raalte was, for the first years of the colony, its financial mainstay and its political leader and guide. Holland township was organized in March, 1847 — the month after Van Raalte had brought the first settlers to the colony — and the first meeting of the group of trustees which Van Raalte arranged to govern the colony — the *Volksvergadering* — was held in his partially built home. This group of prominent citizens raised and debated issues which concerned the colony's well-being, agreed upon regulations, and enforced them. The *Volksvergadering* provided a system of government for the colony at a time when the colonists were not yet citizens of the United States. Federal law required immigrants to wait five years before applying for citizenship, and to register their intention to become citizens at the midpoint of those five years. The county clerk came to the colony, and was much impressed.

> *When the necessary two years and six months had elapsed since their arrival in this country, the Hollanders in order that they could vote in the spring election of 1851 were obliged to take out their first papers, Since there were so many who wished to take the first steps toward naturalization, Dominie Van Raalte asked the county clerk, Mr. Henry Griffin, to come from Grand Haven to make out the papers. He is reported to have said that on that trip he made out papers for about three hundred men in Holland, one hundred in Zeeland, and forty in Drenthe. Since this was wholesale naturalization, Mr. Griffin charged only half price for his work and said that he walked back through the forest to Grand Haven with seventy dollars in his pocket.*

To the Detroit Free Press

County Clerk's Office
Grand Haven, July 10, 1848

Mr. Editor,

Sir: - Having spent the past week among the Hollanders at Black River, and believing some farther account of them may interest the public, the following is at your disposal. About 300 of these people have filed in my office the report and declaration of intention to become citizens of the United States, from the age of twenty-one and upwards, the average being about thirty-five years of age. I think it worthy of notice that only six individuals of the whole number made a mark, two in 100 who could not write their names. In order to enable these emigrants to do this conveniently, at the request of Rev. A. C. Van Raalte, and others, I met the people in their three principal settlements: first *at Holland city, then at Zeeland village and Statesland [Drenthe]. ...Many of those who cut the first tree on their farms last fall and winter have from 5 to 10 acres cleared and in crops of corn, potatoes, etc. that look well, and a few have from 20 to 40 acres cleared and planted.*

Holland City is pleasantly situated, high, dry, and level, the streets partly cleared out. I should think there were about 200 houses of all descriptions, from the rude hut covered with bark, to the well finished and painted frame house, every lot occupied having a fine garden and yard, in front of the house a gate, and at every window on the street the neat white curtain. Here are already several stores and provision groceries where goods are sold as cheap as in any county or village in Michigan. ...I attended their church at this place, in two of their services, and estimated their number at 500 souls, thirteen of whom were Americans; in the evening the Rev. McPason of Comstock addressed the Hollanders very appropriately, which was interpreted by their minister, the Rev. A. C. Van Raalte. They have an English school in this church which is large, about 40 by 60 feet, and before leaving the place I assisted them in organizing a district school, agreeable to our Primary School Law system.

...New settlers are going in every day and they all appear happy and contented; there are few very poor among the Hollanders and they are all provided for by contribution in their churches every Sabbath. Much more might be said in relation to this interesting Colony, but lest my communication be too long I shall close.

Most truly yours,

H. Griffin

The colony thrived. Many years later, tired and lonely toward the end of his life, Albertus Van Raalte wrote, "I must go forward, or give up. The people would be too disheartened if I sat still [and] it would be ruinous for myself." In the early days he must often have been tired but never lonely, and there was no thought of not going forward. Schools, farms, stores, roads, communication and industry — there was work to do on every side. With relentless energy, and a vocabulary which shows his impressive mastery of English, Van Raalte wrote appeals to powerful men in the state and nation, seeking support for roads and a harbor to link the colony with its neighboring cities. His harbor letters alone span more than a decade. The examples given here — the letter to Vice President Millard Fillmore in its entirety and the salutatory opening of two others — give a flavor of Van Raalte's eloquent style.

To His Excellency
The Vice President of the United States
Millard Fillmore
Dear Sir!

We Hollanders settled in Ottawa and Allegan Counties Michigan about two and a half years, take the liberty of addressing you about our Harbor petition, which has been brought before Congress.

Though we know you only by reputation, though we have no recommendation nor any claim, excuse us that we ask from you the favor, to give your attention to our petition; and realize, we pray you, our isolated position in the wilderness, and our want for facilities for navigation, realize our losses on Shore for the want of an Harbor, which are doubly discouraging in our young exhausted state; that we may come in consideration; and by your efforts may be placed in the appropriation bill. -

We know you are in favor of such improvements; but there could arise a doubt in your mind about the expediency of an appropriation for such a young people: but Sir!

here is the largest settlement on the Western side of Michigan; our Lake can be made a Splendid refuge for the Shipping of the lakes, (see the North Black Lake Survey) and is joined with the richest farming land.

By the way of this Lake is the shortest road across Michigan to Milwaukee: - and it is now just the time when we need the appropriation most; now we are exhausted, now we are feeble; when we could come through the difficulties now, then we could go along afterwards: but Sir! you must know, the harbor question is our life question, for what will become of us without suitable facilities for shipping! Therefore Dear Sir! we pray you humbly, but with the most pressure, give your influence to Secure, by an Harbor appropriation, our welfare, that our hopes may not end in disappointment and despair, and the hearts of thousands will be filled with love and gratitude towards you.

Dear Sir!

We remain with the most respect your humble servants
A. C. Van Raalte
in name of the Holland Colony of Michigan

Hon. Alpheus Felch, United States Senate

...knowing your kind willingness to spread blessings and happiness around you, and to help where you can; we are encouraged, to come again before you, with a pressing supplication, to favor the Holland colony; and to keep working for the Harbor interest of that Colony: in the midst of the flood of Congress business, and the stormy debates of agitating principles and politics, will our voice be easily lost, and our interest forgotten, if no quiet persevering and working mind keeps the eye on our lot; therefore Sir! we look to you and pray you watch our interest...

A FEW WORDS FROM THE HOLLANDERS IN MICHIGAN.
To the Honorable Senate and House of Representatives of the United States, in Congress assembled.

Honorable Gentlemen, Defenders of justice, life and property in behalf of our adopted land! We pray you give attention and your assistance in behalf of the weak. We, Hollanders, adopted citizens of Michigan, come with a plain case, stated in but few words. It is again the Black Lake Harbor, in Michigan.

Ten years ago, we began to knock at your doors; since which time we have constantly engaged in a life and death struggle in the wilderness and on a desolate shore, tantalized with an inefficient beginning of our harbor work, and cruelly kept in suspense....

Neither eloquence, nor need, nor reminders of the commercial advantages to the area had any immediate effect. The Hollanders more energetic and more dedicated to their colony's welfare, dug their own channel. "The transition from land-only trade through dense forests to lake trade proved to be a stimulus to the Holland economy and the small factories that thrived over the ensuing years." Within four years the channel became blocked by silt, but in 1859 the Michigan state legislature, in response to a request made by Van Raalte on behalf of the community, granted 11,000 acres of state public lands to finance the harbor project. In this aspect of his role as civic leader, Van Raalte's zealousness resulted, eventually, in development which was a lasting benefit to Holland and the western area of Michigan.

A traveler who has recently visited the settlement of Hollanders in Ottawa County, gives us the following sketch of their situation, character and prospects. ...Some of their first attempts in the way of chopping and clearing the forest, and other kinds of work appear rather awkward, compared with our Yankee fashion of doing the same things; as, for instance, hacking around and girdling a tree to fell it, instead of chopping it in the usual way. - But they readily learn the American style of doing business, already showing a decided improvement in this respect.

...These Hollanders are, on the whole, the most valuable body of settlers that have arrived from any foreign country for many years. They are a very industrious, orderly, quiet and religious people. - They are ambitious of learning our language and our modes of doing business. Tho' some of their manners and customs are different from ours, they are fast becoming assimilated to us in that respect. - They have generally fresh and healthy looking countenances. The women are generally intelligent, with an open-hearted, lively, and sociable manner, and free from that unnecessary timidity, or false modesty that characterizes so many of our American women. They have more exercise in the open air, frequently walking several miles, are not afraid to use their hands at work, and have, consequently, healthy and vigorous constitutions. Yet I believe they are as moral and virtuous as the females of any other nation; and most of them are rather good looking.

Grand River Eagle,
July 6, 1849

What a noble and self-sacrificing spirit do these persecuted emigrants display! How similar to the Puritan settlers of New England! Driven from Holland for his religious principles, but a few years since, with only a few followers, we now find Van Raalte at the head of a mighty and flourishing colony, destined to be a great emporium for Lake traffic, Van Raalte's followers are striving to become as well versed as possible in American affairs, and in a few years they will become acquainted with our language and customs and be called upon to assume the responsibilities of American citizenship, and never were a foreign people more fitted for the arduous duties incident upon sovereignty and independence.

Grand River Eagle
September 9, 1849

Isaac Fairbanks

It was evident to me that when [these pioneers] left their native land, their trust in God came across the ocean with them. When springtime came their songs of praise could be heard in the woods, and I well remember the earnestness manifested by Dominie Van Raalte, not only to care for temporal wants but also to make Holland a godly town. The further development of the settlements was convincing evidence that the God whom they trusted was with them.

Isaac Fairbanks' description of Holland's founding and early days

The progress of the colony, from its earliest days, was impressive, and Van Raalte's vision of his people's "joyful labor to improve their condition in life" was being fulfilled. American newspapers were enthusiastic in their praise, but the love and appreciation for the colony and its leader that were most precious came from those who understood and shared their faith.

The Reverend Isaac Newton Wyckoff

> *My reception, as your messenger, by the Colony was almost literally with a shout of joy. ...To think that we at last felt for them...shot through every heart, and there were many thanksgivings to God for His work of love, and many benedictions on the head of your representative. ..."Out of their deep poverty" shone "the riches of their liberality"... [and] they feasted us with all they had. ...It is a most remarkable community and God will sustain and bless it and I feel that it will be a blessing and an honor to us to be His instruments in that matter.*
>
> Isaac Wyckoff's report on the Holland colony, *Christian Intelligencer, June 23, 1849*

One of the many visitors to the colony in its early days was the man who had supported the immigrants in the first weeks in America, the Reverend Isaac Wyckoff, of Albany, New York. From the first moment of awareness of the proposed Dutch emigration, he was an advocate; from the first acquaintanceship with Albertus Van Raalte, a devoted supporter. He loved the Holland colony, and knew it well through his visits, and through Albertus Van Raalte's visits with him when he traveled to the east. In 1849, Wyckoff visited the colony and reported its success to the eastern churches. In 1866, when Hope College celebrated its first commencement, "the gray Wyckoff" attended and preached. When he died, his work for the colony was remembered as a significant part of his life of service.

> Dr. Wyckoff was the busiest, kindest, most persevering, most enduring of men with them. He listened to all their congratulations and complaints, talked with them about their old home and their new one; counseled, expostulated, scolded (for some scolding was a kindness); raised money for them; looked after their luggage; attended the very dray in its burden of their queer, quaint, conglomerate effects; preached for their cause; listened to their preaching; grieved in their woe; apologized for their errors; and entered into all their wants as a guardian. The Hollanders in America may well, when they get prosperous, make enduring monument to this most devoted friend, who devoted his time and talent to make them a solid home in the new world.
>
> William H. Bogart's eulogy
> on the occasion of the death
> of the Rev. Isaac N. Wyckoff
> *New York World*, April 1, 1869

BOOK II.

TREATING OF THE FIRST SETTLEMENT OF THE PROVINCE
OF NIEUW-NEDERLANDTS.

He was, in fact, the very reverse of his predecessors, being neither tranquil and inert, like Walter the Doubter, nor restless and fidgeting, like William the Testy; but a man, or rather a governor, of such uncommon activity and decision of mind, that he never sought nor accepted the advice of others, depending bravely upon his single head, as would a hero of old upon his single arm, to carry him through all difficulties and dangers.

To tell the simple truth, he wanted nothing more to complete him as a statesman than to think always right, for no one can say but that he always acted as he thought. He was never a man to flinch when he found himself in a scrape, but to dash forward through thick and thin, trusting by hook or by crook, to make all things straight in the end. In a word, he possessed in an eminent degree that great quality in a statesmen, called perseverance by the polite, but nicknamed obstinacy by the vulgar. A wonderful salve for official blunders; since he who perseveres in error without flinching, gets the credit of boldness and consistency, while he who wavers, in seeking to do what is right, gets stigmatized as a trimmer. This much is certain; and it is a maxim well worthy the attention of all legislators great and small, who stand shaking in the wind, irresolute which way to steer, that a ruler who follows his own will pleases himself, while he who seeks to satisfy the wishes and whims of others runs great risk of pleasing nobody. There is nothing, too, like putting down one's foot resolutely when in doubt, and letting things take their course. The clock that stands still points right twice in the four and twenty hours, while others may keep going continually, and be continually going wrong.

Nor did this magnanimous quality escape the discernment of the good people of Nieuw Netherlandts; on the contrary, so much were they struck with the independent will and vigorous resolution displayed on all occasions by their new governor, that they universally called him Hard-Koppig Piet, or Peter the Headstrong, a great compliment to the strength of his understanding.

BOOK V.

CONTAINING THE FIRST PART OF THE REIGN OF PETER
STUYVESANT, AND HIS TROUBLES WITH THE AMPHIC-
TYONIC COUNCIL.

If, from all that I have said, thou dost not gather, worthy reader, that Peter Stuyvesant was a tough, sturdy, valiant, weather-beaten, mettlesome, obstinate, leathern-sided, lion-hearted, generous-spirited old governor, either I have written to but little purpose, or thou art very dull at drawing conclusions.

Washington Irving, *History of New York from the Beginning of the World to the End of the Dutch Dynasty*, Book V, chapter I.

How gladly we would have spoken with them, but we could not.

The heritage of the Dutch in America is unique, but it is also like the heritage of all Americans whose original language is not English — beautiful and sad and hidden, because the children's children cannot easily read the family histories of their past. And, as it has been with other cultures in the past and in the present, there are many tensions: between the generations, and between the old country and the new.

In the 1840s, one of the most hearty, hustling, boosting, go-getter newspapers in western Michigan was the *Grand River Eagle*. The Holland colony was a bonanza for the *Eagle*, providing a wealth of patriotic opportunities to commend the virtues of the new arrivals, condemn the country that sent them forth, and applaud the rapidity with which they were becoming thoroughly American. Less than two years after the colony was named, the voice of a Michigan poet was raised in glowing praise — praise which may been offered without ever having seen either Holland in Michigan, the city with its lofty spires, or Holland in the Netherlands, with its dungeons, rack and steel, where the titled nobles were cowering in terror.

Lines on the Holland Colony

...What reared the city with its lofty spires,
Where Michigan's dark waves upheave the sand
And raise to God and Freedom altar fires
Within those forest aisles, and on that strand?
'Twas stern Oppression, with its iron heel,
Its crown and sceptre, dungeons, rack and steel,
These gave to wind and waves full many a keel,
With self made exiles from their 'father land.'

Yes, Holland! thou wilt deeply rue the hour,
Ye drove these noble hearts across the deep,
E'en now your titled lords in terror cower,
As Freedom o'er thy lowlands stalks to reap
Sceptre and crown, and crumble with its might,
These baubles of the past whose tinsel bright
Shone only to obscure her holier light,
Till roused by Wrong, men forth to Freedom leap.

Grand River Eagle, August 14, 1848, reprinted from the *Michigan Telegraph*

The author of "Lines on the Holland Colony" had a way with words and a lively imagination, but was neither a historian nor a reader of history. The nineteenth century was a time, however, when histories and literature with a historical background were popular in the Netherlands and America. For many Americans, particularly easterners, the nineteenth century was a time of strong interest in Netherlands history. In New York there remained a substantial Dutch presence, and yet memories of Dutch control of the area had, for most Americans, faded into a hazy, charming, amusing past — a distance in time made vivid in the story of Rip Van Winkle, who slept for twenty years in the Catskill mountains, and woke up to a different world.

Washington Irving was born in New York in 1783, and named for George Washington. He created Rip Van Winkle, and became world-famous by celebrating and spoofing the Dutch, so easy to admire for their upright ways, so easy to make fun of for their old fashioned clothes and habits and speech. Today his most famous story, "The Legend of Sleepy Hollow," is often retold or dramatized at Halloween: stuffy, conceited, homely schoolmaster Ichabod Crane is a suitor for the hand of pretty Katrina Van Tassel, but his dashing rival, Brom Bones, sends him fleeing in terror by masquerading as a headless horseman.

One of Irving's most dramatic successes was a burlesque of early New York history, as told by an imaginary Dutch narrator, Diedrich Knickerbocker: *History of New York from the Beginning of the World to the End of the Dutch Dynasty,* which became popularly known as *Knickerbocker's History of New York* (and eventually gave the New York Knicks basketball team their name). The three Dutch governors of Nieuw Amsterdam, Wouter Van Twiller, Willem Kieft, and Peter Stuyvesant, are satirized as Walter the Doubter, William the Testy, and Peter the Headstrong.

On a continuum from the frivolous to the sober, Irving was at one extreme and John Lothrop Motley at the other. Motley was an American historian and diplomat whose life span — 1814 to 1877 — closely paralleled Albertus Van Raalte's, though their life histories were dissimilar. Motley was the handsome son of a wealthy Boston family; he graduated from Harvard in 1831; Oliver Wendell Holmes, Sr., was a classmate and friend who later wrote his biography. He traveled widely, serving as United States ambassador to Austria, and later to England. He was famous in his lifetime and beyond as a historian. His subject was Dutch history and his major works were *The Rise of the Dutch Republic*, in 1855; *The History of the United Netherlands*, published in three volumes, the first issued in 1860 and the last in 1867; and, in 1874, *The Life and Death of John of Barneveld*. A sermon preached after his death in Westminster Abbey eulogized him as "an ardent, laborious, soaring soul whose name will be indissolubly connected with Holland." For Motley, as for many Americans in his time, the sixteenth century struggle between William the Silent and Philip II of the Netherlands was the epitome of the conflict between good and evil, and well into the next century American high school students read descriptions of Motley and excerpts from his works in their literature anthologies.

THE UNITED NETHERLANDS
CHAPTER 1

Murder of Orange - Extension of Protestantism - Vast Power of Spain - Religious Origin of the Revolt -
Disposal of the Sovereignty - Courage of the Estates of Holland - Children of William the Silent -
Provisional Council of State - Firm Attitude of Holland and Zeeland - Weakness of Flanders -
Fall of Ghent - Adroitness of Alexander Farnese

WILLIAM THE SILENT, Prince of Orange, had been murdered on the 10th July, 1584. It is difficult to imagine a more universal disaster than the one thus brought about by the hand of a single obscure fanatic. For nearly twenty years the character of the Prince had been expanding steadily, as the difficulties of situation increased. Habit, necessity, and the natural gifts of the man, had combined to invest him at last with an authority which seemed more than human. There was such general confidence in his sagacity, courage, and purity, that the nation had come to think with his brain and to act with his hand. It was natural that, for an instant, there should be a feeling as of absolute and helpless paralysis.

…A small, dull, elderly, imperfectly-educated, patient, plodding invalid, with white hair and protruding underjaw, and dreary visage, was sitting day after day, seldom speaking, never smiling, seven or eight hours out of every twenty-four, at a writing-table covered with heaps of interminable despatches, in a cabinet far away beyond the seas and mountains, in the very heart of Spain. A clerk or two, noiselessly opening and shutting the door, from time to time fetching fresh bundles of letters and taking away others - all written and composed by secretaries or high functionaries - and all to be scrawled over in the margin by the diligent old man, in a big schoolboy's hand and style - if ever schoolboy, even in the sixteenth century, could write so illegibly or express himself so awkwardly; couriers in the courtyard arriving from or departing for the uttermost parts of earth - Asia, Africa, America, Europe - to fetch and carry these interminable epistles, which contained the irresponsible commands of this one individual, and were freighted with the doom and destiny of countless millions of the world's inhabitants - such was the system of government against which the Netherlands had protested and revolted. It was a system under which their fields had been made desolate, their cities burned and pillaged, their men hanged, burned, drowned, or hacked to pieces, their women subjugated to every outrage; and to put an end to which they had been devoting their treasure and their blood for nearly the length of one generation. It was a system, too, which, among other results, had just brought about the death of the foremost statesman of Europe, and had nearly effected simultaneously the murder of the most eminent sovereign in the world. The industrious Philip, safe and tranquil in the depths of the Escorial, saying his prayers three times a day with exemplary regularity, had just sent three bullets through the body of William the Silent at his dining-room door in Delft. "Had it only been done two years earlier," observed the patient old man, "much trouble might have been spared me; but 'tis better late than never."

Motley, *The United Netherlands: A History, from the Death of William the Silent to the Twelve Years Truce.*

Most of the American leaders who supported Van Raalte enthusiastically, and strongly encouraged Dutch settlement in Michigan, were well-educated and well-read. They were undoubtedly familiar with Motley's writing, and would have imbibed from him a vision of the Dutch as a virtuous and upright people. Albertus Van Raalte would have impressed them as an energetic, eloquent and, above all, righteous person who matched their image of bygone leaders of the Netherlands.

Johan van Oldenbarnevelt (1547-1619)

I propose to retrace the history of a great statesman's career. That statesman's name, but for the dark and tragic scenes with which it was ultimately associated, might after the lapse of two centuries and a half have faded into comparative oblivion, so impersonal and shadowy his presence would have seemed upon the great European theatre where he was so long a chief actor, and where his efforts and his achievements were foremost among those productive of long enduring and widespread results.

There is no doubt that John of Barneveld, Advocate and Seal Keeper of the little province of Holland during forty years of as troubled and fertile an epoch as any in human history, was second to none of his contemporary statesman. ...The ever-teeming brain, the restless almost omnipresent hand, the fertile pen, the eloquent and ready tongue, were seen, heard, and obeyed by the great European public, by the monarchs, statesmen, and warriors of the time...

Dutch influence on American language, however, went far beyond the works of humorists and historians. It has affected everyone. References to the Dutch which came by way of England, where, until the twentieth century, national interests were often seen as opposed to those of the Dutch, were usually ungenerous, but one phrase originally intended to be negative — *Dutch treat* — has come to serve a modern, egalitarian purpose. *Boss* ("baas") is now thoroughly American. Dutch love of good food has given Americans cookies and crullers and waffles, and also the word *snoop*, derived from "snoepen," meaning to sneak sweet treats without permission — to rob the cookie jar. Some lexicographers and etymologists assert that the fine American word *Yankee* has a Dutch origin. "*Yankee* probably comes from the Dutch *Jan Kees*, 'John Cheese,' a disparaging European nickname for the cheese-making, cheese-eating Hollanders since the 1650s. ...By 1663 the Dutch settlers in New York seemed to have turned the term Yankee around, using it as a derisive name for their neighboring English settlers to the north in Connecticut (who thus became the first Connecticut Yankees...)."

The very name of our country, "The United States of America," was borrowed from "The United States of the Netherlands." Many "typical American" activities are Dutch in origin. The immigrants from Holland brought to this country ice-skating, bowling, many forms of boating and golf (which they called <u>kolf</u>). ...To our folklore they contributed the figure of Santa Claus and his reindeer, and the many tales of the Hudson Valley. Examples of their architecture can still be seen on the banks of the Hudson today.

The early nineteenth century interest in literature based on Dutch themes was matched by mid-nineteenth century interest in American literature and history in the Netherlands. While the Americans added to their literature by writing about things Dutch, the Dutch read American literature, in the original English or in translation.

> *Before the middle of the century there existed already an extensive and varied literature on the United States. As a great laboratory for democratic processes of government and social organization, the young republic had always attracted a host of European visitors. Their accounts found a ready sale among their compatriots, who especially after 1830 were becoming increasingly critical of conditions in their own countries. The existence of a free commonwealth across the Atlantic constantly invited comparison between the Old World and the New. America thus became a political issue and was the subject of frequent debate in newspapers, magazines and pamphlets.*
>
> *American literature, too, began to attract the attention of readers in Europe. Above all, Cooper and Irving appealed to the romantic sensibilities of the day. Of the former, thirteen novels were translated into Dutch in the years 1826-1840; among them was* The Last of the Mohicans, *which one critic called "a wild and dreadful novel, by no means to be recommended to the weaker sex." Most readers, however, seem to have possessed stronger nerves, for five years later, in 1839, the editor of* de Gids, *Everhardus Jan Potgieter, was able to write that "the fame of Chateaubriand was eclipsed by that of Cooper wherever panoramas of the wilderness and its natives were concerned."*

Like Albertus Van Raalte and John Lothrop Motley, Everhardus Potgieter was born in the second decade of the nineteenth century and died in the eighth decade. Though passionately interested in America, he never visited the country he deeply admired. He wrote enthusiastically about "a people which, even as ours in its youth, is pointing the world in new directions, believing, and meanwhile working"; translated the works of Irving, Cooper, Hawthorne and Emerson into Dutch; and based his own imaginative writing on American poetry and prose, including a short story patterned after Whittier's poem "Maud Muller," a tale of ephemeral love glances between a beautiful farm lass and a wealthy townsman, ending with the memorable lines, "Of all sad words of tongue or pen, the saddest are these: *It might have been.*" Potgieter's major works were two poems on the theme of slavery: "Mount Vernon" and "Abraham Lincoln." The latter was unfinished at his death. "Mount Vernon," written in 1861, has two parts: "1799," describing Washington's death, and "1861," a lament that Washington's resting place in Virginia has become a part of Confederate territory. When he died in 1875, Potgieter had completed seven stanzas of his second poem: "Lincoln's Election," "Europe Hears the News," "Lincoln at the Capitol," "Fort Sumter," "Lincoln's Proclamation," "The Attitude of Europe," and "The Battle of Bull Run."

Literature provided an important link between American and Dutch intellectuals, and thus was influential in producing and maintaining a climate of mutual regard between the two nations. The concerns of the emigrants who came to America with Albertus Van Raalte, and those who followed over the next few years, were related to issues of survival rather than culture. Letters of introduction, written in English and often carried by people who could not read them, were a necessity. Without a knowledge of English, or the help of Americans, immigrants could not protect themselves against cheats and sharpers, sometimes their own countrymen, who tried to lure them into using overpriced accommodations for housing or travel, or buying worthless goods or property. Some early immigrants arrived without being able to ask for food or help, or to express their thanks for kindnesses.

> *Speedily we noted that we were in a strange land where everything seemed odd to us, but also that we ourselves were looked upon as a very strange kind of people. Our clothing, and particularly the large poke bonnets of our women drew much attention. We could not understand what the people said about us. Unfortunately we could not make ourselves understood when we wanted to buy something so that it was with the greatest difficulty we could get what we wanted. Had we not had Dominie Van Raalte or his friends to guide us, as for example Dominie Thomas De Witt, we would not have known how to make our way. But with the Lord's help everything turned out well.*
>
> Egbert Frederiks' Reminiscences

> *In a day or two we left New York for Buffalo and from there by railroad to Detroit. On a Sunday our train stopped at a town and some of our company got off to see what the place was like. Our train started, leaving us behind. Not knowing what to do, we walked about and passing a church we noticed some men standing outside it. We went to them and tried to tell them about our trouble but they could not understand us. So one of the men took some silver money from his pocket and offered it to us. But we protested we were no beggars. Finally they seemed to understand our plight and put us on the next train which came along and overtook the train which was carrying the rest of our group.*
>
> Recollections of Henry Cook

> *From Mr. Theodore Romeyn, a man of Dutch descent who also understood Dutch, we received directions and also a letter of introduction to Dominie Ova P. Hoyt in Kalamazoo. With little trouble we found Dominie Hoyt who, after reading Mr. Romeyn's letter, immediately ordered the women and children be brought from the station and saw to it that we were well cared for that night. How good those people were toward us! They looked after all our needs, even for the journey to Allegan which had to be made by sleigh, and all without any expense for us. How gladly we would have spoken with them, but we could not.*
>
> Egbert Frederiks' Reminiscences

In 1849, the *Grand River Eagle* reported happily that the Holland settlers were "determined to shake off the customs and manners of the country they left, and become as they term it 'Yankee' as much, and as soon as, possible." As was so often the case, the *Eagle* misjudged. Colonists worried individually and disagreed with each other, about how, when and whether to become Americanized. Albertus Van Raalte advocated assimilation without absorption, and he himself was a superb example of a person who was able to become Americanized without absorption — to acquire a new language and learn new customs without losing a sense of heritage or losing touch with his people. "With an iron will he made the English language so much his own that he could participate in debates and contribute in meetings." However, Van Raalte had motivation and opportunities which others in the colony did not. Learning enough English to become assimilated was a difficult task, and absorption, once the new language was learned, was perceived as a serious temptation to be resisted. In this situation, the church and the home were often in opposition to the influence of the schools.

The old Dutch Reformed churches of the east contributed funds and sent people to the west, and welcomed students from the college to their theological seminary, and wrangled over how much to give and whether a western seminary was needed. The new churches in the west took up collections to send east, enjoyed the visits of eastern colleagues, and squabbled about the eastern churches' theology and practice. There was a deep and important connection between the two groups, but it was weakened by a discontinuity in emigration. People leaving the Netherlands for America did not come in a steady stream from the seventeenth through the nineteenth century. Van Raalte led the beginning of a great immigration, but the interval between the Dutch settlement in the east and the arrival of the first colonists in the west was too great to be easily spanned.

The roots of the Reformed Church in America run deeply in the American past. It was founded in the New Netherlands colony in 1628 under the jurisdiction of the Classis of Amsterdam of the Netherlands Hervormde Kerk. In 1792 in response to the changed political climate of the revolutionary era, it declared ecclesiastical independence from Amsterdam and adopted its first denominational constitution. The denomination numbered 116 churches and 40 ministers in 1791 and was heavily concentrated in New York state and northern New Jersey. During the next fifty years, the Reformed Church became increasingly Americanized and grew steadily, until it totaled 274 churches and 33,000 communicants by 1845. The final Dutch language service was held in 1844, only two years before the beginning of the great Dutch migration of the nineteenth century. The process of Americanization had been hastened by the "Puritan legacy" and the very low rate of Dutch immigration in the post-Napoleonic decades. Until the mid-1840s, immigration averaged only 100-200 persons a year. Such a small influx was obviously insufficient to slow the pace of assimilation of the old Dutch.

Pillar Church

The immigrants to [Holland] "worshipped their Dutch and clung to it with a grip of steel." The community was unlike other Dutch settlements in the cities of western Michigan which contained enclaves of immigrants — these towns were first of all American cities, primarily composed of English-speaking people. The reverse was true in the colony. It was a Dutch-speaking community that contained a number of English-speaking Americans. There was no mistake about Holland's being a town where Dutch was prominent. In what would be considered a small town today, there were three Dutch language newspapers: <u>De Hope</u>, published by Hope College, <u>De Grondwet</u>, and <u>De Hollander</u>. For the first twenty-five years of its existence, Holland had no English newspaper.

As long as Dutch families stayed in the colony, Americanization moved at a moderate pace. Dutch continued to be the sole language spoken in many homes. New emigration from the Netherlands was a powerful influence against change, especially when the newcomers connected the use of the Dutch language with righteousness — a tempting position, which meant that new arrivals were automatically more Dutch, and thus better, than those who had lived longer in the colony. Still, influences that moved the colony toward American ways and language were strong. As the town, and then the city, prospered, English-speaking people moved in; as the citizens of Holland engaged in business, acquaintance among English-speaking Americans expanded, and they needed to learn American speech, customs and laws. The college drew students from other states and other countries; soon not all professors were bilingual. President Phelps, responding to an inquiry from a prospective faculty member, wrote that being able to speak Dutch was not a requirement: "part of the work to be done is to show the people practically that we are in America and expect them to become gradually American."

Nothing in the first decade and a half of the colony's history pushed Holland toward the mainstream of American life more swiftly and thoroughly than the Civil War. Throngs of young men left home, first to be amazed by the sights of distant cities like Indianapolis, and then to endure a long, harsh struggle that, for those who survived, was enlivened by comradeship with fellow soldiers from many parts of the country. The letters they wrote home became an amalgam of Dutch and English. In Kentucky, the kindly farm folk brought in food daily for the Union soldiers, but their cooking wasn't a patch on what Dirk Van Raalte was used to at home. "De boeren die komen nu dageliks in," he wrote to his mother, "met brood en boter and pies de stretchen like rubber en hard genoeg for een foundation voor een huis."

Prior to the rebellion the great mass of the people were satisfied to remain near the scenes of their birth. In fact an immense majority of the whole people did not feel secure against coming to want should they move among entire strangers. So much was the country divided into small communities that localized idioms had grown up, so that you could almost tell what section a person was from by hearing him speak. ...This is all changed now. The war begot a spirit of independence and enterprise. The feeling now is, that a youth must cut loose from his old surroundings to enable him to get up in the world. There is now such a commingling of the people that particular idioms and pronunciations are no longer localized to any great extent; the country has filled up "from the centre all around to the sea"; railroads connect the two oceans and all parts of the interior; maps, nearly perfect, of every part of the country are now furnished the student of geography.

The war has made us a nation of great power and intelligence. We have but little to do to preserve peace, happiness and prosperity at home, and the respect of other nations. Our experience ought to teach us the necessity of the first; our power secures the latter.

Ulysses S. Grant, *Memoirs, pp. 589-590.*

Despite the adventures of the young, Dutch tenacity among the older generation of Hollanders remained powerful. In extended families respect for elders was strong — and they were not reluctant to express their views. Many church members resisted using English, and many within the community — particularly older people and women — spoke no English at all. When Philip Phelps was inaugurated as Hope College's first president he described the refusal to learn English as a "near fatal mistake." The college's position that English would be the primary language accorded with Albertus Van Raalte's earlier urging that the colonists should learn and speak the language of their new country. A portion of Dr. Phelps' inaugural address showed that Van Raalte's view remained controversial twenty years after the colony was founded:

> ...if our church has such traditional regard for education, why have New England influence and New England reputation extended throughout this continent, while the Dutch progress has been kept within so narrow limits? Simply or chiefly because the Hollanders refused to use the English language until it was a century too late to retrieve their almost fatal mistake! What! is the English language so much better than the Hollandish? No, _but whatever God chooses for anything is best_!

Interior of Hope Church, where services were conducted in English

The same mistake that limited the influence of Dutch Reformed churches in the west affected individual families in smaller but more poignant ways. Aleida Pieters, writing in 1923, retained a vivid memory from the previous century, of an early settler who had determined to maintain a little Holland in America by firmly retaining Dutch customs and language.

> The writer well remembers, when a child, being told by the widow of one of the early settlers that this was their intention, and that therefore they did not wish to learn to speak English. The sadness in her tone will never be forgotten as she added, "But we made a mistake." The sadness was all the more touching since this old woman who had not wished to learn English, could not converse with her own grandchildren, as they could not speak Dutch.

*The Reverend Philip Phelps, D.D.
first president of Hope College*

1 8 6 6

H. Woltman
W. Moerdyke

P. Moerdyke
W. B. Gilmore

G. Dangremond
W. A. Shields

A. Buursma
J. W. Te Winkel

He saw in education the hope of the colony. It was his lodestar, the compass by which he steered.

"Dominie Van Raalte wishes the school districts to be discussed." It was Albertus Van Raalte's insistence, beginning at the first meeting of the Holland Classis on April 23, 1848, which put the topic of education on the classis agenda and kept it there. Other topics were far more absorbing, such as "the man with his brother's widow," addressed at the first classis meeting and several thereafter: a man sought permission from the classis to marry his brother's widow and thus to support her and her children, was denied permission, married her anyway, and was excommunicated along with his new wife. At its second meeting, the classis agreed to discuss education, and did so. "Dominie Ypma proposes that the interests of the schools shall be discussed. The discussion takes place, and the judgment is: the schools must be promoted and cared for by the churches, as being an important part of the Christian calling of God's church on earth. All lukewarmness and coldness toward that cause must be condemned and rebuked."

In *de Kolonie* there was no wish to separate church and state, and there was no need for such separation. Holland's population was growing rapidly, but for some time the number of American citizens living there was small, and the number of voters could be counted on the fingers of a man's hands — Mrs. Fairbanks, Mrs. Smith, Mrs. Post all of course being ineligible. Provision of a government was thus largely up to the Hollanders themselves, and, under Van Raalte's leadership, this was accomplished efficiently through the *Volksvergadering* system, patterned after classis meetings, in which trustees met together regularly to discuss, plan, and regulate. Education would be provided in Christian schools. When the community became eligible for state support of its schools, the schools became public. Albertus Van Raalte was elected school inspector and religious topics continued to be taught. Nor was this out of step with the ethos of the time. Schoolteachers generally were expected to be properly religious, and the religion usually expected was Protestant.

Progress was rapid. A school district was formed. School officers were elected: Albertus C. Van Raalte, moderator; Henry D. Post, director; W. J. Mulder, assessor. Van Raalte volunteered to donate a lot on which the school would be constructed, and money raising began. Textbooks — spellers, readers and arithmetic books — were prescribed; adults learned to read from Bibles in which Dutch and English texts were printed in parallel columns. It was some years, however, before the first real school building was completed, and until that time, students were taught in a variety of places, including the versatile Orphan House, which over the years housed classes, offices and a publishing company, but never an orphan, because every orphaned child was welcomed into one of the colony families.

Even the most ignorant Hollander bearing in mind the educational position of the Netherlands, could not be unmindful of the need for elementary schooling. Thus it was that during the very first year, schools were started in the different communities. In the settlement of Holland, an American, Mr. Ira Hoyt, taught the first school in the winter of 1847-1848 in a small building on what [was then] called the Van der Haar farm. During the day the children were taught, but in the evening the men and women came to be instructed in English. A little later the log church at the cemetery was used, and later still the school was kept in a private house on Eighth Street.

> *There was also a school taught by an English schoolteacher, Mr. Hoyt. At first the school was held in Mr. Binnekant's home and later in ours. He had a big house and could easily spare a room.*
>
> from the diary of Grace - Geesje - Van der Haar Visscher

The concern of those in settled places in the east, for the welfare of those in what was then the west, was not confined to the realm of religion. During the 1840s a civic leader in Vermont formed an association whose purpose was to supply schoolteachers for western communities. In 1849, Elvira Langdon, sponsored by this society, came to Holland by a route she described afterwards as "tedious." She rode the stagecoach from Allegan to Singapore — "then a thriving lumbering village near the present site of Saugatuck" — stopped there for a week "until I could get word to Mr. Post, twelve miles distant," and then traveled along the beach — there was no road into Holland — in an open wagon drawn by horses who had to rest often because of the sleet and snow. "Once I tried walking for a change but a big wave from the lake caused me to hurry back to the wagon." Arriving at the mouth of Black Lake where she was "refreshed by a cup of coffee from the *vrouw* of the boat house," she and her large trunk were transported by open boat to Holland. In 1850 Miss Langdon moved farther west and married, but she never forgot the year she worked in Holland, and when she wrote her reminiscences for the Semi-Centennial celebration in August 1897, she noted wryly, "I sometimes felt lonely, and imagined I had privations; I had not yet lived in Nebraska."

> *It was in the middle of the century, 1849, that I was employed by Henry D. Post to teach the first school taught by a woman in Holland. In addition to this I also organized the first English Sunday School in Holland. It was kept up six months and then dropped, owing to sickness and cholera.*
>
> *…There was no schoolhouse in Holland but I had a small, comfortable room in which to open school. I adopted methods in teaching suited to children who were ignorant of the English language. I used oral teaching entirely at first, as I perceived they retained these ideas better than when required to study [from books]. My Sunday School was also on a simple plan.*
>
> *…That winter I taught in a lone house built for orphans. …I never lost interest in Holland, though I dare say I would find none of my Holland friends who would remember the schoolma'm.*

Albertus Van Raalte's gift for enlisting others in causes he believed in was used forcefully for the cause of education in his colony. He looked with pride at the Pioneer School, but from the first he envisioned a college, where young people from the colony could be educated as ministers and teachers. The Reverend John Garretson, secretary of the Board of Domestic Missions of the Dutch Reformed Church, visited Holland and prepared a report, stating the purposes of the academy which Van Raalte proposed to found. "The object of this school shall be to prepare sons of the colonists and others to be educated in Rutgers College, New Brunswick, N.J., and also to educate daughters of the said colonists, and others, in the branches of study ordinarily embraced in a female education in this country."

The classis however being deeply impressed of the urgent necessity of an Academy of <u>religious education</u> for the churches, a religious education not only fit to sharpen the mind but also fit to train the heart; (being learned by experience that teaching without decisive religious influence is apt to cause damage to the churches) takes liberty to ask most humble and urgent the Board of Education to do all what is possible for this part of the Lord's Church and for this steadily increasing Dutch population in the West; to secure to them a religious education of the youth: that those churches of emigrants from the Netherlands may be able to fill well their position trusted to them in the West, and that their increasing wants of Preachers and Schoolmasters etc. may be supplied.

Minutes of the meeting of the Holland Classis, April 1854

Van Raalte saw that basic education must continue in addition to academic preparation for higher education — and from the academy, a college could be born. In 1853, school and academy were separated. Oversight of the Holland Academy became the responsibility of the general synod, in the east, and was placed under the management of the denomination's Board of Education. At a meeting of the Holland Classis in 1853, Van Raalte transferred five acres of land to be used as a campus for a college. Representatives from Overisel volunteered the services of their community to clear the trees from the land. Eastern benefactors donated funds; the most generous donation — $7,000 — was given by Samuel Schieffelin.

TOWNSHIP ELECTION HOLLAND

For Supervisor
Henry D. Post — 132
Anderen en blanken — 4

For Township Treasurer.
Hendrik van Eijk — 131
Anderen en blanken — 5

For Township Clerk
Pieter van den Berg — 134
Al de anderen — 2

For Justices of the Peace
To fill vacancy, for 3 years,
Henry D. Post — 131
Al de anderen — 5
for full term
Hendrik van Eijk — 134
Al de anderen — 2

For School Inspector
Albertus C. Van Raalte — 135
Al de anderen — 1

De Hollander, June 6, 1853

John Garretson assisted Van Raalte in enlisting the help of the eastern churches. His plan called for developing subscription lists for annual contributions over a period of five years, at the end of which time he predicted (over-optimistically) that the institution would be self-sustaining. In the meantime, the Board sent a teacher to the colony. He was Walter Teller Taylor, an elder in the Dutch Reformed church of Geneva, New York, and he arrived in 1851 with his whole family — his wife, their daughters Margaret and Anna and their son Hugh — and Holland's first piano.

The only newspaper was printed in the Dutch language and was edited and published by Hermanus Doesburg, who had two sons. Doesburg also kept a small school for instruction in the Dutch language, which I attended for a time. There was in those days a large frame building [the Orphan House] standing on the square where I think Hope College now stands, in which a Walter T. Taylor with one or more assistants had a school for instruction in English. Whether it was a public or private school I do not know but I remember Mr. Taylor very well. He was an elderly man with a long gray beard and a severe aspect. I know I stood in great awe of him (and so did all the boys that had passed once under his rod), for he greatly resembled the prophet Elijah, whose picture was in our family Bible.

Edward Cahill's Reminiscences

Mr. Taylor was an experienced schoolmaster and accomplished scholar, though with little formal schooling, who had taught himself Greek, Latin, French, German and Dutch. He was not yet fifty years old when he came to Holland, but his physical appearance and personal characteristics made him appear older. He began his teaching duties immediately, and added a Latin class. During his first year, all three of his children were his assistants, but his older daughter and principal assistant, Margaret, died suddenly in July 1852. Her obituary, in the *Grand River Times*, is an example of the florid style of the times (and the *Times*).

This is the first time a death has occurred among the American residents of Holland; and the first victim is the one whom all would have selected as least likely to receive the dread summons. May we all profit by the warning, and may the king of terrors find us all as well prepared to make the journey "to that bourne from whence no traveller returns" as she was.

Despite all difficulties, Taylor gave his heart and soul to teaching, and achieved so well that by 1854 some of his students were ready to study in the east at Rutgers College. But sadly, his situation in the colony suited neither the Hollanders nor himself. He returned to New York after three years, and again opened an Academy, which the *Geneva Gazette*, in an article headed "Our Schools and Mr. Taylor" heralded enthusiastically. "Few places in the country furnish better facilities than Geneva for every grade of education. And now we are to have one more among us — that fine old Roman, Mr. W. T. Taylor, who for more than twenty years was associated, as a chief teacher, with all the real thorough scholarship of the neighborhood... is about to open a school in our midst. There are pupils in abundance for another classical school; and there can be no chance of failure, if our citizens will remember their obligations to Mr. Taylor's great learning, industry and fidelity." Walter Taylor did not live to establish his new school; he died in less than a year. Though his obituary was written in a most admiring style, some of the information, had it been available, might have deterred John Garretson from selecting him to work in the Holland colony.

Walter Teller Taylor

His private study left its mark upon him in some peculiarities of little moment. ...He sought to lay well the foundations of knowledge and never yielded to the temptation to sacrifice the ultimate advantage of the pupil to the allurements of ease or present popularity. ...Somewhat stern as a teacher he could not help being, for it was a serious purpose with him, to bring the untrained and reluctant minds, which were committed to him, under discipline, and to train wayward wits to careful study.

He was often pained by unskillful censure... It was perhaps from a feeling of disappointment at the success of his efforts here, as well as from the conviction that few could be found so well qualified as himself by experience and teaching, and a thorough knowledge of the Dutch language, that led him in 1851 to remove to Michigan to undertake the school in the recent Dutch settlement of Holland.

Dear Dominie,

. . . I have been thinking of the sad misunderstandings which had crept in between you and father — and hoped they would pass away and that all would be bright again. And I think with Father that they were passing away, for he has often spoken of you with great kindness and sympathy and only the night before he died was wishing that he could see you and Mrs. Van Raalte, and the children. But this is not to be in this world.

. . . Dear Dominie forgive all imperfections in this letter. I have written very fast, and then my thoughts would run ahead of my pen. Please write to me. I would be so happy to receive a letter from you. Give my love to all the family,

and believe me,

respectfully yours,

Anna

There was indeed a sad misunderstanding between Walter Taylor and Albertus Van Raalte — it was a misunderstanding about the source of Taylor's irascibility. Van Raalte and the other Hollanders believed, mistakenly, that Mr. Taylor gave his students the rough side of his tongue because he didn't like the Dutch. When people who are members of a group that is looked down upon are treated rudely or unfairly, they often assume the mistreatment occurs because of their group status. (I am an "X"; that person is unkind to me; therefore that person is prejudiced against Xs.) "This people is uneducated," Van Raalte wrote, "*but they must not be despised.*"

Both men had strong feelings and were impetuous. Van Raalte was good-tempered unless roused. Taylor was, by all accounts, habitually bad-tempered. At this point in his life he was old (by the standards of the time), he was far from the place where he had always lived, he worked hard and was paid late if he was paid at all (and he may not have realized that in this regard he was being treated the way all the colony's ministers were). His older daughter, whom he relied on most heavily as an assistant, had died. His temper probably was worse than usual, not surprisingly, but it had been his style for years to be crotchety and cross. Young Edward Cahill, an American, saw Taylor as a grumpy, scary old man. The Dutch children saw him as a grumpy, scary old man who didn't like Dutch people.

In 1853, two ministers of the Dutch Reformed Church, David McNeish and John Newton Schultz, visited places in the west — now the middle west — which were receiving support from the church's Board of Domestic Missions. John Garretson was aware that there was concern about Walter Taylor's effectiveness as principal of the academy, and he had asked them to make inquiries. McNeish was a cheerful Scot who described himself and his colleague as "chiels among them, taking notes." The Scots word *chiel* originally meant *child* but evolved to mean an inexperienced person; the visiting ministers were inexperienced in understanding Dutch language and customs. He wrote in detail to tell Garretson about "the condition of the Academy you labored so hard to found."

We visited the Academy and were all well pleased with Mr. Taylor as a Teacher. His pupils had been thoroughly trained, being very well drilled and had made good progress. This was very gratifying. But while we found Mr. T. to be a good Teacher we found, I am sorry that it is so, that he lamentably failed in securing the good feelings and kind wishes of either pupils or their parents. This is a very great draw back to the prosperity of the school.

When he first went there, he commenced teaching both the district school and the Academy. For the services he rendered in the District School he received the sum of thirty dollars per month - what you gave him I don't know. This connection had subsisted from the time he went out there until a few weeks before we went up. It was obliged to be broken up, because the people would no longer send their children to him. The reason they give is that he treated them more like cattle - and indeed was in the habit of calling them a <u>rough, uncouth, uncultivated, dirty set of cattle</u> and that he did not wish to be troubled with such <u>herds</u> of them. The various clergymen endeavored to smooth matters as much as possible - but did not succeed. The people replied that they had not only discovered a want of sympathy on his part for them, but a disposition to harshly and cruelly treat their children. They said that they would make no objections to their children being corporally punished if necessary - but to have them brow-beaten and upbraided with such opprobrious language they would not have. So vacate the district he must. But his unhappy manner has alienated the affection of the people generally - and he learned that the clergymen of the various colonies had been working with great earnestness to persuade the people to send their children to the Academy. It is all up-hill work for them to sustain him. The ministers are grieved, for they see that it is an Institution of much promise to their Church. By-the-bye Mr. Taylor has been severely afflicted in the loss of his eldest daughter. I presume that the Academy also suffers in consequence of this affliction of the Providence of God.

Albertus and Christina Van Raalte had a gift which is often described as "a way with people." They were kind and caring and their home was a happy place. If Albertus Van Raalte had known that Taylor was the same in the colony as he had been, and would be again, in New York, he might have been able to befriend and guide him. Their mutual love of music might have become a source of shared pleasures. But, as Anna Taylor wrote, that was "not to be in this world." Walter Taylor was dismissed. Albertus Van Raalte wrote to John Garretson that the problem was incurable, but with characteristic kindness and the "alsoo" that marks a letter as Van Raalte's own — "above this we wish to honor him alsoo is our step painfull towards him" — he hoped that the Board would manage the dismissal as gently as possible.

Dear Brother,

...Now something about an dear interest t.w. [to wit] our School. This in confidence. You know Mr. Taylor has been in our district school. Last summer were the clergymen obliged to separate Mr. Taylor's academy from the district school; to avoid disagreeable conflict between Mr. Taylor and the people: we did prepare the orphan house for the Academy: not being able to get timely a teacher in the district School.

...The school is injured by the uncertainty of the institution: most of the time has Mr. Taylor spoken in such a way that he was about to leave the place; then on account of his disgust in the people; then on account of the want of payment. Mr. Taylor is an able teacher therefore I do estimate him highly: but I must tell you in confidence that there is no sympathy between him and the people. He has a too difficult and a too impatient and unforbearing temper. I stood from the beginning between him and the people: it was a trying burden: but I am convinced the evil is deeprooted and can not be cured. ...Mr. Taylor will remain the same till his death...

The subject of the School has been since long ago a cause of great anxiety among us, and we did not know what to do: - we did handle Mr. Taylor always very discreetly and did hush everything: notwithstanding this he has lost the place in the heart entirely.

The step of the classis is unknown to him, and we wish it so, because every body is afraid to have anything to do with him; he is too difficult to handle: and above this we wish to honor him alsoo is our step painfull towards him. We do not wish to damage him but only we must say he can not answer for this people. This people is uneducated but they must not be despised. We want a man who is willing to converse with the people about religion of the heart and who is able to train the hearts of children. Also we ought to have a man who is a real friend of the Dutch church. Without going into details, which is impossible, I am opening my whole heart to you, knowing that I trust my self in the hands of a wise and dear Brother. It can not go; our School looses the place out the hearts of the people and we can not exspect that the church will have benefit of the school on the contrary. Mr. Taylor did tell me that he had written to the board that he was willing to receive his dismission under condition of six weeks notice and his pay; the best way is grant him this and to make an end with him.

VIEW OF RUTGERS COLLEGE AND GROUNDS, AT NEW BRUNSWICK, N. J., 1879.

The young men who had prepared, under Taylor's tutelage, to enter Rutgers College were now about to leave the Holland colony for the sophisticated world of New Jersey — an awe-inspiring, and expensive, step. On September 19, 1854, two of John Garretson's correspondents wrote to him. Cheerful, fluent David McNeish had suddenly died; now John Schultz was the informant. Albertus Van Raalte also wrote, bubbling with ideas and verbiage (with a few words idiosyncratically spelled), and with a sparkle of humor as well as pride now that young men from the Academy were going to the college. "Now dear Brother, New Brunswick being peopled with Hollanders, it will cause you a great deal work."

Kalamazoo Mich. Sept. 19th 1854

Rev. J. Garretson
Ch'st. Brother.

…Dominie Vander Meulen expects to start for New Brunswick next Monday (25 inst.) in order to take his son Jacob and one or two other boys to the College. He will arrive here on Tuesday and be in N.Y. on Thursday or Friday. I told him to go to the Chrn.

Intelligencer Office and inquire for you or a letter from you to direct him onward. The boys have scarcely any means to depend on. ...Upon consultation with Doms. Van Raalte and Vander Meulen it was deemed best taking all things into consideration that two or more go this year. Some of the Hollanders want to see the fruits of the Academy and wish to go, the church expects them, etc. Dom. Van Raalte says that you promised to see to the boys' necessities beyond the supply of the Synod's funds. To aid you I have written concerning this matter in Dom. Vander Meulen's letter of introduction to Pres't. Frelinghuysen.

I will write you again next week about home affairs. We have a fine autumn day - a rain last night and a buoyant air and glorious sky today. But 50 miles riding on the top of a loaded stage coach gives me a strong inclination to sleep.

So good night.

Yours truly,
John N. Schultz

September 19, 1854

My very dear Brother!

The Lord be your shield joy and strength, that you may run the race without being weary, that your life may be spared for the good of Zion, and to glorify God in his redemption work: - Since long ago I would have written, but I was so much hesitating, and surely it wants decision to accomplish such if a person is steadily in the midst of a stream of urgent necessities, which must be done at once. The reasons of my hesitation were that the boys for College did draw back under pretext to be unfit for the ministry. Now after the visit of Dominies McNeish, Schultz and Crispell it is yet settled in the right way. Dominie Vander Meulen will now go himself next morning to bring his son to New Brunswick. I hope you will meet him there or in New York and help him along so much as possible. With them will go the second boy C. Vander Veen. The third... I fear will not go: - His father had an intention to send him to Ann Arbor in Michigan; on account he could do it $100 cheaper per annum: and he could not afford to pay $100 more because his means were to limited. I told him my reasons why I thought it better was to go to New Brunswick, and alsoo that I had a strong hope that you would be willing and able to seek for him by some church that $100 wanted: I wish my dear Brother this request was not to burdensome nor entirely out of your reach. Then I have strong hope that a young man from Rochester t.w. Brother Zwemer will be helped along by the classis of Geneva: he has a desire for the ministry and he is fit for it, so I think. Now dear Brother, New Brunswick being peopled with Hollanders, it will cause you a great deal work; and I am beginning somewhat to fear, that the burden will be to heavy because they are all poor. May God give you Strength to plead the cause of Jesus Christ and give you Speed. -

Our hearts are filled with sorrow, about the sudden and unexpected death of our beloved Brother McNeish. He had been here to preach in the Colony: just when he came home, he was taken sick and did die.- What a blow for his family and Church not only, but also for the West! - The Colony did loose a warm friend; his death has left a deep impression on our mind: it was a clear and loud teaching of the uncertainty of life, and a solemn warning to work while it was yet daytime. It is a great consolation that he is gone to his rest alsoo that God called him away; and nobody else, and that his dealings with his church are wise and good.-

Our dear Brother Crispell has visited us.- He is a man love and high esteem worth; a pearl. May God incline his heart to this appointment, and make him willing to deny himself and to work here for Jesus sake. I pity that church which has to loose him, but I hope you will succeed in finding one good for her: - I am satisfied he is a man able to exert a moulding influence upon a community. I am full of anxiety to hear of the decision.

Dominie de Moen, living in the Netherlands, my wife's own Brother, did receive a call from the church, Overijssel: if he could come (but his sickly wife is most feeble) we would have in him an important addition for our classis.

...We were blessed with a healthy summer and with a prosperous season; but the sudden and extreme change in the weather from heat to cold has brought on quite a deal sickness, and the drought of the past two months has injured some the crops. Several in my family are sick now, my wife alsoo is now sick, but during the summer she has been unusual strong: the symptoms are now good and I have a strong hope that she by God's kindness will be back at her post, where she is wanted so much.

After Walter Taylor left the Academy, the Board of Domestic Missions sent the Reverend F. P. Beidler to serve as principal *pro tem.* Edward Cahill referred to him in his reminiscences as a pleasant gentleman whose name he couldn't remember. A genial man, he attended a classis meeting in 1855 and was greeted cordially. Beidler kept up the work of the Academy and included girls as well as boys in the classes, as Walter Taylor and Elvira Langdon had done. He taught Sunday School, and, for the first time, provided church services in English.

The third principal of the Holland Academy was the Reverend John Van Vleck, who came to Holland in 1855 from the east, where he had just graduated from Rutgers College and New Brunswick Theological Seminary. He was a remarkable young man. One of Van Raalte's biographers describes him as "an intimate friend of Van Raalte, as three of his letters show which he addressed to the latter." This misapprehension fails to take into account that three letters were only a tiny fraction of Van Vleck's epistolary output. Albertus Van Raalte was a great speaker, able to affect and influence his hearers because his powerful words and ideas were in harmony. When he wrote letters, he wrote as he spoke — effervescently and honestly. Van Vleck was a prolific letter writer, and when read together, his letters, which are preserved in different archives, reveal his character.

The Reverend John Van Vleck

Walter Taylor was testy; John Van Vleck was devious. He did indeed write effusive professions of friendship to Van Raalte, but at the same time he was writing letters to John Garretson, full of self-praise interlaced with innuendo and complaints about Van Raalte and the community.

> *I regret to state that I am discouraged with Holland as a field of missionary labor. Excepting my own family, the number of Eng. auditors on the Sabbath may be put down at about four, or perhaps three. And, until a better class of Eng. people move in the place, there is little hope for a better state of things in the future. I have not been here long enough to speak very positively about the prospects of this field. Bro. Beidler, I see, reported a "fine opening," and adds "all the members of our church seem to encourage Eng. preaching very much." Very true, – but there is only one 'member' here viz. Mr. Pitcher! and of the other Eng. people here only one family encourage preaching by their presence! I merely state these things as facts which I think the Board should know. Nothing but a sense of duty would induce me to make such a statement, which I well know may be so regarded as to reflect perhaps discredit upon my qualifications to be an acceptable pastor. It is a matter which weighs heavily upon me. I have however done my best, and endeavored to preach Christ faithfully. And of the few sermons I have preached here, the one you had the misfortune (?) to hear had the least gospel in it.*

> *Oh for more zeal! - more of that love which will constrain me both in the pulpit and out of it; to preach Christ and Him alone to my worldly-minded countrymen here. ...The American population here will probably be considerably increased before long. Already several such families have settled in our vicinity, but they are illiterate and wicked.*

Van Raalte and his new colleague were similar in wishing for expansion of the Academy. Van Vleck wanted, in addition, an assistant and more money — expectations that were understandable but unrealistic. One of the documents in Van Vleck's hand that has been preserved is a small book made of folded paper.

Travelling & Begging Guide
for
Rev. A. C. Van Raalte

Within are extraordinarily detailed directions, beginning (even though Van Raalte was an experienced traveler), "At Detroit purchase through tickets to N. York, via Great Western R. R. to Suspension Bridge - where you change cars." Day by day, he was directed which towns to visit, whom to stay with, when to write to Van Vleck, and what to do: "Rev. DeWitt promised me $120 per annum. Exact that, or else get all you can for the building. His people are rich. ...Do not leave New Paltz without a good round sum." Given Van Vleck's knowledge of the upstate New York area and the people in it, Van Raalte asked him to take a turn with the fundraising.

> *Holland, June 27, 1857*
> *Dear Dominie,*
> *Last evening I received the letter sent by you from Geneva & the one sent from Albany. Of course I was grieved at your poor success in getting the "tin." You ask if I will come & beg. Now dear Dominie, you know, or ought to, that I would do almost anything to relieve you. But in this matter I cannot. I would not raise enough to pay for my traveling expenses. In serious, dead earnest I mean what I say, when I say that I can not beg money, even tho' it be in a good cause. You can. Verbum sapienti sufficit. If you come home, & the money is not raised I will go & try - & the result will most assuredly*

be a failure. I am sorry to tell you this for it adds to your burdens, & implies weakness on my part - but it is better to speak plain truth. Your family are well. Mrs. V. R. seems in much better spirits than she did during your absence last winter. I believe the domestic affairs at your house are going on well - at least I know of no troubles there. The churches seem to be quiet. Your flock seems to be in a tranquil state. I have not heard any complaint of your absence. Bolks preached here on his return from Synod. V. d. Meulen has preached twice. Oggel will preach twice to-morrow. I will prob. the sab. following. There is very little sickness around now - less than usual. Elder Wilterdink has broken his arm.

The building progresses slowly. Schrader is at work for us again. Talsma, Slink, VerBeek & Co we could not get for a day. Suppose we had depended on them! Another mason from Battle Creek will come here within two weeks. The three will then soon lay up the bricks. I hope you will not neglect to send me the cash as fast as you gather it. I have now received of Academy funds all told $1971.25, & have expended $1579.96, leaving a balance in my hands of $391.29. Of this I will have to pay out to night near $200. So I will have about $100 left. So you see I will want the "needful." & it will go from hand to mouth. I fear & tremble. Excuse my vanity - but I think it is almost absolutely necessary for me to be here every day. I think decidedly the best policy for me to remain where I am & for you to stick to it till we have enough. We can ill afford to miss you at examination, but better your absence this year & the presence of a new building next year. May God bless & prosper you. This is my third hasty letter to you. May it reach you! Be strong and patient - your labors may bear fruit when your name is forgotten. Remember that I love you.

John Van Vleck

Academy Building

Reference has already been made to the new building. It is now in process of erection; and is to be of stone, and brick, and finished in the best style of Architecture. Its dimensions are fifty-three by forty-two feet, with four floors. It will accommodate one hundred students, and forty boarders. The private rooms for the Students will be ten by sixteen feet. The boarding department will be conducted by the family of the Principal. Every effort will be made to render it a comfortable and an agreeable *home*; it follows that no person of bad morals, or offensive habits, can be tolerated for a single day; and should any such find their way into the Institution the Principal claims the exclusive right of sending them away, (if need be) unceremoniously.

De Hollander, July 1, 1857

On this trip, Van Raalte raised nearly seven thousand dollars from 712 donors. Samuel Schieffelin gave $100, and there were lesser but substantial gifts from Nathan Graves, who later gave funds to build Graves Hall; Theodore Frelinghuysen, president of Rutgers College; and several members of the wealthy Van Rensselaer family. The average amount per gift was $9.36, and since the range was skewed by the large donations, it is clear, even without examining Van Raalte's meticulous records, that many gifts were very small. Van Vleck, meanwhile, was writing to Garretson: "The whole business connected with the erection of our new building devolved upon me. ...To put up such a building in Holland, where <u>nothing</u> is to be had ready to hand is, I assure you, a perplexing task."

Van Vleck was, briefly, a regent of the University of Michigan. At a Republican convention in 1857, delegates choosing a candidate for regent cast three ballots, with the same man leading the small field in the first two rounds of voting. On the third ballot "Albertus C. Van Raalte, of Ottawa, was declared to be unanimously nominated for the office of Regent of the University." The Democrats then nominated Cornelius Vander Meulen. Looking back at the times, and these men, we can see that it would have been advantageous if Van Raalte or Vander Meulen had served as regent of the University. The man chosen would have brought wisdom and judiciousness to the task, and his service would have extended awareness and appreciation of the Dutch-American community among influential state leaders. However, the *Grand Rapids Daily Eagle*, which reported convention results on March 19, carried a joint message from Van Raalte and Vander Meulen in the following week's issue: "We hope our friends are willing to excuse us in declining this nomination, because, as pastors in the church, we wish to avoid the appearance of being in conflict. ...[In our stead, we] propose John Van Vleck, a native born and trained American - a man whose life has been devoted to educational interests..." A 1906 *History of the University of Michigan* contains a record of Van Vleck's service. "In April 1857, he was elected Regent of the University of Michigan, and entered upon his duties the following January. He attended only a single meeting of the Board, and on October 2, 1858, resigned the office."

In July 1859, having finally left Holland, Van Vleck wrote a lengthy and dramatic letter to Van Raalte in which accusations and expressions of forgiveness, self-justification and self-condemnation, sarcasm and flowery expressions of regard, were tumbled together amid a mass of exclamation points. He acknowledged having "said naughty things about you and yours," recalled an occasion "when your countrymen irritated me a little!" and "cannot forbear adding a little here about 'your countrymen' [because] my <u>limited</u> acquaintance with them has convinced me that they have national faults." One strange passage concerned Pieter Oggel: "His [Oggel's] feelings also became alienated from me. Surely it was the work of the Devil: - perhaps it was a divinely sent punishment for my worshipping him! ...They do tell me that it was a reproof which I once felt called upon to administer to Christian [Pieter Oggel's younger brother] that changed the Dominie's feelings towards me. Impossible!" This was followed by expressions of love and beneficence: "I tell you honestly, if I was rich, and had my present heart, the very first thing I would do would be to put your church out of debt, and fill one side of Mr. Plugger's store with gifts for the poor dear children of God."

Five closely-written pages of the nine-page letter were devoted to two issues. First, he gave five reasons why he should have been allowed to take two Academy students with him to the east: "that they might continue their studies so as to enter the Sophomore class, which they could not do with Van de Wall (for they could teach him): — that they might become a little more refined by contact with good society among Americans: — that I might prosecute my study and speaking Dutch: — that they might aid us in traveling: — that, having mainly brought them to the stand they had attained, I had a certain claim to their society for a few months." Van Vleck had made the plan with the boys without consulting other faculty members or Van Raalte; in refusing to permit it, Van Vleck wrote, "a violence has been done their feelings which they will never forget. ...There was mercilessness (I coin a word) in parting us." The remainder of this section of the letter consisted of elaborate description of financial transactions, which Van Vleck concluded by writing, "Thus, dear Dominie, you see I was all in the right, and you, all in the wrong." The letter closed with a request — "Please write me soon and at length" — and the news that his infant daughter was flourishing. "We shall teach her to lisp your name with gratitude." Later that year, an anonymous letter-writer who signed himself "W" wrote to the *Christian Intelligencer*, to oppose giving any more funds to the Academy. The writer warned against such aid on four counts.

First, have we not been deceived in respect to what Synod voted in 1853, to transfer to the Reformed Church a debt and Free School to be supported for years to come? The Committee was of the opinion that in five years it would be self-supporting. What efforts have been made in the West to make it so? Had I known the secret objects of the movement, I would have voted against it.

Secondly, have we not done all that was asked for?

Thirdly, have not the Holland brethren been allowing themselves to walk too much on crutches? ... How many repair bills will it take to open the eyes of the Synod?...

Fourthly, why are the improvements needed now? There are accommodations for forty students. A Refectory was installed and now the new Principal declines to board the students. Then let him find a residence elsewhere. The Hall was not built to furnish a free residence for a principal, but to house a man who would take personal oversight over the pupils, the burden of boarding them as well. Mr. Van Vleck always paid rent or its equivalent. I see no necessity of a second teacher in the building.

By this time, Philip Phelps had come to head the Academy, and Van Raalte at last had the colleague he needed. He wrote to Phelps, "Let us not trouble ourselves with Mr. V. V. He says he did not write it, but it is his spirit. But I pray you let him alone. He is suspected in the East and they all say it will damage him very much. ..." Philip Phelps wrote two long articles for the *Christian Intelligencer* in response to "W." Van Raalte made two more trips to the east, and eventually raised enough to complete construction of Van Vleck Hall, Hope College's first building, which stands to this day. John Van Vleck opened an academy near Poughkeepsie, but left the field of teaching after three years and then served as a pastor in two upstate churches over a period of two years. He died in 1865.

John Van Vleck believed he was a better, cleverer, more *suitable* person to be in a position of leadership than, for example, Albertus Van Raalte. The contrast seemed great to him between his subordinate status and his natural superiority. History and everyday life provide other instances of people who are overtly deferential to someone who has a claim on their allegiance, but are surreptitiously disrespectful. One such example is revealed in the collected letters of George B. McClellan. On November 1, 1861, early in the Civil War, President Lincoln appointed McClellan commander of the entire Union Army. Two weeks later McClellan wrote to his wife, referring sarcastically to Lincoln by a phrase they were accustomed to using in private: "went to the White House shortly after tea where I found *the original gorilla*, about as intelligent as ever. What a specimen to be at the head of our affairs now... was of course much edified by his anecdotes — ever *apropos*, & ever unworthy of one holding his high position."

Van Vleck Hall was not dedicated until after John Van Vleck had left the Academy and returned to the east, although the building was in use even before construction was completed and he and his family and forty students lived there. Van Raalte could have given the building a different name — why did he not do so? The answer must be conjecture, since there is no indication that Van Raalte wrote about the name, or even thought about it. When he named buildings — or places — he used descriptive names: Orphan House, Pioneer School, Holland Academy, Third Reformed Church. While the building was being erected, Van Raalte was often in the east raising money for it; Van Vleck was in Holland. It is likely that people became accustomed to speaking of Van Vleck's hall.

With all his failings, John Van Vleck had taught well and worked hard, and he impressed many people with his talents as an instructor. Moreover it must be remembered that Van Raalte was unaware of just how troublesome Van Vleck had tried to be.

Van Vleck Hall

Hope College Collection of the Joint Archives

Unless John Garretson gave him some cautions about Van Vleck — and there is no record that he did — Van Raalte never knew about the letters stored in the records of the denomination's Board of Domestic Missions. The fact that he readily named the college's first building for a difficult former colleague is one of many indications that Albertus Van Raalte thought in a different way from many people; one reason he accomplished so much is that he didn't waste his thoughts on fruitless irritation. Like Walter Taylor, John Van Vleck had done some good work and caused some trouble; they were gone and the new principal was a gem. Van Vleck Hall was a handsome part of the college campus, and Albertus Van Raalte probably found it a source of pride.

During Van Vleck's time at the Academy, education for girls and young women — which Van Raalte strongly supported — was abandoned. Philip Phelps restored it. His older daughter Frances and his son Philip Tertius (Philip, the third) graduated in 1882, and Eliza — Lizzie — Phelps graduated in 1885. Sarah Alcott was a classmate of Frances Phelps and Mary Alcott was a classmate of Lizzie's; these were the first four women to graduate from Hope. Fourteen years before Frances Phelps and Sarah Alcott graduated, in May 1868, the Council of Hope College had adopted the following resolution, forward-looking for its time, though flawed from a modern perspective: "Higher education for females seems to furnish the proper medium between that spirit of Oriental barbarism which regards women as fitted only to be mere parent and housekeeper, and the infidelity of 'women's rights' falsely so called." What is most pertinent about the resolution is that the college *did* accept women students, and educated them as people, not as a separate and subordinate class.

The Emperor Napoleon, in 1808, decreeing the curriculum
for a school established for the orphaned daughters of his soldiers

What shall be taught to the young ladies who are to be educated at Ecouen? First religion in all its severity. ...You must bring up women who believe and not women who argue. The feebleness of the female brain, the instability of their ideas, their destination in the social order, the necessity on their part of constant and perpetual resignation and of a sort of prompt and indulgent charity — all this can be obtained only through religion, through a religion that is both kind and charitable.

The nineteenth century, like previous centuries, was not a time of equality between men and women; such an idea never occurred to most people. However, the second half of the century brought progress. In 1860, New York state passed the Married Women's Property Acts — the first in the nation to grant these freedoms: a married woman could buy, sell, and own property, maintain joint guardianship with her husband of their children, and keep her own wages. In 1869, the legislature of the newly formed Territory of Wyoming granted women the right to vote in all elections, though nationally, women's suffrage was hotly condemned. (One authority said it would be a mistake to give women the vote because it would be impossible to guard against fraud: the same woman could vote again and again, because all women looked alike.) When Matthew Vassar founded a college for women, it was ridiculed as "Vassar's folly," on the grounds that women could not survive the rigors of higher education. When Vassar Female College opened its doors — to capacity enrollment — in 1864, he wrote a diary entry comparing himself to Lincoln: "Two Noble Emancipists — one of women — [the other of] the negro."

In a miniature emancipation, Albertus Van Raalte was freed from many burdens. "After Phelps' arrival, Van Raalte was not so much the Atlas on which everything rested. In more than one sense they were spiritual brothers." Perhaps Van Raalte also saw Phelps as a surrogate son, with qualities and shared interests his own much loved sons lacked. Phelps, like Van Raalte, was named for his father, and he was the apple of his father's eye. The senior Phelps kept scrapbooks over the years, lovingly recording every school prize his son was awarded — pages and pages of them — and preserving letters and photographs and reports of his son's newsworthy achievements. Philip Phelps loyally assisted Albertus Van Raalte in every endeavor. He encouraged Van Raalte's fundraising in a pleasanter way than his predecessor had done, and then took up the burden himself. In the first excerpt below, Van Raalte is traveling; in the second he writes from Holland to Phelps, who is fundraising in the east.

> *You say that I must strike while the iron is hot. You are always right, but I wish you were the striker and I were the writer. Three months away from home for a man with an eating cancer of homesickness. Now, gentlemen and professors, will you allow me to come back at the end of January?*

> *I thank you very much for your kind informations, and I rejoice in your success and courage: I am very glad that our friend, Sam B. Schieffelin, did take a scholarship of $2500. ...Such are messengers from Heaven to cheer us on.*
> *I can sympathize with you in suffering from misrepresentations of your motives: Well, we can not avoid this and must expect such: He who has an evil in his heart he expects evil from others... but I must acknowledge that it is hard to bear it: In several hints thrown in my face I heard that my motives in working for the academy were low and mean; but let our life be fixed on what happened to Jesus when crucified: and it will leave us.*

They were partners in enthusiasm. When Hope Church was built, Phelps and his students provided janitorial services. When Holland was threatened by fire, Phelps organized bucket brigades and saved the college buildings, ensuring that the campus would be a place of refuge when the fire came. When the college needed a gymnasium, he and his students built it, and the completed building was dedicated by Dr. Phelps and his students "with the hoisting of the stars and stripes, the reading of a psalm, the singing of a hymn, the offering of a prayer and the concluding utterance of three rousing cheers." In his baccalaureate address to the first graduating class of Hope College, President Phelps spoke movingly of the years together.

Seldom does so special a link unite teacher and pupil, as that which has bound us together. In a sense which can never be repeated here to so full a degree, though it belongs in great measure to the three other of the first college classes — you are my class. I have been to you as preacher, preceptor, counsellor, brother, friend and companion ...Together we have been compelled to touch, however slightly, on almost every division of the curriculum. Together, too, we have gone into the woods, and there and on our own grounds, have labored with our own hands. We have worshipped together, evening and morning, at our academic altar, and on the Sabbath, in the sanctuary. We have passed together through the varied and often trying experience connected with the infancy of our college; and you have been not merely recipients but co-workers. Your habits, your attainments, your characters, your prayers are built on that foundation, which, we trust, will remain until the destruction and restitution of all things.

Dr. Phelps' study in Van Vleck Hall

In the earliest classes of Hope College there were students who left to serve in the Civil War; some returned to graduate and others did not. Over the years, Hope students have left their college for a multiplicity of reasons and many have returned and completed their course of study. Willard Wichers, class of '30, had a purpose for leaving which was, and probably will remain, unique. He was editor of the college yearbook, and his vision went beyond a single year. The first college annual appeared in 1905; earlier classes had no yearbook to be remembered in. There must have been more than a touch of Van Raalte's and Phelps' enthusiasm in this tall young man, because the project he conceived and carried through was a classbook spanning more than six decades. *The Milestone* appeared in 1931; the thick volume is an invaluable historical document. Students in each graduating class are listed and pictured — for the earliest classes, a touching and unusual array, where recently taken photographs of gray-haired elders are side by side with pictures of long-dead youngsters who were their classmates. But in 1931 the country was in the midst of the Great Depression. Merchants who had taken ads, and students who had ordered copies, could not pay. Wynand Wichers was the new college president; his nephew asked him for help in paying the debt. His uncle suggested he get a job. The young man dropped out of college, worked to pay *The Milestone's* bills, and graduated in 1932.

Top row, l. to r.:
A. T. Huizenga,
E. J. Heeren,
G. Bolks

Bottom row, l. to r.:
D.B.K. Van Raalte,
J. Huizenga,
J. De Pree

Hope College Collection of the Joint Archives

The first Class of Hope College are all gone, and I am the only one left of the Second Class. I am eighty-eight years old; and between me of this second class, '67, and the tenth class, '75, but one Alumnus remains - the Rev. J. Meulendyk, '73.

We two are thus distinguished - both are in the eighties, but we are still holding on - Brother Meulendyk rather strongly; I feebly. Yet, as of yore, still deeply interested in affairs a-la-Hope.

We of those early classes were strong, able-bodied men, and there were some expert carpenters in our midst. No Athletic Association in those days, but it was felt that a gymnasium was needed. President Phelps, himself adept at tools, proposed we, ourselves, build one. So we all followed him out to the forests, felled the trees, rolled the logs to the river where they were floated down the stream to the old Pluggers Mill, thence sawed into lumber for our projected building.

Those have been called "the days of small things," but with our finished product which answered the purpose and lasted for many years, we felt this no small job.

Then we assisted in making a huge chandelier - the frame work was of heavy tin, painted black. In this were inserted large letters spelling HOPE, illuminated by tiny kerosene lamps. This was suspended over the platform in our newly erected Gym - which building was also used for some years as the Chapel and Assembly Hall. At that time no one dreamed of electric bulbs.

Pioneer experiences, indeed, but withal a feeling of manly independence and self assurance, gained by discovering that - "Necessity is the Mother of Invention."

Our class numbered six. Three became ministers and of these one went as a missionary to India. One flourished as a schoolmaster for many years. The remaining two held up the business ends of the class.

And now life's curtain is falling fast upon many of us older graduates, and the illuminated HOPE of the past is a little dimmer as we look back, but our HOPE for and of the future, is brighter with a heavenly glow. At the end of my long life, I can still say, "Hope is the College of Colleges."

Gerrit Bolks, class of 1867, *The Milestone* (1930)

Twenty years after the cold February night in 1847 when Albertus Van Raalte reached the wilderness where his colony would be built, Gerrit Bolks and five fellow seniors, including Civil War veterans Dirk Van Raalte and John Huizenga, were beginning their final college term. Van Raalte had followed his lodestar — his guiding light — with perseverance and faith. What he accomplished shines even more brightly in retrospect than it did in his time.

Dominie Pieter Oggel and Dominie Albertus C. Van Raalte

People bound for Zion almost always have trouble with their fellows along the way.

In the first few years after the Holland colony was founded life was hard and there was much suffering, and yet there was also much gratitude for God's providence. In those difficult days, Dominie Van Raalte's unflagging courage and care sustained the people. Holland grew and thrived, and beyond *de Kolonie's* little boundaries America expanded and grew strong. With so much to be proud of, so much to be grateful for, nevertheless in the decade of the 1850s there were troubles in the colony, and in the larger world outside the town as well. One forecast of future trouble appeared, as the decade opened, in a letter responding to an ongoing concern: the community's need for a harbor. Albertus Van Raalte was diligent in petitioning officials, urging support for the project; Senator Lewis Cass was unusual, among the officials addressed, in replying promptly and straightforwardly.

Washington, August 12, 1850

Dear Sir,

I have the pleasure to inform you that appropriation is reported in the improvement bill for $10,000 for Black River, and I assure you that no effort will be spared by the whole of our delegation to procure its final passage. Our present difficulty is the great question which so much divides the country. If that were out of the way we might hope to enter upon the proper business of legislation, and to dispatch it without delay. I hope for this result, but still there is danger that we may adjourn without the restoration of harmony and if we do, we may soon take the consequences.

I am dear sir,

Truly yours,

Lewis Cass

"The great question which so much divides the country" was not a question, but a practice which some believed was necessary and desirable, and others believed was an abomination. This was the practice of slavery, and it was the source from which many terrible questions flowed. A small town in Michigan needed a small appropriation which would result in substantial benefit to an extended area. A myriad of similar needs throughout the country also waited to be addressed. But they were submerged by debates about questions which by this time centered not on ways to end or limit slavery but on ways to protect and promote it: How widely shall slavery spread throughout the expanding nation? To what extent shall the citizens of individual states which have banned slavery within their borders be forced to cooperate with slave states in treating Negroes as property? The questions could be, and were, expressed in a multiplicity of ingenious ways. What couldn't happen, and didn't, was for agreement to be reached about how the questions were to be answered.

As to the harbor, the Hollanders set to work and dug a channel themselves, which remained navigable for four years. The harbor enabled passenger ships to reach the town and mail to be carried by packet boat from Grand Haven. Easier access to other communities and the opportunity for more extensive and rapid communication between the colony and the outside world was economically advantageous for Holland. It also opened the way to further Americanization, which was in turn matched by greater resistance to change.

HOLLANDERS DIG THEIR OWN CHANNEL — 1850

One effect of more efficient mail delivery was that newspapers arrived more promptly. A hundred and fifty years ago, American newspapers were not huge empires bent on devouring their competition; most of them were bumptious little weeklies, serving a particular community or a special interest, and featuring a potpourri of civic news, vigorous commentary, informal items about the local citizenry, and colorfully worded advertisements. They filled out their columns with items clipped from other papers around the country. Then, as now, newspapers printed news designed to alarm as well as to inform. And they were eagerly read.

It is possible for people, and nations, to want opposing things, and to want them vehemently. This period in history was a time when America wanted to grow. It wanted more land — and got it. It wanted more people to settle the land — and they came. It also wanted not to grow, not to change, not to look up and discover that there were people in the next town or street or house who looked different, talked a different language, had different customs, worshipped in a different way. Some Americans came to the conclusion that they didn't want un-Americans

88

around, so they formed secret societies with secret passwords and secret ways of shaking hands, and then they formed a political party and — to the consternation of the two major political parties, the Whigs and the Democrats — they began putting up candidates and winning elections. The new party's name changed around a good deal, but it was usually called the Native American party. Its members would have been richly surprised to know that future generations would recognize Native Americans who had more right to the name than they. The new party's stated purpose was to insure rights for people born here as citizens and to limit or deny rights to others. On the theory that they were likely to be oppressed and persecuted, party members were advised not to give out any information, and, if questioned, to answer, "I know nothing about it." The phrase became a nickname for the political group: the Know-Nothing party.

Know-Nothings hated immigrants and they hated Catholics — groups with overlapping memberships. They aimed to prevent such people from arriving on America's shores, to admit those who did get here to citizenship only after a 21-year uninterrupted residence, and to keep them from holding office even if they lived long enough to become citizens. In the 1854 elections Know-Nothing candidates won major state offices in Massachusetts, and received substantial support in New York, Pennsylvania, and a number of southern states. Because the early correspondence of national leaders is usually collected, studied and reported, we have the opinions of two future presidents on Know-Nothing success. Abraham Lincoln wrote, "As a nation, we began by declaring that 'all men are created equal.' We now practically read it, 'all men are created equal except negroes.' When the Know-Nothings get control, it will read, 'all men are created equal except negroes and foreigners and Catholics.'" Rutherford B. Hayes commented, "How people do hate Catholics, and what happiness it was to thousands to have a chance to show it in what seemed a lawful and patriotic manner."

The party was strong enough, by 1856, to hold its first — and only — national convention. Former president Millard Fillmore, who had served out Zachary Taylor's term, was the party nominee; he carried the state of Maryland and received eight electoral votes. A major feature of the party platform was a Nativism plank. If these policies had been law in 1848, Albertus Van Raalte, because of his criminal record in the Netherlands, would have been barred from entering the country. If they had been enacted after his arrival he could not have become a citizen until 1869 (and not then if the Van Raaltes had taken their 1866 trip to the Netherlands), and then could not have been elected school inspector if an American-born candidate sought the position.

> *Americans must rule America*; and to this end, *native*-born citizens should be selected for all state, federal, or municipal offices of government employment, in preference to naturalized citizens...
>
> [There must be] a change in the laws of naturalization, making a continued residence of twenty-one years, of all not heretofore provided for, an indispensable requisite for citizenship hereafter, and excluding all paupers or persons convicted of crime from landing upon our shores.
>
> Nativism Plank of the Know-Nothing Party, 1856

Men who joined the Know-Nothing party did so because they were alarmed by the vast increase in immigration. Recent immigrants, to the extent that they became aware of the Know-Nothings, were alarmed by their animosity. Dislike and distrust blossomed ominously, side by side. Although most of the Dutch residents of Holland and its surrounding communities did not yet read newspapers printed in English — Albertus Van Raalte, who subscribed to a wide variety of newspapers, was an exception — most were now citizens and they were increasingly interested in politics. (In the Dutch settlement in Iowa, the founder, Hendrik Scholte, had taken the efficient step of editing his own newspaper, the English language Pella *Gazette*, and he used this forum to attack the Know-Nothings in 1854 and 1856.) Although they may not have paid much attention to the opinion of outsiders, many of the Hollanders would have been aware of the ambivalent attitudes about them. They were viewed as admirable, industrious, devout, clean, thrifty; as foreign, peculiar, amusing; and — by a bigoted few — as ignorant, dirty and stupid. In his old age, Henry Cook recalled a lesson he was taught while he was still Hendrikus Kok, a recent arrival from the Netherlands, by people who regarded the Dutch immigrants as less than human.

> *In St. Clair I learned a little more English. One time I accompanied some of our men to a blacksmith shop in order to grind an ax. A boy and a man were standing idly in the shop; they looked at us with some curiosity and the man said to the boy, "Kick him!" The boy's boot hit my shins, which made such an impression that I never forgot the meaning of that simple word. I have frequently wondered what ever became of that rude man and boy. But on the whole the people were very kind to us.*
>
> Recollections of Henry Cook

Like the rest of America, Holland was in flux, but the pattern in which push for change warred with opposition to anything new was the reverse of what was happening on the national scene. Nationally, immigrants were an element of change. In the Holland community, some of the newer arrivals, who had come expecting to find *Holland in Amerika*, were dismayed. They found a town where Americans whose heritage was Dutch lived and worked contentedly alongside Americans whose heritage was English. They saw an Academy where young people were taught in English, and whose principal was expected to provide weekly church services in English. They discovered that the churches in Holland and the neighboring colonies had joined with the eastern Dutch Reformed Churches — churches which no longer held services in Dutch and where hymn singing was rampant. Some of those who had recently come to the colony, and some who had been there from earliest days, set themselves to discover and root out such sinfulness.

Not every newcomer, of course, thought in this way. Pieter Oggel, who came from the Netherlands in 1856 and married Mina Van Raalte in 1860, was both godly and learned. Among church leaders, he was a support and mainstay for Van Raalte, his father-in-law, former teacher and friend. Like Van Raalte and some others, he took a position which, when followed, minimized strife: local consistories, who knew their own parishioners best, ought to have decision-making power in cases which were not matters of basic church doctrine, rather than having every disputed issue ruled upon by the classis.

Through preaching and example, Dominie Oggel sought to lead people to help rather than harm, to be a blessing to others, rather than to attack them. In one of his sermons, he took as his text a passage from the psalms, with the beautiful image of people strengthened by God, who were able to travel through a desert and turn the barren wasteland into a place flowing with precious water.

> **Blessed is the man whose strength is in thee; in whose heart are the ways of them, who passing through the valley of Baca make it a well; the rain also filleth the pools.**
>
> Psalm 84: 5-6, KJV

One of many topics about which there was rancorous disagreement in the classis at this time was a visit from the ever-controversial Hendrik Scholte, who had been invited to preach in some of the area churches. Certain elders and ministers wished this to be condemned. The clerk for this classis meeting was Albertus Van Raalte, whose minutes are often a treat to read. Not only were his summaries clear and precise, they were sometimes witty. Van Raalte — in common with many sensible and busy people across the years — disliked lengthy, fruitless discussions conducted for the purpose of airing animosities; thus he was in accord with Brother Van Hees' view that Scholte's preaching was neither a problem nor a concern of the classis. Nevertheless he sat through the discussion, summarizing its subtopics neatly — Scholte's personal characteristics, Scholte's religious stance, instances of dissension caused by Scholte — and recorded that the discussion was smoothly concluded by Pieter Oggel's motion, which left the matter where it had begun, some hours before.

Dominie Hendrik P. Scholte of Pella, Iowa

The [question] whether Rev. Scholte should be allowed to preach in several churches was taken up. Rev. Van Den Bosch judges this not be allowable. Brother Van Hees believes that it is unnecessary to discuss this at length, since we ought to leave one another free in this, and he, for himself, sees no objection to it, inasmuch as Rev. Scholte has never yet been suspended by any general assembly. Other brethren, however, wish to discuss it. After a long discussion about the person of Rev. Scholte, about his ecclesiastical standpoint, and the mutual alienation in church affairs, the following resolution is moved by Rev. Oggel: The assembly judging that those who have allowed Rev. Scholte to preach have not all done that to indicate thereby any fellowship with the ecclesiastical position of Rev. Scholte, but have merely lent to him their church building, judges that it can not prescribe to the consistories to what they may or may not lend their churches, and that this matter thus lies outside its competence: which motion was adopted.

Minutes of the meeting of the Holland Classis, April 1856

A more serious and persistent controversy arose about actions taken by the classis in 1850. In that year Albertus Van Raalte had led the Holland Classis into union with the churches in the east, where so many members had been solicitous in assisting and guiding emigrant groups from the Netherlands. He attended the Particular Synod of Albany for the purpose of establishing a formal connection between the Holland Classis and that Synod.

... Since the day that we stepped ashore in this new world, our hearts have been strengthened and encouraged by meeting the people of God. The children of God are all dear to us, living in their respective denominations, but in guiding and caring for the interests of our congregations we find ourselves best at home where we are privileged to find our own confessional standards and the fundamental principles of our church government. Thus it was gratifying to us to experience from the other side no narrow exclusiveness, but open, hearty, brotherly love. This awakens in us a definite desire to make manifest our fellowship, and to ask for the hand of brotherly fellowship in return.

For these reasons we have resolved to send as our representative to your church assembly, which in the near future is to be held in the neighborhood of Albany, one of our brethren, namely A. C. Van Raalte, pastor and minister in the church of God, instructing him in our name to give and ask for all necessary information which may facilitate the desired union.

Minutes of the meeting of the Holland Classis, April 1850

The early immigrants from Holland had memories of the warm, protecting welcome they received when they arrived in New York and Albany from leaders in the eastern church. Years later, when Albertus Van Raalte spoke at the celebration commemorating the twenty-fifth anniversary of the colony's settlement, he recalled the aid they had been given. He spoke eloquently of their eastern benefactors: "To us they truly were as angels of God."

The conviction that when God calls us to some task He also offers His helping arm supported me during the storms on the sea, and also in the face of my helplessness and lack of knowledge. ...In New York we were encouraged by the friendly interest of Dr. Thomas De Witt and Elder James Forrester. We have not forgotten the difficulties we experienced upon our arrival as immigrants nor God's friendly and paternal solicitude in offering us the loving help of many people, as for example, Dr. Isaac Wyckoff. To us they truly were as angels of God.

Albertus C. Van Raalte's address to the Ebenezer Commemoration, 1872

After a few years, however, immigrants were not so helpless. Those coming to Michigan were headed for Holland, or Zeeland, or one of the neighboring areas. They came with maps and letters of introduction, information about transportation, cautions about how to avoid being preyed upon by swindlers on their way. Many of them came to join family members; some had received financial assistance from donations collected in the churches of the Holland classis. They were Dutch emigrants, helped by Dutch-Americans. And because of all these advantages, they had no reason to love and honor the eastern churches, and when they arrived in the colony, some of them disapproved vociferously of the connection that had been established.

In 1857, the union established seven years earlier was publicly condemned by a group of elders from some of the Holland churches. A crisis was reached at the classis meeting held in April of that year. Dominie Pieter Oggel presided; Albertus Van Raalte was clerk. The meeting opened with information about charitable giving. The amounts were significant for the times and for the people who gave. An offering of $62.32 had been received for the theological school at Kampen in the Netherlands; $99.85 had been given for the support of newly-arrived immigrants. Another important item of news was that Van Vleck Hall — a project heavily supported by donors from the eastern churches — already had forty students in residence, though construction was not yet completed.

Good news was followed by bad. There were announcements of intention to secede from the classis. Two ministers had withdrawn, one with a statement condemning his former colleagues for "the abominable and church-destroying heresy and sins which are rampant among you." Two congregations announced their intention to leave the denomination, and the church at Graafschap supplied a list of six points on which they believed the other churches in the classis were in error. These included allowing people from other Protestant denominations to participate in communion, neglect of catechetical teaching and house visitation, and consideration of the views of other denominations in choosing Sabbath School materials. Joining with the eastern churches was denounced as an indication "that there are members among you who regard our secession in the Netherlands as not strictly necessary" and a sixth point was that Isaac Wyckoff's report about conditions in the colony — the report in which he had written about how beautiful the colonists' faith seemed to him — gave approval to their errors. The first point on the list, however, was "the collection of 800 hymns, introduced contrary to church order."

Pieter Oggel was first to respond. He expressed sorrow "to see enumerated from the source such serious and unsubstantiated accusations: as, for instance, that the principle of the secession in the Netherlands was abandoned" and he called attention to the contributions regularly made for the theological school in Kampen, an institution of the separatist Free Church. Albertus Van Raalte followed, to explain the practices of the Reformed Church that were misunderstood, and to speak against "ignorance and sectarianism." He tried, without success, to show that there was nothing wrong with a hymn in itself.

Van Raalte had long been troubled by the tendency of those who separated once from an established denomination to engage in further schisms. This had happened among the original separatist pastors in the Netherlands, and it was a danger to the churches of the colony from its earliest days. At a classis meeting in 1850, he had spoken out against "the tendency to found little churches" — little churches formed by the breaking up of larger ones because of differences of opinion. "The starting point is generally a certain discontent, or a certain passion for independence, to secure greater self-government; so that presently anyone who is dissatisfied will …feel free to gather about him some who live at a distance, in a remote corner of the congregation, and to organize them into a new church. The churches will be split up and weakened, with the result that all interests which require unity that they may be rightly promoted, will be enervated and neglected." So, seven years earlier he had protested "against lightly organizing small churches." He still believed just as strongly that such schisms were pernicious.

The schism of 1857 was not extensive. One of the two ministers who had seceded returned at the next classis meeting. However, "it was an expensive option because the basic unity of the children of the Secession of 1834 was broken, and broken with such enmity and strife." The seceded church which had presented the six-point list to the classis had difficulty in obtaining a minister. Elders sent a call to a pastor in the Netherlands — "you received 32 of the 43 votes cast" — stating that they were unable to tell him what his salary would be but that the congregation was committed "to sustain and support you and your family in a manner so that you may have a living above that of the congregation." They gave this further assurance: "As to stability, the consistory will take care of this and in such a manner that the pastor will suffer no danger of ill-disposed attacks if ever such should arise." That call was declined.

My Dear Dominie,

    I wrote to you a few weeks ago and promised you a letter about this time but said that I wished to submit it to Dom. Schultz and here I am simply seated by his fire side. We had a pleasant visit, as I informed you, to our brethren in the Holland Colony. We all felt that it was refreshing to the Spirit to hold brotherly communion with them for a few days. These pleasant interviews recalled to my mind our former visit and I greatly regretted that God in his kind providence had not permitted you to be again with us. Much of the forest you saw is now blooming gardens and fruitful fields. And the vine that he has transplanted here from Holland, he has watered by his grace, so that its branches are greatly spread and still rapidly extending clothed in the verdure of spring and bearing abundantly of the fruitage of the "tree of Life."

    ...You will have marked [a congregation which belongs to] the Associate Reformed Church. This will, of course, be news to many in our church. [This] is the matter I was to say a few words about, that you may be "posted up" in the secret as well as public history of such movements. In the Colony of Graafschap - where you will remember, we called on Dominie Kline - there was a man of some property, but having little influence but what that gave him, who was anxious to invite a friend from Holland to minister among them.

    The name of this Rev. friend of his was V... Unfortunately, he was a man who had conducted himself in Holland so as to incur the censure of his Classis. This friend of his in Graafschap was aware of this and convinced that the members in the church of their colony could not be induced to send a call to such a man but evidently supposed that if he could get V... out among them, they would submit to have him preach rather than remain destitute of the public means of grace. He, therefore, wrote a call, as if emanating from the church, signed it himself and induced one other man, also a member of the Consistory, to sign it and secretly transmitted this to Holland. The Classis in Holland were surprised to receive a call for such a man. But after deliberating on the subject and especially after receiving the humble acknowledgments of V... and his promises of future good behavior, they consented to restore him and to send him here with clean papers.

    The church here, as I have said, had been kept in ignorance of this movement. But being anxious to procure the services of a minister of the gospel, they made out a call in constitutional form on Dominie Kline. This also was transmitted to Holland. He accepted the same and arrived here. But what was his surprise to find that V... had preceded him to the same church. This, of course, produced trouble. The Classis here did all that was in their power to compose the trouble. V... was induced to accept a call made on him by a church across the Lake, in Sheboygan I think; but after he left, the few who had been the means of his coming here, were not satisfied to remain in quietness. This made it uncomfortable for Dom. Kline and he too left them, having accepted a call from our Holland Church in Milwaukee. Thus the church was again left without a minister.

    At this time there was living in Zeeland - the congregation of friend Dom. Van Der Meulen - a young man, by the name of S..., who had been once prosecuting his studies for the ministry. The Classis in Holland under whose care he was had granted to him a written permission to exhort and speak in meetings of the people of God when requested by such people so to do, for the purpose of exercising and improving his gifts. The same man who had been the means of procuring V... now set to work to induce this young man to come among them and discharge the duties of the ministry. The temptation *overcame him and he went, without consulting his own Pastor Dom. Van Der Meulen, or any other member of the Classis.*

Indeed the first thing they learned about the matter, was the reception of a request to come as a Classis and ordain him as Pastor. They replied that they were willing to do so, if he was found on examination, as pointed out by our constitution, qualified. But this very examination was what he dreaded. He took no notice of their answer further than to transmit an imperative demand for ordination. This, of course, could not be complied with. But this same S... had a brother who had been working among the members of an Associate Reformed Church, just one mile from where we stayed all night in Gun-Plains, when on our way to the Rapids. These very excellent people had learned that the Hollanders like themselves sang only the Psalms. They had not neglected to enlarge on the great sin of our Churches in singing Hymns - the mere composition of sinful men.

The young man returned to Graafschap full of this new discovery. The young man who sought ordination at the hands of the Classis and was refused unless he submitted to an examination is next heard of knocking loudly at the doors of the Associate Presbytery for admission there, that he may be found in the bosom of a Pure Church. ...He tells them that he has learned with horror that the Churches in New York "sing human compositions" and that the Classis of Holland has joined such a sinful Body, but that he can not consent to such union. He is therefore before them with his original License from Holland and also with a call from a church in Graafschap - that he craved admission to their pure Body for his Church and for himself admission and ordination. They looked at his License, which was no other than the aforesaid permission to exhort - but it was in the Holland language and of course was as intelligible as if it had been written in Choctaw. ...But one thing they knew and that was that they were sound in Psalm singing, and according to their logic, must be also in Theology. So they admitted to the Church and ordained this poor ignorant young man their Pastor. This then is the history of one of [these] Churches...

To my friend J. Garretson.

David McNeish

Having visited the Holland Colony and learned with sadness the above facts I concur in the above expression of them, as well as the importance of your learning them from us. We expect Doms. Van Raalte and Van Der Meulen at our Spring meeting of Classis at South Bend and hope to enjoy more intercourse hereafter with that worthy people.

Yours truly,

J. N. Schultz

To most church members today the angry condemnation of hymn singing seems strange. For many generations past, singing hymns has been an integral and deeply loved part of church services. It is surprising to learn that in Albertus Van Raalte's time hymn singing was bitterly opposed by many devout members of the Reformed Church. This opposition — whose basis was that hymns are the work of humans, whereas psalms are part of God's word in the Bible — arose in the Netherlands and continued in America.

The Netherlands Reformed Church — the *Hervormde Kerk* — formally introduced hymns into worship several years before Van Raalte was born. He was familiar with these *gezangen*, hearing and singing them in his father's church. Years later, in America, Van Raalte wrote, "in my parental home I had grown up with the hymns, many of which had become precious to me, although I did desire congregational freedom for others."

Hymns were used in the churches of one synod in the Netherlands as early as 1796, and a church commission worked over a period of nearly a decade to produce a collection of 192 hymns, which, as noted in an introduction to the hymnbook, were intended as a means "to guard in our congregations the purity of doctrine in the midst of a stream of manifold dangers and modernities." However, Article 69 of the church order of Dordrecht forbade the singing of any songs except the Psalms of David in worship services. The hymnbook was opposed on this ground, and also because the words of some of the hymns appeared to run counter to the doctrinal purity which had been claimed for them, by failing to emphasize the sinfulness of human nature. During the years that France ruled Holland, protests of all kinds were suppressed, but after the Netherlands was once again an independent nation, opposition to hymns arose again, and became one tenet of the secession movement in which Van Raalte was a leader.

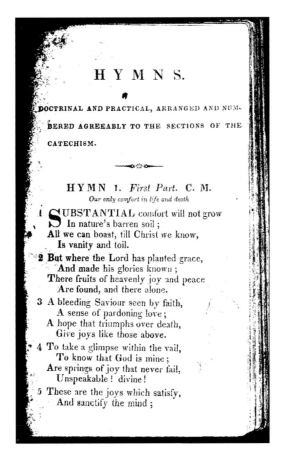

In the Netherlands and in America Van Raalte did not include hymns in worship services out of respect for the beliefs of others, though he himself had no objection to their use. He had come to love many of Dutch hymns, and hymn singing was one of the ways he learned a new language. On the trip to America, the ship's captain taught Christina and Albertus Van Raalte American hymns — and thus they learned English while raising their voices in joy and praise. Years later, one of the passengers recalled the beautiful singing. "When the weather was calm Dominie and Mrs. Van Raalte and the captain would sit in front of the cabin and sing hymns. One I remembered ended with the words: *O that will be joyful to part no more, On Canaan's happy shore!* I never forgot these words even though at the time I did not know their meaning."

Hymns had been part of church services in Dutch Reformed churches in the eastern states for many years. This aspect of worship was enjoyed, accepted, and indeed taken for granted. However, some immigrants who were members of the Dutch Reformed Church — and some churches which had splintered away from other denominations — believed earnestly that the practice was sinful. Some members of *de Kolonie* opposed union with the eastern churches on this ground; however, local church affairs were of greater interest, and, until Isaac Fairbanks led in establishing a Methodist congregation in 1861, there was no hymn singing in Holland churches.

In a few instances, however, the controversy was inflamed for devious motives. Among letters about the Holland colony stored in the records of the Board of Domestic Missions of the Reformed Church in America is the lengthy missive from the Rev. David McNeish, written while he was visiting churches in the midwest which the mission board supported, providing for John Garretson, at denominational headquarters, a careful account of ecclesiastical shenanigans of a sort that was possible before the days of rapid long distance communication.

Although the Dutch loved to sing, and visitors to the colony described the beauty of their singing with awe, playing or listening to music other than that of the human voice, and using music other than the psalms in worship, were regarded by many as sinful. In 1856, Frederick Van Lente, who as *voorzanger* led congregational singing at Van Raalte's church, proposed to establish a church choir; the consistory refused permission. (He then organized a private singing school which became known as "Van Lente's choir" and was a popular part of the Holland community for many years.) In 1858, Christina Van Raalte was criticized for attending a concert of sacred music held at Van Vleck Hall, because the music was not confined to the psalms. It was not until September 7, 1874, that the Holland Classis officially approved of hymn singing during worship.

The desirability, or the sinfulness, of singing hymns was a source of controversy in the classis for more than a quarter of a century. That disagreement was of a sort some people seemed to revel in, and Van Raalte abhorred. Early in his career, when he was one of a small band of friends and colleagues who led the *Afscheiding* — the secession from the established church — it was not exhaustion, or poverty, or persecution that troubled him; it was the dissension among this group of brothers in Christ over trivial matters that made him almost physically ill. "The gap between the faithful in the Netherlands was a deeply felt pain. This made me more afraid than any persecution." Van Raalte's first biographer, Henry Dosker, described Christina Van Raalte's ability to comfort her husband in these trials of the spirit. "We get to know her as a religious and cheerful woman. Her husband was often very depressed under all the arguments and division among the Separatists. She cheered him by reminding him of God's loyalty to His church."

Van Raalte was not only a man of principle; he was a man of understanding. Thus, he could discern what was important and what was not. Throughout his life, he encountered people with more limited minds who were challenged and intrigued by opportunities to take a self-righteous stand — such as the view that hymn singing marked people and churches as wicked — and condemn others roundly for an easily-grasped error. Although it is unlikely that he read Emerson's essays, he would have agreed with Emerson's aphorism: "A foolish consistency is the hobgoblin of little minds."

His strong leadership faltered when bickering about minor matters rose to heights which set neighbor against neighbor. He was not a ruthless dictator who could suppress such quarreling, nor would he have chosen to be so. But this was the one feature of ministering to others which caused him to despair. It is likely that his distress at this kind of strife was especially intense because people whom he cared for showed the worst side of their nature in these foolish, bitter quarrels. In mid-August, 1860, Van Raalte wrote to Philip Phelps, the principal of the Academy, who was traveling to raise funds, and in part of that letter he shared his concerns with his friend and colleague about the quarrel, which was becoming increasingly inflamed by the local newspaper. "Since you left, Dominie Oggel did rebuke the strife and slander against the hymns of the Dutch church in *De Hollander*."

Van Raalte saw little hope for conciliation and coming together: "I see how difficult it will be to battle with ignorance, sectarian spirits, and leaders full of ill-will, who know how to make use of the ignorance and prejudice of the simple-minded but suspicious people." At the end of August, he wrote again, a letter which is probably the most despairing of the letters that have survived: "I see too much strife among the people on my account; the influence of my preaching is injured: they sin against God's gift of the ministry. Many good things are opposed on my account. ...The foul insane fury against hymns is going on."

First Church in Holland Michigan is not the only church where debate about hymns became a frenzy. In Cambridge Massachusetts, in July 1827 — two years before Van Raalte entered the University of Leiden — an established pastor was presented by some of his parishioners with a "memorial" of their complaints. The Rev. Abiel Holmes had served his church for twenty-seven years. The differences between the minister and part of his congregation centered around two concerns. One was the issue of substitute preachers, or of preachers trading pulpits; specifically, whether the ministers who preached at First Church should, or need not, be theologically in accord with church doctrine. It was the minister's position that they should be, and the parishioners' view that such orthodoxy resulted in dreary sermons. The second issue concerned singing hymns. Eleven years earlier, the Rev. Holmes had changed the hymnal used by the church, discarding a popular collection of metrical psalms known by the names of its compilers — Tate and Brady — for a collection prepared by the well-known composer of hymns, Isaac Watts. Watts, known as the founder of English hymnody, published *Hymns* in 1707, and is the author of, among others, "O God, Our Help in Ages Past," "When I Survey the Wondrous Cross," and "Joy to the World!" After more than a decade of using this hymnbook, the parishioners now found fault with Watts. Thus, in this congregation, the concern was not whether hymns should be sung, but which hymnbook should be used, and although this might seem a matter on which agreement would be possible, the dispute was acrimonious and enduring. "Where the minister himself was mild in temper and averse to controversy, his principal deacon... was apparently a Christian warrior of the old-fashioned type. If the minister had at any point been tempted to modify his practice, the militant deacon was there to stiffen his resolve."

Soon a member of the congregation was writing to inform her brother, that "the town of Cambridge... can be called the peaceful little village no longer, as husband is against wife and mother is against daughter." After more than a year, during which committees "badgered each other and the minister with letters, memorials, petitions, protests, and remonstrances," the majority of the parishioners met and determined that "the parish had sufficient cause to terminate its contract with its minister." Within a month, Abiel Holmes gave his last sermon at First Church and became minister of the newly formed Second Congregational Church of Cambridge. The 250th anniversary of the First Church, in 1886 — fifty-seven years later — was the first time when the parishes of First and Second Churches met together again. Hymns by Abiel Holmes and his son, Dr. Oliver Wendell Holmes, were sung, and Oliver Wendell Holmes, Jr., then a Justice on the Supreme Judicial Court of Massachusetts, made a speech.

The Cambridge hymnbook controversy arose long before Albertus Van Raalte left the Netherlands and did not simmer down completely until long after he died. It is likely that he never heard of this vignette from American ecclesiastical history; if he had, he would have seen Abiel Holmes as a fellow sufferer from the passions which can grip a congregation. His own suffering was deep and long-lasting, though he tried to bear it patiently. After this time some of his letters, written when he was most downhearted, contain references to himself as a stumbling block. The bitter accusation must have been made against him that he, like a barrier set in the midst of a pathway, made others stumble and fall.

The metaphor of a stumbling block appears in both the Old and New Testaments. There are references in the books of Leviticus and Deuteronomy, and the latter calls down a community curse on those who violate the prohibition against being a stumbling block: "Cursed be he that maketh the blind to wander out of the way. And all the people shall say, 'Amen'." The image is also used by the prophet Isaiah: "...and he shall be... for a stone of stumbling and for a rock of offence, and many among them shall stumble, and fall, and be broken, and be snared, and be taken." How Albertus Van Raalte must have shuddered to think that he himself, who sought so earnestly to bring people to the Lord, was accused of causing them to fall from grace. In the year after the bitterest of these local church controversies, Van Raalte was awarded an honorary degree for his efforts on behalf of Christian education. His response to the letter announcing this honor is written in a hand unlike his usual flowing script; here the handwriting is cramped and blotted. Rather than thinking of the honor and commendation, he is absorbed by fears of unworthiness. The degree was awarded to him, but he did not attend the ceremony.

> *University of the City of New York, 30th June '58*
> *Rev. A. C. Van Raalte*
> *Dear Sir,*
>   *I am happy to say that the degree of Doctor in Divinity has been this day conferred on you by the institution. I trust your earnest efforts in the cause of Education & especially a Christian Education may be crowned with entire success. Your perseverance in a good enterprise has the admiration of those who know you.*
>   *I am Yours Truly*
>   *In Xn ties*
>   *Isaac Ferris,*
>   *Chancellor*
>
>   *I acknowledge the receipt of your favor of June 30th communicating that the University have conferred on me the degree of Doctor of Divinity. I know the reality of my weakness, unprofitableness, and [here a word is illegible] and will accordingly prefer the shade; And yet tonight to acknowledge thankfully the kindness of my Christian friends, truly they are a precious gift of our gracious God. I value it highly and it is only by the grace that I enjoy the esteem of God's people and am not to them a stumbling block or a destroyer of souls. May that grace keep us, make us more faithfull here and in eternity as examples of everlasting love.   A. C. Van Raalte*

Angry passions, though they are of consuming interest — even those which enrage whole communities or nations — fade with time. There is a quicker way for them to be quelled: more serious troubles may arise; more violent rage may be aroused. In August of 1860, when Van Raalte despaired of finding a way to calm the fury against hymns, a presidential election was in full swing, and a southern newspaper editor was among those who stoked the fires of unrest.

> **...the South has come to the conclusion that in case Lincoln should be elected... she could not submit to the consequences, and therefore, to avoid her fate, will secede from the Union.**

Battle Hymn of the Republic

by Julia Ward Howe

Mine eyes have seen the glory of the coming of the Lord;
He is trampling out the vintage where the grapes of wrath
   are stored;
He hath loos'd the fateful lightning of His terrible swift sword:
   His truth is marching on.

I have seen Him in the watchfires of a hundred circling camps;
They have builded Him an altar in the evening dews
   and damps;
I can read His righteous sentence by the dim and flaring lamps:
His day is marching on.

I have read a fiery gospel writ in burnished rows of steel:
"As you deal with My contemners, so with you My grace
   shall deal."
Let the Hero born of woman crush the serpent with His heel,
Since God is marching on.

He has sounded forth the trumpet that shall never call retreat;
He is sifting out the hearts of men before His judgment seat.
Oh, be swift my soul to answer Him! be jubilant my feet!
Our God is marching on.

In the beauty of the lilies Christ was born across the sea,
With a glory in His bosom that transfigures you and me;
As He died to make men holy let us die to make men free,
While God is marching on.

   Glory, glory, hallelujah! Glory, glory, hallelujah!
   Glory, glory, hallelujah! His truth is marching on.

Nations, like individuals, are punished for their transgressions.

The roots of the Civil War stretch backwards in time. One source of that fiery conflict was the issue of how government should be conceived, a problem which has existed since humans first sought for order in groups. Government is essential, but to organize and maintain a system of government requires that opposing needs must somehow be balanced. How shall individual rights be weighed against the need for order? How shall power be shared among different levels of government? How can liberty and law be attained together?

America achieved independence, with the Peace of Versailles in 1783, by winning the Revolutionary War, but it took four more years for the people of America to form a nation. The grand achievement of creating and adopting a federal constitution produced the Union. Nearly three decades later when the Treaty of Ghent ended the War of 1812, the world was shown that the new nation could withstand threat from without. But the states within the Union and the people within those states were often more divided one from another than they were united, and some who sought to lead their fellow citizens preferred to inflame divisions rather than to heal them. In the early years of the nineteenth century, spared from major external threats, the country was increasingly troubled within itself.

> That is the real issue! An issue that will continue in this country when these poor tongues of Douglas and myself shall be silent. These are the two principles that are made the eternal struggle between right and wrong. They are the two principles that have stood face to face from the beginning of time; and will ever continue to struggle, one of them asserting the divine right of kings, the same principle that says you work, you toil, you earn bread and I will eat it. It is the same old serpent, whether it comes from the mouth of a king who seeks to bestride the people of his nation, and to live upon the fat of his neighbor, or whether it comes from one race of men as an apology for the enslavement of another.
>
> Lincoln-Douglas debates, Alton, Illinois, October 15, 1858

In seeking the causes of the Civil War, one date to look to is 1619. In that year, in the English colony of Jamestown Virginia, a Dutch ship, as John Rolfe recorded in his journal, "sold us twenty negars." Thus slavery entered America, when people who were willing to sell human beings met people who were willing to buy them. Slavery existed, legally sanctioned, in America for nearly two hundred and fifty years, continuing after most other nations had taken steps to outlaw it. Mexico, for example, decreed the abolition of slavery in 1829. European countries ended slavery within their nations and in their colonies, in some cases through a gradual process. In the United States, individual states, beginning with Vermont in 1777, could and did make slavery illegal within their borders. By 1860, in the western hemisphere the institution of slavery flourished only in Brazil, Cuba, and the southern United States.

The effort to hold the nation together and still maintain the institution of slavery was an ongoing struggle — a struggle linked to, and intensified by, the country's rapid expansion. Between 1845 and 1848, the time period when Albertus Van Raalte arrived in this country, the United States acquired more territory than at any other time in its history — more even than was gained through the Louisiana Purchase during Jefferson's presidency.

In President John Tyler's last week in office in 1845, the United States annexed the Republic of Texas, including all of the present state of Texas and parts of the current states of Colorado, Kansas, New Mexico, Oklahoma and Wyoming. During James Polk's presidency the annexation was confirmed, and there were two other extensive acquisitions of land. In 1846, through a treaty with Great Britain, the boundary between the United States and Canada was settled; the Oregon territory included the current states of Idaho, Oregon, and Washington, and part of the current states of Montana and Wyoming. At the end of the Mexican War in 1848, by the Treaty of Guadalupe-Hidalgo, Mexico received fifteen million dollars for ceding territory including the present states of California, Nevada and Utah, and parts of the current states of Arizona, Colorado, New Mexico and Wyoming.

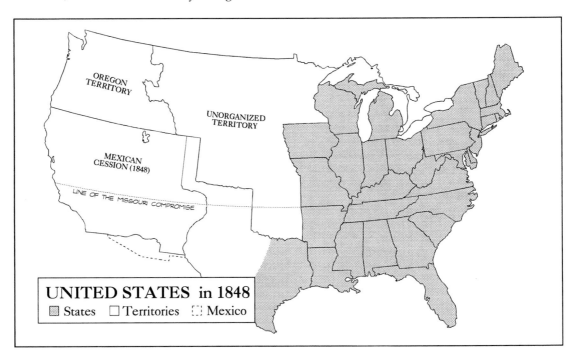

By the terms of the Missouri Compromise of 1820, slavery had been forbidden in all territories north of latitude 36°, 30', which marked the southern border of the newly admitted slave state of Missouri. Beginning in 1820, when both Maine and Missouri joined the Union, new states had been admitted in pairs — one slave, one free — as was the pattern when Arkansas and Michigan were admitted as the twenty-fifth and twenty-sixth states. However, with the admission of both Florida and Texas in 1845, slave states outnumbered free states, and the conditions of Texas statehood allowed it to divide into as many as four separate states. Many Americans believed that the war with Mexico was deliberately provoked, in an effort to expand the territories from which even more slave states could be formed.

President Polk had sent troops under General Zachary Taylor to the disputed border area between the United States and Mexico; in a skirmish there were American casualties. "The cup of forbearance has been exhausted," the President wrote, calling on Congress to declare war, which it promptly did. The action was not taken without opposition, however. Abraham Lincoln, then a recently elected representative from Illinois, spoke in the House to propose what came to be known as the "spot" resolutions, demanding that the President name the spot where American blood had been shed, and tell whether that spot was in American or Mexican territory. In Massachusetts, Henry Thoreau refused to pay the state poll tax and spent a night in jail — an insignificant protest except for its far-reaching effect as the impetus for a famous essay.

> *When a sixth of the population of a nation which has undertaken to be the refuge of liberty are slaves, and a whole country is unjustly overrun and conquered by a foreign army, and subjected to military law, I think that it is not too soon for honest men to rebel and revolutionize. What makes this duty the more urgent is the fact that the country so overrun is not our own, but ours is the invading army.*
>
> Henry Thoreau, *Civil Disobedience*

Among the American officers serving in the Mexican War were General Zachary Taylor, Captain Robert E. Lee, Captain George B. McClellan, and Lieutenant Ulysses S. Grant. Years later, after he had become General of the Union armies and then President of the United States, Grant wrote about the war and its consequences.

> *Ostensibly we were intended to prevent filibustering into Texas, but really as a menace to Mexico in case she appeared to contemplate war. Generally the officers of the army were indifferent whether the annexation was consummated or not; but not so all of them. For myself, I was bitterly opposed to the measure, and to this day regard the war which resulted as one of the most unjust ever waged by a stronger against a weaker nation. It was an instance of a republic following the bad example of European monarchies, in not considering justice in their desire to acquire additional territory.*
>
> *...The occupation, separation and annexation [of Texas] were from the inception of the movement to its final consummation, a conspiracy to acquire territory out of which slave states might be formed for the American Union. Even if the annexation itself could be justified, the manner in which the subsequent war was forced upon Mexico cannot.*
>
> *... In taking military possession of Texas after annexation, the army of occupation, under General Taylor, was directed to occupy the disputed territory. The army did not stop at the Nueces and offer to negotiate for a settlement of the boundary question, but went beyond, apparently to force Mexico to initiate war. It is to the credit of the American nation, however, that after conquering Mexico, and while practically holding the country in our possession so that we could have retained the whole of it, or made any terms we chose, we paid a round sum for the additional territory taken; more than it was worth, or was likely to be, to Mexico. To us it was an empire and of incalculable value; but it might have been obtained by other means.*
>
> *The Southern rebellion was largely the outgrowth of the Mexican War. Nations, like individuals, are punished for their transgressions. We got our punishment in the most sanguinary and expensive war of modern times.*
>
> Ulysses S. Grant, *Memoirs*, pp. 22-24

From its earliest years, the United States was plagued by the issue of slavery. The idea of abolition of slavery was perceived by many in the southern states as so threatening that they saw withdrawing from the Union as a preferable alternative. The idea of the Union's dissolution was seen by many in both north and south as so dreadful and dangerous that they were willing to make one accommodation after another, hoping to buy time in which a solution might be found. Instead, the prediction made by John Quincy Adams that the Missouri Compromise of 1820 was "a title-page to a great, tragic volume" was fulfilled. The political lines drawn to delineate slave and free territories intensified sectional separation. Many white southerners became economically and philosophically shackled to the slave system, and the habit of threatening to secede made secession appear first endurable, then honorable, and finally thrilling.

Most of America's early great leaders were opposed to slavery. Our first president was a slaveholder, but he believed that abolition would, and should, be brought about, and, in his will, Washington freed his slaves. Zachary Taylor, who defeated Michigan's Lewis Cass in the presidential election of 1848 and took office fifty years after Washington's death, owned more slaves than any other American president. "His victories in Mexico, his Southern birth, his ownership of three hundred slaves, his clean political record (in his entire life he had never cast a vote for anyone) made him the most 'available' candidate."

In 1850, the dying John Calhoun of South Carolina sat silent in the Senate and glared out at his colleagues while a fellow senator read his final speech, a catalog of the South's demands, insisting, under threat of secession, that slavery must no longer even be a subject for debate. "I have, Senators, believed from the first that the agitation of the subject of slavery would, if not prevented by some timely and effective measure, end in disunion." The great orator Daniel Webster of Massachusetts and Henry Clay of Kentucky, "the Great Pacificator," now grown old in the service of their country, spoke for compromise to preserve the Union, and achieved it at the sacrifice of their own political ambitions. A part of that compromise was to revise — and make much harsher — an earlier law requiring that fugitive slaves be returned to their owners.

> *[The] accused fugitives could not testify on their own behalf or benefit from trial by jury. In reaction to state refusals to participate in the rendition process, the 1850 law provided federal commissioners, appointed in every county in the country, to enforce the law. They received five dollars if they decided that the black person before them was not a slave but were paid ten dollars if they found in favor of the claimant. ...Under the 1850 act, more than 900 fugitives were returned between 1850 and 1861; Southerners estimated, however, that as many as 10,000 escaped.*

Thus the south was not pacified, and the north was enraged. Opposition to the Fugitive Slave Act and efforts to enforce it escalated together. In 1851 Thomas Sims escaped from Georgia to Boston, where he lived and worked until his owner traced him. "When the federal commissioner found for his owner, 300 armed deputies and soldiers removed him from the courthouse at 4:00 a.m. and marched him to the navy yard, where 250 U. S. soldiers waited to place him on a ship going south to slavery." In 1854 Congress passed the Kansas-Nebraska act, overturning the ban on slavery in northern territories. This legislative triumph for the south polarized political parties, virtually destroying the Whig party, whose members came from both sections of the country.

In 1858, the vigorous debates in the Illinois senatorial race were among the calmest and most rational of political events. Stephen Douglas advocated giving each state power to vote slavery up or down; Abraham Lincoln spoke against the spread of slavery. The shorter candidate — Lincoln was six feet four inches tall and Douglas a foot less — won the election, but Lincoln's powerful words made him nationally known.

We are now far into the fifth year since a policy was initiated with the avowed object and confident promise of putting an end to slavery agitation. Under the operation of that policy, that agitation has not only not ceased but has constantly augmented. In my opinion, it will not cease until crisis shall have been reached and passed.

"A house divided against itself cannot stand." I believe this government cannot endure permanently half slave and half free, I do not expect the Union to be dissolved — I do not expect the house to fall — but I do expect it will cease to be divided. It will become all one thing, or all the other. Either the opponents of slavery will arrest the further spread of it, and place it where the public mind shall rest in the belief that it is in the course of ultimate extinction; or its advocates will push it forward till it shall become alike lawful in all the States, old as well as new, North as well as South.

Lincoln's speech to the Republican State Convention, Springfield, Illinois, June 16, 1858

And if a kingdom be divided against itself, that kingdom cannot stand. And if a house be divided against itself, that house cannot stand.

Mark 3:24-25, KJV

In 1859, the zealot John Brown, with a small group of men, white and black, seized a federal arsenal in Harper's Ferry, Virginia. Federal troops commanded by Colonel Robert E. Lee killed some of the band and captured the rest; Brown was quickly tried, sentenced and hanged. As was so for many others in his time, the words of the Bible permeated John Brown's thinking and speaking. He believed fully that God without respect of persons — without regarding status or power in this world — judges everyone equally. He was wholly convinced that he acted in the cause of righteousness. Because of his brave words and demeanor at his trial and execution, John Brown was transformed into a martyr of the abolitionist cause. "He is not old Brown any longer," Henry Thoreau wrote, "he is an angel of light."

Harper's Ferry, Virginia

> I am yet too young to understand that God is any respecter of persons. I believe that to have interfered as I have done... in behalf of His despised poor, was not wrong, but right. Now, if it is deemed necessary that I should forfeit my life for the furtherance of the ends of justice and mingle my blood further with the blood of my children, and with the blood of millions in this slave country whose rights are disregarded by wicked, cruel and unjust enactments, I submit; so let it be done!
>
> John Brown, his last speech at his trial, November 2, 1859

> And if you call on the Father, who without respect of persons judgeth according to every man's work, pass the time of your sojourning here in fear.
>
> I Peter 1:17, KJV

At the Democratic convention in the following year, Stephen A. Douglas was favored to win his party's nomination — and he did, but the process destroyed his chance to win the election. "Rarely in American history has there been a convention as tumultuous as the one that assembled in Charleston, S. C., in April 1860." The Alabama delegation talked openly about bolting unless a pro-slavery plank was included in the platform, and in a conference before the convention, members of six other delegations — Georgia, Florida, Mississippi, Louisiana, Arkansas and Texas — agreed to follow them.

Douglas' floor leader, the man with the responsibility for insuring that all went smoothly for his candidate, was Charles E. Stuart of Kalamazoo, a former U.S. senator. On the second day of the convention, probably on his own initiative and without consulting Douglas, Stuart delivered a blistering speech attacking the South, and the southern delegates immediately walked out.

The convention chairman then ruled that the votes required for nomination would be based on the number allocated, rather than on the number of delegates present. Although Douglas consistently received twice the combined total of votes cast for his opponents, after three days of balloting and 57 roll call votes, he was still short of the required number. Eventually the delegates agreed to adjourn and reconvene in six weeks in Baltimore, where, with a different decision about what constituted a two-thirds majority, Douglas was finally nominated. Southern Democrats held their own convention, and nominated their own candidate. "The seceders intended from the beginning to 'rule or ruin,' and when they find they cannot rule they will then ruin," said Georgia's Alexander Stephens, "[and] in less than twelve months we shall be in a war, and the bloodiest in history."

The Republican convention considered eleven candidates and chose Abraham Lincoln on the third ballot, over the original front-runner, William Seward. With the Democratic party split, and a fourth party candidate also running, Lincoln won the presidential election handily. Even before all the states' electoral votes were known, Stephen Douglas, realizing that he had lost, went south, where, despite threats on his life and attempts to wreck the trains he rode on, he traveled through the southern states, speaking urgently against secession. But before the end of the election year, South Carolina had seceded.

Louisiana seceded in January. The Louisiana State Military College, later to become Louisiana State University, had been established in 1859 under an energetic, hard-driving superintendent.

Above his office door was a marble plaque engraved with the words, *By the liberality of the General Government. The Union — Esto Perpetua.* When he was certain secession was coming, the superintendent, William Tecumseh Sherman, sent his resignation to the Governor of Louisiana: "I prefer to maintain my allegiance to the Constitution as long as a fragment of it survives."

By the first of February, 1861, Alabama, Florida, Georgia, Mississippi, and Texas had also seceded, and a week later delegates from these seven states met in Montgomery, Alabama, to form the Confederates States of America. The following day — nearly a month before Lincoln's inauguration — Jefferson Davis of Mississippi and Alexander Stephens of Georgia were chosen president and vice-president of the Confederacy.

> *Now the civil war broke out and many of our young people volunteered to serve their country for right and freedom.*
>
> from the diary of Grace - Geesje - Van der Haar Visscher

> We are not enemies, but friends. We must not be enemies. Though passion may have strained, it must not break, our bonds of affection. The mystic chords of memory, stretching from every battlefield and patriot grave to every living heart and hearthstone all over the broad land, will yet swell with the chorus of the Union when again touched, as surely they will be, by the better angels of our nature.
>
> Lincoln's first inaugural address, March 4, 1861.

Despite Lincoln's speech and Douglas' pleas, the voices of "the better angels of our nature," went unheard — smothered by war fever throughout the country, drowned in the torrent of cries for war. One of the most ardent of those urging war was Michigan senator Zachariah Chandler, who enthusiastically welcomed the prospect of the approaching conflict: "Without a little bloodletting this Union will not, in my estimation, be worth a rush."

Fort Sumter, South Carolina,
U.S. commanding officer, Major Robert Anderson

At 4:30 on the morning of April 12, 1861, General Pierre Gustave Toutant Beauregard directed Confederate troops to fire on Fort Sumter. A federal fort in the channel off Charleston, South Carolina, it had not been built to withstand attack from the American shore, and was inadequately armed and provisioned. During thirty-four hours of shelling the interior of the fort was set afire, and several men were wounded, one fatally. On Sunday, April 14, commanding officer Major Robert Anderson surrendered the fort and evacuated the garrison, and the "stars and bars" flag of the Confederacy — three stripes, red, white, red, and seven white stars on a blue field — was raised over Fort Sumter. Major Anderson took with him the tattered United States flag, and exactly four years later, then a general in the Union army, he was present when it was raised again over Fort Sumter. At the celebration, the Reverend Henry Ward Beecher, brother of Harriet Beecher Stowe, delivered an oration honoring the nation's flag: "As long as the sun endures, or the stars, may it wave over a nation neither enslaved or enslaving."

In Michigan, as throughout the North, as war became imminent, the prospect was thrilling. Many years later a man who had been a student at Holland Academy in 1861 recalled the enthusiasm of the time from the perspective of age and knowledge of the terrible years to come: "When last my boyish eyes rested on the town, a war cloud burst upon the land and the flag was bathed in blood."

> *Early on April 12 William and Peter Moerdyk and I started out at early dawn for a fifty mile tramp. Never was there a more beautiful day. We passed through Overisel and breakfasted at Rabbit River, with birds twittering and fluttering, and early spring flowers signaling forth a new season. We sang and we laughed as we communed in nature's forest solitude. We dined and rested at Allegan, then on for Kalamazoo by nightfall. But when we arrived all was excitement. Bells rang, everywhere "Star Spangled Banner" was sung, flags were flying, earnest groups gathered, hot angry speeches mingled with drum and fife. No one stopped long enough to explain. Simply, "Rebels fired on Sumter."*
>
> Henry J. Brown's Reminiscences

Lewis Cass

Lewis Cass was Michigan's most famous political leader. A hero of the War of 1812 in his youth, he succeeded William Hull as governor of the Michigan Territory when he was 31. He was secretary of war for both the seventh president, Andrew Jackson, and the fifteenth, James Buchanan, and United States minister to France for six years. From 1845 to 1856 he served as United States senator from Michigan, and in 1848 he was the Democratic candidate for President. A staunch supporter of the Union, he resigned from the Buchanan cabinet, angered by the president's inaction in the face of southern rebelliousness. Cass' loyalty was to his country. He knew that northern unity must be maintained, and therefore leaders of all political parties should speak out for the Union.

At a patriotic rally in Detroit he spoke movingly about the nation's hero-president George Washington, whose burial place was now claimed by the seceding states. "The veteran statesman and soldier General Cass assured the hearts of his countrymen by kindling words of patriotic energy. ...He contrasted the situation in which he now found himself, with the position in which he had been placed on the same spot fifty years before by the capitulation of General Hull."

...Then our contest was a legitimate war waged with a foreign foe; our war to-day is a domestic one, commenced by and bringing in its train acts which no right feeling man can contemplate without most painful regret. But a few months since, and we were the first and happiest nation on the face of the globe. In the midst of this prosperity, without a single foe to assail us, without a single injury at home caused by the operations of the Government to affect us, this glorious Union, acquired by the blood and sacrifices of our fathers, has been disowned and rejected by a portion of the States composing it — a Union which has given us more blessings than any previous government ever conferred upon man.

...You need no one to tell you what are the dangers of your country, nor what are your duties to meet and avert them. There is but one path for every true man to travel, and that is broad and plain. It will conduct us, not indeed without trials and sufferings, to peace and the restoration of the Union.

He who is not for his country is against her. There is no neutral position to be occupied. It is the duty of all zealously to support the Government in its efforts to bring this unhappy civil war to a speedy and satisfactory conclusion, by the restoration, in its integrity, of that great charter of freedom bequeathed to us by Washington and his compatriots. His ashes, I humbly trust, will ever continue to repose in the lonely tomb at Mount Vernon and in the United States of America, which he loved so well and did so much to found and build up. Manifest your regard for his memory by following, each within the compass of his power, his noble example, and restore his work as he left it, by devoting heart, mind and deed to the cause.

Lewis Cass, speaking in Detroit on April 24, 1861

On April 15, the president called for mobilization of the state militias for a three month period of service, to end insurrections "too powerful to be suppressed by the ordinary course of judicial proceedings." Southern states responded with rage. Virginia, Arkansas, Tennessee and North Carolina joined the Confederacy, bringing to eleven the number of seceded states. Secessionist governors of several border states wired furious refusals: Kentucky "will furnish no troops for the wicked purpose of subduing her sister Southern States"; "Your requisition is illegal, unconstitutional, revolutionary, inhuman... not one man will the State of Missouri furnish to carry on any such unholy crusade." But northern and western states answered the call enthusiastically. As troops poured into Washington, General George McClellan organized the regiments and put them on parade.

Massed troops of the Union Army marched in the nation's capital to a stirring tune written as a camp song for southern soldiers, "Say, brothers, will you meet us on Canaan's happy shore." New words honored the abolitionist John Brown: *John Brown's body lies a'mould'ring in the grave, but his soul goes marching on.* Among the visitors who watched the parade and joined in the singing was Julia Ward Howe, reformer, abolitionist and poet. The music and the cause came together in her thoughts with a Biblical passage about an angry God, crushing wickedness like one who crushes grapes in a winepress, "trampling out the vintage where the grapes of wrath are stored." She sent her "Battle Hymn of the Republic" to the *Atlantic Monthly* magazine, and the editor bought it for four dollars and published it in February 1862.

> 𝔚herefore art thou red in thine apparel, and thy garments like him that treadeth in the winevat?
>
> I have trodden the winepress alone, and of the people there was no one with me; for I will tread them in mine anger, and trample them in my fury; and their blood shall be sprinkled upon my garments, and I will stain all my raiment. For the day of vengeance is in mine heart, and the year of my redeemed is come.
>
> Isaiah 63: 2-4, KJV

The First Michigan Infantry, composed largely of men from the eastern part of the state, was the first of the western militia contingents to arrive in Washington; Lincoln's comment — "Thank God for Michigan!" — has been a continuing source of state pride. Washington was the rallying point for federal troops not merely for organizational reasons or for patriotic display, but because the capital was in danger. State and sectional rivalries existed in America from its earliest days, and the central location of the nation's capital, and the creation of a special district to surround it so that it was a part of no state, were decisions aimed at reducing sectionalism. But now, when rivalry spiraled into war, the nation's capital was on the front line. Lincoln needed troops in Washington because Confederate troops led by General Joe Johnston were massing to the south and west of the city.

The First Battle of Bull Run, July 12, 1861

Maneuvering began in earnest in July. In both armies many of the generals were competing for renown with fellow officers on their own side; most of the troops were raw; means of communication and supply were uncoordinated. In the north as well as in the south, the popular view was that the victory of their side would come easily and quickly. At that time, most ordinary people tended to stay home; they rarely traveled outside their area, their state, their town. (By 1860, Albertus Van Raalte had probably done more traveling than all the other

Hollanders combined, and he had not yet visited the southern states.) So it was easy, as the country became divided, for prejudices to grow stronger; on each side "we" were right and strong and good, and the unfamiliar "they" were wicked and cowardly and wrong. In the coming months and years, prejudices would intensify, but the idea of easy victory would fade.

The first battle of the Civil War was fought across a small river called Bull Run, near the Virginia town of Manassas Junction. It was a horribly disorganized fight and the casualties were dreadful. (Losses in future battles, when thousands upon thousands would die, would overshadow these.) Confederate losses are estimated at 400 killed and 1,600 wounded, 225 fatally; Union losses at 625 killed or with mortal wounds, 950 others wounded, and more than 1200 captured. During the fighting many soldiers on both sides ran from the field, but southerners rallied when General Barnard Bee pointed with his sword toward General Thomas Jonathan Jackson, shouting, "There is Jackson, standing like a stone wall! Rally behind the Virginians!" On the Union side, congressmen who had come down to watch the battle tried unsuccessfully to stop the rout of federal troops.

> There is nothing in American military history quite like the story of Bull Run. It was the momentous fight of the amateurs, the battle where everything went wrong, the great day of awakening for the whole nation, North and South together. It marked the end of the ninety-day militia, and it also ended the rosy time in which men could dream that the war would be short, glorious, and bloodless. After Bull Run the nation got down to business.

> In the November elections Abraham Lincoln was chosen president. [Soon] began the great rebellion, breaking out first in South Carolina... I remained at my carpenter's work in spite of the fact that there was much excitement throughout the entire country. ...In September 1861 Lincoln issued a patriotic call for three hundred thousand volunteers. ...With unbelievable dispatch did volunteers answer his call. On September 18, I and twenty-five other Hollanders volunteered our services, enlisting in Company D, 2nd regiment, Michigan cavalry. Twenty-four thousand strong, we set out for St. Louis Missouri. Thousands of loyal citizens escorted us to the depot.
>
> Jan Vogel's Recollections

> In September 1861, the call came for volunteers. ...I enlisted in a cavalry regiment [which] was Colonel Sheridan's first command. [On our way to St. Louis] we made a short stop at Niles Michigan for an exhibition drill and change of train. We were enthusiastically received, the girls showering us with kisses, flowers and food.
>
> Civil War Recollections of John Nies

On the home front, Albertus Van Raalte was unflagging in his support of the president and the Union. He could not go to war, but he could preach that God's truth was marching on with the Union soldiers. Whether because they disagreed with his views, or whether they were solely impelled by belief in the separation of church and state, some church members complained when political matters were addressed in church services.

> There were some in Holland, Michigan, who were annoyed by Van Raalte's stand against slavery and for Lincoln. Many of these people were his political opponents; religious beliefs clouded politics and vice versa. Van Raalte, however, would not consider leaving out his propaganda, and stated to his consistory that... he refused to separate

his political views from his faith. This position aroused such strong resentment in the hearts of some people that they dared to call him, he to whom they owed so exceedingly much, a "bungler."

Records of a consistory meeting at this time state that the discussion was tabled "because of the profound political changes in which N. N. and others are so deeply involved." This is an intriguing entry — who was the mysterious N. N.? He was, literally, no one who was known; the initials stand for the Latin phrase *Nomen Nescis*, meaning *Name Unknown*. Consistory minutes masked N. N.'s identify only for any future reader unfamiliar with the community and the issue; everyone else would understand that the unknown name was the best known name in the colony: Albertus C. Van Raalte.

Op nu Nederlandsch wakkere zonen!
Burgers van Amerika,
Wilt u uwer waardig tonen,
Volgt der vad'ren voorbeeld na,
Hebt gij eens dit land verkoren
Voor uw tweede Vaderland,
Aan de Unie trouw gezworen,
U aan haar in nood verpand.
Op Bataven! Dan te wapen,
Nu het vuur des oproers brandt!

Arise now, vigilant sons of the Netherlands!
Citizens of America, show yourselves to be worthy.
Follow the example of your fathers. You have chosen this land as your second fatherland,
have sworn loyalty to the Union, pledged yourself to her in need.
Arise Batavians! Take up arms, now the fires of insurrection are burning!

Our oldest daughter was now so far in her studies that she was called to Overisel to teach school. That was six miles from our home but she came home often. Then a call to teach in North Holland where she gave excellent satisfaction. She came home often on Sundays to hear Dominie Van Raalte preach. He was her best teacher. We enjoyed his sermons greatly during those times because he also had two sons in the army.

from the diary of Grace - Geesje - Van der Haar Visscher

The colony of Holland held tenaciously to its Dutch heritage, but during the war it was, in many ways, a microcosm of America. All but the newest immigrants were citizens, and that meant the men could vote and were subject to the draft. They lived in a state — not a territory — and federal and state laws applied to them. They lived in the north, where the press was not under government control, and most newspapers took extreme stands — pro-Lincoln or anti-Lincoln; for war or for negotiated peace; Republican or Democrat; abolitionist or anti-abolition — and printed subtle slander and vituperative attacks.

In politics, Holland was now energetically, vigorously, and sometimes bitterly, a two-party town. Historically, immigrants had found their home with the populist, down-to-earth Democratic party of Andrew Jackson, rather than with the aristocratic Whigs. Now there was a new party, and in the Dutch colony in Pella, Iowa, Hendrik Scholte, who was always newsworthy, had been elected a delegate to the Iowa state Democratic convention, but attended the Republican convention instead, and was welcomed by Lincoln as "my good Dutch friend." In Holland, Albertus Van Raalte was an ardent Lincoln supporter, and thus in favor of the new Republican party, while the editor of the town's largest newspaper remained a Democrat. As political positions polarized, the "radical Republicans" were pro-war and anti-slavery. Older, and thus with a longer history, the Democratic party had split apart on the war issue and many of its members wanted to return to some kind of pre-war footing.

As the Civil War raged on, Northerners who supported the Southern cause were regarded as an insidious threat, like a poisonous snake in the grass, and called "copperheads." (Some tried to make the name a proud one, and wore badges made of copper pennies showing the head of Liberty, but almost everyone who used the name knew it meant the deadly copperhead snake.) Hermanus Doesburg, like Albertus Van Raalte, had sons, and Dirk Blikman Kikkert Van Raalte and Jacob Otto Doesburg went off to war together, with bands playing and people cheering. And both the young men came home, but one came back faster. Dirk commented scornfully about it at the time. "Last week our very beloved, high esteemed friend Mr. Otto Doesburg, left us. He himself says it's due to ill health but I say it's because of being homesick, and for fear of the bullets." Family ties intensified political opinions. Editor Doesburg's desire for his sons to be respected strengthened his opposition to the war. Reaction against misleading information in *De Hollander* was a recurrent theme in the letters the men of Company I sent home. As the war went on, Ben, who was usually easy-going, became increasingly bitter about Doesburg and *De Hollander*.

> *Dear Father,*
>
> *Yesterday evening I received your letter of the 20th. The calling up of 500,000 suits me fine. I have no sympathy for those at home who are being drafted. In Holland they appear to be very scared. Doesburg is putting the fear of death into the hearts of the ignorant masses. They should burn his printing office - he speaks as if everyone who signs up is going to die. It is enough to put the death fear into anyone who has never seen a war. I am not surprised that the young people are running away. He is no better than a Rebel - his writings are shameful for our Holland People. I saw an article in the paper that he was making an estimate of the number of soldiers Lincoln had had in the service and how many survivors there were. It was such a large figure I hardly dare mention it. The way he figured, Lincoln had, through his stupidity, doomed all these men to eternity. But he overlooked the thousands of deserters and those who died of illness. Also those who bought their way out. I can name a couple for him - his own sons, the one a deserter and the other purchasing a substitute. Just a coward.*

It does my heart good that Co. I is so down on the copperheads in the colony. They say if they could re-enlist that it would never be for Holland — they would rather represent Kentucky. Now those at home are doing all in their power to stay there and have been around to collect money from parents who have all their children in the war. They are too old to be in the service themselves but collect money in order to buy substitutes for those who have to go. ...Nice people. ...If I may give advice, never give anyone any money in order to stay home. It would be better to perish.

...We were overjoyed to have Lieut. Kramer drop in and feeling fine. ...He told me you were looking very well again which made me happy. The boys then wanted to know how things were in the colony and he said that it had grown tremendously - we would hardly know the place any more. But in the same breath he said that the place was full of Copperheads. I am sorry to hear it. He said the Copperhead newspapers told such lies and printed such favorable Rebel news to bring fear into the hearts of the people, but I think the shoe is beginning to pinch because they are afraid of their businesses and of the Army. Well, one thing is certain - there is no copperheadism in the army - it is true blue. Gen. Sherman's army is the cream of the country and is bound to crush the rebellion. It doesn't make any difference under what circumstances all that bad news is published in the Northern papers. It is nothing but favoring the Rebs and a pack of lies. The Rebels have not once had the advantage in this campaign but rather the contrary.

Sometimes we have had heavy losses but that has been exaggerated in the Northern papers. Our soldiers are not discouraged because of it or sad about it. On the contrary, they feel they will make it up next time. Such is the Army - the good soldiers who are truly fighting for the cause are found in the front lines and the slackers and good-for-nothings are found in the rear. Then there are those cowards who get their discharge and have so many complaints to make that everyone gets scared. With few exceptions, they favor the copperheads. For that reason I am sorry that the North believes them because it isn't very pleasant for us, besides encouraging the Rebs.

Sergeant Ben Van Raalte and General Ulysses S. Grant often thought alike. At the end of his life, dying and poor, Grant wrote his memoirs, hoping thereby to provide money to support his widow. He wrote, as he had always written, straightforwardly and clear-sightedly.

The copperhead disreputable portion of the press magnified rebel successes, and belittled those of the Union army. It was, with a large following, an auxiliary to the Confederate army. The North would have been much stronger with a hundred thousand of these men in the Confederate ranks and the rest of their kind thoroughly subdued, as the Union sentiment was in the South, than we were as the battle was fought.

Looking backward, there seems an inevitability in historical events. In the Civil War, Union forces won; the Confederate States of America were defeated and disappeared. And we think, "of course." Economically, the outcome must have been inevitable: the northern part of America was more industrialized and had a larger population than the south; thus the Union forces had more men and more equipment. Socially and culturally, the outcome must have been inevitable: slavery is abominable; surely such wickedness could not have been tolerated in America much longer. But there was no such assurance of inevitability at the time.

There was a large population of military-aged men in the north, but how to get and keep them in the army presented gigantic problems. The ninety-day term of enlistment was clearly nonsensical. After Bull Run men enlisted for three years or for the duration of the war, but desertions and discharge for illness, real or feigned, were common, and furloughs were frequent. Letters exchanged between the soldiers of the colony and their families are full of information about someone who's been home and brought news of the others — "P. S. You must have the greetings of B. van Raalte. He is here on a 30 day furlough. He looks heavy and fat. He also told us that you too look heavy and fat."

Creating a manageable fighting force was a major challenge. In the heyday of enthusiasm and individuality at the beginning of the war, well-to-do men formed and outfitted their own companies with uniforms and arms. Zouave uniforms — brightly colored short jackets and baggy pants, sashes round the waist, and fez-style caps — were dashing, and popular on both Union and confederate sides. Patriotic feeling for Michigan inspired the Lancer regiment, for which "lances, which were made in Michigan from Michigan white ash... were to be the regiment's principal, if not sole, weapon in battle." (The regiment never saw action; the army refused to accept it on the grounds of noncompliance with regulations about arms and equipment.)

In the army, the impulse to obey orders was not highly developed, and in some cases — as was true of many of the soldiers in the 25th Michigan Infantry — some of the troops didn't speak English. On both sides in the conflict, short terms of service didn't keep men long enough for them to become efficient soldiers; voluntary enlistment did not produce armies large enough to offset the dreadful losses to disease, maiming and death. In April 1862, as the one-year term for southern soldiers ended, the south passed the first conscription law in America's history, which applied to every able-bodied white male citizen in the confederacy between the ages of eighteen and thirty-five. The U. S. Congress passed an Enrollment Act in March of 1863, under the terms of which there would be a draft in localities which didn't produce a requisite number of volunteers. The practices of allowing substitutes (a man who was drafted could pay someone else, including an immigrant not yet a citizen, to take his place), and paying bounties (localities, states and eventually the federal government raised money to encourage volunteers) made already cumbersome draft legislation even more complex. In the colony, the system worked reasonably well. One way or another, draft quotas were filled — despite his sons' disapproval Albertus Van Raalte raised money for this cause as he did for so many others — but elsewhere, there were draft riots, some of horrendous proportions, lasting for days, with arson and lynchings. Van Raalte, writing to Phelps, described it as a form of lunacy.

> *I foster more contempt than fear for the quarreling North: we have business enough to suppress the rebels in arms: and I hope that they may learn how to deal with mobs too: Is the North crazy? Very well, the Lord will take care of the insane, He is never hindered nor helped in his grand majestic Forward March.*

Throughout the war, Albertus and Christina Van Raalte tried to help their sons in every way they could think of, and their sons were constantly explaining what they didn't need and why. Their families sent money and stamps and clothing and ink bottles so the boys could write neatly, and Albertus Van Raalte decided Ben needed a bullet-proof vest, though he didn't send it. The boys sent money back, and wrote to say they had plenty of everything — they couldn't carry any more — and they apologized but they kept on using pencil. ("I lost my pen in the straw.") Ben asked for one thing, and whether his request was honored during the war we do not know. It certainly isn't honored now. "All I write had better be kept confidential because I sometimes read some strange things in the Hollander and it doesn't sit well here. *Don't let anyone read my letters.*"

above, Ben Van Raalte
inset, Dirk Van Raalte in the early years of the war

The poor Rebs who fall into my hands are going to pay for Dirk's arm.

Although many of the Michigan Hollanders "flocked to the colors before some of them could read the call to arms in the language of their adopted country," not every eligible man enlisted immediately. Albertus Van Raalte, a fervent supporter of the Union, shared with his brother-in-law in the Netherlands the disappointment his family was causing him. "I am not at all proud of the fact that none of my sons has yet taken up arms against rebellion and treason."

In the summer of 1862, the Van Raaltes' oldest son Albertus was twenty-five and thus toward the younger end of the age range of volunteers at this point in the war. However, he was married, with two young children and a third about to be born. Van Raalte's discouragement with his sons was partially satisfied when Ben, then twenty-two, enlisted on August 22, 1862 — leaving him with only his youngest son to lament about.

> *The town of Holland has been aroused to encourage volunteering to avoid the Draft. $4,000 has been subscribed for the volunteers. Sixty-one from this town were sworn in. …Now the married men are allowed to stay home. We have 459 men from 18 to 45 years. The volunteers in the different regiments in the beginning in the war numbered over 60 in Holland. …Dirk has no desire or courage. Benjamin has enlisted. It did cost Mrs. Van Raalte a severe struggle but now she has rest.*

Within weeks, however, Dirk, had enlisted too. He was eighteen years old and a student at the Holland Academy — "but I am afraid he doesn't like it," his father had written at the beginning of the summer. The *Allegan Journal* reported that the Holland Rangers were greeted with enthusiasm when they arrived in that city. "The company carried with them a beautiful silk flag, presented to them by the patriotic Ladies of the Colony — an Ensign we are sure the brave Hollanders will carry in triumph over Dixie. …Accompanying the boys were many of their friends and relatives, among others Rev. Dr. A. C. Van Raalte (who has a son in the company). …The Rangers left for Otsego after lunch amid much cheering."

Van Raalte shared family cares, church matters, and concerns about needs of the Academy with his friend Philip Phelps, the Academy's principal. (The baby mentioned in the letter excerpt below was a granddaughter, Christina Johanna, Mina and Pieter Oggel's second child. She lived for nearly two years, but died before her uncles came home from the war. The Oggels' first child had died earlier.)

> *The boys have organized a Company. Dr. Dowd is Captain: a wounded volunteer Martin De Boe just coming back was elected 1st Lieutenant and Jacob Doesburg for 2nd Lieutenant. - May all this shaking bring us nearer to God, may it make us strangers and*

pilgrims: may it make us holier. Our time has been swallowed up by this war affaire and it works very unfavorable for Church building and every other enterprise.

...I have been busy more than I could stand: and yet my health is well, but being overdone I am troubled with toothache. My health is now better than I had exspected.

...Mrs. Oggel is with her baby very well - after 2 or 3 weeks Dominie Oggel will take her away.

Our kindest regards and best wishes toward your Father and Mother: and be with your Lady assured of our high esteem and love.

Holland Historical Trust Collection of the Joint Archives

Johannes Van Lente

Among the men who enlisted in the 25th Michigan Infantry at the same time as Dirk Van Raalte was Johannes Van Lente, aged 27. Like Van Raalte's sons, he had emigrated with his family from the Netherlands. The Van Lentes, parents and eight children ranging in age from 23 to 7, sailed to America on the *Albatross*, arriving in New York in July 1847 and reaching *de Kolonie* in the early fall. Years later Johannes told his grandchildren how his mother "sat under a huge, cotton, colored umbrella that they had brought with them from the old country, her brood of children around her, every time it thundered and lightninged and poured, before their log cabin was raised that first year." Johannes' father, Frederick Van Lente, was a cooper — that is, a barrel-maker — and also the *voorzanger* for the colony church. At the time no musical instruments were used in church services, and the voorzanger, or fore-singer, led the congregation as they sang the psalms.

Letters exchanged between Johannes and his parents, as well as letters from other family and friends, were preserved, survived the Holland fire, and many years later were translated into English and published by one of his descendants. These letters provide an informative supplement to those of the Van Raaltes. One feature is Johannes' reference to Dominie Van Raalte, as a revered leader who was loving but stern.

> *Now you must understand about our Colonel, or "Father" as many in our Regiment call him. He makes sure that everything is in order and in its place. By nature he is the same as Dominie Van Raalte, according to me: "Do it right or don't do it at all." And on the other hand, he is as good as he can be to his people. He won't allow anyone who has something wrong with him to work.*
>
> Johannes Van Lente to his father, mother and brother, December, 1862

Religion permeates the letters Johannes wrote to his "Worthy and beloved Father, Mother and Sister," and those he received — "Much respected and beloved son, John Van Lente" — and later in the war, the letters he exchanged with his "Esteemed girlfriend, Miss Jantje Bouman." He was earnest in his wish to live his faith: "Oh loved ones, there is nothing too miraculous for the Lord, but I have to tell you that it is something else for a soldier to stay good." For Johannes, the rough language of the camp was shocking. "You should be here sometime," he wrote from Kalamazoo, where his company camped, "and if you could master the language, you could understand the God-provoking language spoken here. It would penetrate you to the very marrow. These are, one and all, souls who have been created for Eternity, that's why I'm telling you that it would be good if there were an end to it." Some of the other young men were less surprised, as is shown by this early, cheerful commentary on camp life.

*Soldier's life agrees with me, it is a merry life. Time flies by and it seems to me as if we have been in the service for only one week. I wish you were here, you would also enjoy it a lot.
...W. van Appeldoorn looks like a rose and C. van Dam about the same as he. How are you doing right now? Are you able to enjoy the winter evenings? Here it's all right. You must understand that we don't have to walk far to see each other. There's a row of tents about 60 feet for the whole Company. We spend the whole night singing and telling stories. What kind of language is used amongst so many boys goes beyond saying, crude and dirty talk. You can imagine that yourself from when we were still together in Holland. Luckily in our Camp, the Hollanders, as well as the English, only swear a little or not at all. B. van Raalte does not do it as much anymore as he used to do at home.*

Ary Rot to Hein Van Lente, November 4, 1862

Before he died, Albertus Van Raalte destroyed many family documents. Much of what remained is scattered among widely-separated archives in this country and in the Netherlands, and is only now being brought together and translated. A great deal is known about his career in the ministry and his business dealings, but there are deep silences embedded in the stories of his children. Among the glimpses we have, the Civil War period provides a treasure trove. Not all the letters his sons in the army wrote reached home, and not all of those have come down to us. The letters which exist — many from Ben, fewer from Dirk — present us with scenes of the war, and glimpses of a family.

In several ways the Van Lente letters parallel the Van Raalte correspondence. Ben and Johannes were from the same home town, served in the same company, and had a shared cultural and religious heritage. Letters home were written in Dutch, although they became more Americanized as the war continued. They enlisted at almost the same time — Ben a few weeks earlier than Johannes — and both served through the entire war, returned to Holland, married, had children, and lived on into the twentieth century. The sons and fathers loved each other, and the sons unknowingly preserved for themselves a niche in history through the letters they wrote to their families. But the two sets of letters have one significant difference. Johannes saw every event in relation to his faith. Ben lived in this world. That it was a world created and ruled by God he did not question, but what he saw was a world full of people to like or dislike, to love and have fun with or hate; and always with daily work to do.

It is possible that the dominie Van Raalte would have preferred sons like those of the voorzanger Van Lente — or that all three of Van Raalte's sons might occasionally have wished for the uncritical outpouring of love and respect that the young Van Lente men received. But uncritical love for his sons was difficult for Albertus Van Raalte to express — throughout their father's lifetime, Dirk was showered with practical advice; Ben was exhorted to pray for his soul. Nevertheless, strength of personality in the Van Raalte family was not confined to one generation. Ben kept on being Ben, and one result of that is a shrewd, brisk, generally sunny account of day-by-day events in one part of the vast war — not a recollection written at leisure after the war by an officer, but a series of letters written to "the music of bullets," intended just for his family, by one of the men of the 25th Michigan.

> *A son of our neighbors, pious people, was also in the army. Dominie Van Raalte had two sons in the war and he was very earnest in his sermons and prayers - so much, that we were given comfort through them.*
>
> from the diary of Grace - Geesje - Van der Haar Visscher

The regiment gathered in Kalamazoo and camped there while troops assembled. On the first of October the soldiers packed into railroad cars and went south, seeing places most of the Hollanders had never seen before — Niles, Michigan City, New Buffalo, Indianapolis — crossing the Indiana-Kentucky border after a few days, and arriving at Louisville, where they stayed until late in December. Dirk was assigned to work in the hospital with William Ledeboer. His father was delighted, and wrote, "I think that you should try to get so far that you can achieve every position of a soldier and officer." He supplied his son with plenty of good advice, and enclosed a pocket-sized physician's manual that Dirk could always carry. He also gave a suggestion for the first lieutenant. Dirk may have decided not to pass it along, but the advice was excellent: an officer with a crippled hand will look authoritative, rather than weakened, if he makes it a habit to hold a stick in that hand, and doing so will have the added benefit of exercising the muscles.

> *Dear Dirk,*
>
> *It is to our happiness that I learn that you and Ledeboer found work at the hospital. ...A good beginning is worth much, let them feel continually that you throw yourself completely in your work, for every one knows that no one can succeed if he is not in it with all of his heart. You know that I am sort of a half-doctor and therefore can give you counsel. There is likely a dispensary in the hospital. Look through that book, always open to the names of the medicines which have been prescribed. Learn the name of the illness, observe very carefully the illness, and also the effect of the medicine they gave. If you investigate the things in such a quiet, unnoticeable way, you can learn in a single year an amazingly great amount. The great secret of becoming a doctor is to stand at a bedside and observe the one who is sick.*
>
> *...I know your present duties are the smallest, but believe me, people quickly notice the small attentiveness toward the sick person. ...To form attentive habits is the best recommendation for you. ...You can quickly make yourself indispensable by doing good and being attentive. Conduct yourself as one who seeks wisdom from God. The fear of God will give you resilience, faithfulness, helpfulness and development. Notice also with Lieutenant De Boe how someone with the simplest plainness, combined with seriousness and diligence, is loved and made indispensable in his group. Tell him from me, that he should always carry a stick in his bad hand.*
>
> *I'm sending you a small medical book written in English. I received it as a present from a Kalamazoo doctor. When you hear a sickness named, you should look it up in that book and at the same time, compare it with the sick person. I'm sending it because it is light, and you can carry it in your pocket.*
>
> *Mother is pleased that blankets have come from the government. She wishes to know whether there is anything she can do for you and anything we can send you. Write as you have opportunity and urge Ben also always to write. Although we in our earthly circle must be earnest, courageous and faithful, realize and don't forget, that your Lord and Savior calls*

out to you, "one thing is necessary," for all earthly concerns pass as clouds over our heads, but that one thing needed remains the great matter, always needed in life, in death and in all eternity. Learn God's gracious will from his Word, and pray to receive the Holy Spirit. God be gracious to you and use you to his honor and for a blessing.
Greetings from mother and the family,
Your loving father,
A. C. Van Raalte

Ben wrote home, sending greetings and messages from members of the company, derogatory comments about men who were lazy, descriptions of camp life, news about the weather — first it was very dry and then there were torrential rains and a snowstorm.

I am enjoying myself. The life of a soldier agrees with me, it is a healthful life if one is willing to take care of himself. ...Dirk has had fever a couple of times but could continue to work - he can take it. He is sturdy and very active. He has more time to write than I have. Sometimes he comes to my tent but then he is always so full of pep that he can't sit down.

We lack nothing. Our company had only five tents and at night we lay so close together that I didn't enjoy it much. So we changed things. Last Saturday I took a squad and got some planks and with them we fixed our tents so we now have a third more space. We banked dirt against the planks and it has been a great improvement. ...We bought a stove from the Indiana Regiment for fourteen shillings - about 10¢ apiece for our group. Now we can have a fire in the morning and evenings.

There is much sickness among the lazy soldiers. Whenever there is work to be done they complain of stomach cramps, etc. We rise at daybreak for roll call and after that it's sweeping the parade ground. Then at eight we mount guard and at nine drill till eleven. Then later battalion drill from two till four. After that dress parade. Other things are also done and so the days pass quickly. ...When we left camp last week it was very cold and snowing hard - about three inches in 24 hours. Ice hung from the trees but now it is much milder. ...The country looks devastated. Fences are rarely seen any more and we take whatever there is to take. So you can understand why the country looks desolate.

Early in the war, the army was beginning as it would go on — living off the land. Ben describes stealing oat sheaves ("or rather, I just took them") from a farm to make bedding down in mud more comfortable for himself and others in the company. General William Sherman, who knew military terminology, advocated the *tent d'abris* for temporary housing — eventually all shelter was temporary for front line soldiers on both sides — constructed from fences or shakes from roofs, or "when boards can be ripped off our neighbors' houses." Eventually not even debris would be left.

Dirk wrote, as his father had requested, describing his work in the hospital. He also expressed his contempt for what he saw as cowardly behavior. Other Holland soldiers wrote light-heartedly about the amazing new experiences that were coming their way, and the pretty girls who put the Hollandish *jonge vrouwen* out of their minds.

Dear Father and Mother,

Now it is again my turn to write to you, which I do twice a week. Benjamin and I are still in good health, and I hope the same is true for you. All of our Holland boys are in good condition, and they enjoy army life.

...We have our hospital in an old church building which is near our campgrounds. The building is as big as Rev. Zwemer's church building. Right now there are about thirteen people sick. They all lie on bunks with straw mattresses. They are much better off than in a hospital tent. Most of the sicknesses are intermittent fever, lung fever, and some colds.

There is a man here in the hospital from Camp C. I do not expect him to live for more than four hours. Most of his lungs have almost gone, and he can hardly get enough air to talk. He was a very strong man, and this is the first time he was sick. Today is the fourth day of his sickness.   He just passed away.

We are camped right near the railroad tracks, and every day we see the cars pass by for Nashville or for Louisville. We have a beautiful view here. Our camp is about a half mile out of town. Nowadays I work full time in the medical department, and I like that work very well, as now I am able to learn something about the medicines too.

...All of us are in good health.

Your loving son,

Dirk Van Raalte

Say hello from me to Rev. Phelps and his wife, also to Maria, Anna, Albertus and his wife, and Lena De Vries. A kiss for Allie and Christine.

Good-by. D. B. K. Van Raalte

P.S. Now it is evening, and my letter is not closed yet. I want you to know that I received your letters of Feb. 9. I was very happy about it. Enclosed I found post currency for 70 cents and in Mother's letter four postage stamps. You should not send money any more. I like to get stamps though for it is rather difficult to get them here. Mother asked me whether we get enough to eat – oh, yes, plenty, as much as we like. Those boys who write home that they do not get enough to eat never had enough at home. So far we have never lacked anything. Last week we got paid. I am sending two dollars along with this letter. Will you exchange them, and give one to Maria and one to Anna, and tell them it is a gift from their beloved brother Dirk Van Raalte! Your loving son, Dirk Van Raalte

Say hello to all of them. Good-by to all of you.

You are asking me why I don't write T. Kroon. Well, friend, I don't want to get into this, but the girls from the Colony are almost out of my mind because there are much prettier girls out here than by you.

...There is in this town a soldier of the female sex. She was wounded in Murfreesboro and there her sex was discovered and reported to General Rosecrans, after which she was discharged from the service. But she said, "I will enlist in the first Regiment I meet with" and when she arrived in Bowling Green, she reenlisted. She came to this town with prisoners, accompanied by her Captain. She is only eighteen years old and has experienced difficult service. She is, so to say, discharged again. ...Once she was in our camp. She is not tall, has a very pretty face, and is very polite. She has served for ten months with the Cavalry.

Wulf Van Appeldoorn, excerpts from letters to Hein Van Lente, January 2 and May 11, 1863

Ben's letters to his mother tended to be livelier than those to his father. It is unlikely that she was reassured by them, but perhaps she took pleasure in remembering little boys who liked to play in the mud, and mischievous boys who were not completely respectful about their father's beloved Academy. As to church-going, mother was the better person to learn that Ben's negative opinion of the company chaplain was based on hearsay, rather than on attendance at services. Ben often stressed his abundant supply of clothes in order to ward off gifts. A persistent theme in letters home was that mother was not to send more clothing, because knapsacks were heavy enough without adding more weight.

Anna Van Raalte was six years old when her brothers went to war. Whether or not the treat she sent Ben was edible when it arrived in camp, her brother loyally tasted it and sent thanks.

At present it is very damp here - it has rained steadily since Sunday evening. Some of the boys are busy digging as the camp ground is covered with water and the tents which were not properly set up are drenched. The mud is terrible. Oh, what fun! Who wouldn't want to be a soldier! I have never had more fun than in camp. We again received an issue of new clothing - pants, shirts and socks, clothing in abundance. ... I do my own washing and Thomson and I help each other a great deal. He is a noble fellow and a good soldier. We lack nothing although we have not had any pay yet.

Dirk has promised that he will write some time. He is getting along very well and I believe they are pleased with his work at the hospital. There is more illness among the English than among the Holland Boys. Our preacher doesn't amount to much. I haven't heard him preach as yet but those who have heard him say that he gives a political speech and not much more. If our boys can get out of it they don't go to hear him, if we can we go to a Presbyterian church. We have no drill on Sundays but we do have inspection. At 4 o'clock we have dress parade. Our boys like our captain - there is none better in the whole regiment. The doctoring which he does is worth a lot to our boys. I haven't had a sick day. A person can do a lot about this himself - cleanliness is worth a lot in maintaining health.

Tell Anna that I received her letter and that I am very happy with the little present - it tasted very good. She wrote that she ate two apples for me every day. Just tell her that if that isn't enough that Mr. Thomson said she was to eat two for him also.

Through the Lord's mercy we are still in good health. ... Yesterday we burned a large house, just like the Holland Academy. It was a beautiful fire and the boys enjoyed themselves.

Ben joined the cavalry. Earlier letters had stressed mother's fears; now father's characteristic decisiveness came to the fore. Dirk was likely to be safe working in the hospital, but Ben would be thrust into much greater danger. Ben's appreciation and practicality — if the money's been paid for something, I'll use it — warred with his experience of traveling with a heavy pack, and a desire not to be the butt of his friends' jokes.

Dear Father,

I received your letter yesterday and was overjoyed to note that you are feeling much better. ...Up to the present we are well and cannot expect to have it any better. Thomson is improving nicely. He has a good appetite but is as thin as a rail.

Regarding your bullet-proof vest I hardly know what to say. When I left home I thought I couldn't get along without some armor and a revolver but I have forgotten about that long ago. The longer one is a soldier, the less danger one feels and for that reason I am indifferent. However, if you have bought one, I will wear it, but if we go into action I would be the butt of some jokes about the "iron-clad soldier." It would be good to have on an expedition but it undoubtedly weighs a lot and that would be bad on a march. Then I prefer to carry as little as possible. My knapsack with clothing weighs 20 to 25 lbs. then a gun of 12 lbs. and cartridges about 6 lbs. Besides we sometimes have a haversack with three days rations and a canteen with water. When you are loaded down with all that there is no danger of blowing away, at least when we are through marching for the day it feels quite comfortable to take it all off.

I have proved that I can take it as well as anyone. At least it was tried on the march to Mumfordsville when half of our regiment fell by the wayside.

In letters to his father, Ben described terrain and tactics. The regiment stayed in Kentucky for nearly a year. "Today it is two months since I joined the cavalry," Ben wrote. "It is a good job. It is healthful and one never gets tired but one does get sleepy." Their first major battle was fought in July at Green River, against the troops of John Hunt Morgan, source of the "Morgan fever" to which both Dirk Van Raalte and Johannes Van Lente attributed an otherwise unexplained illness that sent some of the men from their Corps hastily back to Holland.

The country is mountainous hereabouts and we are camped on a high mountain. We have two pieces of artillery here. Our camp is located about a quarter mile from Green River from which we get our drinking water. ...At the foot of the mountain lies another regiment and two on the other side of the river where they have a fort of sorts. It is a strong position and we are daily awaiting an attack by Uncle Morgan. His purpose is to cut off communications between Nashville and Louisville. We sleep at night with our guns at our sides so we can be ready at a moment's notice. Every morning at 4 or 4:30 we form a line of battle which is done to teach us to fall in quickly and not be half asleep in case the old boy should come as he has the habit of attacking at night.

On July 4, 1863, Morgan attacked the vastly outnumbered Union forces commanded by Colonel Moore. Called upon to surrender, Moore replied, "Present my compliments to General Morgan, and say to him that this being the Fourth of July I cannot entertain his proposition to surrender." The next wave of the Confederate attack was beaten back. The battle was a triumph for the Union forces, and Albertus Van Raalte rejoiced in the victory with the zeal of an Old Testament prophet.

Our boys 200 in number had a tremendous fight with Morgan's division on the fourth of July: the fire and 8 charges they had to endure [over many] hours; Morgan did ask permission to bury his dead, but did not finish his work (our boys had to bury yet 25 of his men) - but left them in haste just at the time when another two thousand did cross the river: Col. Moore had chosen an excellent position on a hill with trees and logs: Sometimes they were overwhelmed and they had to back out to be able to use their guns: - In the evening they did get reinforcements - 1000 cavalry and 700 infantry: then they followed him to Lebanon. All along the road the houses were filled with wounded and dying rebels. They did call our boys groundhogs because they fired out of the ground; they said their number wounded and killed were 250: Morgan did parole one of the wounded soldiers: and said they must make your Colonel General and his boys are all sharpshooters: five of our boys were killed and 20 wounded: and yet they were constant under a rain of bullets: The leaves brush and bark of the trees were so abundant it did hinder constant in their eyes: the Colonel's horse and pantaloon was hit. The Colonel loves very much the Holland Company: they drove them by the tremendous charges to surround them several times. We feel that God's hand did cover them: Morgan's division could have eaten them up: Morgan seems to have been discouraged on account of that unusual number of wounded and dead: our boys did hit them all in the head or breast. I tell you we have had a very pleasant thanksgiving today.

The Holland men took up a collection which they sent to Dominie Van Raalte. "With gratitude to God for sparing them in the battle of Green River, the undersigned [31 soldiers] send a contribution to Kingdom causes." Morgan the raider did not survive the war. Within a month of this battle he was captured and imprisoned; he escaped and returned to lead raids in Tennessee, where he was killed in September 1864. General Ulysses S. Grant was made lieutenant general and commander of all the Union armies. Lincoln defended this decision by explaining how Grant differed from his predecessors. "He fights," Lincoln said. Grant besieged Richmond, while Sherman — and the Van Raalte boys — set up fortifications outside Atlanta. Ben, as usual, wrote more frequently than Dirk, sometimes from his "headquarters" in the rifle pits.

General Ulysses S. Grant

One evening we were shelled very heavily and a piece of shell hit Wilterdink in his side but fortunately he had a Testament in his pocket which saved his life. It hurt him a lot but he stayed with the company. Another was hit but his knapsack saved him.

My opinion is that much will have to happen before this campaign is concluded. Whoever lives through it will have much to tell. Last night I got your letter in which you said that you know the news almost as well as we, if not better. Yes, at the front where you would expect to know it, one hears nothing but the music of bullets.

Much of the Rebellion has been licked and one thing is certain - they do not fight with the courage of our soldiers. They fight in despair and they can see with their own eyes that many soldiers are deserting and that from their best troops. Besides nearly all of their men are under arms, at least all that can carry a gun. Their strength is diminishing and ours is getting stronger daily. All the losses which they suffer cannot be replaced.

We went forward about two miles today. Our Corps is on the extreme left joining the 4th Corps under command of Gen. Howard, the one-armed general. We are all well and have again erected strong fortifications. We have fortified all of Georgia - a pleasant prospect for the Rebs. It is terribly hot here and Kramer said that Michigan didn't know what heat was.

...If I need anything I'll write for it. Remember we carry our clothes closet on our backs. Mother may send me a pair of carrying straps.

I am happy to be able to write and announce that I am still in good health. It is now the third day that we have lain in our breastworks and we have had a very good rest.

...I am sorry that Grant's campaign has not been as successful as we had hoped. Sherman seems to be taking his time. I hear that heavy cannon are arriving daily by train. There is heavy cannonading on the left as far as we can hear. We built a flank to our breastworks as the Rebs seemed to have us in a crossfire this morning. I don't know how it happened but it sometimes occurs on the flanks. Sometimes the breastworks run very crooked because of the way the land lies. They must always be built on the highest elevations. Georgia is becoming a country of breastworks as each army fortifies itself. The farmers will have quite a job to level them all. It seems as if the Rebs have received reinforcements because their lines are nearly as long as ours. Only on the flank not much is to be seen besides cavalry.

Now I must close. It is still very hot and we are having lots of rain. Everything in our path is being destroyed. The boys tear down the houses to construct breastworks. So it goes with everything.

In haste but with much pleasure I can announce that we are still well. The Rebs have been flanked again and are slowly retiring. The fighting began at noon on the 15th. We were opposite Lost Mountain a little to the left. Schofield went forward in the shape of a horseshoe leaving the mountain to his left. We pressed the Rebs so hard they no longer felt safe on the mountain and on the night of the 17th they had to fall back. Since that time we drove at them from all points. It is hard going because of the rains. ...The people at home think we are making slow progress as we are still far from Atlanta but they wouldn't say so if they were here and taking part in the fighting. You must realize that all the roads are strongly fortified and if we didn't proceed slowly and cautiously there would not be much left by way of an Army to take Atlanta. We must first feel out the enemy positions - should you run into a group of masked batteries it is far from pleasant.

...The rebs are getting discouraged and they reserve their best troops for the skirmish line to prevent desertions. The 1st Georgia Regiment is opposite our bridge in the skirmish line and they are about played out. One day sixty deserters came over and now there are more every day so that nearly a whole company has been taken as prisoners. A hundred or more were buried in the field. This is one of their best units so you can imagine what will happen when we meet the others. Now they have to retreat in the mud which isn't so pleasant. The Yanks are full of pep and say "The Rebellion must and shall be put down, mud or no mud." Yesterday we waded through such deep creeks that we had to hold our ammunition above our heads.

I am writing under difficulties so please forgive the writing in this letter. I hardly get any letters and do not know when this letter will go but at least it is ready.

John Nies

At Strawberry Plains, on our march to Atlanta Georgia, I went over to see some of our boys of the 25th Michigan Infantry, and when I arrived they asked me if I had something to eat, and I handed my haversack to them and as it contained some ham, etc., they were glad to get it as they were poor on rations.

When we got home after the war, Dominie Van Raalte sent for me to come and I went and such a spread I never sat down to and it was in my honor because I had given my haversack to the boys, his two sons being among them.

Civil War Recollections of John Nies

Camp one half mile from Atlanta Ga, July 15, 1864

Dear Mother,

Last night I received your letter of the 15th and it made me feel happy. We also received the shirt and socks for me and the ink bottle for Ben. I am very pleased with them and thank you very much for them. I don't think that Ben needs a shirt because not so long ago he threw one away. If he needs one he can speak for himself. You had better not send any more - if I need anything I will let you know. If I permitted you to do so you would send so much I wouldn't be able to carry it. Ben and I are both well and the other Hollanders also. We now lie behind our breastworks with Atlanta in sight. We are shelling Atlanta continuously and sometimes the Rebs send some shells our way. The first day we were here and building our breastworks they shelled heavily but did little damage. We can see Atlanta well from here and can see what effect our shells are having. The night before last we set a house afire with our shells. Father wrote that it seemed to him that Atlanta lay on some heights and that it was strongly fortified. He is right in that. You undoubtedly have heard about the heavy fighting which occurred on the 22nd. The Rebs suffered heavy losses. Yesterday we captured a Reb captain and he told us that they had 12,000 casualties that day. For my part let them make a couple more such charges.

Yesterday our cavalry returned from a raid. They had destroyed the railroad which runs from Covington to Charleston and they brought tobacco, mules and horses which they had captured.

The breastworks we have here are very strong and cannot be captured. The Rebs works are strong too the way it appears to us. But Sherman will not let us charge them - his intention is to take Atlanta without the loss of a lot of men.

...You worry about us too much. You must not do that - it doesn't do you any good or us either. We can bear the hardships very well.

The reason I am not writing with ink is because it is so inconvenient and sometimes I do not have the time to write with ink. Greetings to all of you.

> *Your loving son,*
>> *Dirk Van Raalte*

P.S. The fact that you do not get many letters from me is not my fault. I write frequently. Why doesn't Christina write?

> *Camp 25th Mich. Near Atlanta Ga., July 26 1864*

Dear Father,

We are directly in front of the city and the Rebs have very strong fortifications. Yesterday we went ahead about a mile but the fighting was very heavy - the Rebs made terrific charges and the amount of firing was deafening. They made three charges and in one of them Gen. McPherson was killed which is a heavy loss. The Rebs drove us back and took some of our cannon and many prisoners. Soon after that we were reinforced by another group of our Corps and others and we made a charge, recapturing all the cannon and the prisoners they had taken from us besides taking two thousand of them prisoner. The dead and wounded all fell into our hands. I do not think Gen. Hood gained anything yesterday with his charges.

...We had to build our breastworks under heavy fire, shell fragments flying about our ears. We have to play woodchuck nowadays. I will become an expert shovel-handler here. Yesterday morning Renke De Vries was wounded lightly by a shell fragment. It didn't draw blood but became very swollen but in a day or two he should be back on duty again. We have made our fortifications extra strong as the Rebs have very heavy artillery. I am expecting very heavy shelling as we lie directly in front of a Reb fort but we can also dump as many shells on them that it will be a joy to behold. Maybe they will get tired of it but they may also throw over some "camp kettles." That's what the boys call those big shells. The story is that we took five thousand prisoners to Marietta this morning.

...Now I must finish, hoping that we may be spared and that Atlanta may soon be in our possession. Best regards to all.

> *Your loving*
>> *B. Van Raalte*

p.s. We get very few letters - why I don't know. ...Yesterday we captured seven stands of colors. The Johnnies must be vanquished. Our boys are in good spirits. My headquarters is at present in the rifle pits, in case the Rebs start shelling.

During the battle that Ben describes, General James McPherson's horse returned to the lines, riderless and covered with blood. When McPherson's bullet-riddled body was found and carried back, Sherman wept. Grant wrote later, in his memoirs, "in his death the army lost one of its ablest, purest and best generals."

General William Tecumseh Sherman

When Ben wrote to his sister Christine he wrote in English, showing excellent command of the language without perfect accuracy in spelling. As usual, he joked; this time he punned. Some of the boys had been spared the trouble of *striking* (taking down) their tents because Rebel shells *struck* the tents for them. Although he underestimated the army's abundance of high-ranking officers — "I have had the pleasure to see most of the generals in this army" — he'd had a good look at a good many, and his assessment of them was shrewd. General Sherman probably would have been pleased by Ben's description of him: he did look like an old broken-down farmer, and he was a sharper. Ben's analysis of the battle styles of opposing generals also accords remarkably well with the views of Civil War historians.

Dear Sister,

A few days ago I received your kind letter and was glad to hear that you were in good health and to hear what good times you have had at the wedding. ...Wel, we have such good success in this army that we often feal as much rejoiced as we should be at a wedding. The Rebbels have had such heavy losses in front of Atlanta that it is awful. They fight most desperate, make charge after charge and are repulsed time after time and still they keep on. Gen. Hood seems to be great for charging - it is great foolishnish to try to take strong works by storm for any genaral. We had satisfaction of that at Resaca. The party behinde the works has all the advantage and if they stand firm the works can not be taken. The Rebs have had a loss of at least 20,000 since the twenty-second... We have taken a large number of prisoners and every charge they make the dead and woonded has fallen in to our hands. Our losses have been but small as our fighting has been mostly behinde the works. I hope that Gen. Hood will stay in command then the sotheren confederacy will soon play out. I auften wonder how it is that the Rebs don't charge our Corps. It must bea that our works are to strong. We have never had the luck to fight behinde the works but have had to take it in the open feild. Our corps is now the exstream left. Gen. Howard has taken the olde command of Gen. McPherson, and has had great success - he is a splendid looking man. I think the best looking on the job. Gen. Sherman looks like an old down broken farmer but he's a sharper. I have had the pleasure to see most all our generals in this Army in this campaign. There has been heavy fighting on our right this afternoon. We have not yet heard the results but the report is that we took a large number of prisoners. We are getting so closely on them that they are very un easy. ...Our boys throw shells night and day, once and a while they replie with a hunder pounder or such a matter. A day or two ago they opend all there guns on us. I tell you what, they made us lay low and struck a few tents for the boys. It was fun to hear our guns open they gained the day and the Johnnies had to nock under. Now I must come to a close. The boys are in good health and good spirit. The brass bands play every night to spite the Rebs. Give my best regards to all.

Your brother, B. Van Raalte.

Against Lee's wishes, Jefferson Davis had now replaced canny, cautious Joe Johnston with General Hood. Union forces were led by "the one-armed Christian general from Maine," O. O. Howard.

> *The Rebs sometimes resort to false alarms, making a pretense of coming at us with a lot of yelling but then do not come. The Reb casualties have been heavy in front of Atlanta. A few days ago a lieutenant surrendered and he told us that he couldn't stand the slaughter any more and that Gen. Hood could stand only two more killings. Gen. Howard experienced one of the killings so that leaves only one. Our boys had to laugh to hear the lieutenant talk. Up to this time our losses have not been heavy.*
>
> *...Col. Cooper of the 6th Tennessee is now Brigadier General. ...I think things will get better since he has received his star - he has earned it. He was the first captain of Co. A of the 6th Tenn. to elude capture by the Rebs. There are no better troops. He looks like a Drenthe farmer.*

In the horrors of war the jokes are gruesome. Ben and his comrades enjoyed the captured officer's wit: "Hood can stand only two more killings." His remark was especially apt, because the Union troops were fighting under a general who, having "experienced one of the killings" would equal Hood if he had one more. In the Civil War, some officers on both sides continued to fight after losing a leg or an arm, and some were strapped into the saddle after two amputations (as long as the losses were balanced — one arm and one leg, on opposite sides). Before Ben and Dirk joined the army, Oliver Howard lost his right arm fighting in Virginia in the spring of 1862, at the bloody Battle of Fair Oaks, fought "amid thick woods and flooded clearings where wounded soldiers had to be propped against fences or stumps to prevent them from drowning in the muck" and the Federal advantage consisted of inflicting six thousand casualties while their own losses were only five thousand. John Bell Hood had a useless left arm resulting from wounds suffered at Gettysburg in July 1863. Two months later he was wounded at Chickamauga and his right leg was amputated. He was a relentless fighter — "all lion and no fox," Lee said — and his strategy of attacking regardless of the situation or the odds against his forces gained him adulation from the southern press and caused his troops appalling losses.

Michigan soldiers

In front of Atlanta Ga. Aug. 24, 1864

Dear Father,

Last night I received your letter of the 13th and was happy to learn that you were all well with the exception of Mina's child. I am sorry about Mina's child. [Mina and Pieter Oggel's only living child was just two years old, and when Albertus Van Raalte wrote to Ben, she was very ill; by the time Ben received his father's letter, little Christina Johanna was dead.]

Through God's blessing we are all well. It is very hot but we can stand it just as well as we could in Michigan. The Rebels seem to be fidgety today and are doing a lot of shelling without doing any damage. Our men just ignore it and let them go ahead. We'll catch up later. …We hear that A. J. Smith has arrived here with 30,000 reinforcements and that can change the program a lot. There is also a rumor that our Corps is to go out on a raid tomorrow. It wouldn't surprise me if, since these reinforcements have arrived, a flanking movement will be attempted. We have always been Sherman's flanking machine. …I do not believe Atlanta can be taken by storm. Cutting off communications could make them very uneasy. They have a large army here and although the railroads have been torn up they can repair them. A couple of good lines of breastworks over the roads would change matters. If the reinforcements have come this is likely to happen soon because such a large army needs a tremendous amount of supplies. We know that from our own experience. If you could see the rations used by our army in ten days it would look such a mountain you would think it never could all be used.

General Andrew Jackson Smith was "small and brusque… popular with his men and respected by his superiors." Smith's troops were moved frequently and served under so many commanders that he referred to them as the lost tribes of Israel. This was the last letter that Ben wrote home before Dirk was wounded.

Marietta Ga. 23rd A. C. Hospital, Aug. 29, 1864

Dear Father,

It is with much sorrow that I must announce that Dirk has been wounded. It happened the morning of the 26th at about nine o'clock. Considering everything he is exceptionally well. He and I arrived here last evening. It was a hard trip but he took it with patience, courage and manliness. He was wounded in the right arm - the bone was so badly splintered that it was impossible to save the arm. So it was necessary to amputate. He still is a thousand times better off than many others. There were no wounded at the hospital on the morning of the operation so the doctors could take their time and give it their best attention. Dirk is well acquainted with all the doctors in our Corps and they all think very highly of him. So all the Corps doctors got together and came to the conclusion that it was necessary to amputate the arm with Dirk's consent. Dr. Wilder, the Corps medical director, performed the operation, assisted by Dr. Lauton, the Division surgeon. They did their very best for Dirk and the arm was amputated at the shoulder.

Dirk also was wounded in the face - a flesh wound and it looks very clean. Dirk's general health is excellent and he is not lacking in courage. He enjoys his food, can walk if necessary and sits up to eat. This noon he ate potatoes with his left hand and can get anything to eat he wishes to have. This is an exceptionally large hospital and everything is first class. I am taking care of him and dare not trust him to other hands unless I am present. The captain and the doctor told me I should go with Dirk, the captain giving me a permit. There was no time limit set and for that reason I would like to have you come here to get him as I will not be able to accompany him home. You probably will need a pass from the governor but I do not know what is necessary. Dirk said I was not to telegraph. It is so busy here that it might not get through and by the time you can get here he should be in condition to be moved easily. I couldn't write before because mail was not leaving the front. The positions of the army have been all switched around. There is a rumor that our division had been in a battle yesterday. The morning we left the boys were all well. Dirk says that mother must not be too concerned about him because he will get along fine.

Dirk had been out with the doctor's horse with Bouman on the captain's mule. As they were riding along they came within ten paces from where some Rebels were hiding. They commanded the boys to surrender. Dirk pretended to do so but at the same time gave his horse the spurs. But he risked too much and was shot although we may be very grateful that he is now in our hands. The Rebel cavalry chased him for two miles but couldn't catch him and he escaped. He soon met up with our cavalry and from there [an officer] and I got him. Bouman was captured and Dirk is afraid the Rebs murdered him.

Now I must close. I will write every day. We send our best regards to all. Van Lente, one of our company, is still here and they are doing all they can for him. The chief cook here is also a man of our regiment and when he was sick last year Dirk took care of him. Now he is doing all he can for Dirk.

Your loving,
B. Van Raalte

"He is still a thousand times better off than many others," Ben wrote, and as usual his assessment of the situation was wise. Jantje Bouman, Johannes Van Lente's sweetheart, received the news that her brother had been killed and all the family mourned. But Cornelis was not dead; he was in the dreaded Andersonville Prison.

Situated northeast of Americus, the prison consisted of a log stockade of sixteen and a half acres (later enlarged to twenty-six acres) with a stream of water running through it. ...Disease and death rates were fantastic, with poor sanitation, crowding, exposure, and inadequate diet contributing to the unhealthful conditions. Only enlisted men were confined there, and in the summer of 1864 the number totaled 32,899. There are 12,912 graves in the national cemetery there, and estimates place the deaths at a much higher figure.

When Sherman's troops approached Andersonville, the Confederates freed all prisoners who were well enough to walk. Emaciated and filthy, Cornelis Bouman came back to his old regiment. Johannes Van Lente sent the news to his family. "Daily our prisoners come here to be exchanged and... yesterday C. Bouman also arrived behind our lines. I did not see him myself... but from what the boys told me, he looked most miserable. He had hardly any clothes on and the ones he had on were not worth anything. Oh, it was terrible. They took him to the Company where they gave him clean clothing and then they washed him because he was so dirty. Then they gave him something to eat." Ben wrote, "Bouman has had a hard time of it. He wouldn't have lasted another week as prisoner of the Rebels but it seems he is going to make it."

Ben stayed with Dirk, and the letter sent home on August 30 was a joint effort, with Dirk's writing at the top. His stoic directive — *you must not concern yourselves about me* — was as likely to be followed as a command to put back his severed arm.

> *Dear Parents, I am doing well. I write with my left hand and Benjamin holds the paper smooth. You must not concern yourselves about me.*
>
> *Yours, D. Van Raalte*

There were times in the chaos of war when letters moved almost as rapidly as they do today; more often, for good reason, mail went astray or took weeks to arrive. Albertus Van Raalte wrote to Dirk in mid-September, without having received his sons' letters. Dirk's reply is dated almost a month after he was wounded. "Today I received your letters of September 12. I was surprised that you did not know yet that I have been wounded. I hope that Mother will not worry too much about this."

Albertus and Christina Van Raalte must have received a packet of letters all at once — what terrors they must have felt! Albertus Van Raalte did his best to bring Dirk home, but he got no farther than Nashville, where he was refused permission to go on. Dirk did not return to Holland until after the war was over, in the following spring. He tried to comfort his parents by telling them not to worry; Ben comforted his mother in another style. Like so many other Americans, soldiers and civilians, men and women, north and south, he had seen enough suffering to want vengeance: "The poor Rebs who fall into my hands are going to pay for Dirk's arm."

For a long time, Lincoln doubted that he would be re-elected in 1864. His opponent was handsome, egotistical General McClellan — in appearance and character poles apart from Lincoln. The North was tired of a war which Union forces couldn't seem to win, and Lincoln despaired — not for himself, but for the preservation of the Union. But early in September Sherman's forces marched into Atlanta. The hopes of the Van Raaltes, father and sons, were realized. "Old Abe" was elected to a second term, and in the spring of 1865, the war ended.

Dear Father,

Yesterday I received your letter of April 7th, and I was happy to learn you and mother are better now.

This morning there is some good news. General Lee has surrendered to General Grant; the war is about to be finished. General Lee's troops have been paroled, and they go home provided they do not take up arms any more against the United States before they have been exchanged properly.

Soon General Johnston will find himself in close quarters because Grant undoubtedly will reinforce Sherman to force Johnston to surrender.

I think that Benjamin and our company will be home again within five months.

…Dad, you should try to get a boy to help you because you cannot do without one.

Kindest regards

Dirk Van Raalte

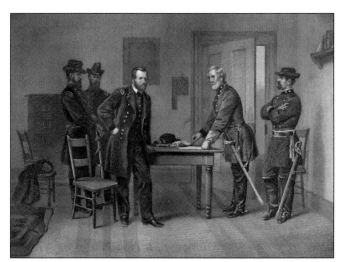

Lee's surrender to Grant at Appomattox Court House

A few more battles and it was ended. From the papers we had learned that our son had been in the last battle and that many had been killed. For a month we didn't hear a thing. Oh, what a terrible suspense — living between hope and fear. In the fifth week we got word that he was alive and shortly thereafter we also got a letter. How grateful we were when he wrote that he had been present when the soldiers had surrendered their guns and flags to the general and that God had saved the lives of him and the other Hollanders.

…But now that the war was ended and the slaves freed by President Lincoln we were saddened by the news that he had been assassinated while attending the theater. He was a good man and did much for his country.

Now we received a letter that the boys were coming home, also our boy though he was still weak. They came home from Grand Rapids by wagon on July 29th, 1865. My husband had gone to town twice but in vain. Then he came home, walking from Holland with our daughter. When I saw him my mind was so overwhelmed with joy that I almost fainted. He was weak and sickly but still in good spirits.

from the diary of Grace - Geesje - Van der Haar Visscher

O sad maimed future! Where is your prime inventor? The ocean covered him with barnacles when the Monitor went down. Where is the saint whose scalpel or microscope was intended to still the scream of cancer? We Federals spattered his skull at Missionary Ridge. …Minister and explorer, balloonist and poet, botanist and judge, geologist and astronomer and man with songs to sing… they are clavicles under leaves at Perryville, ribs and phalanges in the soil of Iuka, they are a bone at Seven Pines, a bone at Antietam… they are in the soil instead of walking, the moss has them.

MacKinley Kantor, *Andersonville*, p. 205

There be of them that have left a name behind them, that their praises might be reported.

And some there be which have no memorial, who are perished as though they had never been; and are become as though they had never been born, and their children after them.

Ecclesiasticus 44: 8-9

Wulf van Appeldoorn

Within three weeks of writing to a friend that "soldier's life agrees with me, it is a merry life," Ary Rot was dead, and buried in Louisville, Kentucky, far from his home. He was the first casualty among the Holland troops and like the majority of those who died it was disease, not injuries in battle, that killed him. Seventy-seven years later, in 1939, the last of Holland's civil war veterans, John Douma, died at the age of 92. The City Council passed a resolution honoring him.

Lewis Cass lived to see the Union reunited. He died in 1866, at the age of 83. Michigan's Cass County, the town of Cassopolis, and numerous streets throughout Michigan honor his name. Defeated for reelection after three terms in the Senate, Zachariah Chandler served for a time as Secretary of the Interior, and was then appointed to fill the unexpired term of the senator to whom he had lost the election. In 1879 he died in his sleep, after delivering a political address in Chicago.

> *More than 620,000 soldiers lost their lives in four years of conflict — 360,000 Yankees and at least 260,000 rebels. The number of southern civilians who died as a direct or indirect result of the war cannot be known; what* can *be said is that the Civil War's cost in American lives was as great as in all of the nation's other wars combined through Vietnam.*

One of the thousands of casualties at the first battle of Bull Run was General Barnard Bee, shot within moments of rallying his troops with the words giving General Jackson the name that was never forgotten. Two years later at the battle of Chancellorsville, a Confederate soldier in Stonewall Jackson's own brigade, mistaking him for a Union officer, shot and wounded him in the hand and arm. Jackson's arm was amputated — Lee said, "He has lost his left arm, but I have lost my right." He developed pneumonia and was carefully treated with all the cruel and useless methods that were the best medical practice of the time. Drifting in and out of consciousness he lived for several days; his last words were, "Let us cross over the river and rest under the shade of the trees." P. G. T. Beauregard survived the war, and, turning down offers from Rumania and Egypt to command their armies, became a railroad president and later supervisor of drawings for the Louisiana Lottery.

In 1863 William Ledeboer died at Bowling Green, Kentucky, and Wulf van Appeldoorn died at Knoxville, Tennessee; Captain William H. Dowd died in the same year — all from disease. Eighteen-year-old Jacobus Grootenhuis enlisted on February 29, 1864, was shot in the leg and head at the terrible Battle of the Wilderness on May 6, and lay untended on the battlefield for four days. He died of his wounds in Virginia while Cornelis Van Dam was dying in Georgia at the Battle of Resaca. Hendrikus Nyland, who had enlisted in 1861, survived three years of war. He reenlisted; he was captured and sent to Andersonville Prison, where he starved to death. Dirk Van Raalte was discharged from the army on April 13, 1865. During a long and prosperous life he was elected to the Michigan state legislature three times. On January 1, 1910, he participated in a ceremony placing a copy of the charter of the A. C. Van Raalte Post of the Grand Army of the Republic in the cornerstone of Holland's City Hall. He died a month later of pneumonia; Renke De Vries, John Wilterdink, and Johannes — then John — Van Lente were pallbearers.

Oliver Otis Howard was appointed Commissioner of the Freedman's Bureau, created to help the freed slaves and protect their rights. Although Howard was honest he was unable to control widespread corruption in the Bureau during the period of Reconstruction. He founded Howard University, which became the largest predominantly Negro college in the country, and served as its president from 1869 to 1874. He died in 1909. Sergeant John Huizenga was discharged on

May 31, 1865, and he and Dirk Van Raalte graduated together from Hope College in the class of 1867. Huizenga went on to study theology, was ordained by the Holland Classis, and served for several years as a missionary in Virginia, where Albertus Van Raalte hoped to establish a new community for Dutch immigrants. He died in 1916 at Rock Valley, Iowa, aged 74, "beloved of all who knew him."

Robert E. Lee became president of Washington College in Virginia, later renamed Washington and Lee University to honor him. He urged reconciliation, telling his fellow southerners, "Make your sons Americans." When he died on October 12, 1870, his last words were, "Let the tent be struck." After Lee's surrender, Jefferson Davis tried to escape to Texas where he hoped to establish a new government and continue the war. He was captured in Georgia within a month, imprisoned at Fort Monroe, Virginia, for two years, and released on bond put up by a consortium of businessmen from the north. He never stood trial, and lived to be 81. The only Confederate officer or official to be executed for war crimes was Captain Henry Wirz, the Swiss-born commander of Andersonville Prison, who was hanged in November 1865.

In 1868 Ulysses S. Grant was elected president of the United States. He served for two terms but his enormous popularity, his talent as a general, and his own honesty were no protection for him, or for the country, from greedy office holders including men in his own cabinet, and his time in office was wracked with scandal. After leaving the presidency, gifts from friends enabled him to travel around the world with his family. A business partnership he formed went bankrupt and he used the last of his savings to pay his creditors. Dying of throat cancer, he began to write his memoirs, hoping that the money earned would support his family after his death.

> *I had been a light smoker previous to the attack on Donelson. ...In the accounts published in the papers I was represented as smoking a cigar in the midst of the conflict, and many persons, thinking, no doubt, that tobacco was my chief solace, sent me boxes of the choicest brands. ...As many as ten thousand were soon received. I gave away all I could get rid of, but having such a quantity on hand I naturally smoked more than I would have done under ordinary circumstances. I have continued the habit ever since.*

The press attacked him; those who knew him best loved him. Mark Twain admired him, and saw to it that his own publishers offered Grant an outstandingly generous contract, despite doubts that he would live to complete the work. "Suffering intense pain but indomitable to the end, he finished in bed the last page of his great military memoirs on 19 July, 1885, four days before death claimed him." In February, 1886, the publishers sent Julia Dent Grant a check for one hundred thousand dollars; in all, she received over four times that amount.

William Tecumseh Sherman was urged to run for president but refused with the famous words, "I will not accept if nominated and will not serve if elected." He wrote a friend, "[I saw Grant] who never swerved in War, bend and twist and writhe under the appeals and intrigues from which there was no escape." He served under President Grant in Washington as Commanding General of the United States Army, a post in which his friend Phil Sheridan succeeded him. When Sherman died on February 23, 1891, eighty-two-year old Joe Johnston was one of the honorary pallbearers, standing bare-headed in the cold wind outside the church. Though a friend cautioned him to be careful of his health, Johnston said, "If I were in [Sherman's] place and he were standing here in mine, he would not put on his hat." Johnston died ten days later of pneumonia.

On July 12, 1866, when Hope College celebrated its first commencement, Civil War veteran Ale Buursma was one of the eight graduates. Charles Eltinge Clark, who enlisted in August 1862, aged 18, did not return to the Academy. He was killed in action on Tuesday, April 4, 1865 — the day President Lincoln walked down the streets of the captured Confederate capital in Richmond; the day Lee reached Amelia Court House with his dwindling army; five days before Ulysses S. Grant accepted Lee's surrender at Appomattox Court House. Johannes Van Lente returned safely from the war, and on August 23, 1865, he and Jantje Bouman were married in a ceremony conducted by Albertus Van Raalte and held at the Van Raalte home. They lived happily and grew old together; a grandchild recollected him singing "Tenting Tonight on the Old Campground" at family reunions. He died, aged 76, in 1911.

Grand Army of the Republic, Albertus C. Van Raalte Post
Memorial Day Parade, 1889

Had Christina Van Raalte been able to look into the future during her anxious concern for Ben when he enlisted, she would have been comforted. Ben rose to the rank of sergeant and was mustered out with the surviving members of his regiment in Salisbury, North Carolina, on June 24, 1865. In Holland, he succeeded John Kramer as commander of the A. C. Van Raalte Post, Grand Army of the Republic. He died peacefully in his sleep on August 22, 1917, the fifty-fifth anniversary of the date on which he joined the Union army. In his obituary an instance of his bravery was recalled. "At Utoy Creek, Georgia, the regiment lost two color bearers and the regimental colors were left on the field when the Union troops were driven back. Van Raalte, during the night, crept through the confederate lines, secured the colors, which he brought back to the regiment, and carried them until the close of the war." Ben's friend Robert Thomson — who told little Anna Van Raalte to eat four apples a day instead of two, so that she would keep him healthy as well as Ben — fell sick soon after that letter was written, was invalided home in 1863, and died in Holland in 1864.

After the war, John Nies gave up farming and became prosperous as the owner of a hardware business in which his sons became his partners. He lived for many years, "rearing a large family in comfort and being one of the most prominent citizens in the town" and died in 1920. His friend Jan Vogel was wounded several times, most seriously in 1864 when a musketball passed through his left leg. With another wounded soldier from the company, he rode fourteen miles on horseback, "and lodged for the night at the home of a rich planter, quite against his wishes; but with weapons in our hands we made him see that in this case might was right." He reached Nashville the next day, and then was shifted from one hospital to another. Although gangrene developed, surgeons were able to treat the wound without amputating his leg, and the wound healed. Vogel was discharged, with the rank of sergeant, on August 1, 1865. He had last seen his family eleven years before, when he emigrated to the Holland colony with the family of a carpenter to whom he was apprenticed.

> *I was eager to accompany them and with [his] help tried to persuade my parents to let me go. My father's mind had long been favorably inclined toward America but owing to poverty he was never able to emigrate. The fact that I was his only living son filled him with apprehension. Yet after long consideration he decided to part with me, hoping that at some future time I might be able to help him go to America.*

Within a few weeks after his discharge from the army, Jan Vogel sailed for the Netherlands, where he was reunited with his parents and sister. With the money he had earned in four years in the army, he paid transportation costs for them and for his sister's husband, and at the end of September they sailed together for America.

At the war's end, as at its beginning, there were speeches. The day after Lee's surrender, a huge crowd gathered on the White House lawn, celebrating and calling for Lincoln. Where others would have made a stirring speech, Lincoln simply asked the band to play a lively tune — one that he thought ought to unite, instead of divide — and listened, and did not stay to hear the peoples' cheers.

> *I have always thought "Dixie" one of the best tunes I ever heard. I have heard that our adversaries over the way have attempted to appropriate as a national air. I insisted yesterday that we had fairly captured it. I presented the question to the attorney general, and he gives his opinion that it is our lawful prize. I ask the band to give us a good turn upon it.*

President Abraham Lincoln

In Holland, Albertus Van Raalte did give a stirring speech, one which was recalled down through the years, because of the poignancy of his words, and because of his powers as a speaker. Without any written notes, he named for the listening crowd a roll of the colony's honored dead: the full name, birthdate, and date and place of death of every man from the colony who had perished in the Civil War. "The impression on his audience was overwhelming. It was as though he drew a moving, bleeding panorama, in which the entire war passed before the eyes of his listeners, and in which the dreadful cost of the war was depicted as if with the single stroke of a pen."

Know all men by these presents: That whereas I, Albertus C. Van Raalte now residing at the village of Holland in the county of Ottawa and State of Michigan am about to go abroad and be absent; as I now expect, for a period of about six months on a journey and visit to Europe, on which journey and visit my wife Christina Johanna Van Raalte is to accompany me, and I being desirous of having a representative and agent to do and transact all my business for me in my absence, and in the transaction of such business to lawfully convey lands and real estate fully discharged and released from all claim on the part of my said wife for dower and right of dower,

Now therefore by these presents I have made constituted and appointed and hereby do make constitute and appoint, and we Albertus C. Van Raalte and the said Christina Johanna Van Raalte do hereby make constitute and appoint, Dirk. B. K. Van Raalte, our son of the said village of Holland, our and each of our true and lawful attorney for us and each of us, and in our and each of our names jointly or severally to do and transact all the business of the said Albertus C. Van Raalte in the State of Michigan during our absence, and for that purpose to have and take possession and control of all his real and personal property and do and perform all necessary acts and things relating thereto in the name of the said Albertus or in our names; to prosecute and defend all suits that may become necessary or material for the said Albertus to prosecute or defend; and for the purpose of this power to enter into and take possession of all such lands, tenements heretowith, and real estate whatever, in the State of Michigan to or in which we or either of us are or may be entitled or interested, and to grant bargain and sell the same or any part or parcel thereof for such sum or price as he shall deem meet, and for us and in our names to make execute acknowledge and deliver good and sufficient deeds and conveyances for the same either with or without covenants of warranty: hereby giving and granting unto our said attorney full power and authority to do and perform all and every act whatever requisite and necessary to be done in and about the business of the said Albertus as fully as he or we could do if personally present, with full power of substitution and revocation hereby ratifying and confirming all that my said attorney or his substitute shall lawfully do or cause to be done by virtue hereof

In witness whereof we have herewith set our hands and seals this tenth day of April one thousand eight hundred and sixty-six

Signed, sealed and delivered
in presence of H. E. Thompson

B. Van Raalte

A. Van Raalte (Seal)
C. J. Van Raalte. (Seal)

State of Michigan
County of Kent   On this Tenth day of April A. D. eighteen hundred and sixty-six personally appeared before me the undersigned Notary Public in and for the said County of Kent the above named Albertus C. and Christina Johanna Van Raalte known to me to be the persons who executed the foregoing instrument and severally acknowledged the execution thereof to be their free act and deed — And the same Christina Johanna Van Raalte, wife of the said Albertus C. Van Raalte, being privately examined by me separate and apart from her said husband acknowledged that she executed the same freely and without any fear or compulsion from her said husband or anyone.

Henry E. Thompson, Notary Public Kent County Michigan

I am glad that my children are on the west side of the ocean. ...the lot in America is far, far better than in the old countries.

Transatlantic travel changed dramatically in the years between the founding of the Holland colony and the end of the Civil War, as steam engines became widely used to supplement sails. Most of the Hollanders, once they arrived in America, stayed there; thus only those who went back to Europe after establishing themselves as Americans experienced directly the improvements in speed, safety and comfort. Jan Vogel's first trip across the ocean, in 1854, was lengthy: the ship was a sailing vessel and the voyage lasted more than six weeks. When he traveled again from the Netherlands to America, in the fall of 1865, the trip took seventeen days.

Hope College Collection of the Joint Archives

When the year 1866 opened, Albertus and Christina Van Raalte were almost in a position to take advantage of these modern advances. To come to America had been a great and daring decision; it had now proved to be a grand success. The little colony had become a thriving town whose civic leaders were discussing the advantages and disadvantages of incorporation as a city. Instead of the small log church there were two growing congregations: stately and beautiful First Church, and Hope Church, where worship services were conducted in English. Both were affiliated with the American Dutch Reformed denomination. The Pioneer School founded in 1851 and reorganized as Holland Academy in 1857 was about to blossom into Hope College, to be incorporated in the summer of 1866 at the time of the first graduation ceremony. The Van Raaltes themselves were leading citizens of Holland. Their home was among the most handsome in Holland, and Albertus Van Raalte's property holdings were extensive. The five children who had come with them from the Netherlands were grown, and American-born Maria and Anna were growing up. Albertus and Mina were married, and there were four healthy grandchildren.

Christina Van Raalte yearned to see her sister Maria again, and Albertus Van Raalte was invited to attend a synod meeting in Amsterdam. But although they appeared prosperous — so much so that some Hollanders had expressed their envy publicly — Van Raalte did not feel financially secure enough to make the trip. In common with other ministers in the Holland area, his salary was paid irregularly and often not fully. He was concerned about his sons' ability to make their way independently. Before Ben and Dirk had enlisted to fight for the Union he had written to a colleague, "I am in a position which, because of the heavy weight of material responsibilities, requires my full time and energies. Although my boys do all the hard work, they lack the teamwork, the love and the patience to do the job. So I must remain at the helm to direct them although I dislike it."

Now, though Albertus' business efforts continued to flounder, Ben and Dirk had returned from the Civil War as mature young men, and Dirk, one-armed but sturdy, was finishing his studies at the Academy. The younger generation could manage at home if their parents decided to travel. The problem was that Van Raalte was land-poor. Much of his property did not yield substantial earnings, and the taxes were a heavy burden. Therefore, the cherished idea of a visit to family and friends in the Netherlands was given up.

142

If Albertus Van Raalte's charismatic talent had been limited to an ability to lead his Dutch compatriots, his American colony could not have succeeded as it did. From the first moment of landing on America's shores, he impressed, and even charmed, American leaders. Citizens with powerful positions in the church, in government and in business assisted actively in the establishment of the colony and many remained Van Raalte's admirers and staunch supporters as long as they lived. One of these was Samuel Schieffelin. A prosperous businessman and an elder in the eastern Dutch Reformed Church, he seems to have regarded assistance to Albertus Van Raalte as a favorite personal charity. In the spring of 1866, Philip Phelps was on a fundraising trip in the east — an ongoing endeavor in which, unlike his predecessors, he willingly and ably cooperated with Van Raalte. He approached the ever-generous Schieffelin, who stepped forward to provide the money for the Van Raaltes' trip. Phelps communicated the happy news to Van Raalte, who reacted with the enthusiasm that continued, in happy times, to be characteristic of him.

Another of Van Raalte's characteristics — one which must have contributed to the friction which developed between him and various colleagues — was his expectation of prompt and thorough assistance, whenever he called for it. Throughout his life, though, there were those who realized that he was demanding, and rather than resisting, took pleasure in assisting him. Now that the Lord had opened the way, Albertus Van Raalte was "at once to work" — and he took it for granted that Philip Phelps would be at once to work also.

> *I am at once to work to regulate and set home matters right: If the Lord may prosper me then I hope to leave the last week in April to take the first steamer in May wishing to be present at the General Synod of the Free Church in session I believe 22nd May in Amsterdam.*
>
> *Please let me know whether I can go [in time] and what kind of paper or rather what pass I need. I keep the matter under the rose til I know from you.*
>
> *All the dominies are willing to supply my pulpit and my Consistory and Church will submit in hopes that my strength somewhat may revive.*
>
> *Tell those gentlemen that I deeply feel their generosity and alsoo I do thank you very much for your kindness.*
>
> *Remember us to Mrs. Phelps - may the Lord cheer her.*
> *…Your grateful Brother*
> *A. C. Van Raalte*

Van Raalte's reply to Phelps is revealing. One feature is that it is written in English. Van Raalte wrote elegantly in Dutch, and good translations present his thoughts in standard English, rather than by using English words and Dutch grammatical constructions. Thus words which mean "In the town of Ommen have I Sunday and Monday preached," for example, are properly translated as "On Sunday and Monday I preached in Ommen." The letter to Phelps, written in English and thus not requiring translation, shows that Van Raalte wrote fluently in English while retaining some Dutch grammatical patterns — *"I am by high prices [and] horrible taxes…. exhausted"*; *"…I do accept that offer very thankfull"*; *"I am at once to work…"*; *"…in hopes my strength somewhat may revive."* He may have acquired the habit of using Latin phrases, or their translations — *"I keep the matter under the rose"*; i.e., *sub rosa*, meaning *in secret* — from John Van Vleck, Phelps' predecessor as principal of the Academy, who was much given to using snippets of Latin in his letters. There are also a very few misspellings, notably *alsoo*, which Van Raalte commonly used — a reasonable error, because the double *o*, in Dutch, is given the long *o* sound (as in *also*). To have acquired the ability to speak and write fluently and powerfully, in a language learned as an adult, was a remarkable achievement; however, throughout his life, Van

Raalte always used the Dutch language in his preaching, and his letters to English-speaking friends, often written in haste, retained a Dutch flavor in the sentence structure.

The letter also illustrates the warm four-way relationship among Albertus and Christina Van Raalte and Philip and Margaret Phelps. The letter was sent to the place where Dr. and Mrs. Phelps were staying. He was traveling; she opened the letter and wrote a sweet, brief note in pencil before sending it on to him, adding "…If Mrs. Van Raalte comes on I would expect to see her before going to Europe. I attended the Anniversary last eve. with Fanie. It went off well." (Fanie, then five and half years old, was the oldest of the Phelps children. Later she was among the first women to graduate from Hope; with her husband she became a missionary to China; she lived to a grand old age, always loving and supporting the college.)

Written in Albertus Van Raalte's flowing and beautiful handwriting, the letter is annotated by two additional hands: those of Mrs. Phelps, and afterwards Dr. Phelps. His notes are written below Van Raalte's postscript.

> *N.B. Please inquire at once for me about the steamers leaving for Europe. If there is no steamer on the first or second May then I have to leave in the last week in April: I do not know whether it is necessary to procure the passage beforehand: mercantile men will know all about it: If it is customary please secure then for me the tickets, that I may know when I must be in New York: if possible I should like a steamer to Rotterdam or to Antwerp next to England.*
>
> *Bremen… fortnightly*
> *N American-Lloyd… April 12 and 26*
> *Hamburg Am. Packet Co… every other Saturday*

The Van Raaltes left from New York a month after deciding to take the trip. In the interval, there was much to be done. The church consistory did indeed submit to his going; fellow ministers agreed to share in the preaching and other church duties. Besides these concerns to settle, it was necessary to obtain a passport, and there were family matters to arrange. Responsibility would, of course, be given to sons, although Christine, the oldest daughter remaining at home, could be relied upon to manage the household cheerfully and well. But the oldest son seemed least fit, of the three, to take charge. One reason was that he had a family of his own to care for — four children now, the youngest not yet two months old. These responsibilities, however, were not the major reason that he was not entrusted with family affairs. Albertus was either unlucky, or inept, at managing business. His father's strong desire to help and change him may not have been useful; he must have known, and been discouraged by, his father's tendency to consult with his younger brothers about his business endeavors. One of Ben's Civil War letters provides a thoughtful answer to a question which must have been something like "What do you think about Albertus' plan for selling and buying land?"

> *You asked me what my opinion was about selling some land to Fijn etc. I cannot help you much because I have been away so long and am not in touch with those things. Buying the swamplands might be a good thing and may work out all right if Albertus is lucky with the mill operation. I am sometimes afraid that he feels like a man standing on ice - a little unsteady. I personally do not like the mill business but, if it is handled right, a good living can be made at it. Don't get me wrong - this is only the opinion of a soldier.*

"I am sometimes afraid that he feels like a man standing on ice" is a perceptive comment for a young man to make about an older brother whom success has eluded. All of Ben's comments are reasonable and kind, responsive but not assertive. "You have asked me, and so I answer. The plan might work or it might not. It's not something I would do, but if Albertus wants to do it then it may work out well. But don't give too much weight to my opinion; I've been away for a long time now, and what I know most about is soldiering." If Albertus were to see — or be shown — the letter, it wouldn't be likely to hurt his feelings much. Dirk would probably have written more firmly, and more critically.

By 1866, all three sons were men and their parents' opinions of them, and their views of themselves, would have been well established. Albertus was the one who couldn't make a go of things. Ben was a hard worker, the one with a sense of humor and a sense of responsibility that enabled him to enjoy or endure. Dirk was smart, quick-tongued and quick-tempered, not a good person to tangle with, the one most likely to succeed. So when Albertus Van Raalte left the country, he put Ben in charge of family matters, and gave a power of attorney to Dirk, who had turned twenty-two on the first of March. The document, signed by both husband and wife, and witnessed by Ben, is accompanied by a formal attestation by the clerk that he had spoken with Christina Van Raalte, "separate and apart from her said husband," in order to be assured that her signature on a legal document had not been coerced.

> *We went to bid them farewell and they were both in a wonderful frame of mind. ....So they left and God protected them since there was a cholera epidemic in the Netherlands and they traveled all over.*
>
> from the diary of Grace - Geesje - Van der Haar Visscher

All of Holland was kept informed about the Van Raaltes' travels through Albertus Van Raalte's letters. He had arranged with his son-in-law Pieter Oggel, a faculty member at the Academy, to have some of the letters he wrote to his family printed in *De Hope,* the newspaper published from the Hope College campus. The Van Raaltes stopped for a few days in Rochester New York, where Dominie Van Raalte was happy to accept an invitation to preach. In Albany they stayed at the home of Philip Phelps' father, and they also visited with Dr. Thomas De Witt, now retired from his ministry at Collegiate Church in New York City. They sailed from New York on April 27, and landed early in May on the Isle of Wight, off the southern coast of England. From there they traveled to London, and then, on a Dutch steamboat, to Rotterdam. "Friday morning, at 11:00, we walked on *Nederlandsche* ground." From Rotterdam they traveled by train through Utrecht and Zwolle to their destination in Kampen.

> *The joy on Mother's face, the pleasant sights of the old country which are so familiar to me and yet so new because of our long absence - so many things fill my heart with joy and thankfulness.*
>
> *An omnibus brought us to Dominie Brummelkamp's house. We were so happy to see one another. Across the road is Dominie Van Velzen's house and on the same street are Dominie de Moen's house and [the home of] our nephew Simon Van Velzen. Soon we were all together in Dominie Brummelkamp's house. To my surprise I found all our loved ones undiminished in strength. Dominie Brummelkamp is gray, but healthier and stronger than before. ... That same evening I had the pleasure of meeting Dominie de Cock.*
>
> *...I have many invitations to preach, but I hope not to be too busy, so that my health may be restored.*

Albertus Van Raalte had arranged the Netherlands trip to coincide with the synod meeting of the church he had helped to found years before — the *Christelijk Afgescheidene Gereformeerde Kerk* of the Netherlands. But the synod meeting was scheduled for May 30 through July 8 in Amsterdam, which meant that it would be impossible for him to return in time to attend events in Holland which must also have been very important to him: incorporation of the upper school of Holland Academy as Hope College, inauguration of Philip Phelps as president, and the college's first commencement ceremony.

His motives for choosing as he did are a matter for speculation. The official record of college events on July 12 through 17 states only that "Rev. Dr. Van Raalte was absent, having been constrained to spend some months in Europe, on account of the impaired health both of himself and Mrs. Van Raalte." Yet his own ailments would not have been sufficient to deter Van Raalte from attending an occasion marking a triumphal point in his struggles to establish strong educational institutions in his colony, especially since to travel required far more effort than to stay at home. Anxiety about his wife's health combined with an opportunity — which could be viewed as a responsibility — to strengthen denominational ties between the church in the Netherlands and the church in America would, however, have weighed heavily in favor of making the trip at this time. The Van Raaltes were a loving couple, and he may have believed that if his Christina did not visit her family in the Netherlands now, she would not meet them again in this world.

It is also conceivable that Van Raalte himself wanted to be away — that, far from being torn by wishing to be in two places, he saw the Netherlands trip as an opportunity to avoid the celebratory events in Holland. Perhaps he believed that if he were present, he would draw attention which rightfully belonged to Philip Phelps, his friend and protégé. Van Raalte was a powerful leader of his people, but he had never been inclined to seek adulation.

Had it not been for his leadership, Holland Michigan would never have come into being; had it not been for his modesty, it might not have become Holland. "People have asked me what name I wish to give to our township. Some wanted to call it after a member of the Association," he wrote in 1846 to his brother-in-law Antonie Brummelkamp, "but I could think of no better name than Holland. The petition for that I have already sent to the officials in question." Surely the "member of the Association" whose name others suggested was *Van Raalte*. There is a small town in the Netherlands named Raalte where the original members of the Van Raalte ("from Raalte") family must have lived. If he had wished, the name might have been on Michigan maps as well. Jackson, Marshall and Monroe; Niles, Jenison and Schoolcraft; Cassopolis and Fennville; Ann Arbor and Ypsilanti — these might have been joined by Van Raaltestad.

The merciless criticism to which Van Raalte had been subjected over the past several years, however, may have been a more compelling reason to leave than feelings of personal humility. Some of his neighbors and parishioners in the colony judged him with great harshness. His biographer Henry Dosker alluded to the adage that "some people can't see the forest for the trees" when he wrote, "The woods encircled them too closely. They were unable to see the expanse of this truly great life." It may have been wounds from these attacks that caused Van Raalte's refusal to attend ceremonies in the east when he was twice awarded honorary doctoral degrees. "I know the reality of my weakness [and] unprofitableness," he wrote, "and will accordingly prefer the shade …it is only by the grace [of God] that I enjoy the esteem of God's people and am not to them a stumbling block or a destroyer of souls."

Though the celebrations at the college were conducted in the absence of its founder, many of those who had long loved and supported the college were there. Dr. Mancius Smedes Hutton, president of the Board of Education of the Reformed Protestant Dutch Church, had come to deliver the oration at Philip Phelps' inauguration, and the Reverend Isaac Newton Wyckoff of Albany, Phelps' former pastor, was there to see the fruition of the immigrants' dream, and to deliver the charge to the president elect. Dr. John L. See, of New Brunswick, New Jersey, and the Reverend William H. TenEyck, of Astoria, Long Island, were part of a deputation sent from church headquarters in the east to consider plans for theological instruction at Hope College.

The inauguration ceremonies were held on the evening of Thursday, July 12. They included the singing of an English hymn and a Dutch psalm, and "by invitation of the President elect, Rev. Cornelis Vander Meulen of Grand Rapids, Mich., one of the oldest of the Hollandish pastors and leaders, opened the exercises with prayer in the Hollandish language."

Students at all levels of instruction participated in speaking, singing and reciting during the following days. "The Intercalary exhibition of the Institution took place in the gymnasium, comprising the delivery of original addresses by the members of the junior, sophomore and freshman classes of the College, with the recitation of selected pieces by members of the preparatory classes, all interspersed with singing by the college choir; and it was intercalated among the different services of the week as a substitute for Junior and other exhibitions." On Saturday there was, by invitation, an excursion to the mouth of the harbor.

Dominie Cornelius Vander Meulen

Sunday morning, the Reverend Wyckoff preached at Second Reformed Church of Holland (Hope Church, where Dr. Abel T. Stewart was the pastor) and the Reverend Hutton preached at First Reformed Church of Grand Rapids. In the evening, President Phelps preached the baccalaureate sermon in the First Reformed Church of Holland. His text was a verse from the book of Job, and he opened his address with these words: "The Bible has one very plain way of denoting the distinction between sin and righteousness. Sin is synonymous with foolishness, and righteousness with wisdom. The sinner is foolish — the saint is wise. It is the fool who hath said in his heart, 'There is no God.'"

> Behold, the fear of the Lord, that is wisdom;
> and to depart from evil is understanding.
>
> Job 28:28, KJV

Hope College Remembrancer.

JULY 17,   FIRST COMMENCEMENT.   1866.

On the evening of Tuesday, July 17th, the first Commencement of Hope College was celebrated in the gymnasium with the following programme:

   Prayer by Rev. S. BOLKS.
   Music.
   Oration—Latin salutatory, PETER MOERDYK, Kalamazoo, Mich.
   Music.
   Oration—Hope, WILLIAM B. GILMORE, Fairview, Illinois.
   Music.
   Oration—Public Opinion, HARM WOLTMAN, Holland, Mich.
   Music.
   Oration—Trials and Triumphs of Liberty, WILLIAM MOERDYK, Kalamazoo, Mich.
   Music.
   Oration—Man, as he was, is, and is to be, WILLIAM A. SHIELDS, Fairview, Ill.
   Music.
   Oration—*De Pen is magtiger dan het Zwaard*, JOHN W. TE WINKEL, Clymer, N. Y.
   Music.
   Oration—Skepticism, ALE BUURSMA, Holland, Mich.
   Commencement Ode—Words and music prepared for the occasion, and sung by the graduating class
   The conferring of Degrees.
   Oration—Valedictory, GERRIT DANGREMOND, Overyssel, Mich.
   Doxology.
   The pronouncing of the Benediction by the President.

Tuesday evening, July 17, graduation ceremonies were held in the college gymnasium, the building that Phelps and his students had constructed. The decorations, also designed and arranged by the students, were possible only because there were no fire code restrictions at the time. "The students had very tastefully decorated the building — one of the features being a chandelier of ninety brilliant kerosene burners so arranged as to form in large letters the word HOPE."

Each of the graduates' speeches was printed in full in the *Remembrancer*, a commemorative booklet prepared by President Phelps. *The Remembrancer* honored two benefactors: the Inaugural portion was most respectfully dedicated "to Thomas De Witt, D. D., *clarum et venerabile nomen*," and the Commencement portion most gratefully dedicated "to Samuel B. Schieffelin, Esq., whose sympathies and liberalities have been enlisted in behalf of Hope College, from its germinal to its present position." Words and music of a Commencement Ode were also included, the words by Dr. Phelps and the music by William B. Gilmore, tutor in Music at Hope College, and a member of the graduating class. Three years later, in a Virginia town called Amelia Court House, Will Gilmore would marry Christine Van Raalte.

In the Netherlands, the Amsterdam synod meeting was a stimulating occasion. "When Van Raalte was given the floor to speak, he urged ties of unity. Van Raalte was concerned that any people going to emigrate to America should know about the Dutch Reformed Church of which he was a part. Then he was questioned about the *Hollandsche Gereformeerde Kerk,* as the Dutch Reformed Church in America was known in the Netherlands. …He made a noble defense of the denomination he had joined… [and] the synod extended the right hand of fellowship to the American church through Van Raalte." After the synod meeting, the Van Raaltes visited families of people in the Holland colony, and Van Raalte traveled widely, often speaking to large crowds.

During these travels, besides the more formal letters which were printed in *De Hope,* Van Raalte wrote to Ben, who stood in his place as head of family affairs (while Dirk managed business matters). Now, as always, the letters to Ben began with exhortations, though these are relatively gentle: "A person who does not put all his interests in God's hands can expect nothing but disappointments — a person struggling through life without God has lost his Master and misses the true central point of activity and rest. Oh, Ben, my dear child, you are missing life's highest purpose. …Do not become discouraged because you feel you are lacking but may it lead you to seek Him in prayer."

Mother and I are both well. …It seems to me that Mother has already gained weight and her cough is better so we have much to be thankful for. Since we got off the ship I have been able to eat much more than I have been able to in recent years and this is making me stronger. The meeting of the Synod in Amsterdam has been concluded, much to my satisfaction. For me it was an extraordinarily pleasant experience to attend the meeting and I was welcomed with so much love and cordiality that I felt ashamed and embarrassed.

...I would love to look around the corner to see you in your work and in your comings and goings. I must warn you about one thing - watch your health; if anything is wrong go to Ledeboer and ask him for remedies because that is a thousand time better than waiting until he has to come to visit you. My further advice is this: None of you must overwork - take the needed rest. Patience and dogged persistence are necessary to develop land on the scale you are attempting. ...you must exercise thoughtful, careful supervision over the whole operation and think ahead to plan the work which must be done before the time comes to do it. ...I can well understand that with the limited means at your disposal you may have difficulty working all that land, and because of that you may have to alter your plans. You will surely have a lot of expense with the threshing machine at haying time. Planting corn without manuring the land seems to me will lead to failure. ...Please write and keep me informed [about the peach and apple crops] or, if you are too busy, have someone else write. Don't dissipate your strength by doing too much building. You must wait until you have more means. ...Have someone write me what success [Allie] is having in raising chickens. Little Chrisje No. 3 must help Mamma and Annie must learn to do so also. [Mamma was Helena Van Raalte, Albertus' wife, and the children mentioned are theirs.] *Mother sends her love to all.*

Despite the happiness the Van Raaltes were experiencing, they observed much that was troubling. "In the provinces of North and South Holland and Utrecht the pest among the cattle has become epidemic," Van Raalte wrote, "although it has not spread over the entire country." This pestilence was anthrax, a disease whose name is derived from a Greek word meaning *coal*, used because the disease, which can be transmitted from animals to humans, is characterized by black swellings which appear suddenly. Anthrax raged from prehistoric times — some scholars believe it was one of the ten plagues of Egypt — until Robert Koch discovered, in 1876, the bacillus which caused it and, in 1883, a method of inoculation against it. Like many other afflictions which Van Raalte was familiar with, humanity was not released from its scourge during his lifetime.

Worse than the pestilence among the animals was the cholera outbreak in the Netherlands and other northern European countries. In a town near Leiden where he preached at the beginning of August — a town no bigger than Holland — 150 people died within six weeks. "In London we hear that more than a thousand have died," he wrote. "In the Netherlands many families are dressed in mourning because of cholera, which walks among us as a secret angel of death from God." Moreover, the economic situation of the country was not good. "The failure of banks and large commercial establishments is also adding to the misery." And although the Netherlands was at peace, constant hostilities among their more powerful neighbors, each competing to expand their power and influence, was an ongoing problem for a commercial nation.

The tension created by the threatening attitude of the armed and opposing forces of Austria, Italy and Prussia is very detrimental to trade and commerce. ...The life-style does not appeal to me in many ways and the worst of all is that painful searching and struggling for the means of making a living. ...I cannot tell you how many unpleasant things I have noticed in these few days concerning this. ...I am glad that my children are on the west side of the ocean... the lot in America is far, far better than in the old, overpopulated countries.

Resolution of the Common Council

Whereas, The Rev. Dr. Van Raalte is about to leave his residence among us, to find a new home in Virginia.

Resolved, That the Common Council of the City of Holland in behalf of the City desire to express their deep regret for the removal of the founder of our City and Colony, their appreciation of his successful efforts in planting the Holland Colony, and laying the foundations of a large and prosperous community here, and their hope that he will be as successful in the future in his enterprise in planting a Colony as he has been in the past. That he carries with him to his new home our best wishes for his future prosperity and happiness, and that we cherish the hope, that although leaving his residence here, he will still retain his interest in the welfare and prosperity of his old home.

I thirst after an opportunity to free myself of these annoyances and to devote myself entirely to the Kingdom of God.

In October, 1866, the Van Raaltes returned from their trip to the Netherlands. It had been a time of much joy and satisfaction for them. A part of their pleasure was in knowing that Ben was caring for the family at home and that he would fulfill the responsibility well.

> *We are enjoying our vacation and rest immensely and the pleasure of seeing so many of our relatives, of whom many are still living, is very enjoyable. We are showered with love and consideration - wherever we go the best is none too good for us. Truly, the rest we are getting is most pleasant. We feel very thankful and appreciative toward our children and yourself that you were willing to assume the care of the family and carry the burden of that care to assure us of being able to get this rest.*

To see old friends and family members, to be treated as honored guests — all this was indeed pleasant. But it was also a pleasure to find no reason to regret the move to America. Despite many problems, their new country was healthier, more economically sound and safer from outside threats. And by now the American style of getting things done, as he experienced it in Michigan, suited Albertus Van Raalte better than the slower *Hollandsche* ways. Americans — and he and his sons were Americans now — were better farmers. He had considered finding a man who wished to emigrate and hiring him to help on the farm, but now he thought better of the idea — Americans were better workers.

> *You can well imagine that I am keeping my eyes open here but, although the farms in the better districts are fine, I have found nothing here to impress me. I have found nothing here that we do not possess in America as well. I have seen many beautiful cattle but none any better than those in America. I saw no horses as fleet as Dirk's. Horses here are like the people - they take things pretty easy. For that reason I have hesitated about hiring a man - they are too easy-going and besides are not accustomed to doing a variety of work.*

America had become the homeland. There was joy in returning to Holland and the family. There were five grandchildren now: young Allie (Albertus Christian Van Raalte IV) was already six, his sisters Christina Johanna and Anna Helena were five and three, and little Carl was five months old. Their cousin, Christina Johanna Oggel, Mina's daughter, had just had her first birthday. Also the first commencement exercises at Hope College, and the inauguration of Philip Phelps as the College's first president, were fresh in everyone's mind, and there was much news of these events to hear.

✳✳✳

To the Common Council of the City of Holland

At the close of the first year of our corporate existence as a city, I am happy to be able to report that, according to our Treasurer's report, all outstanding city orders are paid. All accounts which have been presented against the City have been settled, and we have a balance on hand of $91.51.

The City has a very good fire apparatus, Fire Engine, Hose, Ladders, Hooks, Hose Carriage and a convenient place to keep them, five good wells, which are living reservoirs for us in case of fire, a fine set of Record books, and a convenient case to keep them in, which are all in perfect order, and all are paid for.

I am happy to report that (with the exception of the Marshal and Street Commissioner) all officers of the city have worked together harmoniously, and have performed the duties required of them faithfully and well. And in taking leave of them, and of the council, officially, I hereby express my satisfaction with the manner in which they have performed the duties of their respective offices.

Isaac Cappon

✳✳✳

Dominie Van Raalte had left his colony and returned to it — but his place there now was that of an older man from an earlier time — honored and respected, but no longer perceived as an essential force. The wilderness into which he had led his people was transformed into a thriving community with businesses, factories, farms, handsome homes, newspapers, schools, even a college, and — at last — a harbor. Holland was preparing to become incorporated as a city under the laws of Michigan. Other leaders had arisen in business and politics. Twenty years ago, young and almost penniless, Isaac Cappon had sailed to America, traveling steerage, selected by his fellow immigrants as an assistant cook for the voyage. When Holland became a city, in 1867, Cappon would become its first mayor. The colony was, in a sense, Van Raalte's child, but that child had grown to be confident and independent. He was the father of the colony — the patriarch — but the citizens of Holland did not depend on him to plan and provide for them, nor did they need him to serve as their advocate and interpreter in a country whose laws and language were unfamiliar.

Albertus Van Raalte was still "the dominie," but there was no longer only one church, one congregation, one pastor. Members of the denomination who wanted services in English attended a second Reformed church — Hope Church — founded in 1862. Membership in the colony's first church —— the Pillar Church — continued to swell; there were now some 500 members. Van Raalte saw that dividing the congregation to form a third church would not only better accommodate the needs of the parishioners but confirm the importance of the denomination in a community where there was already a Methodist church and plans for an Episcopalian church.

He accomplished the formation of the new church and the apportioning of membership with his usual combination of decisiveness and endurance. Market Street — which later became Central Avenue — would be the dividing line; families to the east would remain as members of the First Church; families to the west would join the new Third Church. This system was efficient and would minimize opportunities for strife; nevertheless, as he knew, there would be much discussion before the plan was agreed to.

> *...the work had become too much for him and he had urged that [another] church be established. But nobody wanted to do that. After much discussion it was, nevertheless, decided that it was the best thing to do. ...Now subscriptions were taken for the formation of a new church which was built in 1868. Dominie Vander Meulen of Kalamazoo was called. The city had been divided according to streets and so we, according to the new division, were obliged to become members of the new church. We looked to God and joined.*
>
> from the diary of Grace - Geesje - Van der Haar Visscher

Originally Van Raalte had expected to remain as minister of First Reformed Church, where he had served for twenty years. However, even before the trip to the Netherlands, he had tried to obtain agreement from his consistory for assistance in his pastoral duties. After his return the discussions continued, fruitlessly.

Never, in any of his many endeavors, did Albertus Van Raalte establish a claque or coterie of assistants to serve him, but he deeply needed one person who shared his beliefs and goals, and who would willingly shoulder burdens along with him. In many aspects of his life, his wife fulfilled this function. As Henry Dosker wrote, "she was an excellent wife for a preacher and many burdens were deftly taken from his shoulders by the hand of love." In the early days in the colony, Bernardus Grootenhuis was his right hand; then Henry D. Post was his friend and fellow-worker as he worked to establish the colony on a sound American footing. In his efforts to build schools and a college he finally found such a colleague in Philip Phelps. What he needed now in his ministry was the solace and support of an enthusiastic collaborator.

If the consistory of the church he had served for so long had granted his request, it is probable that his own energy and enthusiasm would have been renewed. It is conceivable that if Van Raalte, assisted by a younger pastor, had remained minister of First Church while maintaining collegial relations, as he always strove to do, with fellow ministers at Third Church and Hope Church, dissension within the Reformed Church would have been allayed, and would not later have escalated into schism.

Third Reformed Church

From the point of view of the consistory, however, halving the congregation seemed to constitute adequate relief from overwork. On this point, Van Raalte was unable to lead. He could fight and win battles of principle, and his influence would prevail on most questions of practical planning. But here what was at issue was how his own efforts and energy would be expended, and he could not, or would not, apply the full force of his personality in order to meet his own personal needs. Thus he was torn. He could not bear to exhaust himself in a task which now seemed of little benefit to the people he sought to serve and lead; but he must be engaged in the Lord's work.

For another person in his situation, the solution to the problem Albertus Van Raalte faced might have seemed easy and pleasant. He was fifty-four years old. He had a loving wife and a wide circle of friends. The Civil War was over and his sons who had gone to be soldiers had come home and were prospering. He was known and respected by important people in Michigan and the northeast; he had twice been awarded honorary doctoral degrees. He was a substantial landowner (and could, if necessary have sold land, which would have reduced his tax burden). His home was elegant and imposing. He was tired, and he might have decided to rest.

He was tired — but not that tired. Unlike the people he had observed on his trip to the Netherlands, he was not easy-going, and he was accustomed to doing a variety of work. Idleness held no appeal for him, and yet he wanted to escape from the petty controversies that were afflicting the church.

In 1867 he resigned as minister of First Church, where in May of 1869 he was succeeded by Dominie Roelof Pieters, who left the Alto Reformed Church in Wisconsin in response to a call from the church in Holland. This was a choice that Van Raalte approved: "...the young men from New Brunswick without my antecedents, [who are] living proofs of the orthodoxy and excellency of our Professors, are more adapted to the field: especially Dominie Pieters is fit to supply my place and is acceptable to the people." Moreover, Roelof Pieters was one of the young men whom he himself had called to the ministry. Aleida Pieters recounted her father's story in her history of the colony.

> ...In another place he found a carpenter, with a shelf of books above his bench, and a strong Bible class in the local church. Van Raalte bade him leave his tools and, adult though he was, take up the study for the ministry. The young man obeyed, and eventually succeeded Van Raalte as pastor of the Old First Church.

Dominie Roelof Pieters,
minister of First Reformed Church, 1869-1880

Now if he could not influence his congregation in one way, he would try another. During his visit to the Netherlands, he had learned more about international missionary efforts, and he saw missionary work as an exciting way to link the church in the Netherlands and the church in America. At the same time that he resigned as minister, the Holland Classis formed a Missionary Committee, and appointed him chairman. The committee's task of seeking a missionary for the Classis to send would be easy to fulfill, because for at least five years Van Raalte himself had been confiding to close friends his wish to enter the mission field. After Giles Van de Wal left Holland Academy to go with his family to Bloemfontein, South Africa, Van Raalte wrote first to him, and shortly afterwards to Philip Phelps.

> *My spirit does not enjoy the idea of spending my life resting upon the laurels of the victory won here. I also feel that my life could end in a manner which would be of more benefit to the people. God reigns, and whatever He does will be well done. He will lead me.*

> *...I am exceedingly anxious to devote the remainder of my life exclusively to the enlightenment of souls... I thirst after an opportunity to free myself of these annoyances and to devote myself entirely to the Kingdom of God: I hear fields of thousands are destitute of preaching.*

Some people seem to be born enthusiasts. Will Rogers said he never met a man he didn't like; Albertus Van Raalte never envisioned an opportunity that didn't excite him. He wasn't perennially optimistic, but he was a spontaneous optimist. Throughout his life his heart leapt up at the thought of new challenges, and he reacted to the possibility of new endeavors with the thought, "I could do that! I could do that *well!*" Eventually it grew more and more difficult for him to walk and not faint, to run and not be weary — but it was always in his power to mount up with wings like an eagle.

> **But they that wait upon the Lord shall renew their strength: they shall mount up with wings as eagles; they shall run, and not be weary; and they shall walk, and not faint.**
>
> Isaiah 40: 31, KJV

So he looked forward to serving as a church missionary, and soon his vision became a plan for a second emigration. As before, he would found a new colony. He would draw there people from established Dutch communities in America, and encourage a resurgence of emigration from the Netherlands. And he would escape from disagreements, criticism and attacks. Emigration, like a kind of little death, would release him from troubles. The similarities between emigration and dying were noted by Van Raalte's earliest biographer, Henry Dosker, in discussing Dutch emigration in the 1840s.

> *In those days America seemed to be situated outside the world and the journey there demanded a farewell that closely resembled a deathbed. At that time emigrants were still moral outcasts, mostly people who had a bad reputation and were <u>put</u> <u>off</u> by friends and relations.*

In many ways, Van Raalte's experiences in leaving the Netherlands fitted this analogy. He left the world he knew, parting, presumably forever, from friends and family who remained behind. He left a place where, although he had followed the dictates of his conscience, he had experienced abuse and persecution, and had been treated as an outcast.

Now he was again persecuted and abused — not by governmental action, nor by gangs of hoodlums; he was protected from both by the laws of the United States — but by some of the very people he had helped and cared for. One parishioner had written and spoken most bitterly against him, making the bizarre allegation that each of Van Raalte's sermons represented a personal attack upon him. A member of the community had written a letter to the newspaper alleging that Van Raalte was enriching himself at the expense of his fellow townspeople. For years, *De Hollander,* which had seemed such a promising instrument for unity when it was founded, had fomented quarreling in the colony and published attacks on Van Raalte, his family and his supporters. An inflammatory article denouncing Van Raalte while appealing to anti-Catholic prejudices, titled "The Pope and His Cardinals," was written for and published in that newspaper. The reading aloud of a scurrilous anonymous letter about the Van Raaltes at a classis meeting was interrupted by the shocked listeners, and a rule was passed that thenceforward only church council papers would be read at classical meetings. To think of himself as being a cause of dissension — as "a stumbling block" to his people — tormented him. To leave the colony for a good purpose would be a way to escape.

The parallel between dying and emigration is especially close, in the case of Albertus Van Raalte, because he feared neither. He had full knowledge of the horrors that often accompanied dying, but, as a fervent Christian, his vision of death itself was a joyous one: union with Jesus, reunion with blessed loved ones, and release from the sufferings of this world. When his own death was near, he comforted his children with this assurance: "Do not cry; as I shut my eyes you can be sure that I will rejoice in the hallelujahs before the throne."

To die was to have the burdens of life lifted, and to enter a place where sin and sorrow and dissension are no more. Emigration seemed to promise some of these joys in an earthly setting. Albertus Van Raalte was, by nature, benevolent — a person who wished for the good. What sickened and exhausted him was the quarreling and strife which, in a way he could never understand, absorbed and excited so many others. Malevolence seemed to him to be a kind of insanity; he hated and feared it, and throughout his life, when he could bear no more, he moved away from it.

Once again, he would move away. And this time, as he had done before, he chose an unlikely location to go to. When Van Raalte brought his people to Michigan in 1847, he settled them in a sparsely inhabited forest. His choice of an isolated location was purposeful. If the colony was to remain a cohesive group of godly folk who maintained their heritage as they learned the ways of their new country, immersion in the life of established towns and cities must be avoided. Moreover, land in this new area could be cheaply acquired. Twenty years later his second colony was again a place where land could readily be purchased. In one sense, it was also out of the mainstream of American life, because it was not, legally, within a state. The town of Amelia Court House was a drab, depressed place, located in the former and future state of Virginia, but then part of Military District #1. When the bullet fired by John Wilkes Booth killed Abraham Lincoln, the president's generous and wise plans for healing the rift between north and south died with him. What had been the proud state of Virginia, home of presidents, became conquered, occupied territory.

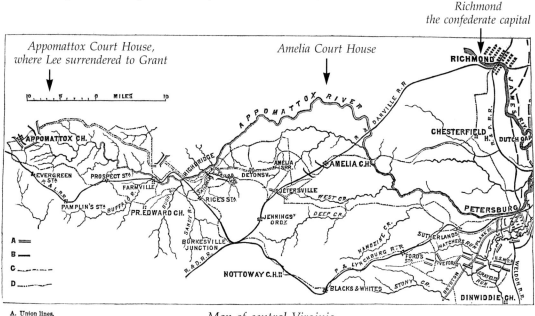

Map of central Virginia,

A. Union lines.
B. Rebel lines.
C. Union routes of march.
D. Rebel routes of march.

At the beginning of the Civil War, Amelia Court House was a small, quiet southern town, a stop on the railroad line running southwest from Richmond to Danville, a county seat, like other Virginia towns with "Court House" as part of their names. Four years later, for a few days in the spring, history touched Amelia Court House.

157

Sunday morning, April 2, 1865, was warm and sunny in Richmond. Southern ladies dressed in their best for church; the beautiful weather lifted everyone's spirits. Then, just as his minister proclaimed, "the Lord is in His holy temple: let all the earth keep silent before him," Confederate President Davis was summoned from church. Word had come from General Lee that the capital of the confederacy could no longer be defended. By midnight, government officials had boarded the last trains on the line running from Richmond to Danville — the last section of railroad in Confederate hands — and retreating Confederate troops were blowing up offices and warehouses and the arsenal, leaving the city a mass of flames and exploding shells, and its citizens in fear of a rioting mob. During the night, 80-year-old Mayor Joseph Mayo left the city to find a Union officer so that he could surrender the city.

Richmond was the site of the notorious Libby Prison, situated on the James River in a commandeered warehouse. Captured officers were separated from enlisted men in the Confederate prisons, and Union officers were held in Libby. In 1866, when Will Gilmore addressed those assembled to celebrate Hope College's first commencement, his topic was "Hope," and he recalled for his listeners "that foul enclosure known as Libby prison — and the sound of that name strikes a chill into every heart — where our loyal men were driven, stripped, tortured with hunger and thirst, scorched with the heat of the sun by day, and exposed to untold suffering from cold and dampness by night." It was *hope*, he said, that "supported and cheered the captive despite all his distress." On Monday, April 3, 1865, federal troops marched into Richmond, put out the fires and restored order. The doors of the terrible Libby Prison were opened and the wretched prisoners were freed.

Danville, Virginia. April 4, 1865.
To the People of the Confederate States of America

...We have now entered upon a new phase of the struggle, the memory of which is to endure for all ages, and to shed ever increasing lustre upon our country.

Relieved from the necessity of guarding cities and particular points, important but not vital to our defense, with an army free to move from point to point and strike in detail the detachments and garrisons of the enemy, operating on the interior of our own country, where supplies are more accessible, and where the foe will be far removed from his own bases; nothing is now needed to render our triumph certain, but the exhibition of our own unquenchable resolve. Let us but will it, and we are free; and who, in the light of the past, dare doubt your purpose in the future?

... I announce to you, fellow-countrymen, that it is my purpose to maintain your cause with my whole heart and soul; that I will never consent to abandon to the enemy one foot of the soil of any one of the States of the Confederacy. Virginia, with the help of the people, and by the blessing of Providence, shall be held and defended, and no peace ever made with the infamous invaders. ...Let us not then despond, my countrymen, but relying on the never-failing mercies and protecting care of our God, let us meet the foe with fresh defiance, with unconquered and unconquerable hearts.

Jeff'n Davis

President Lincoln came to Richmond on Tuesday, sailing up the James River on the *River Queen*, stopping short of the harbor which had been mined when Confederate Admiral Raphael Semmes had blown up most of what remained of the Confederate navy the day before. He was rowed ashore, and with his young son Tad by his side and accompanied by Admiral David Dixon Porter, the President walked to the Confederate White House, a mile and a half away. Newly freed slaves flocked around him, and some knelt. Lincoln said, "You must kneel to God only, and thank Him for the liberty you will hereafter enjoy." Meanwhile Jefferson Davis had reached Danville, and from there, despite the Confederacy's desperate situation and Lee's warnings, he issued a proclamation urging southern soldiers to fight a guerilla war.

Lee was trying a desperate last maneuver. He hoped to avoid Grant's advancing army by crossing and recrossing the meandering Appomattox River and marching his straggling, starving troops to Amelia Court House. He expected the regiments that had retreated from Richmond to meet him there, and he ordered supplies to be sent. If they could reach Amelia Court House, a stop on the Richmond to Danville railroad line, he could get provisions for his starving soldiers, and then, with luck, join forces with General Johnston's army in North Carolina. On April 4, Lee reached Amelia Court House. The Richmond troops had not yet arrived, and there were no supplies.

> *To The Citizens of Amelia County, Virginia*
>
> *The Army of Northern Virginia arrived here today, expecting to find plenty of provisions, which had been ordered to be placed here by the railroad several days since, but to my surprise and regret I find not a pound of subsistence for man or horse. I must therefore appeal to your generosity and charity to supply as far as each one is able the wants of the brave soldiers who battled for your liberty for four years. We require meat, beef, cattle, sheep, hogs, flour, meal, corn and provender in any quantity that can be spared. The quartermaster of the army will visit you and make arrangements to pay for what he receives or give the proper vouchers or certificates. I feel assured that all will give to the extent of their means.*
>
> *R. E. Lee*
> *Gen'l*

There were no supplies to be had. No rations were issued, and soldiers ate corn meant for the horses, when they ate at all. After waiting two days at Amelia Court House, Lee moved westward. There was one more fierce battle at Sayler's Creek; Sheridan's troops captured 6,000 prisoners, including six Confederate generals. Lee retreated toward Appomattox Court House, where on April 7, Grant sent a message to him, urging him to surrender: "The results of the last week must convince you of the hopelessness of further resistance." On Palm Sunday, April 9, 1865, General Grant accepted Lee's unconditional surrender of the Army of Northern Virginia. Five days later Abraham Lincoln was shot, and on April 15 he died. If he had lived he might have been able to lead the nation to conciliation and reconciliation, as he earnestly sought to do. His death let loose a frenzied passion against the south which Andrew Johnson, who succeeded to the presidency, could not have restrained even if he had wished to do so.

> With malice toward none; with charity for all; with firmness in the right, as God gives us to see the right, let us strive on to finish the work we are in; to bind up the nation's wounds; to care for him who shall have borne the battle, and for his widow and his orphan — to do all which may achieve and cherish a just and lasting peace among ourselves, and with all nations.
>
> Lincoln's second inaugural address, March 4, 1865

Much of history suggests that hatred is, for a short time, an easy, satisfying emotion. People who are *cast down* are easily *caught up* by it. At first, hatred is exhilarating — there is an upsurge of righteousness, a rush to action. But hatred is a poison so powerful that to touch it is as destructive as to be touched by it. After the horrors of war, the United States might have risen to Lincoln's patriot dream of a nation whose people worked together with malice toward none and charity for all. Instead there was mutual hatred between south and north, incited and exploited for selfish gain. Socially, politically, and economically the southern states suffered first, but the whole nation was impoverished because more effort was put into hating than into finding ways to restore and energize all parts of the country after the war.

The southern system of agriculture had depended on slave labor. Crops which depleted the soil could be grown year after year because high yield was less important when a few people owned vast plantations and labor cost little or nothing. After the war even subsistence farming — raising enough to keep a family going from year to year — was a nearly hopeless task. "The loss of every third horse or mule and almost half the agricultural machinery in the South meant reduction in productivity and in some states reduction in the acreage cultivated. Two mules and one plow could not do the work of three mules and two plows."

The war-ravaged, conquered south was the place where Albertus Van Raalte's second colony was begun, and the answer to the question — *why there?* — has been heatedly, though not widely, debated. Whether they were motivated by charitable impulses or desire for gain — or both — it is probable that some of the New York financiers, including Samuel Schieffelin, who had long been supporters of Albertus Van Raalte's religious and educational enterprises, saw the economic advantage of buying large tracts of land cheaply, and selling some of it to energetic, hardworking emigrants who could make the desolate area prosperous. This was a time when many northern entrepreneurs saw possibilities for improving agricultural methods in the south, and doing well for themselves in the process. General William Sherman — whose style ranged from the elegant to the colloquial — pointed out to a wealthy friend that land and climate in many of the southern states were suitable for northern methods and northern crops. The country, he wrote, "is not Southern but Northern — where water freezes and wheat grows — where the hickory, oak and chestnut groves are Northern, and it is a misnomer to call it Southern. Because slavery ever existed there don't affect the laws of Nature." He proposed that lands in the former confederacy "be taken up in small farms by Germans or Yankees," and then "the social question and even the political question would soon be settled."

Van Raalte saw additional advantages of this unlikely location. Not only was the land cheap, and easily purchased if financiers were interested in the project, but the climate was warm and thus there was a long season for farming. Much of what an emigrant group needed — and that the early settlers in Holland did not have in their colony's early years — such as railroads and easily accessible cities to be markets for the crops that would be produced, was already in place. Though the national trend was to follow the popular advice — "Go west, young man!" — Van Raalte saw no need for everyone to move in the same direction. "The main argument against

Virginia," he wrote to Pieter Oggel, "seems to be that settling here is against the stream. But this is not the case with people from the Netherlands in whose interest this settlement was begun. They shorten their trip by 300 hours and pay for only a sea voyage ...and at the same time they locate themselves 300 hours nearer to the great ocean ports. ...Now even if several Hollanders should want to move from the West to the East such an unnatural decision would not turn the world up-side-down."

For Van Raalte himself, the south could be a fertile area for missionary work. Ambitiously, he planned three churches, and a school with both primary and advanced levels. To help finance church development, President Phelps, Van Raalte's soulmate in enthusiasm, made a loan of $2,100, from Hope College funds. Phelps' beneficence cannot be faulted, but in this case his judgment was poor. College funds are not now, and were not then, the equivalent of present-day foundations (i.e., a source of monies to be given for charitable purposes). Nor was the Amelia Colony a sound investment. The college could not afford to lose the money and though it was repaid, making such a loan jeopardized Phelps' position.

Emigrants came to the Amelia colony from the Netherlands. Some came also from the Holland community and other Dutch settlements in America, but many of these looked over the prospects, turned around and went home. Returning to Europe was not an option for dissatisfied emigrants from the Netherlands, but they could and did complain. Those complaints are summarized in a lengthy letter Van Raalte wrote to a man who was considering emigration. One of the roles Van Raalte accepted in the Holland colony, was that of business leader, and as he used his business skills, "he was, at the same time, developing into an entrepreneur. ...He became a businessman in America out of personal necessity and possibly because he enjoyed business life."

One source of his enjoyment must have been exercising his talent for conceptualizing complex situations in business terms. He opened his letter with a cost-benefit analysis of emigration. He then summarized the problems facing this part of the country, and the advantages in settling there for people who were willing to manage frugally and work hard, and who were willing to farm. Not everyone who comes to America would want this kind of life, however, and for some he recommended going to cities where factory work was available. He also gave a clear description of share-cropping, although he did not know the term and could not envision the despicable way avaricious people would use the system in future. At this point, he was aware of a factor that he had not planned for: the emigrants' unrealistic expectations. In Europe it was difficult to acquire land or to find work, but cities were built and farmlands were prepared. In America there was land to be had, but it had to be developed. Building something new — "it does not take place, sleeping."

Amelia Court House Virginia. August 3, 1869

Dear Friend,

...It is my conviction that the transplanting of a generation is a great gift from above; but the heart of man must be attuned to it and determined to it, for it is a difficult thing. ...it does not take place, sleeping!

The easiness of the old world where one inherits cultivated land, cities and villages from the fathers, makes many unfit for the difficulties here. Many hear of what their poor acquaintances have become in America, but they do not take into consideration how much this required. They come here and find these blessings are not ready, but rather they must be sought and worked out with persistent effort. This fact irritates and disappoints them, and they complain. But we, who have been here a long time smile about it, for we

161

know that all find their place at last and get possessions and are able to find work for their children.

But be assured that to arrive in a strange land without money and without knowing the language, and where one has to learn anew about work is very hard at the beginning. - much harder than one can imagine. And yet I rejoice when they arrive on this side of the waters. ...The great safety for the emigrant is to acknowledge God and keep on seeking His advice.

...These are the reason why some from the middle states have begun a settlement here in Virginia. They escape the brief summers and cold winters; people in the north are much troubled by them. Here the fruits have time to ripen. One can keep on long in sowing; and keep on plowing even in the winter season. Also the region is sparsely populated, but roads, bridges and railroads are ready, and because large cities are nearby, products bring higher prices than in the west.

...Slavery has spoiled this region and the war has impoverished everything. Great lords' houses are built on large plantations, surrounded by Negro huts. Along the railroads one sees little that can bear a name, little of what may be called farms. If the conditions were different, there would be no need of new emigrants and the land near the railroads and cities could not be bought for thirteen dollars an acre. ...Great effort is necessary to make the land prosperous, but this is true of all settlements. Men who come here and only look for high wages despise these regions, and they are better off in the cities where there are factories.

Those who want to own land should buy in places that have just begun to develop. This is the reason why many from the north come here and settle, especially along the railroads - these are only a little distant, along the foot of the mountain range. These regions are chosen, as I have said, by the Hollanders on account of the cities, which are markets, and the railroads. The region is warm, but not like the states farther south where cotton is cultivated. Here the usual grains and tobacco are grown. I have spent the summer here and for fifteen days the heat was oppressive. The remainder of the time was agreeable. But we frequently experience such hot days in America. In the mountainous areas which are nearby the soil is more difficult to plow, but richer, and there are beautiful scenes of nature, but our people do not want to farm there. Some buy entire plantations and then they get large houses. The Negro huts are a miserable sight, but those who buy small pieces of land often do not find a house on what they buy and must get along in these huts or are obliged to build a shack, unless they can live for a time with friends.

This slavery-ruined and war-impoverished land must be rebuilt, economically and socially. But it is easier to do this in places where one has to begin from the bottom. The original inhabitants have become the prey of the old slavery, and hardly know how to make the best of life in harmony with the new order of things. The best thing for those who cannot afford to buy farms is to get land and cultivate it for the owners - such arrangements are made at Christmastime. When the new person furnishes horses and other equipment, he receives one half of what he earns by farming. When the other partner furnishes everything, the person who works the land receives one fourth. People who come here without money should buy cows, because they can easily be kept on pastures or corners of land that are not used, and cows produce and are easy to take care of. But if you and your family want to have an income from the beginning, move to a city, especially if there are factories. There everything is easy and ready. Paterson, New

162

Jersey, is such a city where many Hollanders are living. Philadelphia is also reported to be a good city. There one should apply to a Reformed minister for advice. If you wish to go west, go to a place where you have friends. And don't be in a hurry; either experience or knowledge is necessary. If you come to a place like Virginia, I advise farming. If you have money to bring, buy little land, and invest all that you can in milch-cows.

For the rest, my friend, I commend you and yours to the gracious Hearer of Prayer. For Him it is so easy to make our path smooth and straight. Our God is good, merciful and helpful - a pardoning God. ...May the Lord's peace be on you and your family in Christ Jesus by His Holy Spirit.

Your friend and servant,

A. C. Van Raalte

Three congregations are beginning to organize here, and at the center of the country the foundations are laid for higher and lower schools of education, about which I rejoice.

Other letters — family letters — provide vignettes of colony life, interspersed with family news. Christine was an excellent correspondent — far better than her brothers, as she pointed out to them. Some of her comments echo her father's letters written from the Netherlands: the Van Raalte family had Dutch tenacity and American know-how, and it was certainly discouraging to see folks who did not — among them the dispirited Confederate veterans, the "Johnnie Rebs."

Dear Ben and Dirk,

I wish to express my deepest thanks for the long letter which you wrote to me but I will not pay you wages according to what you have earned. Maybe you are so busy now that you do not have time to write but you must not forget me entirely. I am just as anxious as the rest of the family to get a letter from you occasionally.

We are having very warm weather here and it is especially hot in the kitchen over a hot stove. There we spend most of our time since we do not have a maid. So there is always plenty of work for us and it is fortunate that we learned how to work - at least if we hadn't learned more about work than these southern girls things would be in a mess. What poor creatures they are - don't know anything - not even how to make a bed or how to sweep. Cherries have been ripe here for a week and our hired man is now picking some for canning. I wish you were all here now, then I would give you a whole pail full. They are very good and as sweet as sugar.

Dear Ben,

At first I didn't like this place because I found everything so strange but I and the others are getting accustomed to it and are well satisfied. It is true our house is rather rickety - the downspouts are hanging loose and there are several broken windows, but we have put up some blinds and with a little money we can make it look quite respectable. One good thing - even though it looks rather slovenly, the Johnnies pay no attention. They are so used to it after the war that they think it can't be any different.

...Oh Ben, how backward these southern people are compared to those in the north when it comes to farming. Father has a very good garden and a good hired man to work it. The garden and the land are being tilled in the northern way, and when some of these

southern gentlemen come to see it they are amazed. Yes, you would get a good laugh because you know a lot more about farming than Father. If you were to farm here they would probably think that you were a wonder from Heaven.

...Anna feels like a big lady because everyone here calls her Miss Annie. Every day more people are coming here. Today a surveyor and his son arrived to buy land here. His wife and two other children are still in Richmond. He is quite a gentleman and I am glad to see men of his type come here. One would be ashamed of many of the people here as some of the men stand around working dressed in nothing but their red flannel underwear.

Now Ben, will you please write me? I would appreciate a letter very much and ask Dirk if he will please answer my letter. ...Kiss the children for me, especially that sweet Karel.

Your loving sister, Christine

Emigrants continued to come to the colony, though the circumstances of some were very hard. As is true of much of what we read in letters from the past, each account leads us to wish we could learn more about some small mystery.

Quite a few emigrants are arriving and we are now waiting for about forty more to come. Saturday that nasty man's family arrived. I say "nasty man" because he is the one who treated Father so shabbily. I pity his poor wife. He just left Holland quietly, taking all his money with him. When he got here he wrote her telling her to come and that she had better borrow some money from her friends. This she did and now she is here, doesn't know where her husband is and doesn't have a cent. She said she came to America only for her children's sake and not for her husband because she was unhappy with him and feared him very much because he was so cruel.

In the Van Raalte family, as in many loving families, letters usually ended with family news and loving messages: Christine sends a kiss to Albertus' youngest child, now two years old, and looks forward to seeing him, along with other family members, when they journey to Amelia for her wedding. Soon after Christine wrote, Will Gilmore came to become principal of the school and to assist his father-in-law in preaching and pastoral cares.

He and Christine Van Raalte married, and spent their honeymoon in the beautiful Appalachian mountains. Little information about the wedding celebration has come down to us, except for an allusion to it in one of her father's letters to Philip Phelps, expressing a male point of view which has tended to last over the years: how can women make such a to-do about a wedding, and enjoy it?

> *Amelia C. H., July 15, 1869*
>
> *Dear Brother,*
> *...We are well by God's kindness, though I am weak. My wife is a wonder in my eye. The marriage festivities are past: they are gone to the mountains...*

One of his letters to Ben concluded gloomily: "...my strength is not improving. I feel like an old man and walking is becoming very difficult for me. I miss my easy chair here. The children are well although, because of the chilliness and draftiness of the house, they have colds but are still not exactly sick." Then comes a flash of his characteristic decisiveness: "I know one thing — we must get stoves and have the house repaired even if I have to sell some building lots. Sickness is too costly — too much time lost. The Lord bless all of you. Love to all. Kiss the children for us. Your very loving father."

In his analysis of the causes of emigration from the Netherlands to America, Gerrit tenZythoff uses a *push* and *pull* metaphor. Some factors pushed the emigrants away from their homeland; other factors pulled them toward America. Albertus Van Raalte was gripped by this kind of push and pull a second time when he chose to move from Michigan to Virginia. However this time the push factors were real, but the pull factors were largely illusory. Moreover, in this replica-in-miniature of the emigration from the Netherlands, Albertus Van Raalte was the person who felt most strongly pushed away from Holland. Earlier, people who experienced religious persecution and economic misfortune made the decision to emigrate, and Van Raalte was moved to accompany them as their pastor and protector. Now it was Van Raalte who needed to escape with dignity from stresses in the Holland community.

He was drawn toward a place where he believed he could recreate an earlier success, but he misjudged. In his early enthusiasm he compared the site in Virginia with the Michigan wilderness and saw advantages in the ways the two places were similar, such as ease of land acquisition, and in the ways they were different, such as warmth of climate. He hadn't considered that both he and America had grown older. America was no longer an unknown, mysterious place; it had become the land of promise — and when those promises weren't immediately fulfilled, the newcomers were annoyed. And while emigrants from the Netherlands had an inaccurate vision of America, they had no vision at all of Albertus Van Raalte. He was not an energetic, charismatic leader who was their lifeline in strange territory; he was an aging gentleman who thought he knew better than they did. In the Michigan wilderness, Van Raalte and his people met Americans, and despite some ambivalence on both sides, connections were made. As Van Raalte and his family perceived the people in Virginia, there was nothing to admire or emulate, nor were any of the "Johnnies" eager to learn from the Hollanders.

The clincher, for Albertus Van Raalte, was that settling in the Holland colony was irrevocable. Bad times there might be, but it was home because there was no other home to go to. This time, his new colony in Virginia was not out of the world, as the Michigan forests had been, years before. He could leave this place, and go home.

Mrs. Van Raalte did not stay in the new colony long. The colonization in Virginia was the one venture, of all her husband's grand plans, that she had quietly opposed, although when he could not be dissuaded she accompanied him as a matter of course. But it was neither her disapproval of the project nor her discomfort in a difficult environment that took her from her husband's side. She was mother as well as wife, and though she was needed in Virginia, she was needed in Michigan more.

It is probable that she and her oldest daughter were especially close. When little Johanna Maria Wilhelmina was three, with an older and a younger brother, she would have been happy to have a baby sister; she would have been old enough to share some of her parents' sorrow when, after a little more than a year, the baby died. On Mina's eighth birthday the Van Raalte family — father, mother and five children — were one day away from arriving in America; she was old enough to have been her mother's helper on that long and tempestuous voyage. Four more sisters were born in *de Kolonie*; and Mina would have assisted at the times of birth, helped to care for the children, and mourned when two of the little girls died. When her youngest sister was born, Mina was seventeen, already a grown woman. At nineteen she accompanied her mother to the first public concert held in Holland, and they experienced together afterward freely-expressed disapproval of their attendance. When Mina was twenty-two, she married Pieter Oggel, who had been a student at her father's school in Arnhem when she was a child. Like each of her sisters after her, she married a man who devoted himself to the realization of her father's dreams.

In August of 1869, Christine and Will Gilmore had been married for several months, and already they were expecting their first child. Mary, who was now eighteen, would stay on to assist them and to teach in the academy where Will was principal. The household there was as comfortable as love and cheerfulness and energy could make it. Her husband might stay if he wished, but Christina Van Raalte would return to Holland. On August 3, Albertus Van Raalte wrote to Philip Phelps, "Mrs. Van Raalte's mind is bent upon Michigan, hearing from our Mina that Oggel is not better."

> *[That winter] Dominie Oggel died of tuberculosis. He was an upright good Christian who possessed a great talent for preaching and teaching. He had been a preacher before he was twenty and was almost forty-one when he died. Dominie Vander Meulen preached the funeral service taking as his text, "He was as a lighted and burning candle and Thou hast permitted him to send forth his light for a short time." It was a severe blow for both church and school and all mourned his passing. His dear wife was particularly lonely. She had only one daughter and had lost two small sons and a girl, or rather they had preceded her to heaven.*
>
> from the diary of Grace - Geesje - Van der Haar Visscher

Dominie Pieter Jan Oggel died, aged 40, on December 13, 1869. In the nine years he and Mina had been married, four children were born to them: in 1861 a son, in 1862 a daughter, in 1865 a daughter, and in 1867 a son. At the time of her husband's death Mina was thirty-one and their third child, Christina Johanna, named for her grandmother, was four years old. None of the three other children had survived; their first little girl, an earlier Christina Johanna, was the longest lived of the three, dying just after her second birthday. Mina needed her mother's love and presence, and Christina Van Raalte needed to be with her daughter, who was also her friend.

A person with many responsibilities can always continue to work. Albertus Van Raalte had a way to separate himself from the unsatisfying tasks in Virginia without being, or feeling, idle. He would go once more to New York, and try to make the eastern church leaders and benefactors of the college understand the importance of a western site where young men could be prepared for the ministry. Writing to Philip Phelps on August 3, 1869, he announced his intention to leave, God willing, in a week, to accompany Mrs. Van Raalte to Holland, to "attend to Michigan matters, [and then] to leave Holland early in the fall for the East and the Endowment Work." After going to New York, Van Raalte returned to Virginia, "to bring the property into a secure position," and then joined his wife and family in Holland.

Will and Christine Gilmore stayed in the Amelia colony for several years, with Mary to assist in the school and be a companion and helper for her sister. The Gilmores' first two children — Albertus Christian Van Raalte and William— were born there. The array of Albertus Van Raaltes in the generations after Holland's founder were known by ingeniously differentiated names: Will and Christine's son was known as Raalte. Like his father, he was musical, and he organized Hope Church's first chorus choir. He died in 1955 in Zeeland at the age of eighty-four. The Gilmores' second son, named for his father, died at birth.

When Will Gilmore accepted a call from a church in Manito, Illinois, the Reverend John Huizenga, another Hope College graduate, replaced him. He struggled to keep the school, the churches and the colony going, but crop failures and the departures of colony members who were often angry and in dire financial straits were dispiriting to everyone. John Huizenga moved on to serve churches in Iowa, and the Amelia colony disappeared like dust blown from a dry and barren field. As decisive as his friend, and with the advantage of wealth, Samuel Schieffelin made sure that Van Raalte would not suffer financially from the Amelia venture. In 1871 he wrote to Will Gilmore, commending him for his work, and stating, "I do not wish Dr. Van Raalte to have any responsibility or anxiety in the matter or be liable for one cent." He bought the land which Van Raalte had purchased, at a cost of over $5,100 — approximately $28 an acre.

Albertus Van Raalte's colony at Holland Michigan grew like a snowball does, rolling along steadily with new material sticking to it on all sides. People came to it from the Netherlands, but they came also from neighboring communities in Michigan and from other states and countries. Today Holland is a city whose annual celebration of its Dutch heritage draws huge crowds of visitors and whose businesses and educational institutions welcome newcomers from around the world. A strong heritage links the past to the present. In Virginia, after the Civil War, the times, the people, the place — perhaps the climate — could not produce snowballing growth. The people who came and the people who were already there didn't connect. Then no more people came, and eventually most people who had emigrated to join the colony left and the few who stayed were too few to maintain a strong cultural identity and were absorbed. Long before the Amelia colony dwindled away, Albertus and Christina Van Raalte had come home to Holland.

Christina Johanna De Moen Van Raalte

The world loses its color with such a blow.

One of a minister's tasks is to care for others — one meaning of the word *minister* is to attend to others' needs. It is a task at which Albertus Van Raalte excelled, because he was able to feel for people who suffered — not always in everyday affairs, where he had a tendency to drive others as hard as he drove himself — but in times of special need. Death comes to all, and those who are left behind grieve. Dominie Van Raalte had gifts which enabled him to comfort the grieving. He had deep and abiding faith. He possessed the gift of sympathy, so that the suffering of others became his suffering too. And he had the gift of words — so that what he believed and what he felt were clothed in beautiful and memorable language.

Now, as in every period of history, death is not always a peaceful ending to a long life. Dying is often a time of great pain, and infants, children, young people, men and women die before they have lived a full span of years. In the lifetime of Albertus and Christina Van Raalte, early deaths were more common than they are today, but families' pain was no less deep. Hendrik Scholte was the minister who had examined and ordained Van Raalte at the first Synod of the separatist group, and when his wife died suddenly in 1844, Van Raalte immediately wrote to the man who had been a friend and colleague.

> *Yesterday evening after coming home I heard with great surprise the great tragedy that has befallen you - which was so completely unexpected!*
> *...The world loses its color with such a blow, yet we know God does give solace. The Lord will heal your wounds. And for her, who has exchanged the eternal for the mortal, the passing away is a great gain.*

For Albertus Van Raalte, the beauties of this world were dimmed within a few years of returning from the failing colony in Amelia. "The strong, loving helper, granted by God," his beloved Christina Johanna, wife of 35 years, died at 10:30 in the morning of June 6, 1871, in their home in Holland.

> He was the ideal preacher, she the ideal wife — inseparable from him, true to him and bound to him in the best sense of the word; a woman, who in the humblest and most natural manner, presented herself as the helpmeet of the man whom we honored as God's servant. They belonged together.
>
> Funeral address for Christina Johanna De Moen Van Raalte

Her funeral service was conducted by Dr. Christian Vander Veen, who had prepared for his career as a minister at the Holland Academy under Walter Taylor, and then at the theological school in New Brunswick, New Jersey. He spoke to the mourners of someone he had known and loved from the earliest days of the colony, when, as a boy, he watched her cradle a baby while listening to her husband preach.

Scholars who explore the published materials and archived documents which relate to the Van Raalte family will find themselves intrigued, and often troubled, by questions which now, after the passage of many years, may never be answered. And besides unanswered questions, there are questionable answers. Much of what has been written about Christina Van Raalte is interpretation, colored by an author's views of what women are like, and what a woman's role should be. The result is sometimes a blend of truth and speculation, perceptiveness and prejudice. *Ideal wife, helpmeet* — at her funeral the words were spoken with admiration as well as love. But over the years, those who have written about Christina Van Raalte — chiefly women — have fixed their attention on such words, and interpreted her life based on them and on their own vision of human nature and religion. Often the resulting picture is that of a martyr.

> *Every great man puts his work first, even before the woman he loves. And every great woman who loves her husband and her God would have it so, though it may mean suffering and deprivation.*

Here we have a judgment that can safely be made, since a woman who would prefer her husband to concentrate his attention on her, at least during part of their time together, can be relegated to one or more of the disqualifying categories: not husband-loving, not God-loving, not great. And it provides a way for a woman to be great — through self-abnegating submission to a man who will become famous enough for her to get into the history books with him.

Albertus Van Raalte did, in terms of time spent, put work ahead of family, and while Christina Van Raalte accepted this as a feature of her life, she missed him when he was away. He also missed her, and though it was his decision to travel, he never became fully accustomed to their separations. But his work did not produce, for either of them, a lifetime of suffering and deprivation. One mitigating factor was that he truly wanted to be with her, wrote to her often, and did not ignore the fact that she felt lonely. A year after their marriage, he wrote, "Dear wife, I hope you will not become hopeless because I am so busy."

It is tempting to call Albertus Van Raalte a tireless worker, but in a literal sense he was not: news of how tired he was forms a running theme in his letters. Some people — and Van Raalte was one — see many possibilities for things to do and to try, and are interested by each of them. This can lead to a life of accomplishment; it can also be exhausting for them, and for their families as well. A sense of humor helps to bring perspective, however, and though humor wasn't Van Raalte's most dominant characteristic, he was clever, he had a subtle wit (shown on occasion in minutes of church meetings when he was clerk) and he recognized a trenchant comment when he heard one. "A certain gentleman," he once wrote to Philip Phelps, "did call the Holland Academy my first wife and Mrs. Van Raalte my second wife."

The history of Holland Academy is full of incident, and the other object of Albertus Van Raalte's loving care, his Christina, led an eventful life also. In the first ten years of their marriage — the years of persecution in the Netherlands — she had six children, and moved three times. The Van Raaltes' fourth child died aged only fifteen months, so we know there was a time of great anxiety for the sick little girl, mourning after her death, and then three living children to console. Yet Christina Van Raalte was remembered as a serene hostess, and as a woman whose home — wherever it was — echoed with her singing.

Dominie Carel Godefroi De Moen
Christina Van Raalte's brother

Dirk Blikman Kikkert Van Raalte
Christina Van Raalte's youngest son

In the photograph of Christina Van Raalte which we have, she looks solemnly out at future generations. Meeting her gaze, a first impulse is to wish it were possible to comfort her. The down-curving mouth draws attention away from her lovely eyes and brows, and her beautiful dark hair. An interpretation of her character should not rest on a single feature, however. In many families, a distinctive feature is passed from generation to generation; Christina De Moen and her brother in the Netherlands shared, and Dirk Van Raalte inherited, the characteristic De Moen mouth. A longer look at her picture lets us imagine that, when the photographer has finished adjusting his complicated apparatus, and popping his head in and out of the black-curtained box through which he peers at her, her mouth may crinkle into a smile.

Christina Van Raalte was strong enough to accept her husband's passion for his work, and she was strong in other ways as well, despite descriptions which present her as physically feeble. By one of the most important standards of her time, Christina Van Raalte was sturdy and strong. She survived bearing ten children over a period of nearly twenty years, at a time when childbed fever was lethal to many women. In her diary of life in the colony, Geesje Visscher described such a death, one which left a young father to care for four children and a newborn infant.

> *My dear sister died after having given birth to a lovely boy. Three days after childbirth she became feverish and the fifth day she was... sure she was going to die... [but] she lingered, torn between hope and fear, sometimes fully conscious. The fever became worse and on the tenth day, at seven o'clock in the morning, she succumbed. It was heart-breaking for the husband and four children to have wife and mother die.*
>
> from the diary of Grace - Geesje - Van der Haar Visscher

The diary entry continues with a description of the sermon Dominie Van Raalte preached to provide comfort in a time of loss. His text, taken from the gospel of Luke, is an account of one of Jesus' miracles of healing. As he often did, Van Raalte adapted the text to the family's loss: "Jesus says, 'Weep not, I will take care of the children.'"

> **And it came to pass the day after, that he went to a city called Nain, and many of his disciples went with him and much people. Now when he came nigh to the gate of the city, behold, there was a dead man carried out, the only son of his mother, and she was a widow; and much people of the city was with her. And when the Lord saw her, he had compassion on her, and said unto her, Weep not. And he came and touched the bier; and they that bare him stood still. And he said, Young man, I say unto thee, Arise. And he that was dead sat up, and began to speak. And he delivered him to his mother.**
>
> Luke 7: 11 - 15, KJV

Puerperal fever, or childbed fever, was deadly because its cause at the time was unknown. The women who died from it were suffering from an infection, introduced into their bodies by those who were caring for them. In the middle of the nineteenth century, a young European doctor, Ignaz Phillip Semmelweiss, asserted that members of the medical profession were the carriers, coming as they did directly from operating or conducting autopsies to attend births. As First Assistant in the Maternity Hospital of Vienna he was able to cut the mortality rate among women giving birth from 18% to 1% by requiring strict cleanliness, but his theory was regarded as an unproven fad, and he was hounded out of the medical profession. He was haunted by inability to prevent such deaths, and he died in an asylum for the insane. In America, youthful Dr. Oliver Wendell Holmes, then unaware of Semmelweiss' work, also infuriated his fellow physicians.

> [He] raised a storm of hostile argument by a paper, "On the Contagiousness of Puerperal Fever," which he read in 1843 to the Boston Society of Medical Improvement. The <u>improvement</u> on this occasion was regarded as an insult by certain old-fashioned practitioners. Holmes regarded the dissecting room as a source of infection, and he advised washing the hands and changing the clothes before attending a confinement. The simple suggestion met with nothing but opposition and abuse. Holmes answered his critics with dignity, observing that "medical logic does not appear to be taught or practiced in our schools." ...Fifty years later he wrote of [the paper], "Others had cried out against the terrible evil before I did, but I think I shrieked my warning louder and longer than any of them... before the little army of microbes was marched up to support my position."

Albertus Van Raalte, among his other roles in the colony, attended many women in childbirth. His Dutch cleanliness must have contributed to their safety.

There is no question that Christina Van Raalte was sometimes ill. A person can be sick, without being sickly. The old days were not always a time of rosy-cheeked children brimming with health, and sturdy energetic adults living to a grand old age. Ill health was commonplace, and there was little protection against it. The letters of the time reflect this fact. People today include health news in everyday correspondence if there's something important to say — I've had the flu; the baby has the measles; the twins need braces — but letters usually begin or end with other kinds of general information — we've had a lot of rain; everything's going along well. Because we can't control the weather, and we can't control the whole collection of events that affect our lives, we customarily write to inform or reassure our correspondents about those topics. In the nineteenth century, health was a factor which couldn't be controlled, and it was usual for letters to begin or end with health news. Albertus Van Raalte was in the habit of reporting on his wife's health at the end of his letters, but during the five years before her death there are letters which refer to serious symptoms of illness. The Van Raaltes' trip to the Netherlands in 1866 was undertaken, at least in part, because of hopes that the visit would bring an improvement in her health.

> *Middelburg, the Netherlands, July 30, 1866*
> *...I have had good days, because God gives strength and power, and with all this traveling and preaching I have become strong and sturdy. And as for Mother, who is sitting next to me writing, she also is gaining in strength even though her cough has not disappeared.*

> *Amelia Court House, Virginia, May 4, 1869*
> *...[She] is in reasonably good health although I sometimes fear for her. She misses the family, is bothered with rheumatism and frequently has cramps at night.*

> *Holland, Michigan, March 12, 1871*
> *...Mrs. Van Raalte is suffering: the fevers are destroying the vitality. Sometimes I see spells of easiness which makes me hope against common sense.*

The illness or illnesses which caused her death were painful. Not all suffering is physical, however. To persecute one member of a loving family is to give pain to many people. Throughout his life, as he served and guided and led others, Albertus Van Raalte was often admired and appreciated, but he also endured much criticism and cruelty, often from people and groups who enjoyed or took pride in their unkind words and actions. Though the cruelty was aimed at him, he was not the only one it hurt. Christina Van Raalte suffered for her husband because she loved him, but she also suffered directly. There is nothing weak or feeble about experiencing pain which is inflicted by others, and she endured bravely and with dignity.

In the Netherlands during the period from 1834 to 1846, the ministers who separated from the established church were harassed by state officials. When Christina Van Raalte was a bride, hostile soldiers were quartered in her home, her husband was attacked by gangs and then he himself — rather than his attackers — was imprisoned. Officials looked the other way when the separatist ministers and their families were set upon, which pleased the street youths greatly. When she was a young mother, noisy groups of ruffians sometimes surrounded her home, pounding on doors and windows, shouting and throwing trash. In later years, although the Van Raaltes were leading citizens in the Holland colony — or perhaps because they were — they had both outspoken and anonymous attackers. Some complainers protested a fault which modern readers are not likely to find unpleasant: they said there was too much laughter in the Van Raalte home, especially on Sundays.

Albertus Van Raalte's letters make it clear that feuding within the church was painful for him to experience or observe. It is a reasonable inference that Christina Van Raalte was also greatly troubled by such division and by its consequences. Toward the end of her life, troubles in the recently formed Third Reformed Church must have reminded the Van Raaltes of earlier difficulties of their own, and they must also have been deeply saddened by the pain caused to children of people they loved.

Jacob Vander Meulen, son of Van Raalte's loyal friend and colleague Cornelius Vander Meulen, was called to become the first pastor of Third Church, where the Visscher family were among the parishioners. Young Dominie Vander Meulen became ill, and substitutes periodically preached in his stead, including William Visscher, who was then completing his theological studies. Controversy arose within the congregation about whether the minister should be let go, and Visscher attempted, unsuccessfully, to mediate in the dispute. Vander Meulen resigned, but the trouble continued, and was manifested in a way which must have evoked painful memories for Albertus Van Raalte of his own experience in being denied ordination, years before, because of a quarrel in which he had only a minor part.

> *Now our son had to take his final examinations. The professors passed him with flying colors - they were well satisfied with him. But now he had to be examined by the Classis which proved to be something different. There were preachers and consistory members who felt animosity toward him because of his activities in the Vander Meulen matter. They said they couldn't accept him because it indicated that his thinking was unsound. While he passed his examinations all right they felt he had defied church regulations. We had feared this might happen but the professors had said they wouldn't dare to do such a thing - that it would be dishonoring the church school. So it was a bitter disappointment for them as well as for us since we had prayed so much together that God might make him worthy of preaching His gospel.*
>
> from the diary of Grace - Geesje - Van der Haar Visscher

Christina Van Raalte was a capable woman, with much to enjoy, although not everyone has described her in that way. In biographical sketches written long after her death, much emphasis has been placed on her delicate physical and emotional nature, which is presumed to be a natural result of her femininity.

The brunt of the hardship of pioneering has often fallen upon the women and children. To many men, pioneering is the acme of living; it appeals to the innate desire to conquer and possess, which is common to men. But few women share that desire with their menfolk. To them pioneering spells deprivation and hardship and danger and fear. Mrs. Van Raalte was no exception. By nature and training she was not at all fitted for pioneer life. She was not hardy and rugged, but gentle, sensitive, dependent, used to the comforts and niceties of life. Therefore we admire her the more as we read of her devotion to her husband and his life's work.

Folktales and historical accounts enable us to envision people who are fitted for pioneer life, like "the chaps from the Wolverine state" that Davy Crockett spoofed in his Almanac of 1845 as "half wolf, half man, and 'tother half saw mill." But real people who are pioneers by nature are memorable because they are unusual. Neither in our time nor a hundred and fifty years ago do we find many people — either men or women — who are naturally fitted for a life of discomfort, strangeness and threat. Christina Van Raalte was not, and neither was her husband, but they both faced difficult situations courageously and successfully, strengthened by their faith in God and their love for one another, and by their natural gifts and talents.

One of Christina Van Raalte's many talents was that she could cook. Cookery was not exclusively a woman's domain in the Dutch community. Emigrant men, among them Isaac Cappon, were elected cooks and assistant cooks on the long voyages to America. A birthday message from Christina Van Raalte to her son Ben told him to "bake a good cake and think of us when you are eating it." Nevertheless, the Hollanders were thoroughly in tune with American culture in the shared assumption that it was women's responsibility to prepare the family's food.

In the early days of the colony, housewives faced great difficulties. Food supplies brought from the Netherlands eventually ran out; stores where food could be bought were distant from their isolated settlement; and they had no kitchens to cook in. Bread consisted of balls of dough baked in the ashes. Almost every biographical sketch of Christina Van Raalte includes the same brief story about bread. Perhaps she was told about outdoor cooking while she was the guest of Judge Kellogg and his family in Allegan; perhaps she cleverly devised a practical baking method herself. Although no one seems to have been interested enough to record what the process was, all the sources assure us that "Juffrouw Van Raalte showed many of the women a better method of baking bread."

> How often do we see the happiness of a husband abridged by the absence of skill, neatness, and economy in the wife! Perhaps he is not able to fix upon the cause, for he does not understand minutely enough the processes upon which domestic order depends, to analyze the difficulty; but he is conscious of discomfort. However improbable it may seem, the health of many a professional man is undermined, and his usefulness curtailed, if not sacrificed, because he habitually eats *bad bread*.
>
> Mrs. Cornelius, in *The Young Housekeeper's Friend*, 1850.

A talent which brought great comfort to her and joy to others was her musical ability. People who heard her sing remembered it long afterwards. "She could sing so sweetly that the room continuously re-echoed the melody."

Although Mrs. Van Raalte had been brought up to a life of refinement, comfort and ease, she adapted herself with remarkable skill and courage to the restricted means of a poor village preacher of a persecuted sect [in the Netherlands]. With her charm and graciousness she won the hearts of the parishioners. She invited to her home the young people attending the classes in catechism, served them chocolate and cookies, and then led them in singing, for she was proficient in both vocal and instrumental music.

When Albertus Van Raalte remembered the early days of the colony, he said "I thank God that my wife without hesitation, and with the singing of psalms, occupied our unfinished house."

There were very few musical instruments in the colony. The first piano we know of belonged to one of the American families in Holland in 1851. [This was the family of Walter Taylor, first principal of the Holland Academy.] Many colonists had scruples even against the use of organs in the church. They were introduced very gradually and not without opposition. In time, with greater prosperity and more liberal concepts, pianos and organs became more numerous and many families owned one or the other. However, in the church, the voorzanger still remained for a long time a dominant figure. The first concert in the colony was given in Holland in 1858. Despite the fact that it consisted only of sacred music and was performed in the chapel of the Van Vleck Hall, it aroused considerable criticism, especially since de Juffrouw — the Dominie's wife — and her daughter attended.

As the wife of the Dominie, Christina Van Raalte had a variety of interesting responsibilities, and held a high social position. Her signature — C. J. Van Raalte — appears as witness on many of the certificates for the marriages her husband performed, including the first one held in the colony, between Lambert Floris, 27, and Jantjen Meijering, 28, "in a church meeting in the woods near the house of A. C. Van Raalte, in the presence of G. Van Rhee and C. J. Van Raalte." In 1858, the local newspaper reported that she was appointed chair of the committee to decorate the interior of the new Pillar Church "fittingly and respectfully, preventing any impropriety." Geesje Visscher noted in her diary visits from both the Van Raaltes — "we had a pleasant time talking about religion" — and from Mrs. Van Raalte along with others. "Mrs. Van Raalte and other women spent a day at my home. (Dominie Van Raalte is away in the east raising money for the Academy.) We spent a pleasant day talking religion much of the time."

In their social life, the Van Raaltes were at home among with those who spoke English as well as those who spoke Dutch. Visitors to the community naturally spent time with the Van Raaltes; she was a gracious hostess, and he held the floor as a raconteur. Henry Post's wife was a special friend. As Anna Post's recollections show, Christina Van Raalte could make a pleasant impression in a situation where only French was spoken.

I very soon made the acquaintance of Rev. and Mrs. Van Raalte. I was struck with his youthful appearance, as he had been described to me by a mischievous friend, who had met him in Lansing the previous winter, as a venerable looking man, with a long white beard. In those early years they were our most intimate acquaintances and the pleasant visits with them are among the brightest recollections of those times. Mr. Van Raalte possessed rare conversational powers; and every sentence he uttered was worth remembering. His noble wife was a lady of culture and refinement.

...In the early settlement many visitors were attracted here by curiosity. We had been here but a few weeks, when Rev. McPason, of Galesburgh, came here on a Saturday afternoon bringing a letter of introduction from Judge Booth of Allegan. The next morning, being Sunday, we all went to hear Rev. Van Raalte preach in the old church. In the afternoon Rev. McPason preached the first sermon in English ever delivered in Holland. After the services we were all invited to tea at Rev. Van Raalte's.

I remember about this time were was quite a sensation caused by the arrival of a family from Paris. They rented a log cabin, opposite us, and the frequent appearance of an unusually beautiful boy with long dark curls and large lustrous eyes made me the more anxious to meet his mother. Mrs. Van Raalte and myself, armed with an interpreter, soon went to call upon her. We found a fine-looking French lady, dressed very neatly with a showy kerchief crossed on her bosom and a becoming cap upon her head. We exchanged bows and curtsies in abundance; and there was some parlez-vous-ing with our interpreter. At length, casting a scrutinizing glance upon us, she asked the interpreter: "Where were these ladies educated that they do not speak French?"

Anna Post's Reminiscences

The Van Raalte home, in later years

In the early days of the colony, the Van Raaltes lived in a roughly built log house. Later their home was stately and beautiful, with three living rooms, and a sweeping cherry wood stairway leading to eight bedrooms on the second floor and Dominie Van Raalte's study which occupied the entire third floor. The cellar floor was made of solid planks of cherry wood, and there was a tunnel leading to the carriage house. In one of the living rooms there was an elegant piano, and Christina Van Raalte's grandchildren told their grandchildren how beautifully she played and sang.

The house no longer stands, but many people in Holland today still recall it. When he was a student at Hope College, Elton Bruins photographed it, and so we have a glimpse of the pillared porch, and the trees that shaded it long after Christina and Albertus Van Raalte were gone and their once lively home left vacant. It was set on seven and a half acres, at the eastern side of the city. Purchases made from the colony store included many trees and fruit-bearing bushes for the Van Raalte home:

> In 1853: *2 English walnut, .50; 2 Spanish chestnut, .50; 1 early walnut, $1; 4 dwarf pears, $2; 6 raspberries, .75; 2 quince, .50; 3000 second size apple seedlings, $4.50.*
>
> In 1854: *6 apple and 2 peach, $2.30; 8 dwarf pear, $4.00, 1 Concord grape, 1 Catawba, .45; 1 Delaware, 1 Diana, .40; 1 Hartford Prolific, 1 Isabella, .10; 1 Osage orange .10.*

Christina Van Raalte was competent and fortunate; she was also a virtuous woman. That is an old-fashioned phrase. To be told that someone is virtuous does not immediately evoke an impression of someone who is happy, and indeed we know that Christina Van Raalte experienced sorrow and fear and physical pain and loneliness. But her virtues contributed to her happiness and to the happiness of those around her. We can tell from what her husband said about her, and what others remembered about her, that she possessed the virtues of loyalty, sweetness, composure and good sense.

Without these virtues, she might have been more greatly indulged in her marriage, however. It was not every minister who had a helpmeet as patient and uncomplaining as Albertus Van Raalte's wife. When Sara Scholte died, causing Van Raalte to think of how bleak life would be if he were to lose his Christina, Hendrik Scholte must certainly have mourned her. He soon married again, however, and his pretty, wayward Maria found it paid her well to show a conspicuous lack of loyalty, sweetness, composure and good sense.

On hearing that her husband intended that they would emigrate to America, Maria is said to have swooned. A gossipy letter from one of Scholte's friends to another reported a scandalous rumor: "Scholte and his wife have reached such disagreement upon the last moment before migration that they have been after each other with knives, so that the police had to be called." Whether or not the disagreement really escalated to that dangerous point, Maria's swooning and annoyance inspired vigorous attempts to mollify her.

> *To encourage his wife, the Dominie pictured an America of great prosperity and agreed to include Hubertina, her sister, in the move. He promised to build a beautiful new home and to reproduce their large Dutch library in every detail.*

In the years since Christina Van Raalte's death she has been described admiringly by people who have written about her from radically different perspectives. In her lifetime she cared for many people, and she loved her God, her children and her husband. Her life was worthwhile, and those who were dear to her loved her deeply.

Mrs. Van Raalte died after a lingering illness She was a true believer and a happy Christian,. In days of health or illness she always sang a great deal. It was a heavy blow for the family since the daughter who had lost her husband the previous year was also living with them. Dominie Van Raalte felt the loss of wife and mother keenly.

from the diary of Grace - Geesje - Van der Haar Visscher

The death of his wife was the hardest thing that Van Raalte had to bear. ...Since the morning of March 15, 1836, when she gave her hand for life to the candidate of the hated Afgescheidenen in the city hall of Leiden, she was a support, help and consolation to him. She was an excellent wife for a preacher and many burdens were deftly taken from his shoulders by the hand of love. She had great influence over Van Raalte and he took her judgment into consideration whenever decisions had to be made. She was a woman with a healthy outlook, a tender heart, inner spirituality and piety, a faithful companion and self-sacrificing mother.

Five years later, when Albertus Van Raalte was dying, his thoughts were of a joyous meeting in heaven with the wife whom he had called "Mother" for almost all their years together. "Oh, if only I could rest my head on Mother's breast for a while... but I will see her, Jesus and her will I see."

The saints die not; they fall asleep in Jesus. ...Our sister sleeps.

Funeral address for Christina Johanna De Moen Van Raalte

HOLLAND CITY NEWS

FIRST ISSUE!

S. L. Morris, Editor
Saturday, February 24, 1872

SALUTATORY

This is a new paper published in the city of Holland. We present our little paper to you today for the first time, with a degree of timidity unexpected, yet prompted by a desire to foster the interests of the city and county, and a more selfish, and to us important fact that we hope the experiment will prove a success forces us to apply to you for support. For a medium for the transmission of ideas tending to promote the general interests of Western Michigan is a desideratum that cannot be gainsayed.

The fact that a city of the commercial importance of Holland, the great Rail Road center of the Michigan Fruit Belt, with her college and schools of learning, her churches, her agricultural and mineral resources, and her facilities for Lake transportation being suppressed from the American reading people for the want of proper expression in the English language and this want being keenly appreciated by a large portion of our citizens, are sufficient reasons why this enterprise has been undertaken.

We propose to make the NEWS a compendium of facts relating to the resources of Ottawa county and Western Michigan and to such a class of people as cannot be reached through any other language. We hope to be able to convince the man of science, the capitalist, the manufacturer, the mechanic, the laborer and the man of leisure that Holland offers superior inducements where a sure return from proper investments may be reasonably anticipated.

...We can with a united effort dig out from the ruins of the 9th of October last, and with proper display of energy, become a relative of importance in the constellation of Michigan cities. Readers, we have started this enterprise; its continuance must be supported by you; if you wish it enlarged, send in your subscriptions and patronage and as soon as it will warrant, it shall be done. The future of the NEWS is in your hands; we promise to do the best we can for you. Will you patronize it?

The Fire King has devastated nearly our entire City, throwing men, women and children upon the charities of the world.

The death of Christina Van Raalte in June of 1871 was a loss to the colony, and a deep personal tragedy for her husband. Four months later, catastrophe fell upon the entire community. *Holland was, en is niet.* That bleak sentence — *Holland was, and is not* — opened the account, in an issue produced jointly by three of Holland's newspapers, *De Hollander, De Grondwet*, and *De Wachter*, of one of the most devastating fires in Michigan's history.

As is true for many cities and towns, events in Holland of vital significance to its inhabitants are often discussed only in local histories, and recorded only in municipal documents or family papers. Information comes from modern summaries and analyses of long ago happenings, or is laboriously gleaned from records of that past time. For the Holland fire, however, there are three, rather than two, sources for information. Besides histories written recently, and contemporary descriptions in historical archives, there is an account of the fire published fifteen years afterwards which describes not only the fire, but its aftermath: "The Burning of Holland, October 9, 1871," by Gerrit Van Schelven, a prominent citizen of Holland and the city's first historian.

Those who experienced the fire which destroyed most of Holland in a period of two hours tell of its destructiveness and their own terrors; modern historians can focus their attention on the cause. The fires "resulted from a lack of concern with fire prevention. ...Branches that were cut off the main trunk of the trees were simply left on the ground in piles; after a dry summer any spark could ignite them."

Van Raalte had settled his people in the forest where lumber for housing was available to poor and rich alike, and there were several reasons why tree branches were left in ditches: the colonists were still learning about lumbering, and it was a simple method of garbage disposal to leave worthless wood to rot where fires would break out spontaneously and clear it away. It would have been folly, however, for the people in *de Kolonie* to have given no thought to protecting their settlement against fire. And the Hollanders were not fools.

In fact, from the colony's inception, the dangers of fire were taken very seriously. The *Volksvergadering* was the forerunner of a city council, two decades before Holland was a city, and years before the Hollanders themselves were American citizens. This group of citizens discussed local concerns, and made regulations to meet the community's needs. They did not think in terms of fire prevention, but protection against fire was an early topic for their planning.

> *What with wooden buildings, underbrush still in the partly cleared forests, and with the regular fires in the spring when men were burning up logs and underbrush, the danger of disastrous destruction to the young community was very great. Accordingly at the meeting of the Volksvergadering on February 7, 1849, a fire commission consisting of eight members and the president of the trustees was appointed to make a plan for fire protection. This commission through its chairman… made the following suggestions at the meeting on February 21. They said that a bell which could be used for an alarm should be procured; that each householder should have three pails and a ladder twenty feet long; that three cisterns should be dug at different places in the village; and that one log pole should be kept at each one. Carelessness in these matters on the part of any one should be punished by a fine.*

Startlingly, the recommended fine is listed as one thousand dollars. Aleida Pieters' early history of the colony, from which this excerpt is taken, is an excellent account, well-written and carefully researched. She translates and reports the actions of the *Volksvergadering* accurately, and then attributes the imposition of such a huge fine to the seriousness with which the members of the *Volksvergadering* regarded the dangers of fire. "The importance to the settlers of this regulation is evident from the size of the fine which is so much heavier than any levied for other offenses." However, the correct explanation is different. It appears in the minutes of the next biweekly meeting, on March 7.

Article I.
    The President requested Mr. Verhorst to read the notes aloud from the last meeting. These were approved except for one comment: the $1000 fine was not instituted by the fire commission: but is according to the <u>law of the land</u> which the commission examined. This is the fine set in the safety and fire prevention laws of the state.

                                                    from the minutes of the *Volksvergadering*, March 7, 1849

In the Holland settlement, and later in the city of Holland, the citizens and their elected officials continued to provide ways and means of fire protection. In October of 1867 the newly incorporated city held a special election at which a one per cent property tax was approved "for the purpose of purchasing a fire engine and other expenses of the organizing of the fire department of said City." Mayor Cappon's report on April 1868 stated that funds had been expended for the purposes proposed. "The City has a very good fire apparatus, Fire Engine, Hose, Ladders, Hooks, Hose Carriage and a convenient place to keep them, [and] five good wells, which are living reservoirs for us in case of fire."

Holland could rightfully take pride in its new equipment. Eagle fire engines were used in major cities, and the members of the new Holland fire department called themselves Eagle Fire Company #1. The engine was equipped with a hand pump, and pulled by horses or the firefighters themselves. It was not fully "state of the art," however, because some cities had begun switching to steam-propelled fire engines, with Cincinnati leading the way in 1852.

For their times, the citizens of Holland had done a great deal to protect themselves against fire. Although in less than three years most of the city was burned, only one person died in the fire. Property was lost, but people were not, because the city was prepared with an alarm bell, fire equipment and wells located throughout the city. The fire department, private citizens, and students at Hope College, fought the fire valiantly. Other communities suffered far greater tragedies.

The early 1870s were a time of drought in much of the east and middle west. In Amelia Court House, Virginia, where Will and Christine Gilmore had remained to lead the struggling Dutch colony after Van Raalte departed, the crops failed because the weather was so dry. Throughout the summer of 1871 and into the fall the drought was so severe in several states that streams dried up and small forest fires kept breaking out. In Holland, the summer was hot and dry; peaches and apples ripened before their time. For weeks during the early fall there was no rain.

Climate conditions were ripe for fire, and in this year, at the same time, two of the worst fires in the history of the world occurred. Encyclopedias listing disastrous fires of history begin with four: in the year 64 A.D., Rome burned; in 1666, London; in 1871, Chicago and Peshtigo. In the great city of Chicago, an estimated 300 people died; in the small town of Peshtigo, in Wisconsin, the death toll was 800 — more than the number who died in the San Francisco earthquake and fire of 1906.

Although Peshtigo suffered the greatest devastation, there were massive fires, and hundreds of deaths, in communities across Wisconsin and Michigan: "Peshtigo, White Rock, Forestville, Elm Creek, Huron City, Bingham, Verona, Holland, Manistee — the names read like a roll call." Peshtigo is located on Green Bay, about forty miles north northeast of the city of Green Bay and twenty miles west of Menominee. At the time of the fire it was a company town, developed by

Chicago industrialist William B. Ogden to house lumber workers and their families. The town was built in an isolated area in clearings on both sides of the Peshtigo River and in the early fall of 1871 approximately 2,500 people lived there. Its buildings were wooden, the sidewalks were wooden, and sawdust was used to keep the streets from being dusty.

On Sunday, October 8, most of the citizens of Peshtigo attended church. As the day wore on, the skies darkened from the smoke of many fires on the outskirts of town. People worried, but stayed in their homes; there was no plan for evacuation and they had nowhere to go and no means of communication that could tell them how great their danger was. At eight o'clock in the evening, a noise like thunder came from the southwest and grew louder; survivors said it sounded as if huge freight trains were racing toward the town at top speed. What they heard was the sound of a crown fire, the most deadly form of fire. With the land parched by drought and the ground thick with dead branches, fires broke out and winds rose — and the fire leaped into the treetops and began to burn there. This is crowning: the top of the forest was on fire and the fire itself hurled chunks of flame into its forward path. The fire reached the town first in a storm of flaming embers which rained down, burning houses and blowing the fragments away, killing people as they fled; then there was a steady blaze which swept through the town, consuming everything. In an area approximately sixty miles in a north-south direction and twenty miles east-west, only one house remained standing.

THE GREAT CALAMITY OF THE AGE!

Chicago in Ashes!!

Hundreds of Millions of Dollars' Worth of Property Destroyed.

The South, the North and a Portion of the West Divisions of the City in Ruins.

All the Hotels, Banks, Public Buildings, Newspaper Offices and Great Business Blocks Swept Away.

The Conflagration Still in Progress.

By midnight a 150 mile stretch of land in northeast Wisconsin was burning, and on the southwest coast of Lake Michigan Chicago was ablaze. Winds spawned by the fire created a gale which blew across the lake. Smoke and ashes darkened the sky. Ships which attempted to cross the lake had to turn back.

So deep and dismal was the darkness caused by the immense volume of smoke that the sun was totally obscured for a distance of two hundred miles. The boat left Escanaba for Green Bay on the fatal Sunday night at 12 o'clock but only made her way 12 miles out when forced to return by the stormy sea beneath and the sea of fire overhead. The air was red with burning fragments carried from Peshtigo and other places along the shore, a distance of fifty miles.

In Holland, Gerrit Van Schelven wrote later, the long drought parched everything that was combustible in and around the city. "The greater part of the southwest addition, but recently platted and sparsely settled, was nothing less than a wooded wilderness, and the ravine along Thirteenth Street was filled with logs and timber."

As fall arrived in the colony, people's eyes smarted from the smoke of many little fires that kept breaking out. On the first of October a fire started at the south end of the city, which threatened the Hope College campus. There was "much attendant danger but, with a strenuous effort, [the fires were] luckily put out." A week later, on Sunday October 8, fires outside the city were spread by swirling winds. A gale from the southwest, blowing with hurricane force, carried ashes and sparks from fires in the woods south of Holland. Though the citizens of Holland were unaware of it, the city of Chicago was also in flames.

Sunday afternoon church services were hastily concluded when Holland's fire alarm bell sounded, and "the townspeople turned out *en masse* to fight fires that were flaring up on the southern and southwestern part of town." President Phelps organized the students of Hope College into brigades carrying water to soak the college buildings. Thanks to this effort, the campus was almost entirely undamaged by the conflagration — a student described it as "barely singed" — and it became one of the havens where people fled for safety. In the smoke-darkened afternoon, Geesje Visscher peered out from her home at the eastern edge of the colony.

> *Now a strong wind came up and the city was in real danger. It was Sunday, October 8th and the people were hastily dismissed at the afternoon services. All of our family had gone to church - I was home alone. I prayed God constantly that He avert the tragedy of a fire and save His people from such a calamity. Now my husband and children came home and told me how near the fire was to the city. One son had stayed in town to help fight fire. My husband and several others now went back also and didn't come home till 10 o'clock in the evening.*
>
> from the diary of Grace - Geesje - Van der Haar Visscher

The men of Eagle Fire Company #1 desperately fought a fire in the woods at the edge of the city. Between these woods and the inhabited part of town was a "slashing," an area where branches and trimmings were stacked. Here, firefighters realized, "the stand must be taken; for if [the fire] passed the woods, it came to a slashing, and the doom of the city was inevitable, as the wind was towards it."

Although on Sunday afternoon it appeared for a time that the fire might be held back, it eventually leapt forward: "the fire got over — got into the slashings, and from that in a few minutes into the city." All over the city, people were struggling to save their homes, then to save possessions from homes which had to be abandoned, then to save themselves and their loved ones when possessions and homes were about to be consumed. Only the last of these endeavors was successful. Houses burned; possessions which were buried were lost because the roaring flames burned into the ground down to the waterline. But the Holland fire differed from the fires which were raging simultaneously in the states of Illinois, Wisconsin and New York. Out of the city's population of 2,400, only Sara Ooms Tolk, an elderly widow who stayed too long in her home in an attempt to save some belongings, was a victim of the fire.

But in those hours of terror, many were in desperate fear for their lives. Some fled to Black Lake, others to the Van der Haar farm or the Van Raalte home; many found refuge on the Hope College campus. One serendipitous result of the outpouring of practical help which was sent to the city after the fire is that there exists a vivid first hand account of one family's experiences on that dreadful Sunday afternoon. The narrative is part of a letter of thanks, written by Charles Post in the closing days of 1871, to a woman in Dedham Massachusetts who, in the outpouring of gifts for Holland, had donated a blanket and pinned her address to it.

> *My house is in the southern part of the city, about midway East and West. As I stood on my roof the fire swept nearly all west of me, moving from southwest to northwest, so that it passed me by. It seemed as though the fire leaped from roof to roof, from house to house, faster than a person could run.*

Post's wife had taken their two children to her sister's home in the northeast section of Holland, and he remained, pouring water on the roof of their home in order to protect it from the advancing flames. As he struggled, Mrs. Post returned; fire was threatening her sister's home as well. They decided she should go toward the east.

> *No building had burned there yet, and I thought we were safe, though the heat and smoke were so great as to be unbearable almost. As I still carried water upon the roof, I turned my eyes south. I saw a large field of timber, hitherto untouched by fire, but now just caught; the flames leaped from tree to tree and rolled in vast sheets over the timber on the ground. ...I saw no chance to save my house now; I was almost blinded with smoke, so I gave up and went in search of my wife and little ones.*

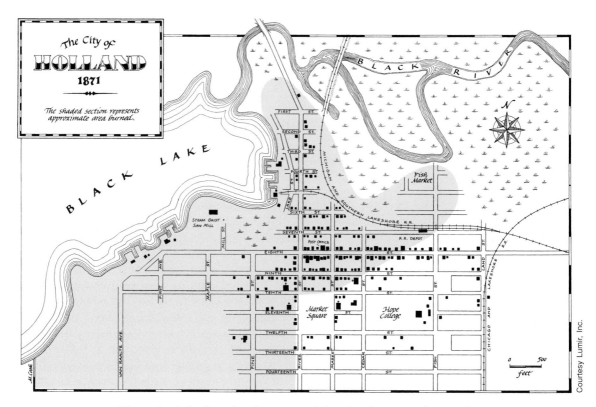

The path of the fire, showing areas of the city that were destroyed

Courtesy Lumir, Inc.

The danger of a great fire is intensified by wind blowing with terrifying force — gales created by the fire itself. Fire consumes oxygen, and the depletion of oxygen at the center of the fire produces an area of low pressure which sucks in air from the periphery. As hot air rises and cooler air rushes in to replace it, the wind on every side of the fire blows toward the fire, whirling with the power of a hurricane or tornado. Mrs. Post fought her way through blinding smoke and high winds with her two children — a baby girl and a determined five-year-old boy — and a small wheelbarrow from which her son would not be parted.

> *Baby was about eighteen months old; she had been ill during the summer; my wife carried her, though the wind was so strong that several times she had to throw herself on the ground until the fury of the wind had passed, and then struggle on. ...Once the wind took both the boy and his wheelbarrow clear from the ground and carried them some little distance; still, Walter would not let go the handles, though his hat was gone and his eyes full of sand.*

Mr. Post was able to share a particularly happy ending with the Massachusetts benefactor — not only were all the family uninjured, but the Post house was not burned after all — though three hundred other Holland families lost their homes and all their possessions. Late Sunday evening, as the flames swept on, the winds grew even stronger.

Holland during the war times, River Street looking north, intersected by Eighth Street

This rare picture which survived the Holland fire gives a view of downtown Holland, more than 130 years ago. (When it was printed in 1911, "war times" still meant the Civil War.)

Just after midnight, on the west side of the city, the colony's devastation was foreshadowed by an attack on its two mainstays — religion and business. Third Reformed Church and the Cappon and Bertsch Tannery went up in flames. At the Van der Haar farm, while the men slept in exhaustion and the younger children slept peacefully, Geesje Visscher and her older daughter watched through the late night and early morning hours.

> *We looked out of the windows to see whether we could see any fire but the smoke was so dense that we could see nothing of the city. We feared the worst for the city and prayed God for deliverance. Beyond the city we could see flames in the distance. The wind was so strong that we couldn't hear the fire bell but at twelve o'clock my husband and sons got up since it looked to us that matters were getting worse.*
>
> from the diary of Grace - Geesje - Van der Haar Visscher

The church and the tannery were burning, and the blaze consuming them was about to scatter fire throughout the city. Gerrit Van Schelven's history describes the fire's rapid spread and resulting destruction, and lists the major buildings that remained.

> *From thence on, the devastating fire fiend had a full and unmolested sway. The burning shingles and siding of this new and large church edifice and the flaming fragments of bark were blown toward the center of town, sweeping everything in the northward course. At this fatal moment the wind turned more westerly and thus forced the fire toward the center and more eastern parts of the city — this sealed the fate of Holland.*
>
> *Within the space of two short hours, between one and three o'clock, Monday morning, October 9, 1871, this entire devastation was accomplished. ...The entire territory covered by the fire was mowed as clean as with a reaper; there was not a fencepost or a sidewalk plank and hardly the stump of a shade tree left to designate the old lines.*
>
> *...The heart of the city, including the entire business portion thereof, was destroyed. [All] that remained of the once thriving and prosperous city [was] a strip of houses along the extreme western and southern parts of the city, all south of Tenth and east of Market. ...Hope College, Plugger Mills, Heald's Planing Mill, Union School, First Reformed and True Reformed churches, both our railroad depots and the townhouse. [These formed] a kind of nucleus around which clustered the faint hopes for the future of Holland. And especially was this so in the case of Hope College, not so much for the money value of the buildings but for what these buildings represented historically, and for the connecting link it had left between the Holland colonists and their true and most faithful friend who had stood by them from the very hour of the arrival upon American soil, under whose fostering care they had gradually developed from the emigrant into the American.*

On Sunday October 8, Albertus Van Raalte had preached in Muskegon. He returned on Monday to find that his beloved colony was no longer a flourishing city of beautiful churches, thriving businesses, and attractive houses lining tree-shaded roads. Holland lay in ruins. Forgetting his own sadness, ignoring the physical weaknesses of advancing age, the colony's "true and most faithful friend" sprang into action. In the pattern of the *Volksvergaderings* of the colony's early days, a citizens' meeting was called on October 10th, and Van Raalte addressed the throng of people who gathered, many of whom now had neither homes nor means of livelihood. As he had always been able to do, he brought comfort and inspiration through his words: *"With our Dutch tenacity and our American experience, Holland will be rebuilt."*

A local relief committee was formed, chaired by Mayor Bernardus Ledeboer, who was one of the city's physicians. Van Raalte and Phelps were members; Henry D. Post was appointed secretary. Subcommittees were formed to receive and distribute food and clothing, to receive and distribute lumber, to receive tools and distribute them, and to appeal to the public for aid. A letter was prepared and distributed to Michigan newspapers; Van Raalte himself wrote immediately to the *Christian Intelligencer,* which printed excerpts from his letter.

Dr. Bernardus Ledeboer
Mayor of Holland, 1868-1870, 1871-1872

> *After finishing our labor in Muskegon, on the 9th inst. we rode through an intense heat of forest fires to Holland. Here we found the railroad-bridge on fire, and heard, "Holland is in ashes!" Reaching my home with great difficulty, I found it was safe from the east side, but threatened from the southwest, and was full of refugees. The scattered people lay all around in an exhausted condition, and no one had strength enough to work in the eye-inflaming and suffocating smoke. To flee into the country was impossible. Most of the roads were inaccessible on account of the forest fires. [The calamity had begun] on Sunday afternoon [and] all the churches were suddenly vacated through the sound of the alarm-bell, and the strong wind drove the fire into the city. It entered first in the vicinity of the Third Church, which, with its parsonage and adjoining buildings was soon consumed.*
>
> *The fire then swept over in the direction of the lake, and ignited the great tannery of Mr. Cappon. The wind now veering more to the west drove the fire to the great mass of hemlock. When these combustibles began to burn, the hurricane spread it as a rain of fire over the city, driving away every human being, and destroying almost the whole. Everyone now fled for life, and to save their families. ...This happened at one o'clock in the night and in two hours the entire city, from Tenth to Second Street, was swept away.*
>
> *...The heart of the business place, all the stores and storehouses and workshops, together with from two to three hundred dwelling houses are in ashes. ...The Second and Third Reformed and the Methodist Churches are burned. ...All the printing establishments are destroyed, except that of De Hope. Dominie Van Der Veen has lost everything, Helping others, he came too late to save his own. He could only bury a few books.*

Within a few days, Van Raalte was traveling to enlist aid for the colony. In response to his appeal, and those of others, the Dutch Reformed Churches in the east took offerings, and sent $40,000. By this time in Holland's history, many of its citizens had come from the east, many had friends and family living there, and the generous help came in many forms. When Geesje Visscher wrote to her son William, who was studying in Albany, he immediately appealed to his friends, and was able to send two large boxes of blankets.

Locally, the response was generous and virtually instantaneous. The citizens of Grand Haven immediately loaded a train with food. Although the tracks surrounding the city had been destroyed, the train came near enough to be unloaded by the grateful Hollanders. "These stores consisted not only in what the grocery and bakery could supply, but the kitchen and pantry had also been emptied — a loaf of bread partly cut, a solitary biscuit, doughnuts, the remnants of a roast, a part of a ham, etc. — creating in the minds of the hungry recipients the indelible impression that this contribution — so timely forwarded — was the spontaneous act of sympathizing friends and generous hearted neighbors."

Record-keeping was superb. On October 13, the *Grand Rapids Daily Times* was able to report that clothing sent to Holland included "71 coats, 144 vests, 204 pairs of pants, 266 pairs of boots and shoes, 205 shirts, 209 dresses and skirts." At its meeting on October 27, in the second week after the fire, the City Council met to consider, to plan, and to express its appreciation for their neighbors' assistance, and their plans for the future, in weighty resolutions.

Whereas in the providence of God to whose will we humbly submit, the Fire King has devastated nearly our entire City throwing men, women and children upon the charities of the world, reducing hundreds from affluence to poverty, leaving thousands with no shelter except the canopy of high heaven homeless and penniless without food or raiment, with no remunerative labor to perform, no place of business where supplies could be obtained and immediate relief having been cheerfully supplied.

Therefore be it resolved by the Common Council of the City of Holland, on behalf of the Citizens thereof, that we tender to our neighboring Towns and Cities our grateful thanks for their prompt relief afforded us in feeding the hungry and clothing the destitute in this hour of our calamity.

Resolved: That though our once beautiful city is in ashes, our fortunes fallen, and desolation surrounds us, yet the spirit is not broken, and we pledge those who aid us in our extremity with the help of Divine Providence and the strong arm of industry and perseverance to rebuild upon a more strong foundation and attain a relative position of Honorable distinction with our Sister cities of Michigan.

Report of the Common Council October 27, 1871

Rebuilding was planned immediately. Isaac Cappon, whose tannery had been among the first buildings to burn, took the lead. "Cappon ensured that Holland was rebuilt after the fire... by insisting that his firm would rebuild here rather than move inland." Despite their horror as the full extent of the calamity became understood, many people reacted with hope, even in the midst of their shock and distress.

> *All those beautiful homes, churches, stores and factories reduced to rubble and ashes. We thought, 'What is going to be done about this?' but then, when we looked back and realized what God had done for us in the twenty-five years we had been in America, we realized that He could help us again no matter how dark things looked at the moment.*
>
> from the diary of Grace - Geesje - Van der Haar Visscher

Hopefulness expressed in religious terms was coupled with vigorous civic boosterism, whose fervency even required the creation of brand new terms. Some time after the fire the *Holland City News* commented on the energy of a local businessman, describing him as "one of the heaviest losers by the great fire; yet with his characteristic go-a-head-ativeness, [he] is bound to win. Success attend him." Holland's newest newspaper was remarkable for its florid style.

> Fellow citizens, must the ill luck of a moment deprive Holland of her future greatness? It can not be! It must not be! Men of means are rushing forward, rising Phoenix like from their own ruins, men of wealth, who seeing the advantages of our position, are stepping into the places made vacant by those who are unable to resume business. Although severely smitten by the scourge of fire, Holland is not dead, the prospects of our future are not in the least dimmed.
>
> *Holland City News*, February 24, 1872

At first, however, prospects for the local economy seemed bleak, and despite a remarkable overall recovery, some Holland business leaders never regained their former prosperity. Gerrit Van Schelven's estimate of the total losses was $900,000; only about five percent of this was covered by insurance — and most of that amount was never collected. The small amount invested in insurance is explained by the habits of the time — it was less common to insure property then than it is now — and the religious scruples of some Hollanders. Some people in the colony believed insurance conflicted with faith in the providence of God.

Gerrit Van Schelven, Holland's first historian

In 1870, members of Holland's Ebenezer Literary Society had held a debate on the subject: "Resolved, that insurance protection is contrary to the principles of Christianity." The fact that most of the insurance on the properties that were insured was not collected would have enlivened the literary society's debate, if anyone had been ingenious enough to envision how such a situation could arise. The cause of that additional financial blow was that Holland was not the only place where businesses were destroyed. Of the Hollanders who did have insurance, most were insured by companies which were burning in Chicago while Holland was in flames.

The generous help which poured into Holland after the fire was a blessing — but not an unmixed blessing. State officials set up a fund to assist the regions which had been damaged by fire, but they deducted from the amount assigned to an area the funds contributed to that place by charitable groups or individuals. Governor Henry Baldwin visited the colony and explained the situation to Van Raalte, and in November, Van Raalte notified President Phelps that supplies would be given, but no money. After speaking with the governor, Van Raalte sought donations in the form of contributions to the college. The Ebenezer Fund, to which Van Raalte himself gave generously, was established and the impressive sum of $36,000 was subscribed. The fund provided financial support for Hope College students preparing to enter the Christian ministry until the college's endowment was lost in the Depression. Gifts from churches replenished the fund, and a committee still meets annually to allocate this resource.

> *Dear Brother,*
>
> *A few remarks: Today Governor Baldwin was here, showing his interest and inquiring what the people did expect... [however] there is no expectation of distributing money, but rather they expect to give building material for 300 houses in the city and 100 out of the city and procure for them stoves, bedding and some furniture. He urged us to make appeals for money to Christian friends as a loan to help the manufacturers or as a donation to Hope College.*
>
> *...Clear enough did he state that no money must be expected from the State.*

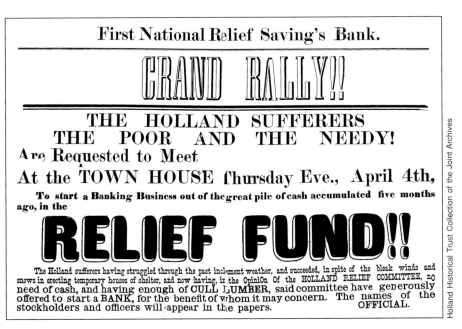

According to an advertisement which appeared in April, 1872, the city's Relief Committee was so successful that a "great pile of cash" and salvaged lumber accumulated.

If Albertus Van Raalte's life is visualized as a tapestry, there is a broad and variegated band running through it — this is the life of his colony. Crossing that band, at irregular intervals, are dark cords, representing the crises that came upon the colony from without. The fire of 1871 is one of these cords. Beside each is a bright, strongly colored stripe — perhaps combining the orange of the Netherlands and the blue of the American flag — illustrating Van Raalte's strong, inspiring response to every challenge. But along with these beautiful and dramatic parts of the tapestry there is another recurring thread in the pattern, thin, but coarse and ugly. The fire was tragic; the response to the fire was courageous. But immediately there were rumors, mutterings that the fire was the fault of the Hollanders themselves, ignorant folk so bound by their church rules that they wouldn't put out a fire or ring a bell in warning, just because it was Sunday. With only one Holland newspaper able to function, an enraged Henry Post published a notice in *De Hope*, three days after the fire, defending his friends and fellow citizens.

> Our attention has been called to reports of the fire at Holland, which are in material false, and calculated to do us great injury by diverting the sympathy of the public from us. It has been stated that the Hollanders refused to aid in extinguishing fires for the reason that it was Sunday. It is also stated that the churches would not permit their bells to be rung, fearing that it would disturb the congregation, etc. Nothing could be more false and slanderous than these statements.
>
> If the Hollanders' ability equaled their courage our city would soon be restored, fairer than before. Shame on those who would mock at our calamity, and tell lies to deprive us of our just share in the sympathy of our neighbors.
>
> Henry D. Post, in *De Hope*, October 12, 1871

In the aftermath of the fire, it was not easy for Van Raalte to look to the future with an attitude of "go-ahead-ativeness." He was exhausted. Despite the fact that the colony was on its way to renewal, meanness and spitefulness sapped his energy as nothing else could. But he knew himself well when he wrote, "I must go forward, or give up. The people would be too disheartened if I sat still [and] it would be ruinous for myself."

front row: Kate Ledeboer Van Raalte, Ben Van Raalte holding his grandson Andy Reimold, Christine Van Raalte Gilmore, John Kleinheksel, Ann Van Raalte Kleinheksel, Gerrit Kollen; *behind Kate Van Raalte (group of 2):* Lou Reimold, Gertrude Keppel(?); *behind Kate Van Raalte (group of 2):* Wilhelmina Van Raalte, Ben Van Raalte, Jr.(?); *behind Christine (group of 4, left to right):* (unidentified), Albertus Van Raalte III (Allie), Adeline Huntley Van Raalte, Christina (Tia) Pfanstiehl Van Raalte; *behind John Kleinheksel (group of 2):* Christine Van Raalte Van Putten, Albertus Van Raalte (Dirk's son); *behind Ann (group of 2):* Anna Van Raalte Keppel, Estelle Kollen Pelgrim; *behind Gerrit Kollen (group of 2):* Jay Pelgrim, A. C. Van Raalte Gilmore (Raalte).

front row: Kate Ledeboer Van Raalte, Ben Van Raalte, Christine Van Raalte Gilmore, John Kleinheksel, Ann Van Raalte Kleinheksel, Gerrit Kollen; *behind Kate Van Raalte (clockwise, group of 6):* Philip Reimold, Orlando Reimold, Albertus Van Raalte (Dirk's son), Lou Reimold, holding Andy; Gertrude Keppel; *behind Ben (left to right, group of 3):* Helene Van Raalte, Christine Van Raalte, Wilhelmina Van Raalte; *behind Christine (group of 4 in two rows, left to right):* (unidentified), Albertus Van Raalte III (Allie), Adeline Huntley Van Raalte, Christina (Tia) Pfanstiehl Van Raalte; *behind John Kleinheksel (group of 3):* Christine Van Raalte Van Putten, Bastian Keppel, John L. Kleinheksel (?); *behind Ann (group of 2):* Anna Van Raalte Keppel, Estelle Kollen Pelgrim; *behind Gerrit Kollen (group of 3):* Lena Kollen, Jay Pelgrim, A. C. Van Raalte Gilmore (Raalte).

194

God's temporal deliverances are many; each settlement and family has a history of its own.

The children of Christina and Albertus Van Raalte can be grouped in different ways. Six were born in the Netherlands; four were born in America. Of these ten children, seven were female and three were male. Three died as babies; seven lived to be adults. Of this group of seven, all married and had children; two had no descendants beyond the next generation.

Family photographs are a grand way to look at groups. Often they capture a moment in time where many family members from different generations are together. Looking back at those photographs later, it is the passage of time that first catches our attention and structures what we say: "you weren't even born when this picture was taken; that's your cousin when he was just a baby; there is your grandmother — you never knew her but she was a wonderful woman." A photograph album owned by one of Albertus and Christina Van Raalte's great-great-granddaughters, now a beautiful woman rich in years and memories, illustrates this customary way of classifying family members. The date of these photographs can be fixed with some certainty as the summer of 1911 — a determination based on who is, and who is not, in the picture. There is a brief poem written by Ogden Nash, whose light verse sometimes touched a bittersweet chord, called "In the middle" — *When I remember bygone days I think how evening follows morn; so many I loved were not yet dead, so many I love were not yet born.* In the photographs, there is a child, the younger of Ben Van Raalte's two grandsons, shown once in the arms of his mother, and once on Ben's lap. Andy was born in March, 1910 — a month after his uncle Dirk died. The stately woman in the dark dress, seated at the left in the front row, is Dirk's widow.

Two pictures tell us even more. We can guess that the younger men set up chairs for the oldest generation, and that serene Aunt Christine persuaded everyone to gather — and to stay gathered. The short interval between taking the pictures was enough time for Orlando Reimold Jr. — little Andy — to wiggle and be handed back to his mother; for Christine to call her grandnieces and Lena Kollen away from arranging the picnic food; for their parents to urge young Philip Reimold and his first-cousin-once-removed John Kleinheksel to join the group; for Ben Jr. to take over the camera from the first photographer — who was probably Orlando Reimold (who probably brought the camera), eagerly assisted by his son, Philip, and his nephew, John, and their grown-up cousin Bastian Keppel.

Every person in the photographs is related in some way to Albertus Van Raalte by birth or marriage; children and children's spouses; grandchildren and the people they married; great-grandchildren. What are their stories? One way of knowing is closed; the picture was taken long ago; none of the people who look out at us is alive today. That is something that must be — the generations pass. Another way of knowing about those nearest to him is closed because this family lived in this place and time.

In 1871, when Albertus Van Raalte, newly a widower, was within weeks of his sixtieth birthday, the great Chicago fire destroyed most of that city within two days. In New York, *The Christian*

Intelligencer informed its readers that "the Chicago fire made sad havoc among the newspaper establishments, eighty-nine of which, embracing dailies and monthlies, were burned. The Illinois Historical Society lost by the Chicago fire its fine building, with all its books, papers, and invaluable collections. The society had been specially active in collecting material for the future history of the West, and its loss is therefore, in some measure, a loss to the whole country." As Chicago burned, Holland burned. Within two hours, past issues of the local newspapers for more than twenty years were consumed by the flames. Everything about Holland families that would have been of absorbing interest locally — and ignored elsewhere — all the records of births and marriages and deaths, of events at churches and schools, of social occasions and trips — all became ashes blown in the winds.

From the beginning of *de Kolonie*, the Van Raaltes were its preeminent family, and they must have been mentioned often in the news. The first child born to them in America died, shortly before her first birthday, before there was a colony newspaper, but by the year 1871, *De Hollander* would have chronicled the births of their last three children and the death of one of these little girls. Articles would have described the marriages of three of their children, and given information about the families into which they married. The births of ten grandchildren, and the deaths of three, would have been announced. Family business ventures, family trips, and family participation in colony social events would have been reported. In 1866, there would surely have been a week-by-week narrative of the Van Raaltes' visit to the Netherlands. Before he died, Albertus Van Raalte destroyed personal papers. He may not have realized how much of his family's history had already been obliterated five years earlier.

He would have known that, inevitably, one source of information about himself would endure because he was a man of the church. Church records abound. Important causes which he championed and supported are documented, in the Netherlands and then in America, and contentious disputes which swirled around him are condensed into official language — providing a rich and ongoing resource for analysis and publication. Because he was a modest man he may have thought little about the other form in which descriptions of a part of his life had already begun to accumulate. These were the pioneer reminiscences.

History requires both doers and chroniclers. Albertus Van Raalte was a doer. There are many chronicles of his earliest years in America, because he lived long enough to become an honored patriarch of his colony, and many of the early colonists lived long enough to write their reminiscences of him. An exciting collection of these documents exists because of the efforts of Gerrit Van Schelven, who, over a period of years in the late nineteenth and early twentieth centuries, interviewed many European-Americans and Native Americans who could recall events which happened some sixty years before.

Church records, and the recollections of the pioneers, and their predecessors, who survived into old age — these richly record two vitally important aspects of Albertus Van Raalte's life. But because the massive accumulation of information about his work for the church and his founding of the colony weighs so heavily when compared with the existing information about other parts of his life, there is a risk that the understanding of his life may be unbalanced. It has been common to assume that this *was* his life — and to infer that the lives of his wife and children were not only secondary, *for him*, to these two powerful interests, but also less full and less happy *for them* because Albertus Van Raalte was such a powerful man. Although the full truth cannot be known, there remains sufficient information about Christina Van Raalte and her children to show that this is not the truth.

Interpretive material, written long after Albertus and Christina Van Raalte and all their children were dead, has, in the past, tended to present a somewhat gloomy picture. Often this is because family letters and biographical information were either inaccessible or in Dutch, or both, and because translated materials were archived but not yet researched. Additionally, writers have sometimes emphasized negative information because it appears more interesting, despite available information which is predominantly positive. An important instance is contained in excerpts taken from Albertus Van Raalte's correspondence with Philip Phelps, where he condemns first all his sons, and then his youngest son, for failing to enlist in the Union Army. Among those who have read about the Van Raalte family, Albertus Van Raalte's comment, "Dirk has no desire or courage," is probably as well known as the story that Christina Van Raalte taught the women of the colony how to make good bread under primitive conditions.

Presumably the bread-making story has a sound foundation — though it will probably remain in the category of family folklore because it's unlikely that Albertus Van Raalte wrote to anyone about it, or that his wife's letters, if she did write about it, were preserved. Dirk's alleged cowardice, on the other hand, is a myth, created from the downside of some of his father's good and interesting qualities — love of the Union cause, impulsiveness, fluency, and affection for his colleague Philip Phelps — which led him to expect his boys would rush into the army just as he assumed he would have done at their age, and to dash off his thoughts of the moment in letters to his friend. To enlist at eighteen, fight bravely when other young men from the colony were shirking, write letters home which invariably minimize distress and rarely mention danger, escape from attacking confederate soldiers by galloping for two miles with a shattered right arm while hotly pursued, and endure stoically the subsequent amputation of that arm at the shoulder — these are the actions of a courageous person, and it is a shame that the earlier slur is remembered. Albertus Van Raalte is at peace, but had he known how his impulsive comment would be spread abroad, he would have been deeply distressed.

"Each settlement and family has a history of its own." Albertus Van Raalte was a wise and generous man; when he addressed the assembled crowds at the grand twenty-fifth anniversary celebration of the settlement's founding, he did not dwell on the largest of the cities that had grown up since 1847, nor on the best known of the founding families. Each settlement, each family was important to the area's history, and they knew it. The Ebenezer celebration in 1872 was a time for settlements and families to share their pride. Each family has a history of its own also, and to tell the whole story of a family, even across only two generations, would require a library full of books.

Albertus Christiaan Van Raalte III,
    first child of Albertus and Christina Van Raalte, was born on July 1, 1837, in the province of Overijssel in the Netherlands, while his father was pastor of the congregations at Genemuiden and Mastenbroek. The Van Raaltes' first-born son was named for his father and grandfather. In the same year, also in the Netherlands, Helena Hoffman was born. Albertus and Helena married in Holland, Michigan, in 1858. They had five children: Albertus Christiaan Van Raalte IV, ("Allie"), born December 12, 1859; Christina Johanna Van Raalte, born June 8, 1861; Anna Helena Van Raalte, born September 17, 1862; Carl De Moen Van Raalte, born March 3, 1866; and Wilhelmina Van Raalte, born January 1, 1870. Of these children, all lived to be adults; all but Wilhelmina married and had children.

It is sometimes hard to be the firstborn child and namesake of a famous person. It was hard for Albertus. In John Van Vleck's last letter to Van Raalte one of his many complaints is about the Van Raalte children. "The boys were very bitter against me. Albertus said at your table that

I had treated him as a boy. The girls too said hard things of me." It is easy to imagine the school sufferings of the founder's oldest son, in the midst of quicker pupils, taught by a swift-tongued, unkind teacher. Outside of school, people compared him to his father, and his father compared him to his brothers. One running theme in Van Raalte's letters about business ventures concerns Albertus' attempts and failures. In protecting his son, the father wrote to others in a way that would have humiliated Albertus had he known, and though he would not have seen the letters, he surely must have sensed that his father was asking — and receiving — his younger brother's advice about him. "Write and let me know how the rye looks and how the horses are doing. Are they still as good as when I used to drive them? Is A's mill ready? It's a silly thing to build a mill at a time like this rather than pay attention to the farm."

Helena Hoffman Van Raalte,
in later years

Albertus got away from home — only a little way — by marrying very early. He and his wife were both nineteen. Even at the wedding, his father held center stage. Recalling the event years later, what a guest remembered was the dominie telling how "when the bridegroom was an infant, he, the dominie, had been thrown into prison for preaching contrary to the law." As it turned out, one thing Albertus could do well was to father children. After six years of marriage, there were four.

There is a mystery about Albertus — a secret which is not a secret. Family members know it and do not hide it, but anyone coming anew to the Van Raalte family records and letters begins, gradually, to become more and more puzzled, and then to make a discovery — "There is what seems to me a fascinating problem about Albertus III..." — and then to find that everybody (the small group of everybody who is familiar with Van Raalte family history) knew it already.

The first puzzlement comes from records such as the power of attorney the Van Raaltes gave to a son, when they traveled to the Netherlands in 1866. Their sons, at the time, were 29, 26 and 22. Naturally, the oldest son would be given power to conduct the family's business affairs — but not so, the youngest, at twenty-two, was given full legal control; his twenty-four year old brother witnessed the document. Perhaps the oldest son lived elsewhere? No, he is married and has lived all his adult life in Holland. Perhaps he was incapacitated or ill; genealogies give 1869 as the year of his death. But his last child was born in 1870 — ah, she would have been a posthumous child, and that should help to bring us closer to the date of Albertus' death; it could not have been earlier than May, 1869. All this history is before the Holland fire, so it is not surprising that no published obituary exists. Odd though, that family information is so sparse, that his wife and children are mentioned in letters though he is not. And then the researcher discovers another letter — "Geliefde Dirk" — a birthday letter from Albertus Van Raalte to his youngest son, written while the Van Raaltes were visiting Christine and her husband.

Manito, Ill, February 27, 1874

Geliefde Dirk:
The reminder that you have reached the age of thirty and that Albertus is already thirty-eight years old stirs up mixed emotions in me. This fact makes plain to me that my life's evening is at hand.

Our loved dead do not grow older. On March 1, 1874, Dirk would be thirty. Albertus, whose birthday was in January, *is already thirty-eight years old*. And then someone more knowledgeable says, of course — that's a little fiction in the genealogical records. No one knows when or where Albertus died (or if they do, we Hollanders aren't aware of it). Albertus left. He went away, and no one knows where, and no one knows what became of him, though some say he died of cholera in New Orleans. He left his pregnant wife, his four young children, his farm, his friends, his brothers and sisters, his mother and father, and all his life history behind, and he never came home again.

Johanna Maria Wilhelmina Van Raalte,
second child and first daughter of Christina and Albertus Van Raalte, was born on October 19, 1838 in the province of Overijssel in the Netherlands, while her father was pastor of the congregations at Genemuiden and Mastenbroek. She was named for her maternal grandmother, and known as Mina; later this was sometimes anglicized as Minnie. Her naming also honors her aunts and mother: the names Johanna or Maria, or both, were given to each of the De Moen daughters: Maria Wilhelmina, Christina Johanna, Johanna Maria.

In 1860 Mina married Pieter Jan Oggel, who was older than she by nine years. They had four children. Judging from the best records available, their first child, a son, died in infancy. Christina Johanna Oggel was born in July, 1862 and died August 19, 1864. A second daughter, also named Christina Johanna Oggel, was born on August 25, 1865, and a son Jan Oggel, or John, was born in April, 1867 and died a year later. Dominie Pieter Oggel died, aged 40, on December 13, 1869. On May 30, 1876, a few months before her father died, Mina remarried; her second husband was Teunis Jan Keppel, a widower with five children. Keppel's son Bastian married Mina's niece, Anna Helena Van Raalte, Albertus' second daughter, who thus became her aunt's step-daughter-in-law. Teunis Keppel died, aged 73, on June 27, 1896; Mina Van Raalte Oggel Keppel died on January 22, 1897, aged 58. Christina Johanna Oggel died unmarried, December 13, 1911, the last of Mina's children and her line.

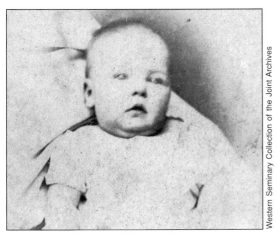

Christina Johanna Oggel,
oud 5 maands, geb. 25 Aug, 1865

Western Seminary Collection of the Joint Archives

Mina was six when tall, blond, fifteen-year-old Pieter Jan Oggel was a student at her father's school in Arnhem. Years later, perhaps Mina and her Pieter remembered that little girl and that serious young man, who didn't know that they would love each other across a wide ocean, in a new land. The young Oggels lived first in Holland, amidst a wealth of family — they both had an abundance of younger brothers and sisters — and Dominie Pieter Oggel was a mainstay and support for his father-in-law at the Academy and in church affairs. Pieter Oggel was staunch in Albertus Van Raalte's defense, but like Van Raalte, he was not a person who reveled in controversy.

Dominie Oggel was invited to fill Giles Van de Wal's position at the college when Van de Wal left for missionary work in South Africa but he declined and accepted a pastorate in Pella, Iowa. Christina and Albertus Van Raalte visited them there, taking with them their daughter-in-law Helena and her children. Some of Van Raalte's most delightful grandfatherly comments come from letters written while he was visiting his daughters. "Here we are in that nice, cold, distant

Pella," he wrote to Dirk, "My room is the warmest. Often I have little Albertus with me and Annatje for help or to be assistant nursemaid. At the moment she is writing a letter in all seriousness to Mietje, and the little one runs around." But he worried about Mina's baby: "The wetness is difficult for our Oggelje." The baby picture on the previous page, with Mina's handwriting on the back, *Voor Moeder*, is of the second Christina Johanna, when she was five months old. In 1865 the Oggels returned to Holland, where Pieter Oggel taught at the college until the illness that led to his death in 1869. Christina Johanna Oggel's obituary, in 1911, notes that she was born and died in Holland.

Teunis Jan Keppel

Mina Van Raalte's life also raises questions which have no answer. We can be sure of her closeness to her mother, can infer the happiness of her first marriage and the deep sadness she must have experienced when her children died, and when her husband died. It is her second marriage that is puzzling. Mina was 37, a widow with a ten-year-old daughter, when she married Teunis Keppel, a man closer in age to her father than to her. Geesje Visscher noted in her diary that Mina's remarriage "caused considerable comment" — and well it might, since her new husband, far from being a well-educated, calm pastor who admired and supported her father, was a tough, stalwart, self-made Dutchman who was frequently one of Van Raalte's noisiest opponents.

Dr. Van Raalte was THE leader of his people. As such he stood single and alone. He felt his responsibility and never evinced any longing to share this with any one. Nevertheless he needed assistance. By reason of the newness of things, isolation of locality, foreign tongue, and absolute unacquaintance with everything that pertained to their new condition — being strangers in a strange land — the early pioneers depended entirely upon him for guidance in everything, and it took just about one generation before along civil and non-ecclesiastical or church lines the community was sufficiently developed to take care of itself. His people 'were a peculiar people,' as Dr. Phelps used to say, and Van Raalte knew this, better even than they knew it themselves. In what theses peculiarities consisted — and to some extent, especially with the new-comers, still consist — is not a topic to expand upon on this occasion. So for want of any other line of support, and undoubtedly also actuated by a due respect for the office, Van Raalte resorted to the training of an efficient eldership. Of what service these men have been in the past, and how well they realized the importance of their position, the written and especially the unwritten history of the good old Colonial days can be made to tell *ad infinitum*. Of this school of elders the deceased was one. As such he came down to our time from the early days of the settlement here. It was this, added to his energy and activity which gave him such a commanding position in the troublous days of '82, when he revolutionized even the denominational and historical relations and moorings of the Old First Church. It is as Elder Keppel that the deceased was most potent. He was the last survivor of the school of elders in our midst, that came to us from the Puritanical past. They leave us no successors. Neither would they be approved of.

"Death of Teunis Keppel," June 27, 1896, *Holland City News*

Benjamin Van Raalte,

third child and second son of Albertus and Christina Van Raalte, was born on May 8, 1840, in Arnhem in the province of Gelderland in the Netherlands. He was named for his maternal grandfather, Benjamin De Moen. Ben and Julia Gladdis Gilmore married on November 27, 1872. Their two children were Julia, who was called Lou, born November 23, 1873, and Ben, Jr., born February 7, 1876. Both children married, and Lou and her husband had two sons. His first wife died in January, 1911, and Ben married again, to Abbie Connel, in November, 1912. He died in 1917, aged 77.

Lou Van Raalte graduated from Hope College, earned a master's degree, and taught history, physiology, botany and English at Holland High School. *Educators of Michigan* noted, "her work has been marked throughout by efficiency and thoroughness." Orlando S. Reimold was the high school principal, and they became engaged. Reimold spent three years in the Philippines in teaching and educational work following the Spanish American War; he and Lou were married on September 10, 1902, in Hong Kong. In 1905 he joined the World Book Company, of which he later became president; in 1948 he retired as chairman of the board. Ben Van Raalte and his father were partners in business, and their success was applauded in a record of successful citizens of Holland and surrounding towns.

B. VAN RAALTE
Farm Implements and Machinery

Mr. Van Raalte, as a descendant of the famous "father of the city," being born in the Netherlands in 1841 [in fact, 1840], is too widely known to need any introduction at this time. He served three years in the war, after which he established his business in 1866, and has steadily progressed until his house is one of the largest in Ottawa county. he has two stores, sixty by eighty feet, and a warehouse forty by eighty feet, filled constantly with every implement used upon a farm, together with a large line of carriages manufactured by the best makers. Some conception of the extensive business conducted by Mr. Van Raalte may be gained from the fact that his annual receipts aggregate some $35,000.

In the conduct of his business Mr. Raalte [sic] is most ably assisted by his son, B. Van Raalte, Jr., a thorough young business man of this period.

Ben Van Raalte and Ben Van Raalte, Jr.

Christina Catharina Van Raalte,
   fourth child and second daughter of Christina and Albertus Van Raalte, was born on February 21, 1842, in Ommen, in the province of Overijssel in the Netherlands, while her father was pastor of the separatist congregation there. She was named for her mother and her paternal grandmother, Catharina Christina Harking Van Raalte. Christina died in Ommen, on May 24, 1843, aged one year, three months, and twenty-two days.

Dirk Blikman Kikkert Van Raalte,
   fifth child and third son of Albertus and Christina Van Raalte, was born on March 1, 1844, in Ommen, in the province of Overijssel in the Netherlands. He was named for Dirk Blikman Kikkert, a business partner of Albertus Van Raalte's in the Netherlands who was also his brother-in-law through marriage to Van Raalte's older sister, Johanna Bartha Van Raalte. In 1884, Dirk married Kate Ledeboer, and they had two sons: Albertus Christiaan Van Raalte, born August 29, 1889, and Dirk Blikman Kikkert Van Raalte II, born July 4, 1891. Both sons married and had children. Dirk Van Raalte died February 10, 1910, aged 65.

In many ways Dirk was the antithesis of his brother Albertus. He served in the Civil War, and came home and graduated from Hope College. He married late and his wife was from a well-to-do Holland family; her father had served two terms as mayor. Dirk was shrewd and successful in business and he prospered as a prominent business leader and banker. He had two children, both sons; he named the older for his father, and the younger for himself. Albertus Van Raalte lived to see his son elected to state office for his first term. Dirk was re-elected on the day his father died. Perhaps that made him reluctant to run for office again, because it was not until 1909, thirty-one years after his second term ended, that he ran again. As a third-term legislator, his seniority gave him his choice of seats in the House chamber. He chose to sit in the farthest back row, immediately opposite the Speaker's table, and it was reported that his powerful voice could be heard throughout the House and on into the meeting rooms beyond. "With his ringing voice and fine command of English, Van Raalte is no mean opponent in scathing debate, and the representatives who can better him in sarcasm and ironical oratory may be counted upon the fingers of a single hand." He was noted for his strong defense of the House Speaker; as he used his oratorical eloquence to support his leader, he may have recalled unjustified attacks on his father, and wished that he had then been of an age and in a position to have defended him.

Christina Catherina Van Raalte,
   sixth child and third daughter of Christina and Albertus Van Raalte, was born on March 31, 1846, in Arnhem, in the province of Gelderland in the Netherlands. She was named for her mother and her paternal grandmother, and for the little sister who died three years before. In 1869, in Amelia, Virginia, Christine Van Raalte married William Brokaw Gilmore. They had four children, Albertus Van Raalte Gilmore, born April 4, 1870; William Gilmore, born and died in June, 1872; Margaret Anna Gilmore, born August 27, 1873, and Frank Edwin Gilmore, born January 23, 1876. Frank died on February 13, 1879, and Margaret died eight days later. The Reverend Will Gilmore died, aged 50, on April 24, 1884. Christine Van Raalte was the longest-lived of all Albertus and Christine Van Raalte's children; she died April 12, 1933, aged 87. Her son Raalte died unmarried, aged 84, in 1955, the last of Christine's line.

Albertus Christiaan
Van Raalte Gilmore

Holland City News
February 22, 1879

Deaths.

GILMORE — In Manito, Ill. on Thursday, Feb. 13, 1879. Frank Edwin Gilmore, aged 3 years, 2 weeks and 6 days.

Holland City News
March 1, 1879

Deaths.

GILMORE — Of Acute Bronchitis, in Manito, Ill., on Friday, Feb. 21, 1879. MARGARET ANNA GILMORE, daughter of the Rev. W. B. Gilmore and Christina C. Van Raalte, aged 5 years, 5 months and 24 days.

Maria Wilhelmina Van Raalte,
    seventh child and fourth daughter of Christina and Albertus Van Raalte, was born on September 16, 1848, in Holland Michigan, and died there, aged eleven months and seventeen days, September 2, 1849. She was the first child born to the Van Raaltes in America.

Maria Wilhelmina Van Raalte,
    eighth child and fifth daughter of Christina and Albertus Van Raalte, was born on September 21, 1850, in Holland Michigan. On Christmas Eve, 1879, Mary married Gerrit John Kollen. They had one daughter, Estelle Kollen, born July 21, 1886, who graduated from Hope College, married a minister, Jay Carleton Pelgrim, and had two daughters. Estelle Kollen Pelgrim, longest lived of all the Van Raalte grandchildren, died July 30, 1984.

D.B.K. Van Raalte requests
the pleasure of your company
at the marriage reception
of his sister Mary W. Van Raalte
and Gerrit J. Kollen,
Wednesday evening December 24th
from 7 to 9 o'clock
Holland Michigan 1879.

Mary Van Raalte Kollen

President Gerrit Kollen

Van Raalte came to the farm home of a widow with three sons, and told her that the youngest, whom he had been told by the village teacher was a bright boy, should be sent to college. The mother protested using the Old World argument that they were farmers, and the boy must not be brought up above his class; to which came the American answer, that this was not the Netherlands, but a land where each one could do the work for which he was best fitted. The mother obeyed the summons — as who did not — the boy went to college, and later became one of the most successful presidents of that institution.

Gerrit J. Kollen, LL.D. ...brought to his task a commanding personality, an intimate acquaintance with the character, aims and needs of the institution, a rich and varied experience along financial lines, and an enthusiasm and optimism that refused to be overcome by obstacles.

Anna Arendina Harking Van Raalte,
    ninth child and sixth daughter of Christina and Albertus Van Raalte, was born on April 4, 1853, in Holland Michigan, and died there on March 6, 1854, aged eleven months and two days. "Our dear youngest child of eleven months, a lovely flower has God taken from us: this bitter cup was sweetened very much by our Father: we could trust the little one with perfect easiness in the hands of our blessed Saviour."

Anna Sophia Van Raalte,
    tenth child and seventh daughter of Christina and Albertus Van Raalte, was born on July 27, 1856, in Holland Michigan. She was given the same first name as her sister who had died; Sophia was the name of her aunt by marriage in the Netherlands, wife of her mother's brother, Dominie C. G. De Moen. She married John H. Kleinheksel, who was a professor at Hope College, working closely with his brother-in-law, President Gerrit Kollen. They had four children: Paul Edwin Kleinheksel, born June 16, 1885; Anna Vera Kleinheksel, born February 20, 1889; Frank De Moen Kleinheksel, born May 5, 1892; and John Lewis Kleinheksel, born July 11, 1896. Vera Kleinheksel died, aged 21; her brothers married and had children. Ann Kleinheksel died on February 2, 1914, aged 57.

Albertus Van Raalte wrote to his friend John Garretson, at the Board of Domestic Missions, and shared family news along with accounts of the new school. "My dear wife has got a baby, now three months old. She was first healthy but now are the lungs affected, So that notwithstanding she is growing we can not exspect that she will grow up. The glorious light of Gospel truth makes it all well." Ann did grow up, had children, and like all her brothers and her sister Mary, her line has continued.

As in many families, the generations spread apart. Although Holland was home to many in the second generation, and has continued to be the home of many in later generations, the descendants of Albertus and Christina Van Raalte live in many parts of America and the rest of the world. The generations spread apart in time, as well. Albertus was seven years older than Dirk, but Albertus' first child was born in 1859, Dirk's first child thirty years later. More than three decades — 37 years — passed between the births of the first and last of the Van Raalte grandchildren. More than a century — 123 years — separated the first and last deaths in that generation, from the first dead infant mourned by Mina and Pieter Oggel to the death of Mary and Gerrit Kollen's only child, Estelle Kollen Pelgrim, at the grand age of 98, in 1984.

Albertus Van Raalte's family honored his name by using it often. Albertus Christiaan Van Raalte IV, was Allie, pronounced *ah-lee*, and descendants wondered how they were related to the Ollie they heard talked of. When he died in 1932, an newspaper article identified him as "the grandson of Dr. A. C. Van Raalte, founder of Holland, who settled in this wilderness before a tree was cut..." and went on to describe his own interests: "Mr. Van Raalte was quite a horseman in his day and for many years owned 'Turk,' considered Holland's 'wonder horse' forty years ago." Albertus Christiaan Van Raalte Gilmore was known as Raalte — perhaps even as a child, when he was tucked in beside his visiting grandfather on cold winter nights. "The little Van Raalte sleeps with me," Albertus Van Raalte wrote to Dirk. "He is a precious talker. I hope that God will use him as a preacher of the gospel." It was yet another Albertus Christiaan Van Raalte, whom his grandfather never knew, who grew up to become a minister — Dirk's first son, born a generation later than his first cousin with the same name.

Christina Van Raalte's name was also given to many Christines across the generations. Like her brothers-in-law Pieter Oggel, Gerrit Kollen and John Kleinheksel, Christine Gilmore served her father's college. Gilmore Hall honors her name.

One of Holland's Leading Women Is Taken Away
WAS THE ONLY REMAINING CHILD OF FOUNDER VAN RAALTE STILL LIVING
Funeral to Be Held From Hope Memorial Chapel

Holland and vicinity were shocked to hear of the death of Mrs. Christine Van Raalte Gilmore, the only surviving member of the family of Dr. Albertus C. Van Raalte, the founder of Holland...her birthday anniversary having just occurred, when she received congratulations and floral tributes from hosts of friends.

...Mrs. Gilmore became dean of women of Hope College in 1887, following out the wishes of her illustrious father, who had told her to do what she could for the "College of Hope." She held that position for a quarter of a century. She was vice-president for the Western Board of Domestic Missions, and organized the Federation of Women's Societies, which she served as president for many years. The society contributed to medical missions in Inhambone, East Africa, and the Christine Van Raalte Gilmore home there is named in her honor. Interment will take place in Pilgrim Home Cemetery, near the spot where the first log church was built by Dr. Van Raalte and his followers.

Christine Van Raalte Gilmore

THE ORPHANAGE THAT WAS NEVER USED — 1847

He was the virtuoso orator of God's word.

Albertus Van Raalte spoke with great power, had great personal energy, and knew himself to be a servant of God. He was a patriot and a leader who believed wholeheartedly in the righteousness of his cause. There are pages in history marked with blood, where the stories of others with power, energy and intense belief are recorded. Great leaders can use their power to create havoc and war, and can inspire their followers to hate and destroy.

There was something lacking in Albertus Van Raalte. Though he could speak with a voice like thunder, with words that burned in the hearts of his hearers, he did not create rage; he did not inspire his followers to rage against others. Instead, the fire within him spread warmth and light. What he lacked was selfishness. He did not place himself beside God and so he did not perceive criticism of himself and his causes as attacks on God which must be avenged.

Van Raalte Accused of Not Teaching the Catechism.

Brother B... having accused Dominie Van Raalte of not preaching the Catechism, he replied that he, precisely because of his special love for the truth in the Catechism, will take all possible means, in his work on Sunday afternoons, to make the Catechism intelligible to his hearers; that to this end he will always draw out from his hearers all kinds of objections and remarks, by which he himself is greatly profited, so as to be able to labor the more efficiently.

Holland Classis Minutes , October 14, 1851

Van Raalte's manner of instruction did not seem to one of the classis members to be the right kind of teaching — indeed did not seem to be teaching at all. It was not formal lecturing and a question and answer drill; he talked, and encouraged the learners to talk and even to question and express doubts. When he was accused in a formal meeting, he did not retaliate, or deny, or apologize and promise to reform. He explained his method and its benefits; and afterwards it is likely that he continued to teach the catechism, blessedly undistracted by angry thoughts about the man who had accused him.

As our family came from Racine, Wisconsin to help Van Raalte with the lumbering and ship building, they left everything behind including their religion, which was Catholic. Dominie Van Raalte gave a Dutch sermon in the morning but his congregation would not allow English spoken in the church. So in the afternoon he gave an English translation in someone's home. My great-grandmother figured this was better than no religion, so they attended in the afternoon.

Maxine Hopkins Robbert's account, from her father, of how her family came to join Hope Church

---

Dominie Van Raalte didn't exhaust himself trying to persuade his consistory and parishioners to change their views about how closely the church and the Dutch language should be linked. Instead when his colony was no longer peopled solely by Dutch-speakers, he preached in the morning, and met in the afternoon with people who wanted to hear the biblical message in English. He knew that the people who came to hear him were welcome to God; therefore they understood that they were welcome to God's servant. In his lifetime, three Dutch Reformed churches were founded in Holland, and they accommodated the diversity of Dutch and English language speakers. The first church began outdoors.

Sundays [this was in the summer of 1847] we held religious services under the trees near his house. Dominie Van Raalte stood behind a table which served as a pulpit and his listeners sat around him on logs on which boards were placed. Those Sundays truly were an inspiration for us because of the spiritually pithy sermons we were privileged to hear for encouragement to labor and endure. However, because holding services in the open, even though under trees, could not continue very long, it was decided to build a church. This church had to be built of logs, exactly as in the case of our houses, for we lacked all other building material. Southeast of the city of Holland, near the spot where Dominie Van Raalte's house stood, a structure was erected of squared hemlock logs. It cost us much difficulty, labor, and expense, but it served for a considerable time as the meeting house for holding public religious services.

The mortality [in that time] had left us a number of abandoned orphans. To care for these we went to work to build an orphanage; but this soon proved an unnecessary undertaking, for sympathetic friends took them into their homes. Yes, also in this respect it was discovered that the Lord does not need rich funds of gold in order to carry out His promises that he will support widows and orphans in their distress. He knew how to maintain them in all need, in our poor Kolonie where nearly every person lived in poverty. He abundantly blessed not only those who cared for the orphans, but later also showed His rich favors to those who were cared for in this manner.

Egbert Frederiks' Reminiscences

In the summer of 1847, the people of Holland would gather in the virgin forest near his house, and Van Raalte, standing on a rude wooden platform, preached to them. Sermons in these days were no twenty minute exhortations. The service began in the morning at nine-thirty and lasted from two to three hours. Those who came from a distance brought a lunch and ate it at noon so as to be on hand for the afternoon service beginning at two. Those living nearer went home to a hastily prepared meal and returned in time for the afternoon meeting. ...Sunday was a day of rest from all worldly occupations, none save necessary work was done. The housewife spent her Saturday in baking and cooking so that none of that work need occupy her time on Sunday. To the children it was often a long day, for no games were allowed, but to the elders it was a day of spiritual and intellectual uplift. On this day especially they worshipped God in his house, and heard the Word interpreted by their pastor.

The solemnity of the long service did not hinder certain kindly disposed women from surreptitiously handing to the restless children the delicious round, white peppermints taken from the pockets of voluminous skirts. These pockets contained not only a delight for the little ones, but a more delicate refreshment for the women, in the form of a tiny silver box with a hinged cover called a "colognedosje." In this box was a sponge saturated with cologne. When handed down the pew, it was considered etiquette for each woman to smell of it and then pass it on to her neighbor.

The sacrament of the Lord's supper celebrated quarterly was an occasion of sacred and solemn enjoyment. ...[A] long table covered with a white cloth, upon which the elements were placed, was set in front of the pulpit. After the sermon, during the singing of a psalm, the minister came down and took his place at the middle of the table facing the congregation, and the people one by one came forward and took their places around him. In the earliest days, elders watched to see that no one who had not the right to partake of the sacrament took a seat. After the usual service of the blessing and prayer, the bread and wine were passed around the table, and then with the singing of another psalm, these people returned to their seats and others took their places. ...It is reported that during the first summer, when service was held under the trees near Van Raalte's house, there was no table and that the people received the sacrament standing, while Van Raalte compared them with the Israelites who having their loins girded for the journey ate the passover standing.

And thus shall ye eat it; with your loins girded, your shoes on your feet, and your staff in your hand; and ye shall eat it in haste: it is the Lord's passover.

Exodus 12: 11, KJV

In the little clearing beside the log house where Albertus and Christina Van Raalte and their children lived, colonists gathered for Sunday worship, and to mourn at funerals and rejoice at weddings and baptisms. Christina Van Raalte's signature regularly appears as witness on marriage certificates.

Worship services were held in the open air at first while the weather was favorable. A clearing was made in the forest. The logs were rolled in rows and used as pews. The pulpit was one of the tree stumps. The firmament was the roof. The surrounding trees were the walls. Not only were church services held in the open air, but marriage ceremonies were performed in the open air as well.

This is to certify that Hendrik Grijpmast Michmershuizen... and Hendrika Johanna Rozendom... are joined in marriage by me in a Church meeting held in the great temple of God's creation, in the woods of Michigan, near the village Holland, on the 8th day of August, in the year of our Lord, 1847.
In the presence of

H. Matting   *A. C. Van Raalte Minister of the Gospel*
C. J. Van Raalte

His message to these newlyweds illustrates his ability to connect an overarching message to a particular event. It was summer, and the roses were in bloom. Everyone came to his cabin for wedding refreshments, made ready by the *Juffrouw*. The dominie made a play on words to link the bride's name — Rozendom — with *rozeboom*, meaning rose tree, and cautioned the married couple that their life together would be a mixture of joy and sorrow, saying, "There is a rose tree under the window of my home, but there are sharp thorns on it."

Albertus Van Raalte was able to be "the virtuoso orator of God's word" because the words of the Bible were in his mind as well as in his heart. In his time, Biblical references were abundant in everyday talk and public speaking, in personal letters and published writing, and they were readily recognized and understood. Van Raalte was not a scholar who analyzed the Bible, but his knowledge of the Bible was wide and deep. His own gracious nature enabled him to use this knowledge to enlighten, comfort and inspire.

the first log church

The guidance of an ingenious professor at the University of Leiden was the spark that forever influenced his preaching style. Like other students, Albertus Van Raalte was required to give a sermon, which would be critiqued. His situation at the university was not a comfortable one; his friends had graduated and gone out in the world and caused trouble. To most of his professors he was an irritating remnant of that very annoying group; to most of his classmates he was an oddity. The text he chose for his sermon was about the peace which is felt by those who know their faith justifies their actions.

> **𝕿herefore being justified by faith, we have peace with God through our Lord Jesus Christ.**
>
> 𝕽omans 5: 1, 𝕶𝕵𝖁

Toward the close of his university course it was necessary to preach a sermon which was to be heard and criticized by students and faculty. A large group of students had gathered to hear this heretic, this member of an independent group. The professor in charge was Professor Clarisse, who stood by Van Raalte and defended him on many occasions. The young student, who was nervous over the event, had written out his sermon with great care and placed it in a pocket in the back of his long coat. Professor Clarisse accompanied his student as far as the platform, and as the young man ascended the steps the professor dexterously removed the sermon, which he saw sticking out of the pocket.

Here is a tale that clutches at the heart of everyone who has ever suffered pangs of nervous anticipation about public speaking. Reading this part of the story, it is clear there will be a happy ending: Albertus Van Raalte survived the shock of discovering he had no notes, spoke with power and vigor, and "preached an excellent sermon that astonished his professor and held the earnest attention of the students who had come to mock him." One part of that conclusion does not ring true: the astonishment of Professor Clarisse. The story is so pleasing because it illustrates many of the good qualities of two good people: professor as well as student. If the professor had been merely playing a prank to see what would happen, Albertus Van Raalte would not have remembered him affectionately. This was a professor with some of the best gifts a teacher can have: he cared about his student, he knew his student, he backed his judgment by taking a risk which paid off handsomely. The profession of teaching is sometimes frightening for thoughtful practitioners; every day may be the day that one student will remember throughout life, and what will that memory be? Professor Clarisse is of blessed memory in the biographies of his most famous student. The story also illustrates an array of

Albertus Van Raalte's gifts. Besides quick wit, the story provides one more evidence of qualities which he showed throughout life: courage, the habit of preparing well for the tasks at hand, love of the Bible, and a tendency to see the best in people. It took real bravery to begin to speak to a hostile audience without the prop so carefully prepared. But he had thought long and deeply about the passage which was his text, and he loved God's word, so he was not adrift and stammering without his notes; instead he could speak freely and from the heart. And then, when he recounted the event at the time and in after years, he did not make it a story about his own success despite professorial mischief: he told about his professor's ingenuity and wisdom.

Eloquence was a natural talent, nurtured by the confidence he gained through this experience, and afterward by year after year of preaching — to the devout, to the troubled, to those who came to heckle and harass and find fault, to the rowdy boys in the back row and the elders at the front and the families filling the pews and crowding the church so that bigger churches were needed to hold them all.

Having learned that he could speak without notes, he usually did. Therefore the few sermon notes which have survived are small and cramped, not in his usual beautiful handwriting. They are clearly not intended to be read, or even referred to, during preaching; they are notes to be looked over before a sermon, and added to afterwards. Scholarly attention to his sermon notes has provided proof that Van Raalte gave the same sermon more than once — an unusual preacher indeed! — because the notes are annotated with dates and places where the sermons were given. However, thanks in part to the freedom Professor Clarisse gave him, sermons he repeated were not identical to one another.

Van Raalte spoke to his hearers in a place and at a time in their world and in the individual lives of particular people in that audience. He preached the timeless word of God, and gave it meaning for each person at the moment that he spoke, and left no doubt in the minds of his hearers that God was concerned with every part of their lives. Throughout his life he believed firmly that religion and the civic life of the community and the country were inextricably linked — a view which caused him to be severely criticized during the Civil War and at other times as well, by people who did not share his opinions. When there was only one church in the colony, Sunday services were the best possible times to give guidance and direction — or orders. An early example of this kind of instruction occurred when four irate Ottawa tribesmen and their interpreter told Van Raalte, after a Sunday morning service, that Dutch colonists had taken the metal containers which they kept attached to sugar maple trees to collect sap. Apparently the colonists thought these trays would make excellent small troughs for pigs. Van Raalte was enraged, and assured the men that he would see to it that no such thing would happen again.

> *Dominie Van Raalte so worded his sermon that afternoon that he said that this incident, which had been reported to him during the noon hour, was a shame for the reputation of the Hollanders. He ordered those who had made themselves guilty of these low-down acts to leave the colony, the sooner the better.*

The most tragic events in the colony were the funerals. In every period of history including our own, death is not orderly. Sometimes the young precede the old, and parents must endure the death of a child. In the nineteenth century children died of diseases which a few decades later became readily preventable or curable. Many sad accounts were recorded in family histories; many more of these losses have been by now wholly forgotten.

Cornelius Vander Meulen, as a young man, was brought into the *Afscheiding* movement in the Netherlands, and then into the ministry, because of his need to seek God after his two children died on the same day. He and his wife had five more children. Two were sons, and both became ministers. "He had made a promise, after the death of his two children in Rotterdam that, should God grant him another child and that it should be a son, he would consecrate him to the service of the Gospel." All his daughters died in childhood. In America, Anna died in March, 1849, aged eight, and then two more daughters were born: Sara, and then another little Anna. On the same cold and bitter day in February 1857, "for the second time in his life, he lost two of his children in one day: Sara, hardly eight, and Anna, four." In a blinding snowstorm, the sexton tried to heap the earth into a high mound to mark the little girls' grave. "But the aged dominie stopped him, exclaiming, 'It is enough, God will know his own.'"

Albertus and Christina Van Raalte also knew the pain of watching children die. Other parents recalled their ability to bring solace through their visits, and all the congregation remembered the power of Dominie Van Raalte's sermons. On one occasion, when a young boy had drowned in Black Lake, Van Raalte used as a text David's lament for his son Absalom, treating his words first as those of a state leader, then as the words of a believer, and then as the words of a father.

> And the king said unto Cushi, Is the young man Absalom safe? And Cushi answered, The enemies of my lord the king, and all that rise against thee to do thee hurt, be as that young man is.
> And the king was much moved, and went up to the chamber over the gate, and wept: and as he went, thus he said, O my son Absalom, my son, my son Absalom! would God I had died for thee, O Absalom, my son, my son!
>
> II Samuel, 18: 32-33, KJV

> *The families of Post and Van Raalte often exchanged coffee visits. The latter was fine in conversation. Once he entertained us by relating his experience in the old country in being tried for schism. He had many trials with his people. He lost an infant and conducted the funeral service himself in English. Mr. Post and myself were there to sympathize with them as Mrs. Post was ill. We were the only Americans present.*
>
> Elvira H. Langdon: School Reminiscences

Elvira Langdon was the schoolteacher Henry Post had engaged to teach in the colony, Fifty years afterwards, an efficient Semi-Centennial Committee found out she was still living and wrote to her with a request that she send them an account of her memories of the colony's early days. She remembered that Van Raalte's descriptions of controversy and persecution in the Netherlands were entertaining; the Dominie was a renowned conversationalist and these were stirring tales of strange events in a distant land. She also remembered hearing him preach a funeral sermon for his own child. Two of the four Van Raalte daughters born in the colony died in infancy, but because we know when Elvira Langdon was there, we know that this was Christina and Albertus Van Raalte's first child to be born in America: Maria Wilhelmina, born September 16, 1848; died September 2, 1849. From Miss Langdon's reminiscences one fact can be learned, and another can be inferred: Van Raalte's sermon was powerful; Miss Langdon remembered it wrong. In yielding his child to God, he moved the hearts of his hearers — and the Dutch listeners heard his words in Dutch, which is surely the language in which he spoke, and an English-speaking listener heard him so vividly that later, in her memory, it was as if he had spoken to her in her own language.

Most of the people Albertus Van Raalte knew were active, convinced, professing Christians. In general they were not consistently good and kind and sensible and appealing, but they did, however, believe in salvation and were confident that they were saved. Van Raalte preached to them — eloquent, passionate, doctrinally sound sermons — but he was not a revivalist, and he did not try to identify which people in his congregation or among his friends who thought they were among God's elect, might not be. Nevertheless, there are letters which show that he was deeply worried about the state of some souls, and that those who knew him valued such care and remembered it, even when their faith was lacking.

Among his other gifts, Albertus Van Raalte had the truly remarkable capacity to pursue those he loved relentlessly, urging them to look to their souls — and to do so without losing their love and friendship. In the face of repeated exhortation, the response Van Raalte hoped for was a joyful conversion; other possibilities would have been feigned acquiescence, or an abandonment of the relationship. Instead there were people who knew their lives did not meet the standards of his faith, and they did not turn away from him nor wish him to turn away from them. There was a longstanding friendship and alliance between Albertus Van Raalte and Henry D. Post. Hollander and American, believer and questioner, they worked as a team for years. From the early days of the colony to the end of Van Raalte's life, Henry Post was staunch in the defense of his friend, and his friend's people. His biblical reference to the widow's mite evokes a vivid image of the wealthy easterners and the poor but devout Hollanders whose gift he was sending to the Board of Domestic Missions.

> *Mr. J. S. Bussing, Treasurer, Board of Domestic Missions*
> *February 13, 1851, Holland, Ottawa County, Michigan, Black River*
> Dear Sir:
>   *Enclosed is thirteen Dollars from "the Missionary box" for the First Reformed Dutch Church of Holland. The amount is small, but it has <u>cost</u> more than $10,000 would have cost some of your old rich New York churches. It is in more respects than one, like the poor widow's two mites. It is also the <u>first fruits</u> from a people struggling with privation in the wilderness. May it do much good to the cause to which it is given. You will please acknowledge its safe receipt by letter to me.*
>   *With much respect,*
>   *Yours in Christian Bonds,*
>   *H. D. Post*

> And Jesus sat over against the treasury, and beheld how the people cast money into the treasury: and many that were rich cast in much. And there came a certain poor widow, and she threw in two mites, which make a farthing. And he called unto him his disciples, and saith unto them, Verily I say unto you, That this poor widow hath cast more in, than all they which have cast into the treasury: For all they did cast in of their abundance; but she of her want did cast in all that she had, even all her living.
>
> Mark 12: 41-44, KJV

In 1858, Post and Van Raalte had known each other for more than ten years. A letter from Henry Post to Albertus Van Raalte stands as the statement of an honest and honorable man, troubled by the gulf between his own life and the Christian ideal, and by actions he observed among confessing Christians. Some years after this letter was written, Henry and Anna Post, along with Philip and Margaret Anna Phelps, were founding members of Hope Reformed Church.

> *May 9th, 1858*
>
> *Dear Sir,*
>
> *I promised to write you on the subject of my religious feelings and, with some little feeling of reluctance, I take up my pen to redeem my pledge. I cannot doubt your sincere solicitude for my spiritual welfare, although I have almost learned to doubt whether there is such a thing as sincerity. My religious feelings have been for a long time like the talent which was hid in a napkin and although conscience has constantly warned me that I was neglecting my duties to God and to my fellow men, still, upon different pretexts, they have been put off. I frequently resolve that I will begin to live the life of a Christian, as I feel I ought, but when it comes to the point of beginning, I shrink from it from a sort of feeling of shame and dread of the ill natured remarks of those who surround me. When it comes to taking up the cross my heart fails me. And I have many strong feelings and prejudices to overcome. The point of loving one's enemies seems beyond reach. I am aware of cherishing very strong friendships and enmities, although they are not always manifested outwardly. It is hard to forgive a deliberate willful injury, coolly inflicted with malice. I think, so far as my observation goes, there are few persons who do. Yet I feel that a sincere Christian must be able to do so, and must do so. I cannot degrade the standards of Christian duty to the level of professing Christians around me, as I do not feel justified in my own conscience in doing so. Although I have much enthusiasm in my nature, I am not excitable, and what would move most people to deep feeling does not affect me in the least. For that reason my most serious feelings have been in solitary communion with my own conscience.*
>
> *The necessity of coming out, and standing alone and unsupported seems a great difficulty to overcome. But it is the position I occupy, and I cannot change it by vain regrets. I thank you for your kind feelings for me, and hope you may yet see your prayers in my behalf answered.*
>
> *Yours truly,*
>
> *H. D. Post*

The most vivid example which has come down to us of Albertus Van Raalte's earnest endeavors to bring a soul to salvation is found in his letters to his son Ben. In both interactions, the documents are one-sided: we hear one voice and infer the other. We have the words of Henry Post responding to Van Raalte; on the issue of Ben's salvation, we have only his father's voice.

Parental love can be beautiful, but that love is sometimes manifested in parental terrors — *what will become of my child?* — and in persistent, overbearing efforts to make things come right. Albertus Van Raalte was frantically concerned about what would become of his sons when they died. Dirk was no more religious than Ben — in one of Christine's lively letters she refers to Dirk as "the same old scoffer and teaser" — but Dirk was showered with practical advice, while Ben was warned again and again to beware of damnation. In his mid-teens his father wrote, "that you labor diligently in the use of your time is fine, but you wear the curse of God upon all that you do, if at the same time you neglect your God"; in his late teens, "you must understand my language or you will be eternally lost"; in his twenties, "consider for a moment that you are a sinful being and consider your awful destiny."

> *...Another matter, my child: that you labor diligently in the use of your time is fine, but you wear the curse of God upon all that you do, if at the same time you neglect your God, your soul, and the means of grace... Oh, my child, how awful, how terrible that is: to incur a curse upon yourself in everything: and truly, that is what you do as long as you disregard God. I predict that God will contend and struggle with you: I do not know how long, but as long as He does not forsake you your path will be one filled with bitterness and obstacles: and I would be happy in the hope that you will humble yourself before your God. But woe be to you, my child, if you, with your hardened heart, get your way here below: for then I see you becoming ripe for damnation: and then you will probably be swept away suddenly. Oh Benjamin, you are not ready to die, to meet your God, for you will have nothing to do with God: you harden your heart, and surrender only to the world, which will betray, deceive and destroy you. ...Oh, dear child, will your bosom always remain closed to the love of God? Turn, my child, to your God and seek His fellowship.*

> *Benjamin, I often think about you, I pray to God for you often. ...God has given you repeated remarkable warnings but you have hardened yourself. The thought that you will be damned in your resistance disturbs me. ...I pray of you, seek that above all else: the loss of the soul means everything is lost, irrevocably lost, lost for ever! ...everything in this life will be a disappointment to you...*
>
> *... Oh, my child, you must understand my language or you will be eternally lost: and if you do not understand it, or cast it from you and neglect it, some day you will understand it, but, alas, then it will be too late, with the terrible remorse on your death bed: and oh, if you do not allow yourself to be led, my child, how my warnings, and also this warning, will torment you in the eternal damnation. Flee to God's throne. Bare your heart to our Savior, and submit yourself to a prayerful study of God's Word, which can make one wise unto salvation.*

> *I felt the need to write a hastily composed letter to send our regards and express my father love since in a few days you will be celebrating your birthday anniversary. Your welfare is very important to us. ...Just consider for a moment that you are a sinful being and consider your awful destiny. Life is short, passing swiftly and preparing for eternity is of the greatest importance,. Dear son, look up! My heart is with you - may there never be any separation to all eternity.*

Those letters are painful to read. Some readers may see the son as a lost soul; others may see narrowness in the father's beliefs. Yet the interchange can be seen as reflecting the good in both son and father, in the pursued as well as the pursuer. Ben might have told his father forcibly to leave him alone — it is possible that his younger brother Dirk did just that — but he didn't; the letters continue down the years. Ben might have crumpled the letters angrily and thrown them away, but he didn't; he saved them, and they endured to be preserved in historical archives. He didn't pretend to beliefs and feelings he lacked, but he had much of his father's native good spirit, so he didn't become anguished and bitter. He loved and honored his father, and was himself a happy man. The nature of both father and son made their mutual love possible.

Holland, September 22, 1875
Soldiers Reunion of the 25th Michigan Infantry

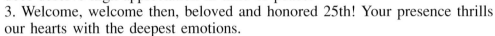

1. The officers and soldiers of the reknown 25th of Michigan infantry! In the name of the Mayor of the city and its inhabitants we welcome you to our midst. We rejoice to receive you as our guests. We thank you for the honor to hold your reunion in our city.

2. Your self-sacrifice for our country, so much fought for, and thought of, in time of danger, does deserve high appreciation in time of peace.

3. Welcome, welcome then, beloved and honored 25th! Your presence thrills our hearts with the deepest emotions.

a. We tasted the cup of bringing our beloved ones on the altar of our country. And yet, though there are among us tears and sorely bleeding hearts, yet how many are given back to us. You all are monuments of God's sparing mercy and love!

b. We partake feelingly in your ennobling reunion, your reflections, meeting. Your presence revives to us history never to be forgotten! Here rises up that impressive parting meeting. There that house of God, our place of prayer for you, while you fought our battles. Yonder that post office, which we dayly did take by storm with its thrilling tidings. Days never to be forgotten! Surely your presence is a solem voice within us. Bless the Lord, O my soul (and forget not all His benefits). Yes, while He did spare, sustain, and inspire you, with the great object and calling, He did give that calm wisdom, confidence, and firmness to stand like rocks in the storm. That memorable 4th of July on that Green River Bend posterity will remember. And that heroic stand, by which the threatening tidal wave of destruction over the northern regions was stayed, will receive its just dues as a most important link in our victory, securing the salvation of our invaluable union, and in the deliverance from our African slavery, and the peace of our country. Yea, we say, Bless the Lord, O my soul! (And while we enjoy peace on earth, thanks and glory be to our God on high!)

In the same time (finally, therefore, before close) we desire greatly to acknowledge our indebtedness to you who did defend at the peril of your lives our great blessing of order, security, law, and liberty, our national life, while we enjoyed home comforts. May none of us ever ungreatful forget it.

And to you, the leader of our beloved 25th, Cornell Moore, gratefull we avail ourselves of the opportunity to express our highest esteem, our love, our thanks. You were to those entrusted to you, our dear ones, a caring and sparing father, a confidence and courage inspiring leader. You are, under God, the cause that we may see our 25th covered with honor. we (express) acknowledge our indebtedness to you and express most emphatically our hearty thanks.

Closing with the sincere wish that you may enjoy peace, that we may be spared from the dire necessities of war, that gospel wisdom may prevail on earth, and that you all may earn that never fading crown in the higher battles under our Captain of Salvation, Jesus Christ.

Closing wish — dues to the leader — indebted to you — matter of thanks — History listing — experience

216

Ten years after the end of the Civil War, Albertus Van Raalte gave a major address in English. This required effort and courage, because the one purpose for which Albertus Van Raalte did not use the English language was for preaching, although he would willingly meet with groups on Sunday afternoons to give a translation of his morning sermons. Delivering this speech was more like giving a sermon than like announcing, conferring, conversing, discussing, exhorting, explaining, expounding, persuading and parleying, which he could accomplish effectively in English or Dutch. He had been asked to address the veterans of the 25th Michigan Infantry. His audience would include his sons Ben and Dirk, other members of the Albertus C. Van Raalte Post of the Grand Army of the Republic, their friends and families, and most of the proud citizens of Holland and surrounding areas.

Because this was one of the few occasions where Van Raalte doubted his own fluency, we have his speech as he wrote it out, complete with topic headings and the spelling and grammar that show his impressive, but not absolute, mastery of English. *Cornell*, for example, is a brave attempt at the unfathomable spelling of *Colonel*. The force of Van Raalte's support for the Union cause, ten years after the war's end, is apparent in his pointing out the sites that evoke memories: the railroad station where the troops left in triumph for a struggle which would last so much longer than anyone anticipated, and bring such pain; the church where fervent prayers were raised; the post office "which we dayly did take by storm" for tidings of loved ones.

> *It was as a pastor that Van Raalte was best loved, revered and remembered in the hearts of his people. From the beginning he took charge of the little congregation at Holland; he visited them in their homes, upon occasions of sorrow and of joy; he buried their dead, baptized their children, married their young people, ...and he preached to them. At the midweek meeting on Wednesday evening, on Sunday afternoon, ...,but especially on the Sabbath morning, he fed their souls. "The whole man was often completely under the power of Eternal truth - all aglow with it. It swayed, inspired, and moved him on. It made him eloquent. When in the pulpit, he seemed like a mighty electric battery. The lightning flashed, the thunder roared. Himself ablaze, he set his audience on fire. His utterances burned their way into human souls. Thus we have witnessed and felt."*

Albertus Van Raalte saw himself and all the world around him in the light of eternity. For him, the present and the past were seamlessly one, and he knew that believers were blessed by the surrounding presence of a great throng of those who had witnessed to their faith at personal cost. He was the servant of the Lord and of his people, and he was remembered by many as a source of great strength. The man who had to stand on a platform to be seen by all his congregation was a towering preacher.

America, the Beautiful

by Katherine Lee Bates

O beautiful for spacious skies, for amber waves of grain,
For purple mountain majesties above the fruited plain!
America! America! God shed his grace on thee;
And crown thy good with brotherhood from sea to shining sea!

O beautiful for pilgrim feet, whose stern impassioned stress
A thoroughfare for freedom beat across the wilderness.
America! America! God mend thine every flaw,
Confirm thy soul in self-control, thy liberty in law!

O beautiful for heroes proved
    in liberating strife,
Who more than self their country loved,
    and mercy more than life!
America! America!
May God thy gold refine,
Till all success be nobleness,
    and every gain divine!

O beautiful for patriot dream
    that sees beyond the years
Thine alabaster cities gleam
    undimmed by human tears!
America! America!
God shed His grace on thee,
And crown thy good with brotherhood
    from sea to shining sea!

Oh beautiful for patriot dream that sees beyond the years.

Few other people are as powerfully connected with a single place on earth as Albertus Van Raalte is connected with Holland. His character and the events of his life combined to bring him to Holland Michigan, and to keep him here when he sought to go away. The main result of his one major failure as a leader — his effort to build a second colony in Virginia — was to bring him back to his people and his place. "He lived for his people, planned conscientiously for his people, and died with his people."

Dying took a long time, as if his spirit and energy could not be easily overcome. For more than four months the people of the Colony talked of the Dominie's declining health, and prayed for his recovery, amid their daily concerns. Death came late in the fall of 1876, but reports of his illness began to appear in the summer.

> Rumors have been floating about town for a few days past that Rev. Dr. A. C. Van Raalte, the founder of the Holland colony, is confined at his residence with a serious illness from which he cannot recover. The doctor has been an indefatigable worker, whose energy has been exercised for the benefit of the colony, and whose labors and sacrifices will long be remembered by those who have walked hand in hand with him during the inception and growth of this city and vicinity.
>
> *Allegan Journal*, August 5, 1876

On the same day in Holland, a brief news item referred to a continuing, painful illness. Newspapers, then as now, need to fill their columns, and one strategy the *Holland City News* used was to include a lengthy "Jottings" column, a weekly potpourri of news, weather, civic and social announcements, commentary, and advertisements, as these excerpts show:

August 5, 1876
- The weather is beautiful and dry.
- Dr. Van Raalte is not improving, he remains a terrible sufferer.
- If you want to be a tee-totaller and have a nice refreshing drink anyhow then call at Andrew Flietstra's and try his excellent cider or pop.

August 26, 1876
- Grapes and Peaches are on the market.
- On Wednesday and Thursday the weather was sultry and hot.
- Hope Church will be opened again tomorrow, and Prof. Scott will fill the pulpit.
- It is rumored on the street that Dr. Van Raalte is failing, and will not survive many days.

October 7, 1876
- Have you paid for your paper?
- Five weeks more and all the campaign agonies will be over.
- Don't fail to read what Dr. Aikin has to tell a suffering people.
- The Penobscot Indians, to the number of 800, are attending the Centennial.
- Dr. Van Raalte still remains a sufferer, and apparently gradually declining.
- The hum of the pensive mosquito is becoming more and more faint nightly.

October 21, 1876
- The weather is changeable.
- Only two more issues before election.
- Seamen's wages at Detroit range from $1.50 to $1.75 a day.
- Dr. Van Raalte is gradually declining by terrible suffering.

For much of this time Dominie Cornelius Vander Meulen was also seriously ill. Older by about ten years, his experiences had paralleled those of Van Raalte, to whom he had consistently been a faithful colleague and friend. Thirty years earlier, in the Netherlands, a large group of people in the province of Zeeland formed an association to plan for emigration to America. They called Dominie Vander Meulen to be their pastor, and paid the passage for him and his family. In 1848, a year after Van Raalte established *de Kolonie*, the group from Zeeland arrived in the outskirts of Holland, calling their new settlement by the name of their former home in the Netherlands. Vander Meulen was pastor of the Zeeland congregation from the settlement's inception until 1859; he later served congregations in Chicago and Grand Rapids. He died, aged 75, on August 23, 1876, and was buried in Zeeland. It was said of him that "in his most difficult hours he never lost the peace and unchanging convictions of his heart; he was continuously content with the will of God."

As Van Raalte's illness worsened, his children gathered — not around his bedside, because he did not wish to go to bed — but around his arm chair, where he sat fully dressed, from coat to well-shined boots. At the end of October his chest congestion was so great that he nearly suffocated. Dominie Pieters, his successor as minister of First Reformed Church, held a special hour of prayer; for a time he seemed to be recovering, but then he grew steadily weaker. He could no longer see clearly, his breathing was labored, and it became difficult for him to speak. His daughters were with him constantly: Helena, Albertus' wife, who was like a daughter; Minnie Keppel, his oldest daughter; Mary Kollen; and the youngest of the Van Raaltes' children, Ann Kleinheksel. In his suffering he longed for the comfort which his wife had always brought him, saying, "Oh, if only I could rest my head on Mother's breast for a while …but I will see her, …Jesus and her will I see, have patience." Dirk, for whom the autumn had been a time of campaigning for state office, came to be with his father; then Benjamin came. Christine Gilmore, traveling in haste from Illinois, did not arrive in time to see her father again before he died.

On the last evening of his life he celebrated Communion with his children. Now, when he could no longer exercise his lifelong gift for speaking fluently and powerfully, his brief words were still beautiful. He thought of his own life with humility — "I have done something with God's help, but it could have been so much more" — but he thought of the future with confidence and joy. "My boat dances on the rushing waves; soon I will enter the harbor," he whispered, and he urged his children not to weep for him. "Do not cry; as I shut my eyes you can be sure that I will rejoice in the hallelujahs before the throne."

He remained in great pain. At five o'clock in the morning he asked for something to eat, but when it was given to him he put it aside. Later he asked for something to drink, and Dirk gave him a spoonful of water, which he was able to swallow. He said *dank je* — thank you — and those were his last intelligible words. He shut his eyes and tried to speak, but no one could understand. He smiled and pointed upward toward heaven, and at seven-thirty he died.

> *At that time there was much activity throughout the country and also in Holland in connection with the elections which were to be held in November. Both the Democrats and Republicans were busy and one evening there was a rally held by both parties. A torch light parade was held by both parties until late at night and political speeches were made in both Dutch and English. There was activity every day until November 7th. ...But on the morning of election day Dominie Van Raalte died and his death made everyone so sad that election day passed quietly.*
>
> from the diary of Grace - Geesje - Van der Haar Visscher

Thirty years earlier, he had been nearing the shores of America — it was November 17, 1846, that Albertus and Christina Van Raalte and their children arrived in New York. He died on Tuesday, election day. The funeral was held on Saturday, November 10. It had been delayed because people were coming from a distance, including Thomas W. Ferry, then vice-president of the United States. "It was the most beautiful of our beautiful fall days. The air was soft and sweet, the sky blue with here and there a white cloud that drifted off like a ship in full sail. ...Everything breathed peace and calmness." The whole city was in mourning, and there was silence throughout the city during the funeral. Young Henry Dosker, later to become Van Raalte's first biographer, was there. "At that hour among the closely packed crowd in the gallery, staring at the coffin, I took on the decision, if God spared me, to study and write about this man's life."

> **Hij neigt zijn oor, ik roep tot Hem al mijn dagen,**
> **Hij schenkt mij hulp, Hij redt mij keer op keer.**
>
> metrical version of Psalm 116: 2
>
> **Because he hath inclined his ear unto me,**
> **therefore will I call upon him as long as I live.**
>
> Psalm 116:2, KJV

Isaac Cappon led the funeral procession, followed by the members of the City Council and Town Board, and the pall bearers flanked on both sides by consistory members. Then came family members, ministers and elders of the congregation, the President and trustees of Hope College, college faculty and representatives from the public school, students, judges of the city and area, representatives from the press, people on foot and then those riding in carriages. The first part of the procession had already reached the cemetery before the last part had started.

And it came to pass. when the Lord would take Elijah into heaven by a whirlwind, that Elijah went with Elisha from Gilgal. And Elijah said unto Elisha, Tarry here, I pray thee; for the Lord hath sent me to Bethel. And Elisha said unto him, As the Lord liveth, and as thy soul liveth, I will not leave thee. So they went down to Bethel. And the sons of the prophets that were at Bethel came forth to Elisha, and said unto him, Knowest thou that the Lord will take away thy master from thy head to day? And he said, Yea, I know it; hold ye your peace.

And Elijah said unto him, Elisha, tarry here, I pray thee; for the Lord hath sent me to Jericho. And he said, As the Lord liveth, and as thy soul liveth, I will not leave thee. So they came to Jericho. And the sons of the prophets that were at Jericho came to Elisha, and said unto him, Knowest thou that the Lord will take away thy master from thy head to day? And he answered, Yea, I know it; hold ye your peace.

And Elijah said unto him, Tarry, I pray thee, here; for the Lord hath sent me to Jordan. And he said, As the Lord liveth, and as thy soul liveth, I will not leave thee. And they two went on. And fifty men of the sons of the prophets went, and stood to view afar off: and they two stood by Jordan. And Elijah took his mantle, and wrapped it together, and smote the waters; and they were divided hither and thither, so that they two went over on dry ground.

And it came to pass, when they were gone over, that Elijah said unto Elisha, Ask what I shall do for thee, before I be taken away from thee. And Elisha said, I pray thee, let a double portion of thy spirit be upon me. And he said, Thou hast asked a hard thing: nevertheless, if thou see me when I am taken from thee, it shall be so unto thee; but if not, it shall not be so.

And it came to pass, as they still went on, and talked, that, behold, there appeared a chariot of fire, and horses of fire, and parted them both asunder; and Elijah went up by a whirlwind into heaven. And Elisha saw it, and he cried, My father, my father, the chariot of Israel and the horsemen thereof. And he saw him no more: and he took hold of his own clothes, and rent them in two pieces.

He took up also the mantle of Elijah that fell from him, and went back. and stood by the bank of Jordan: And he took the mantle of Elijah that fell from him, and smote the waters, and said, Where is the Lord God of Elijah? and when he also had smitten the waters, they parted hither and thither, and Elisha went over. And when the sons of the prophets which were to view at Jericho saw him, they said, The spirit of Elijah doth rest on Elisha. And they came to meet him, and bowed themselves to the ground before him.

II Kings 2: 1-15, KJV

The services were in Dutch and English. Philip Phelps preached on the text, "Know ye not that there is a prince and a great man fallen this day in Israel?" Roelof Pieters' text was taken from the story of the prophet Elisha receiving the power of Elijah, when that great prophet was taken up into Heaven: "My father, my father, the chariot of Israel and the horsemen thereof!" As Van Raalte had requested, the congregation sang Psalm 116 in Dutch.

But there was no Elisha to inherit the power of this prophet. Van Raalte's wisdom, his charismatic leadership and his generosity of mind had often held people together, but "[his] moderating presence was gone after 1876." After he died, controversies sprang up, almost as if there was a spirit in and around his colony that had been waiting for a great and pacifying leader to be gone.

It was tempting then — as it is now — to take an easy and exciting path, attempting to feel and appear righteous by pointing at others as evil or wrong. Differences of opinion over whether it was right to join a group with exclusive membership and rules and rituals which were secret, escalated into a fierce battle purporting to be about good and evil. The Masons were a secret society; and what, people asked, were those secrets? In Holland, as elsewhere in America, traveling speakers drew crowds to lectures in which frightening tales were told, sinister rites depicted. One such lecture was given at First Church, and Hermanus Doesburg, never one to minimize a quarrel, editorialized that the event was "a disgrace to the city and especially to that church, and we believe firmly that if the spirit of its first pastor could rise and speak, he would say 'To what use is this my temple put?'"

Passions escalated between those who feared and opposed the Masons and those who belonged to the several lodges in Holland, between those who tried to compose the quarrel and those who found pleasure or profit in exacerbating it. Roelof Pieters' influence was reduced when he became ill; he died in February 1880. Henry Utterwick, the pastor of Third Church, left Holland and joined another denomination. First Church split away from the Reformed Church of America, and joined the Christian Reformed Church, which had been established in 1857. Today denominational differences are respected and there is friendliness among members of the different churches; then it was not so.

There was controversy at the college as well as in the churches. Without his friend and leader, Philip Phelps was unprotected. The money he had lent to support the development of the Amelia Colony had been repaid, but his financial rashness was roundly condemned by denominational leaders. College funds were depleted; plans to develop a theological seminary seemed greatly unwise to church members in the east, where there already was a perfectly good seminary to which people could travel. In 1878, the General Synod of the Reformed Church passed a resolution, calling for the resignation of Philip Phelps and Cornelius Crispell. "It sometimes becomes necessary to sacrifice men to save institutions... for the President of Hope College, we, with every member of this Synod of the entire Reformed Church have a profound respect. ...[T]he Reformed Church owes him a debt of obligation which can it never repay... still the truth must be spoken. Confidence in Hope College such as is absolutely essential to its salvation cannot be restored to the eastern churches save by a change both in the presidency and the chair of theology." Phelps and Crispell resigned, and all the college faculty submitted their resignations also, but only those of Phelps and Crispell were accepted. The Reverend G. Henry Mandeville of New York City was named Provisional President; Professor Charles Scott was named Acting Vice President. Mandeville stayed in the east to raise funds; Scott served as administrator of the college.

It is hard to pursue in our own lives the great goal envisioned in the psalms, to seek to know what is true and do what is right, ourselves, and to think of others gently and work for peace. Albertus Van Raalte could do that, and often he could lead others to do so. He could not always prevail in his lifetime, however, and for a time after his death, many people took a different path. Yet his influence remained, and has endured, for good.

> 𝔐ercy and truth are met together; righteousness and peace have kissed each other.
>
> Psalm 85: 10

We need to read about heroes. More than that, we need to walk a middle way between hero worship and distrust. Perhaps knowledge of Albertus Van Raalte's life may inspire leaders, and followers also, to judge thoughtfully but without rancor, to cultivate the habit of respect, and to become accustomed to learning from the good in others. "The history of every country," Willa Cather wrote, "begins in the heart of a man or woman." Holland is a small part of America, its founding a small piece in the huge, variegated panorama of American history. But the city truly began in the heart of Albertus Van Raalte, who chose where it was to be, and set it on a path of growth and goodness. And all things and people combined to bring him to this place: the scourge of cholera, the enthusiasm of his friends, the pettiness of those in authority at the university and in the state, the love and devotion and talents of his wife, the skill of the Southerner's captain, the support of De Witt and Wyckoff and Romeyn and Duffield and Kellogg, the loyalty and admiration of Bernardus and Janna Grootenhuis, of Henry and Anna Post, of Philip and Margaret Phelps, the gifts and talents of the man himself.

In a narrative about emigration from the Netherlands, a picture has this caption: *De separatistenleider in de provincie Overijssel en de "Mozes en Aäron" figuur in de gescheidenis van Holland-Michigan.* Albertus Van Raalte was indeed the leader of his congregation in the Netherlands, and of his colony in Holland Michigan. It was a special gift to him, and blessing to them, that he could be for them both their Moses and their Aaron. Moses was a great leader, but he was "slow of tongue," and the Lord provided his brother Aaron to speak for him. Albertus Van Raalte was both leader and orator, and his ideas and words were glorious.

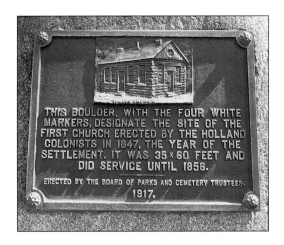

> And 𝔐oses said unto the Lord, O my Lord, J am not eloquent, neither heretofore, nor since thou hast spoken unto thy servant: but J am slow of speech and of a slow tongue. …And the anger of the Lord was kindled against 𝔐oses, and he said, Is not Aaron the Levite thy brother? J know that he can speak well. And also, behold, he cometh forth to meet thee: and when he seeth thee, he will be glad in his heart. And thou shalt speak unto him, and put words in his mouth: and J will be with thy mouth, and with his mouth, and will teach you what ye shall do.
>
> Exodus 4: 10, 14-15, 𝔎𝔍𝔙

Dominie Van Raalte lived in a handsome home at the eastern end of town. Stately Van Raalte Hall, central to the Hope College Campus, was built and dedicated during the presidency of his son-in-law, Gerrit Kollen. Van Raalte Memorial Hall was almost as versatile as Van Raalte himself. Over the years it housed science classes and laboratories; the first faculty offices and a pingpong table; student service organizations, a Theater Club and rehearsal hall, and an interfraternity room; the first bookstore and the first coffee shop, both student-run; business offices, the registrar's office, the alumni office, the president's office. It was designed "to stand as a monument to the memory of the founder of Holland." The Van Raalte home stood vacant for many years, and was eventually razed to make way for handsome and vigorously used athletic fields. Van Raalte Hall burned in 1980. Where those buildings stood, there are beautiful grounds where people work and play and learn and see the beauty of the changing seasons.

Where is his monument today? Theologian Martin Marty makes an unusual statement in his introduction to a text on the secession in the Netherlands and the Dutch emigration: "this story is not only for the Van Raalteites, very few of whom would know that that is what they are." What is a Van Raalteite? The writer does not say; he only tells us they exist, without awareness of that heritage, but he expresses an important truth about Van Raalte's legacy. Most of the people whose life has been affected for the better because he lived do not even know that he lived — his name is unknown to them. It can truly be said of Albertus Van Raalte, *if you seek his monument, look around you*. And his influence has been such that it can also be said, *if you seek his monument, look within you*.

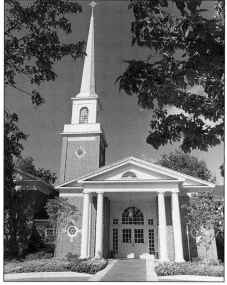

Schoon zijn uw heem'len uitgebreid,
Op velden govend graan.
Op bergen vol met majesteit,
En 't dal met ooft belaan.
Amerika, Amerika
God gaf Zijn gunst u mee.
Gij staat gekroond
War eenheid troont
Van zee tot blauwe zee.

Over the years, many people have praised Albertus Van Raalte. When those early residents of the colony who had lived to old age recollected him, they remembered him with great admiration. Because he was so powerful a person, their memories of him were not blurred and bland, though they were sometimes overstated. Henry Brown said that Van Raalte's leadership was so firm and successful that "grumblers went with wolves and bears from this redeemed waste," but the evidence is clear that not every grumbler did disappear. Those who read the reminiscences of people who knew Van Raalte will note that Henry Brown grew up to be a lively raconteur, willing to stretch a point to make a good story. Edward Cahill, who also had a gift with words, expressed an idea that endures.

> *Dominie Van Raalte lived at the eastern end of town in a very comfortable frame house. I met a short man, [riding on] horseback, dressed in white overalls, strong voice, nervous, quick, and shortspoken. He did not seem sympathetic, but resolute and thoughtful. He was a man of extraordinary faith and devotion. He could look out of woods and swamps by faith to see what industry and thrift could do. Nor did he falter from doubt or fear to lay foundations out of all proportions to their surroundings. Holland now justifies his shrewd foresight, and grumblers went with wolves and bears from this redeemed waste.*
>
> Henry J. Brown's Reminiscences

> *In the sixty years since I knew him, three generations have been born and have grown or are growing to manhood and womanhood in the Colony. Most of these never saw the Founder and only knew him by tradition. He was a great man, whom everybody who came within the circle of his influence respected and loved. He had a gentle but most persuasive personality. He was a gentleman of the old school; but he was more than that, for he was one who loved his fellowmen and labored unselfishly for their good. May his memory be forever kept green in the Colony which he founded and which has done so much for the welfare of this state of their adoption!*
>
> Edward Cahill's Reminiscences

"After him was no one like him," a biographer wrote, "and he was the best of all. So people say, and such talk is easy to understand." There were people in the colony who wouldn't have agreed with that — who wouldn't have said it and who wouldn't have wanted to hear it. Most of those people would have been surprised to find — what seems probable, given the character of Albertus Van Raalte — that he himself would not have wanted to hear it, and would never have believed it. He, who always looked to a bright future, would not have wanted the best to be in the past. "When people were angry at him, he smiled; when people complained he talked of hope and pointed to the future." When he died, he smiled and pointed upward.

References

Barraclough, Geoffrey. 1982. *The Times Concise Atlas of World History.* Maplewood NJ: Hammond.

Bartlett, John. 1968. *Familiar Quotations, Fourteenth Edition.* Boston: Little Brown.

Boatner, Mark Mayo III. 1959. *The Civil War Dictionary.* NY: David McKay.

Boorstin, Daniel J., ed. 1966. *An American Primer.* NY: Penguin.

Boorstin, Daniel J., ed. 1975. *Portraits from The Americans: The Democratic Experience.* NY: Random House.

Bradford, Ned, ed. 1956. *Battles and Leaders of the Civil War.* NY: Appleton-Century-Crofts.

Bratt, Katherine. 1947. Mrs. A. C. Van Raalte. *The Young Calvinist, (November), 26-27.*

Brooks, Van Wyck. 1944. *The World of Washington Irving.* Cleveland: World.

Brooks, Van Wyck, & Bettmann, Otto L. 1956. *Our Literary Heritage: A Pictorial History of the Writer in America.* NY: E. P. Dutton. .

Bruins, Elton J. 1971. Holocaust in Holland. *Michigan History, 15,* 289-304.

Bruins, Elton J. 1974. What Happened in 1857? *Reformed Review, 27,* 120-126.

Bruins, Elton J. 1977. Albertus C. Van Raalte and His Colony. In *Albertus Christiaan Van Raalte 1811-1876-1976. Centennial Studies. Reformed Review 30,* 83-94.

Bruins, Elton J. 1983. The Masonic Controversy in Holland, Michigan, 1879-1882. In Peter De Klerk and Richard R. De Ridder, eds. *Perspective on the Christian Reformed Church: Studies in Its History, Theology, and Ecumenicity.* Grand Rapids MI: Baker Book House.

Bruins, Elton J. 1991. Albertus Christiaan Van Raalte: Funding His Vision of a Christian Colony. Paper presented at the *Eighth Biennial Conference of the Association for the Advancement of Dutch American Studies,* September 19 and 20, 1991. Hope College.

Bruins, Elton J. 1995. *The Americanization of a Congregation, Second Edition.* Grand Rapids MI: Eerdmans.

Bruins, Elton J. 1996. "An American Moses"; Albertus C. Van Raalte as Immigrant Leader. Paper presented at *Sharing the Reformed Tradition: The Dutch-North American Exchange, 1846-1996,* November 15. The Historical Documentation Center for Dutch Protestantism, the Free University, Amsterdam, & the Roosevelt Study Center, Middelburg, the Netherlands.

Brummelkamp, Antonie. 1847. *Holland in Amerika, of De Hollandsche Kolonisatie in den Staat Michigan.* Arnhem, the Netherlands: J. W. Swann. Translated by Henry ten Hoor, 1976.

Brummelkamp, Antonie, & Van Raalte, Albertus C. 1846. *Landverhuizing of Waarom Bevorderen Wij de Volksverhuizing en Wel Naar Noord Amerika en Niet Naar Java?* Amsterdam.

Buechner, Cecilia Bain. 1976. *The Pokagons.* Berrien Springs MI: Hardscrabble Books. Originally published in 1933.

Buley, R. Carlyle. 1951. *The Old Northwest: Pioneer Period 1815-1840. Volume Two.* Bloomington IN: Indiana University Press.

Butterfield, Roger. 1957. *The American Past.* NY: Simon and Schuster.

Capers, Gerald M. 1959. *Stephen A. Douglas, Defender of the Union.* Boston: Little Brown.

Catlin, Janice Van Lente. 1992. *The Civil War Letters of Johannes Van Lente.* Okemos MI: Yankee Girl Publications.

Catton, Bruce. 1956. *This Hallowed Ground.* NY: Doubleday.

Catton, Bruce. 1960. *The American Heritage Short History of the Civil War.* NY: Dell.

Catton, Bruce. 1961. *The Coming Fury.* NY: Doubleday.

Catton, Bruce. 1965. *Never Call Retreat.* NY: Doubleday.

Catton, Bruce. 1984. *Michigan: A History.* NY: Norton.

Classis Holland: Minutes 1848-1858. 1950. Translated by a Joint Committee of the Christian Reformed Church and the Reformed Church in America. Grand Rapids MI: Eerdmans.

Clevely, Hugh. 1958. *Famous Fires.* NY: John Day.

Commager, Henry Steele, ed. 1949. *Documents of American History.* NY: Appleton-Century-Crofts.

Davis, Burke. 1959. *To Appomatox: Nine April Days, 1865.* NY: Rinehart.

Deedy, John. 1976. *Literary Places: A Guided Pilgrimage.* Kansas City: Sheed Andrews and McMeel.

deKruif, Paul. 1932. *Men Against Death.* NY: Harcourt Brace.

Descola, Jean. 1963. *A History of Spain.* NY: Knopf.

Dosker, Henry Elias. 1893. *Levensschets van Rev. A. C. Van Raalte, D. D.: Een Man Krachtig in Woorden en Werken.* Nijkerk, the Netherlands: C. C. Callenbach.

Drabble, Margaret., ed. 1985. *The Oxford Companion to English Literature, Fifth Edition.* NY: Oxford.

Dunbar, Willis F. 1903. *The Michigan Record in Higher Education.* Detroit MI: Wayne University Press.

Dunbar, Willis F., & May, George S. 1995. *Michigan: A History of the Wolverine State, Third Revised Edition.* Grand Rapids MI: Eerdmans.

Duncan, Russell, ed. 1994. *Blue-eyed Child of Fortune: The Civil War Letters of Colonel Robert Gould Shaw.* NY: Avon.

Duyckinck, Evert A. 1861. *National History of the War for the Union, Civil, Military and Naval, Volumes I, II and III.* NY: Johnson, Fry.

Educators of Michigan. 1900. Chicago IL: J. H. Beers.

Ergang, Robert. 1939. *Europe: From the Renaissance to Waterloo.* Boston: D. C. Heath.

Evans, Ivor H., ed. 1981. *Brewer's Dictionary of Phrase and Fable: Centenary Edition, Revised.* NY: Harper & Row.

Evans, Richard J. 1992. Epidemics and Revolutions: Cholera in Nineteeth Century Europe. In Terence Ranger & Paul Slack, eds. *Epidemics and Ideas: Essays on the Historical Perception of Pestilence.* Cambridge England: Cambridge University Press.

Everett, Franklin. 1878. *Memorials of the Grand River Valley.* Grand Rapids MI: Grand Rapids Historical Society.

Fellman, Michael. 1995. *Citizen Sherman: A Life of William Tecumseh Sherman.* NY: Random House.

Flexner, Stuart Berg. 1976. *I Hear America Talking: An Illustrated History of American Words and Phrases.* NY: Touchstone.

Foote, Shelby. 1958, 1963, 1974. *The Civil War: A Narrative, Volumes I, II & III.* NY: Random House.

Garrett, Wilbur E., ed. 1988. *Historical Atlas of the United States, Centennial Edition.* Washington DC: National Geographic Society.

Gildea, Robert. 1986. *Barricades and Borders: Europe 1800-1914.* NY: Oxford.

Grimm, Joe, ed. 1987. *Michigan Voices: Our State's History in the Words of the People Who Lived It.* Detroit MI: Detroit Free Press.

Grant, Ulysses S. 1865-1866. *Personal Memoirs of U. S. Grant.* NY: Webster & Co.

Grootenhuis, Bernardus. (1888, 1912). Our History. *De Grondwet,* April 16, 1912. Translated by Peter T. Moerdyk.

Grun, Bernard. 1991. *The Timetables of History: Third Revised Edition.* NY: Simon & Schuster.

Guthrie, Douglas. 1946. *A History of Medicine.* Philadelphia: J. B. Lippincott.

Haggard, Howard W. 1996. *The Doctor in History.* NY; Barnes & Noble. (First published in 1934.)

Hall, Kermit L., ed. 1992. *The Oxford Companion to the Supreme Court of the United States.* NY: Oxford.

Harrison, Frederic. 1924. *William the Silent.* NY: Scribners.

Herold, J. Christopher. 1987. *The Age of Napoleon.* Boston MA: Houghton Mifflin.

Hickey, Donald R. 1990. *The War of 1812: A Forgotten Conflict.* Urbana IL: University of Illinois Press.

Hinsdale, Burke A. 1906. *History of the University of Michigan.* Ann Arbor MI: University of Michigan.

Hitchcock, Charles B., ed. 1968). *These United States: Our Nation's Geography, History and People.* Pleasantville NY: Reader's Digest Association.

Hope College, First Catalog and Circular. 1865. Holland MI: Hope College.

Hope College Remembrancer. 1867. Holland MI: Hope College.

Hope Church Historical Booklet: Our Time for Rededication. 1982. Holland MI: Hope Church.

Hyma, Albert. 1947. *Albertus C. Van Raalte and his Dutch Settlements in the United States.* Grand Rapids MI: Eerdmans.

Inaugural Addresses of the Presidents of the United States From Goerge Washington 1789 to Lyndon Baines Johnson 1965. 1965. Washington D.C.: United States Government Printing Office.

Irving, Washington. 1864. *History of New York from the Beginnning of the World to the End of the Dutch Dynasty.* NY: George P. Putnam.

Jacobson, Jeanne M. 1996. Remembering the Early Days. *Joint Archives Quarterly, 7,* 1, 4-5.

Jenks, William L. 1944. Michigan Immigration. *Michigan History, 28,* 67-100.

Katzman, David M. 1978. *Seven Days a Week.* NY: Oxford University Press.

Keegan, John. 1988. *The Mask of Command.* NY: Penguin.

Kennedy, John F. 1986. *A Nation of Immigrants, Revised and Enlarged Edition.* NY: Harper & Row.

Kerber, Linda K., Kessler-Harris, Alice, & Sklar, Kathryn Kish, eds. 1995. *U. S. History as Women's History.* Chapel Hill NC: University of North Carolina Press.

Ketchum, Richard M., ed., 1959. *American Heritage Book of the Pioneer Spirit.* NY: Simon & Schuster.

Lagerwey, Walter. 1985. Dutch Literary Culture in America. In Robert P. Swierenga, ed. *The Dutch in America: Immigration, Settlement, and Cultural Change.* New Brunswick NJ: Rutgers University Press.

Large, E. C. 1940. *The Advance of the Fungi.* NY: Henry Holt.

Lewis, Lloyd. 1932. *Sherman: Fighting Prophet.* NY: Harcourt, Brace.

Lord, Walter. 1960) *The Good Years: From 1900 to the First World War.* NY: Harper & Brothers.

Lorant, Stefan. 1968.*The Glorious Burden: The American Presidency.* NY: Harper & Row.

Lucas, Henry S. 1947. *Ebenezer: Memorial Souvenir of the Centennial Commemoration of Dutch Immigration to the United States held in Holland Michigan 13-16 August 1947.* NY: Netherlands Information Bureau.

Lucas, Henry S. 1955a. *Dutch Immigrant Memoirs and Related Writings.* Assen, the Netherlands: Van Gorcum.

Lucas, Henry S. 1955b. *Netherlanders in America: Dutch Immigration in the United States and Canada.* Ann Arbor:University of Michigan Press. .

Lyons, Paul Robert. 1976. *Fire in America!* Boston MA: National Fire Prevention Association.

Mahon, John K. 1991. *The War of 1812.* NY: Da Capo.

Marty, Martin. 1987. In tenZythof, Gerrit J. *Sources of Secession: The Netherlands Hervormde Kerk on the Eve of the Dutch Immigration to the Midwest.* Grand Rapids MI: Eerdmans.

Massie, Larry, & Massie, Priscilla. 1990. *Walnut Pickles and Watermelon Cake.* Detroit MI: Wayne State University Press.

Martis, Kenneth C. 1982. *Historical Atlas of U. S. Congressional Districts, 1789-1983.* NY: Macmillan.

May, George S. 1967 *Pictorial History of Michigan: The Early Years.* Michigan Historical Commission.

McCullough, David. 1992. *Brave Companions: Portraits in History.* NY: Simon & Schuster.

McPherson, James M. 1988. *Battle Cry of Freedom.* NY: Oxford Press.

Meijer, Reinder P. 1971. *Literature of the Low Countries.* Assen, the Netherlands: Van Gorcum.

Merriam-Webster's Medical Desk Dictionary. 1993. Springfield MA: Merriam-Webster.

Morison, Samuel Eliot. 1965. *The Oxford History of the American Nation.* NY: Oxford.

Motley, John Lothrop. 1904. *The United Netherlands: A History, from the Death of William the Silent to the Twelve Years Truce - 1609, in Four Volumes.* London: John Murray.

Motley, John Lothrop. 1904. *Life and Death of John of Barneveld, in Two Volumes.* London: John Murray.

"Mrs. Cornelius." 1850. *The Young Housekeeper's Friend.* Quoted in *The Country Kitchen 1850.* 1965. Scotia NY: Americana Review.

Mulder, Arnold. 1947. *Americans from Holland.* Philadelphia PA: Lippincott.

National Party Conventions: 1831-1972. 1976. Washington DC: Congressional Quarterly.

Nevins, Allan. 1950. *The Emergence of Lincoln, Volumes I and II.* NY: Scribner's.

Nevins, Allan. 1959. *The War for the Union, Volumes I and II.* NY: Scribner's.

Oostendorp, Lubbertus. 1964. *H. P. Scholte: Leader of the Secession of 1834 and Founder of Pella.* Doctoral Dissertation: Vrije Universiteit te Amsterdam.

Pereboom, Freek, Hille, H, & Reenders, H., eds. 1984. *"Van scheurmakers, onruststokers en geheime opruijers…": De Afscheiding in Overijssel.* Kampen, the Netherlands: IJsselakademie.

Pieters, Aleida J. 1923. *A Dutch Settlement in Michigan*. Grand Rapids MI: Reformed Press.

Pokagon, Simon. 1893. *The Red Man's Rebuke*. Hartford MI: C. H. Engle.

Portrait and Biographical Record: Muskegon and Ottawa Counties, Michigan. 1893. Chicago: Biographical Publishing Co.

Powers, Tom. 1994. *Michigan in Quotes*. Davison MI: Friede.

Quaife, Milo Milton, ed. 1940. *War on the Detroit*. Chicago: Lakeside Press.

Rapport, Samuel & Wright, Helen, eds. 1952. *Great Adventures in Medicine*. NY: Dial.

Ravitch, Diane, ed. 1991. *The American Reader: Words that Moved a Nation*. NY: HarperPerennial.

Rhea, Gordon C. 1994. *The Battle of the Wilderness: May 5-6, 1864*. Baton Rouge LA: Louisiana State University Press.

Rietveld, Ronald D. 1986. Hendrick Peter Scholte and the Land of Promise. *The Annals of Iowa, 48*, 135-154.

Roetman, H. 1986. *Rondom den Herdenbergh. (Round about the Hardenberg)* Historical Society of Hardenberg and Vicinity, the Netherlands.

Schoolland, Marian M. 1951. *The Story of Van Raalte*. Grand Rapids MI: Eerdmans.

Schoolcraft, Henry Rowe. 1839. *Algic Researches: Indian Tales and Legends, Volumes I and II*. Reprinted 1992. Baltimore MD: Genealogical Publishing Co.

Schrier, William, ed. 1966. *Winning Hope College Orations, 1941-1966*. Holland MI: Hope College.

Seldes, Gilbert. 1928. *The Stammering Century*. NY: John Day.

Severan, Bill, & Severan, Sue. 1963. *The State Makers*. NY: G. P. Putnam's Sons.

Shaw, Archer H. 1950. *The Lincoln Encyclopedia*. NY: Macmillan.

Shepard, Richard F. 1996. *The Paper's Papers: A Reporter's Journey through the Archives of the New York Times*. NY: Times Books

Sherman, William T. 1957. *Memoirs of General William T. Sherman*. Bloomington IN: Indiana University Press.

Shorter, Edward. 1987. *The Health Century*. NY: Doubleday.

Smith, Mrs. A. A. 1981. *A Pioneer Woman*. privately published, Joanna B. Smith, Lansing MI. (Originally published in *Grand Traverse Herald*, 1892.)

Stegenga, Preston. 1954. *Anchor of Hope*. Grand Rapids MI: Eerdmans.

Stimpson, George. 1946. *A Book about a Thousand Things*. NY: Harper & Brothers.

Stimpson, George. 1952. *A Book about American Politics*. NY: Harper & Brothers.

Swierenga, Robert P. 1965. The Ethnic Voter and The First Lincoln Election. *Civil War History, 11*, 27-43.

Swierenga, Robert P. 1980. Local-Cosmopolitan Theory and Immigrant Religion: The Social Bases of the Antebellum Dutch Reformed Schism. *Journal of Social History, 14*, 113-135.

Taylor, A. J. P. 1995. *From Napoleon to the Second International; Essays on Nineteenth Century Europe*. NY: Penguin.

ten Zythoff, Gerrit J. 1977. The Americanization of Albertus C. Van Raalte: A Preliminary Inquiry. In *Albertus Christiaan Van Raalte 1811-1876-1976. Centennial Studies. Reformed Review 30* (2), 77-82.

tenZythof, Gerrit J. 1987. *Sources of Secession: The Netherlands Hervormde Kerk on the Eve of the Dutch Immigration to the Midwest*. Grand Rapids MI: Eerdmans.

Thoreau, Henry David. (1906). *The Writings of Henry David Thoreau: vol IV, Cape Cod and Miscellanies*. Boston MA: Riverside Press.

Tilton, Eleanor M. 1947. *Amiable Autocrat: A Biography of Dr. Oliver Wendell Holmes*. NY: Henry Schuman.

Tuchman, Barbara W. 1981. *Practicing History*. NY: Ballantine.

Van Hinte, Jacob. 1985. *Netherlanders in America: A Study of Emigration and Settlement in the Nineteenth and Twentieth Centuries in the United States of America*. Robert F. Swierenga, general editor, and Adriaan de Wit, chief translator. Grand Rapids MI: Baker.

Van Loon, Hendrik Willem. 1940. *Van Loon's Geography: The Story of the World*. NY: Garden City Publishing.

Van Schelven, Gerrit. 1886. The Burning of Holland, October 9, 1871. *Report of the Pioneer and Historical Society of the State of Michigan, IX*. Reprinted in Lucas, 1995a (q.v.), pp. 1-13.

Vennema, Ame. 1920. Rise and Progress of Hope College. *Michigan History, 4*, 287-298.

Versteeg, Dingman. 1886. *The Pilgrim Fathers of the West*. Grand Rapids MI: C. M. Loomis. Translated by William K. Reinsma.

Wabeke, Bertus Harry. 1944. *Dutch Emigration to North America: 1624-1860*. NY: Netherlands Information Bureau.

Wagenaar, Larry J. 1989, 1996. *Guide to the Collections of the Joint Archives of Holland*. Holland MI: Joint Archives of Holland/Hope College.

Wagenaar, Larry J. 1991. *Supplement to the Guide to the Collections of the Joint Archives of Holland*. Holland MI: Joint Archives of Holland/Hope College.

Wagenaar, Larry J. 1992. *Early Political History of Holland, Michigan 1847-1868*. Unpublished Master's Thesis, Kent State University.

Wedgwood, C. V. 1944. *William the Silent*. New Haven CT: Yale university Press.

Weeks, Edward, & Flint, Emily, eds. 1957. *Jubilee: One Hundred Years of the Atlantic*. Boston MA: Little Brown.

Wichers, Willard, ed. 1930. *The Hope Milestone of 1930: Alumni Number*. Holland MI; Hope College.

Wichers, Wynand. 1964. Holland Academy in the Civil War. In Willis F. Dunbar, ed. *Michigan Institutions of Higher Education in the Civil War*. Lansing MI: Michigan Civil War Centennial Observance Commission.

Wichers, Wynand. 1968. *A Century of Hope 1866-1966*. Grand Rapids MI: Eerdmans.

Woodward, C. Vann. 1951. *Origins of the New South*. Baton Rouge LA: University of Louisiana Press.

Zylstra, Henry. 1942. A Mid-Nineteenth Century Dutch View of American Life and Letters. *Publications of the Modern Language Association of America, 57*, 1108-1136.

Endnotes

Reference sources used throughout all chapters include encyclopedias, atlases, maps, almanacs, Bibles and Bible commentaries, dictionaries including topical and foreign language dictionaries, dictionaries of quotations and biographical dictionaries; resource texts cited in endnotes are listed in the Reference Section. Many materials used are from archives, and abbreviations are used when they are cited: JAH-HHT: Holland Historical Trust Collection, Joint Archives of Holland, Hope College, Holland, Michigan; JAH-HOPE: Hope College Collection, Joint Archives of Holland, Hope College, Holland, Michigan; JAH-WTS: Western Theological Seminary Collection, Joint Archives of Holland, Hope College, Holland, Michigan; CCA-ACVR: Calvin College Archives-A. C. Van Raalte Collection, Calvin College, Grand Rapids, Michigan; RCA-BDM: Reformed Church in America, Board of Domestic Missions, New Brunswick Theological Seminary, New Brunswick, New Jersey. Letters are identified by sender and recipient, date, and archive; e.g., ACVR to Phelps, July 15, 1869, JAH-HOPE; the names of Albertus and Christina Van Raalte are abbreviated: ACVR and CVR; their children are referred to by first names: Ben, Dirk, Christine. Other adults are listed by last name, e.g., Oggel, Schieffelin, or by first and last name, e.g., Will Gilmore. A record of events kept by a woman who was part of the *Afscheiding* movement in the Netherlands, emigrated to Holland and was active in colony and city affairs, has been a valuable resource; it is archived JAH-HHT. The diarist was known as *Geesje*, a name difficult for English speakers to pronounce: a rough transliteration of the sound is *Hay-sha*. She married Jan Visscher and they and her two brothers Hein and Wouter Van der Haar were among the first to build houses in the colony; the place they lived was known for years as the Van der Haar farm. Many immigrants eventually anglicized their names, and there was sometimes variation in the names selected. One of Geesje Visscher's daughters was Gesina, and the diary's translator gives the diarist's name as Gezina. In family records of the Van der Haar family in *Portrait and Biographical Record...*, however, Mrs. Visscher's name is given as Grace. Throughout this book, the boxed diary entries are credited to *Grace - Geesje - Van der Haar Visscher*, and she is referred to in the text as *Geesje Visscher*, and in the endnotes as Grace Visscher, and her diary excerpts are referenced as *Visscher*. Other archived reminiscences and recollections are included through the text; in the endnotes below they are referenced only by last name; archival information is as follows: Rieks Bouws, JAH-HHT, Van Schelven: *Bouws*; Henry J. Brown, JAH-HHT, Van Schelven: *Brown*; Edward Cahill, JAH-HHT, Van Schelven: *Cahill*; Isaac Fairbanks, JAH-HHT, Van Schelven: *Fairbanks*; Egbert Frederiks, JAH-HHT, Van Schelven, *Frederiks*: Edward Harrington, JAH-HHT, Van Schelven: *Harrington*; Elvira Langdon, JAH-HHT, Van Schelven: *Langdon*; "The Civil War Recollections of John Nies," JAH-HHT: *Nies*; Anna Post, JAH-HHT, Van Schelven: *Post*; Jan Vogel, JAH-HHT, Van Schelven: *Vogel*; Evert Zagers, JAH-HHT, Van Schelven: *Zagers. The authors have vigorously attempted to ensure accuracy in the endnotes, as we have throughout the text; perspicacious readers who identify errors are encouraged to write to us, at Hope College, Box 9000, Holland Michigan, 49422-9000.*

CHAPTER ONE: **"Had he been placed by Providence at the head of a nation, he would have made a wise and powerful ruler ."** The title quotation is taken from Albertus Van Raalte's obituary in the *Holland City News*, November 11, 1876. The opening illustration shows a maquette, created in 1922 by Leonard Crunelle for Holland's 75th anniversary celebration. Sources that point out that Van Raalte was "short of stature" include biographies and recollections of those who knew him, as well as the two records cited - one from the city jail at Zwolle in the Netherlands, where Van Raalte was imprisoned early in 1837; the other the U.S. passport issued to Albertus and Christina Van Raalte in 1866. After the sesquicentennial celebration of the founding of Holland, Michigan, Van Raalte may no longer be remembered as short: a nine-foot statue will be erected in the city's Centennial Park. Quotations include "born a Frenchman, grew up a Dutchman...": tenZythoff 1977, p. 77; and "Napoleon, who knew only as much geography...": Van Loon, p. 212. A prolific, popular author whose books were translated into many languages, Hendrik Willem Van Loon (1882-1944) was, like Albertus Van Raalte, a transplanted Netherlander who made America his home. Information about the Napoleonic era is drawn primarily from Herold; for further background, see Taylor and Ergang. Quotations about Louis Bonaparte - ""while his actions in private life...", "I advise you to cultivate in private life...", and "did not halt in his flight..." are all from Herold, p. 246. Information about Van Raalte's birth comes from tenZythoff, 1977, p. 77, and from biographies and archived materials, which also provide information about his family and early years. The school certificate of "the excellent youth Albertus Christiaan..." is quoted from Hyma, p. 28; the anecdote about rabbits is from Pieters, p. 159. Sources for early nineteenth century United States history include Buley, Dunbar & May, and Morison. The quotation, "Although the inhabitants of the Michigan Territory...," is from Buley, p. 32; it should be noted (see Dunbar & May, p. 113) that John Griffin was not appointed until 1806. Samuel Huntington, Jefferson's first selection, declined: he was Chief Justice of the Ohio Supreme Court and had hoped to be named governor of the Michigan Territory; accepting a lesser position would have meant a salary reduction. Information about uniforms in Hull's militia is from Dunbar & May, pp. 116-117; also from this source: the Catholepistemiad, pp. 188-189, and tuition and admission at the University of Michigan, p. 284. Descriptions of Woodward as "brilliant and erratic" and "crafty and cantankerous" are from Quaife, p. 222, footnote, and Buley, p. 33, respectively; for the length of his service see Dunbar & May, p. 187. The quoted phrase "tangle of land claims" is a reprise of the quotation from Buley on the previous page. Sources for information about Native American nations include Buechner, Buley, and Dunbar & May. Information about Henry Rowe Schoolcraft is drawn primarily from Brooks, especially pp. 395-398. Schoolcraft was the author of *Algic Researches* (1839); he created the word *Algic* by combining *Alleghany* and *Atlantic*, to indicate the area in which the Algonquian nations lived. There has been a tendency among modern scholars to dismiss Schoolcraft's work for stereotypism, especially on the grounds that it inspired Longfellow's poem "Hiawatha." Such criticism should be balanced by appreciation of Schoolcraft's unique and comprehensive research. The quotation "In their dispositions the Indians of the lakes are peaceable..." is from James H. Lanman's, *History of Michigan, Civil and Topographical* (1839), p. 310, which is quoted in Buechner. Information about the War of 1812 is drawn primarily from Hickey, and Mahon, and additionally from Dunbar & May, Herold, Morison, and resource texts. Sources for quotations are "We pen these lines in mid-May, 1940...", Quaife, p. xiii-xiv; "By this increase in territory...", Herold, p. 310; "The core of the American navy...", Mahon, pp. 7-8; "few fir built frigates...", Mahon p. 9. Statistical information is also from Mahon, p. 7. Both Hickey and Mahon offer useful explanations of impressment. McCullough, pp. 200-201, provides an interesting brief anecdote about the Madisons' stay at the hexagonal Octagon House. Sources for the origin of "The Star Spangled Banner" are primarily Ravitch, p. 44-45 and Hickey, pp. 203-204. The song was not declared the U. S. national anthem until 1931.

Information about the Battle of New Orleans is taken primarily from Hickey, pp. 204-214 and Mahon, pp. 354-368. Note that though the pirate chief's name is sometimes spelled Lafitte, *Laffite* is the spelling preferred by most historians. Sources for quotations are "Bounded by a cypress swamp…", Ketchum, p. 128; "these d____d Yankees…", "hurled in as fast as we could bring them…", and "our lamented general's remains…", all Hickey, p. 212; "this species of milito-nautico…", Hickey, p. 297. Information about the Treaty of Ghent (the Peace of Christmas Eve) and the speed record in getting peace news to Boston are from Hickey, p. 296 and p. 298; for the quotation from the treaty, see Hickey, p. 296. The quotation, "After the War of 1812, the soldiers who returned…", is from Brooks, p. 396; this book is a useful resource for information about Schoolcraft, especially pp. 393-398. The quotation "where they would have room…" is from Grootenhuis, p. 4; he was referring to the needs of the Dutch colonists. Information about the land bounty is from Mahon, p. 335. The quotation "for the Indians…" is from Dunbar & May, p. 138. The surveyors' report is quoted in Grimm, p. 33. The rhyme "Don't go to Michigan…" appears in a number of sources, including Powers and Dunbar & May. Rude comments about developing territories were not uncommon; it is said (Stimpson, 1946, p. 398) that hot-tempered Philip Sheridan, later to become famous as a Civil War general, was asked how he liked Texas and answered, " If I owned Texas and Hell I would rent out Texas and live in Hell." Information about Cass and Mason as governors is taken primarily from Dunbar & May; for further information about Mason, see Severan & Severan. Mason was elected for two terms as governor, but the state experienced money problems and he became so unpopular that the legislature refused to read his farewell message. He moved to New York state and died there in 1843. In 1905 his remains were disinterred and buried with honor in Detroit's capital square. The quotation from Paul Fried's speech can be found in Schrier, pp. 37-38. Information about "the Toledo War" is drawn primarily from Buley, Catton 1984, and Dunbar & May, where the quotation from John Quincy Adams is given on p. 217. Buley, p. 193, maps the disputed boundary lines clearly. "Come all ye Michiganians…" is quoted in Grimm, p. 44. "Old Brown" was Brigadier Joseph Brown of the Michigan Militia; "this rebel Lucas" was Ohio's Governor Robert Lucas. If Ohio had chosen to name the county it created after an earlier governor, Return J. (Jonathan) Meigs, it could have been aptly named Return County. Catton 1984, gives information about the Stickney family. The map showing United States territory in 1837, prepared by Mark Cook, is based primarily on Barraclough, Garrett, and Martis. Michigan's state motto is patterned after a Latin quotation: *Si monumentum requiris circumspice.* (If you seek his monument, look around you.) It is the epitaph for the British architect Sir Christopher Wren, and is inscribed on a tablet in his most famous building, St. Paul's Cathedral in London.

CHAPTER TWO: "The idea of emigration swept over the land like a breath of God." The title quotation is taken from Brummelkamp and Van Raalte, in their pamphlet discussing the advantages of emigration to North America rather than to Dutch-controlled Java. Information about this period in Van Raalte's life in the Netherlands can be found in Dosker; Pereboom, Hille, & Reenders; Pieters; and Roetman; for further information about the secession see Oostendorp, tenZythoff 1987, and Wabeke; Gildea is a useful source for comparative information about emigration to America from European countries during this time period. Pieters, Chapter I, "Reasons for Emigration," is an especially helpful source. The phrase "walked … as a secret angel from God" is from a letter written by Albertus Van Raalte during his trip to the Netherlands in 1866, when another cholera pandemic had struck Europe and North America, ACVR to the colony, June 30, 1866, JAH-HOPE. Van Hinte, pp. 89-90 discusses the effect of the cholera epidemic in the Netherlands on Van Raalte and Vander Meulen. Information about cholera and the six devastating cholera pandemics is taken primarily from R. J. Evans, which is the source for these quotations: "an affliction that killed rapidly, remorselessly…", p. 154, and "massive vomiting and diarrhoea…", pp. 153-154. (Note the earlier spelling, -rrhoea..) The term "the health century" is taken from Shorter, p. 2. Edward Dimnent, fifth president of Hope College and later a faculty member, wrote a drama about Albertus Van Raalte and the founding of Holland, titled *"The Pilgrim: Seventy-fifth Anniversary Pageant,"* JAH-HOPE, for a college presentation. Women's roles included various kinds of weather (all bad), and diseases. Cholera's lines began dramatically: "I am cholera. When once I come within thy villages, when once I find a victim there, then go I not away." Additional quotations include "the Lord sent a striking angel…", Roetman, p. 191; "The death of his two only children…", Jacob Vander Meulen in Lucas, 1955a, p. 367; "I desired nothing so much…", Dosker. Information about Bilderdijk is drawn primarily from Meijer, pp. 184-196; the quotation, "had not the curse that came from Babel clipt the wings of poetry," is from Meijer, p. 188. Additional quotations include "Oh, that the people were one!", Van Raalte to Groen Van Prinsterer, September 21, 1846, Lucas 1955a; "and may God reward the noble Groen van Prinsterer…", Dosker. It should be noted that one unusual feature of some Dutch and French names of this period is the double surname, unhyphenated. Thus Gezelle Meerburg, Groen Van Prinsterer, and Merle d'Aubigne are all last names; the full names are George Frans Gezelle Meerburg, Guillaume Groen Van Prinsterer, and J. Henri Merle d'Aubigne. Confusion about this leads to indexing the names improperly, and thus making it more difficult to find information about them (when, for example, Gezelle Meerburg is listed as *Meerburg* in one text and *Gezelle Meerburg* in another). Additional quotations include "under God's blessing at some place in America we soon shall grow…", Van Raalte to Groen Van Prinsterer, September 21, 1846, in Lucas 1955a; "natural arrogance" (Budding, describing Scholte), Oostendorp, p. 77; "de profs hoeven mij geen liegen meer te leren…", Reenders, p. 101, and see also Oostendorp, pp. 37-38; "Van Raalte replied that like all other students…" and "if he too wished to push himself into the church…", Pieters, p. 162; "there is for example a law…", Pieters, p. 164. The story of the girl in the purple cloak appears in Pieters and also in Bratt; it is Pieters who credits a family member as the source. Family information is taken from genealogies. For *"Scheurmakers, onruststokers en geheime opruijers …"*, see Pereboom et al.; a translation of the three articles from the Napoleonic Code which were used in an attempt to halt the secession from the Hervormde Kerk is given in Pieters, p. 13; a slightly different translation of these articles is given by tenZythoff 1987, p. 49; "unfortunately, …the Dutch government did not understand..", is from Wabeke, pp. 88-89; *"eene zekere Van Raalte…* (A certain Van Raalte…) is quoted in Roetman, p. 195. Other quotations include "before Van Raalte moved to the more centrally located Ommen…" and "the horse is fresh and frisky…" *(Het paard is frisch en dartel…)*, Roetman, p. 197; "found friends and peace", Van Raalte's "Biographical sketch of Christina Van Raalte, written by A. C. Van Raalte, soon after her death," translated by Harry Boonstra, CCA-ACVR. Major sources for information about the potato murrain (pronounced *murr'-in*) are Large, and Wabeke; the latter is the source for the quotation, "every other night accounts are settled…", p. 91; the other quotations are from Large, pp. 16-18 and 31-36; see also Gildea, p. 8. "Two factors help to explain…" is from Wabeke, p. 95. (Note that Bertus Wabeke's book, published during World War II, is dedicated "To My Mother and Sister in Occupied Holland.") "Petitions for divine guidance..." is from Pieters, p. 38; Hendrik DeKruif's "The Ocean Voyage of Dr. A. C. Van Raalte" is archived, JAH-HHT; the quotation, *"Valsche munt..."* is from Johannes Kolvoord's acccount of Jan Kolvoord's travels from the Netherlands to *de Kolonie*, JAH-HHT; "and how sad a funeral is on the ocean..." is from the Reverend Gerrit Baay's description of his trip to Alto, in a letter to "My dear friends in the Netherlands," January 4, 1849, JAH-HHT. Wabeke, p. 109, describes the burial of a child at sea: the Biblical text quoted is part of Revelations 20: 13. The map showing United States territory in 1837, prepared by Mark Cook, is based primarily on Barraclough and histories of the Netherlands.

CHAPTER THREE: "Ik wist geen beter naam dan: HOLLAND" The title quotation is taken from a letter from Albertus Van Raalte to his brother-in-law Antonie Brummelkamp, in the Netherlands, 1847; a longer excerpt is quoted later in the chapter. The lengthy letter was published by Brummelkamp as *Holland in Amerika, of De Hollandsche Kolonisatie in Den Staat Michigan*, and is a source for information about the founding of the colony. The picture facing the title page shows East 14th Street in Holland when the road was under construction; the Biblical passage from Isaiah was used as an introduction to *Holland in Amerika*. Major sources for this chapter include Bruins 1977 and 1996, Dosker, Dunbar & May, Grootenhuis, Lucas 1955b, Pieters, Van Hinte, Versteeg, letters and newspapers of the time, and Van Schelven, "Historical Sketch of Holland City and Colony," JAH-HHT. Archived accounts and reminiscences are from *Bouws, Fairbanks, Frederiks, Harrington, Vissscher*, and *Zagers*. Quotations include "well known, because of his kindliness toward Dutch immigrants...", the diary of Hendrik Van Eyck, JAH-HHT, Van Schelven; "in Albany it was Wyckoff who most aided...", Pieters, p. 45; "the emigrants came with high hopes,...", Pieters, p. 43. Information about the Erie Canal is taken from Butterfield, Dunbar & May, and Morison; the story of the "Wedding of the Waters" and the quotation, "may the God of the heavens and the earth smile propitiously...", are from Butterfield, pp. 76-77. Additional quotations include "in those days the travel to the west...", **Johannes Kolvoord's acccount of Jan Kolvoord's travels from the Netherlands to *de Kolonie*, JAH-HHT**, Van Schelven; "the interference of the government..." in "Emigration from Holland", JAH-HHT, Van Schelven; "Our trials rose to the highest point...", Van Raalte's speech at the Ebenezer Celebration, in Lucas 1947; information about the meetings in Detroit and the resolutions passed there are from Pieters, pp. 52-55. For information about the Smiths and Old Wing Mission, see Smith, and *Fairbanks*. The anecdote about the naming of Pasadena is from Massie and Massie, p. 83; the quotation "As soon as we commenced..." is from Grootenhuis. For information about land acquisition, including treaties with Native American nations, see Barraclough, Buechner, Dunbar & May, and Morison; for an excellent summary of land cessions and compensation, see Dunbar & May, chapter 8: "Exit the Fur Trader; Enter the Farmer," especially pages 146-154. For information about the attitudes of the Dutch settlers and the Native American residents, see interviews with Chief Blackbird, and with Hoyt Post, JAH-HHT, Van Schelven. The quotation, "in 1848 Mr. Smith..." is from the Reverend George Smith's obituary in the *Grand Traverse Herald*; **note that *Waukazooville* is spelled *Wakazooville* in the obitua**ry. Buechner and Powers are sources for the information about the Columbian Fair and Simon Pokagon. Henry Dosker's poem, "O somber oord" is quoted in Lagerwey, p. 245. Versteeg, chapters XIII and XIV, "Losing One's Way," and "Clearing the Forests," are useful sources for information about the wilderness where the colonists arrived; the anecdote about the young man who lost his way is from Versteeg, p 79; note that the Dutch is dialect of the time. The quotations "small notches and large chips..." and "notwithstanding all such difficulties..." are from Pieters, p. 68, and Versteeg, p. 84, respectively. Information about food shortages in the colony's first year are drawn from Dosker, Grootenhuis (source for the quotation, "no matter how zealous the cooks..."), Pieters and Versteeg, as well as archived reminiscences. The antimacassars purchaseed at the colony store were lacy doilies placed over the backs of upholstered chairs; their original purpose was to protect fabric from being stained by men's hair oil, and that explains their name: Macassar Oil was much used in the nineteenth century, and anti-Macassars were devised to save the furniture. The quotation from Oscar Wilde about servants is from Bartlett, p. 840; the story about Christina Van Raalte is from Arvilla Smith's recollections (Smith); she spelled the name as she recalled speaking and hearing it: "Van Raalta." Other quotations include "often I have little Albertus with me...", ACVR to Dirk, February 7, 1861, CCA-ACVR; "I like these people very well...", Grimm, p. 75; "there is no place where one is more lonely...", Katzman, p. 8. Letters from A. B. Taylor and George Duffield are archived JAH-HHT; information about Fourier is drawn from Seldes and from Herold pp. 96-97; the quotation "Fourier was magnificent..." is from Seldes, p. 199; information about Ransom's address to the legislature is given in Jenks, where the lengthy passage about the Holland colony, excerpted in a boxed section of this chapter, is quoted. Additional quotations include "fever, malaria and dysentery were common...", Pieters, p. 77; "the great mortality of that season...", Van Schelven, "Historical Sketch of Holland City and Colony," JAH-HHT (for further information about the Orphan House, see Bruins, *Historic Hope College: A Guide for a Walking Tour of the Campus.* Hope College, p. 9); "Our trials rose to the highest point...", Van Raalte's address to the Ebenezer celebration, Lucas, 1955a, p. 28; "the worst year was 1852...", McCullough p. 97; "the climate stood like a dragon in the way," is from Robinson, *Fifty Years in Panama*, which McCullough quotes on p. 96. Information about mail and stage deliveries is taken from reminiscences and from Pieters, pp. 89-90; the quotation, "the isolation of the community...'" is from Pieters, p. 89. Information and quotations about Henry Griffin's visit to the colony are from Pieters, pp. 157-158, and Griffin's account of his visit, JAH-HHT, Van Schelven; see also Lucas, 1955a. Van Raalte's letters about the need for a harbor include "To His Excellency, The Vice President...", February 5, 1850, JAH-HHT; "Hon. Alpheus Felch, United States Senate,...", January 31, 1850, JAH—HHT; A Few Words...", December 1857, JAH-HHT; for further information, see Wagenaar, 1992. Citations for information about Isaac Wyckoff are given within the chapter; the quotation, 'the gray Wyckoff' is from *Hope College Remembrancer;* see also many references in Pieters. Wyckoff's report to the *Christian Intelligencer* is included in Lucas, 1955a.

CHAPTER FOUR: "How gladly we would have spoken with them, but we could not." The title quotation is from the second excerpt from *Frederiks* (archived). Sources for information about the life and works of Washington Irving include Brooks & Bettman, pp. 8-16; Brooks, especially pp. 163-175; Deedy, pp. 34-43; Drabble, 497; and for John Lothrop Motley, Drabble, p. 674 and Brooks and Bettman, 3, 45, 52, 98-99. In the excerpt from Irving's *History of New York...*, the now out-dated word *trimmer* is used. The metaphor comes from trimming (adjusting) the sails of a ship as the wind changes - so a trimmer is a person whose principles change when public opinion shifts. In the boxed excerpt (pp. 1-3) from Motley's *The United Netherlands...*, a history of events in the sixteenth century, the "foremost statesman in Europe" refers to William the

Silent, the "most eminent sovereign in the world" to Queen Elizabeth of England, and "the industrious Philip" to Philip II of Spain, whose palace, the Escorial, had been constructed to serve also as a crypt for Spanish royalty. The excerpt from Motley's *The Life and Death of John of Barneveld*, beginning "I propose to retrace the history..." is from pp. 1-2. Biographies of William the Silent include those by Harrison and Wedgwood; for information about Philip II, see Descola, pp. 308-322; this section includes a description of the Escorial, pp. 319-320. Information about Dutch-Americanisms is taken from Flexner, pp. 129-133 and 458-459. H. Carol Trenery suggests, as an alternate explanation for the second syllable of *Yankee*, that the Dutch referred derisively to the English, whose symbol was John Bull, by combining *Jan* with a feminine ending, *Jan-tje*, which sounded to non-Dutch ears like *Yan-kee*. Sources for quotations are "the very name of our country...", Kennedy, p. 12, and "before the middle of the century...", Wabeke, p. 95. The latter quotation refers to the French author and diplomat, François René, Vicomte de Chateaubriand, whose romantic novels were popular in the nineteenth century. Information about Potgieter is drawn from Meijer, p. 209, and Zylstra. The first of two archived excerpts from *Frederiks* refers to "the large poke bonnets of our women." These were large headdresses with a wide brim in front. The excerpt from Henry Cook's recollections is from Lucas (1955a), vol. I, p. 50. Sources for quotations are "with an iron will...", Dosker; "determined to shake off the customs...", *Grand River Eagle*, February 9, 1949; "The roots of the Reformed Church run deeply...", Swierenga 1980, p. 115; "The immigrants to [Holland]...", Bruins 1995, p. 36; "part of the work to be done...", a letter from Philip Phelps quoted in *Hope Church Historical Booklet*; Dirk Van Raalte's letter to his mother: "De boeren die komen nu dageliks in...", is quoted in Schoolland, p. 130; "...if our church has such traditional regard...", *Hope College Remembrancer,* p. 15; "The writer well remembers", Pieters, pp. 130-131.

CHAPTER FIVE: "He saw in education the hope of the colony. It was his lodestar, the compass by which he steered."
The title quotation is taken from Van Raalte's first biographer, Henry Dosker, quoted in Wichers (1968), p. 99. Pictures of the class of 1866 appear, p. 276, in the *Milestone*, Willard Wichers, editor. Contemporary writing and recollections boxed and quoted in this chapter are archived: *Cahill, Langdon* (including her description of her trip to the colony and the quotation, "It was in the middle of the century,... "), and *Visscher*. Quotations in the first paragraph - "Dominie Van Raalte wishes...", "Dominie Ypma proposes..." and information about "the man with his brother's widow" are from *Classis Holland: Minutes 1848-1858*, JAH-WTS, as is a latter boxed excerpt, and the information about Van Raalte's donation of land, and Overisel's offer to clear the land. Pieters, in her chapters VII and VIII, discusses education and government in the colony; for election of school officers and Van Raalte's donation of land, see Pieters, p. 132. The quotation, "Even the most ignorant Hollander..." is from Pieters, p. 131. In addition to Pieters, early history of education in Holland is discussed in Stegenga, 23-95; Van Hinte, 390-403; Wichers 1968, 27-61; and summarized in Dunbar, pp. 155-156. John Garretson's report on the planned Academy, "the object of this school shall be to prepare...", which includes the prediction that the school would require no support from the Board of Domestic Missions after five years, is in RCA-BDM. Van Hinte, p. 393, gives information about the donation from Schieffelin. The major source for information and quotations about Walter Taylor (in addition to the sources cited above) is George M. B. Hawley, *Biography of Walter Teller Taylor*. JAH-HOPE. "Few places in the country furnish better facilities than Geneva ..." is from "Our Schools and Mr. Taylor," *Geneva Gazette*, April, 25, 1856; "his private study left its mark upon him..." is from Taylor's obituary, December 12, 1856. The phrase used in Margaret Taylor's obituary, "that bourne from whence no traveller returns," is from Shakespeare's *Hamlet*,: "The undiscover'd country from whose bourn no traveller returns" (act iii, scene i, line 89). Archived letters include "Dear Dominie, ...I have been thinking...", Anna Taylor to ACVR, CCA-ACVR; "We visited the Academy...", McNeish to Garretson, December 11, 1853, (which includes the quoted phrase, "the condition of the Academy you labored so hard to found"), RCA-BDM; "Dear Brother, ...Now something about an dear interest...", ACVR to Garretson, April 18, 1854, RCA-BDM (note that Van Raalte, writing in English, did indeed write "an dear interest"); "Rev. J. Garretson, Ch'st. Brother. ...Dominie Vander Meulen expects...", Schultz to Garretson, September 19, 1854, RCA-BDM; and "My very dear Brother! The Lord be your shield...", ACVR to Garretson, same date, RCA-BDM. Information about Beidler is limited; see Pieters, p. 138, Stegenga, p. 69 and Wichers 1968, p. 39. Information about Van Vleck's term at the Academy (1855-1859) is given in histories of education in the colony (sources listed above). The quotation, "an intimate friend of Van Raalte, as three of his letters show..." is from Hyma, p. 264. Van Vleck's interest in obtaining an assistant is evident in letters to Garretson, e.g.., December 27, 1856, RCA-BDM: "Now, dear Brother, it would not require a very labored argument to show that in such a school there is imperative demand for more labor than one man much more talented, & learned than I am could bestow." Van Vleck's letters include "I regret to state that I am discouraged...", to Garretson, December 1, 1855, RCA-BDM; "Oh for more zeal!:". to Garretson, August 18, 1857, RCA-BDM; "Dear Dominie, Last evening I received the letter...", to ACVR, June 27, 1857, CCA-ACVR; "The whole business connected with...", to Garretson, August 18, 1857, RCA-BDM. The *Travelling and Begging Guide*, in Van Vleck's handwriting, is archived, JAH-HHT; for information about the amount Van Raalte raised, see Bruins (1991). In Van Vleck's letter refusing Van Raalte's request to come east to help with fundraising ("Dear Dominie, Last evening I received the letter..."), he uses the Latin phrase *verbum sapienti sufficit*, which means "a word to the wise is sufficient"; the saying was sometimes abbreviated: *verb. sap.* The boxed item about the Academy Building is an excerpt from "Circular of the Holland Academy," written by Pieter Oggel, Van Raalte and Van Vleck, and published serially in *De Hollander* (JAH-HHT). Information about Van Vleck as regent is given in Hinsdale, p. 186, which also includes information about Van Vleck's work after leaving Holland, and his death. The nine page letter from which excerpts are taken, beginning with "said naughty thing about you and yours" is Van Vleck to ACVR, July 1859, from Ulsterville NY, CCA-ACVR; anonymous letters signed "W" were printed in the *Christian Intelligencer* in the fall of 1869. Van Raalte's letter to Phelps, "Let us not trouble ourselves with Mr. V. V....", is dated December 17, 1859, JAH-HOPE. The excerpt from George McClellan's correspondence with his wife (November 17, 1861), "I went to the White House shortly after tea..." is quoted in Holzer, p. 45. Pieters, p. 143, notes that education of girls and women was abandoned during Van Vleck's principalship; the 1868 statement of the Hope College Board of Trustees (JAH-HOPE) relating to the education of women is quoted in Pieters, pp. 143-144. The boxed quotation from Napoleon, "What shall be taught to the young ladies who are to be educated at Ecouen?" is from Ergang, p. 721. The view that all women look alike, used to oppose giving the vote to women, was held by James M. Buckley, "brilliant editor of the *Christian Advocate*," Lord, p 275. Information about Matthew Vassar, and the quotation "Two Noble Emancipists..." is taken from Boorstin (1975), p. 139. Excerpts from Van Raalte's letters to Phelps are "You say that I

must strike while the iron is hot...", ACVR to Phelps, December 26, 1859, JAH-HOPE and "I thank you very much for your kind informations...", ACVR to Phelps, April 17, 1865, JAH-HOPE. Sources for information about Phelps' and his students' energy include *Hope Church Historical Booklet* (janitorial services); Bruins 1971, p. 293 (bucket brigades); *Hope College, First Catalog and Circular*, p. 46 (building the gym). The phrase used to describe Philip Phelps - "the apple of his father's eye" - has an interesting history; *apple of the eye* refers to "the pupil, because it was anciently supposed to be a round solid ball like an apple. Figuratively, anything held extremely dear or much cherished (I. H. Evans, p. 44). A biblical reference is in Deuteronomy 32: 9-10: "For the Lord's portion is his people; Jacob is the lot of his inheritance. He found him in a desert land, and in the waste howling wilderness; he led him about, he instructed him, he kept him as the apple of his eye." President Phelps' baccalaureate address, from which the excerpt beginning "Seldom does so special a link unite..." is printed in full in the *Hope College Remembrancer*. Nell Wichers (Mrs. Willard Wichers) is the source for information about Willard Wichers' work on the *Milestone*, which includes pictures of the class of 1867, p. 277, and, on p. 275, Gerrit Bolks' report on the class of 1867.

CHAPTER SIX: **"People bound for Zion almost always have trouble with their fellows along the way. "** The title quotation is from Catton 1965, p. 461, referring to attacks on President Lincoln. The opening illustration shows Van Raalte with his son-in-law Pieter Oggel. In at least two published texts, a picture of Oggel has been used as a picture of Van Raalte: "A. C. Van Raalte" (Pereboom et al., p. 99) and *"Jeugdfoto A. C. van Raalte, als student"* in Roetman, p. 192. The letter from Lewis Cass - "I have the pleasure to inform you..." is archived: CCA-ACVR. The picture showing harbor construction is Number Eleven in the First National Bank's Heritage series of drawings, used by permission of the bank (now First of America). For information about the Know-Nothing party, see Butterfield, p. 127; Lorant, pp. 216, 223-224; McPherson, pp. 135-144; and Stimpson 1952, pp. 151-158. Lincoln's letter is quoted in Shaw, p. 178, where the source is given: letter to Joshua F. Speed, August 24, 1855; for Hayes' letter, see Stimpson 1952, p. 154. The boxed excerpt from the party's 1856 platform is from *National Party Conventions: 1831-1972*, p. 33. For the effect of the Know-Nothing party on the Dutch settlements, see Oostendorp, pp. 184-186; Swierenga 1965, pp. 32-36; Van Hinte, pp. 427, 434-435; and Wagenaar, 1992. The excerpt from Henry Cook's recollections is from Lucas 1955a, vol. I, p. 50. For Dominie Oggel's sermon text, see *Visscher* (archived). Information about actions and discussion at the Holland Classis, including two boxed excerpts, are from *Classis Holland: Minutes 1848-1858*, JAH-WTS; the letter from McNeish to John Garretson, December 11, 1853, is archived: RCA-BDM. (In the letter, S... and V... are named.) A useful summary of the hymn controversy in the Netherlands is given by tenZythoff 1987, pp. 50-53; Van Raalte's letter, "in my parental home I had grown up with the hymns...", is quoted on p. 25. Note, however, that tenZythoff gives two dates - 1806 (p. 146) and 1807 (p. 50) - for the introduction of hymns, and that he is in error (p. 146) in stating, "hymns had been introduced into the Reformed Church when Albertus Christiaan Van Raalte was five years old (1806)"; Van Raalte was born in 1811. For information about controversy in the colony, see Bruins 1974; for "Van Lente's choir," see Bruins 1995; the same source, p. 22, gives the date the Holland Classis officially approved of hymn singing during worship. Sources for quotations and information include "the gap between the faithful...", Dosker; "a foolish consistency...", Emerson's essay, "Self Reliance"; "since you left, Dominie Oggel did rebuke..." and "I see how difficult it will be...", ACVR to Phelps, August 14, 1860, JAH-HOPE; "I see too much strife..." and "the foul insane fury against hymns...", ACVR to Phelps, August 31, 1860, JAH-HOPE; information about the hymn singing controversy in Cambridge, Massachusetts, Tilton, pp. 44-48, 394-395; letter from Chancellor Ferris to ACVR and ACVR's reply, June 30, 1858, CCA-ACVR. The boxed quotation, "[The South] has come to the conclusion..." is from the *Louisville Daily Journal*, August 13, 1860, quoted in McPherson, p. 230.

· **CHAPTER SEVEN**: **"Nations, like individuals, are punished for their transgressions."** The title quotation is taken from *Personal Memoirs of U. S. Grant*, p. 24. Major sources for information about the Civil War, and American history leading up to it, include Boatner, Butterfield, Foote, Lorant, McPherson, Morison, Nevins (1950 and 1959), the memoirs of Generals Grant and Sherman, and the Civil War histories of Michigan's most famous historian, Bruce Catton. The boxed excerpt from Grant's *Memoirs* (from which the title quotation is taken) begins, "Ostensibly we were intended to prevent filibustering in Texas." Today, *filibustering* usually means speaking uninterruptedly in a legislature to prevent action being taken on a bill that would otherwise pass. The word comes from a Dutch noun - *vrijbuiter* (freebooter) - which the Spanish adapted as *filibustero*. Filibustering meant freebooting - plundering, pirating - and a filibustere, a soldier of fortune, came to mean an American mercenary looking to make a fortune in Mexico, or Central or South America, often by fomenting revolutions. Contemporary writing and recollections boxed in this chapter are archived: *Brown, Nies, Visscher* and *Vogel*. The map showing United States territory in 1848, prepared by Mark Cook, is based primarily on Barraclough, Garrett, and Martis. Sources for quotations include "a title-page to a great, tragic volume", Morison, p. 405 and 615; "his victories in Mexico...", Lorant, p. 191; "I have, Senators, believed... ", Morison, p. 571; '[the] accused fugitives could not... ", Hall, p. 320; "When the federal commissioner found for his owner...", McPherson, p. 83. (The phrase "found for" refers to a legal decision: the court's decision, or finding, was in favor of the slaveowner.) In a footnote on pp. 83-84, McPherson tells what happened to Sims after he was sent south. "Sims' owner subsequently sold him at the slave auction in Charleston. He was taken to New Orleans and sold to a brickmason in Vicksburg, Mississippi, where Sims was living when federal troops besieged the city in 1863. He escaped into federal lines and obtained a special pass from General Ulysses S. Grant to return to Boston, where he arrived in time to watch the presentation of colors to the 54th Massachusetts Infantry, the first black regiment recruited in the North. A dozen years after the Civil War, Sims became a clerk and messenger in the office of the U. S. attorney general, under whose auspices he had been remanded to slavery a generation earlier." One source of information about black regiments in the Civil War is the collected letters of Colonel Robert Gould Shaw, edited by Duncan. A chapter titled "The Revolution of 1860" in McPherson, pp. 202-233, is a useful source of information about John Brown. The quotation, "He is not Old Brown any longer..." is from "Plea for Captain John Brown," Thoreau, p. 438. Nevins (1950), p. 98, gives information about the African Americans who fought and died with Brown: "In Oberlin [Ohio] citizens erected a monument to three negroes: Lewis Leary, killed in following Brown, and Shields Green and John Copeland, who had been hanged. Copeland's letters to his family made a great impression in the North. He would rather die a rebel than live a slave, he declared, and hoped his name might be preserved with that of Crispus Attucks. 'Believe me when I tell you, that though shut up in prison and under sentence of death, I have spent some very happy hours here.'" Information about the Democratic and Republican conventions is drawn primarily from

Capers, Lorant and *National Party Conventions 1831-1972* (NPC). Lorant, p. 233, includes pictures of the eleven leading Republican candidates in 1860. Sources for quotations: "Rarely in American history...", NPC, p. 35; and "The seceders intended from the beginning...", Capers, 203-204. John Dryden's *Absalom and Achitophel* is the source of the phrase "rule or ruin": "In friendship false, implacable in hate, Resolv'd to ruin or to rule the state." Alexander Hamilton Stephens - "little Alec" - opposed secession, but accepted the post of vice-president of the Confederacy. After the war he was imprisoned for six months; he was elected to the Senate, from Georgia, in 1866, but the Congress refused to seat him; he was elected to the House of Representatives in 1872 and served for ten years. Information about William Tecumseh Sherman, including his service as founding superintendent of The Louisiana State Military College is drawn from Fellman, Lewis, and Sherman's memoirs. Keegan p. 196, refers to Sherman as "President of Louisana University." In Lincoln's first inaugural address, he referred to "mystic chords" which stretch from patriotic grave to hearthstone and swell when touched; the metaphor is mixed, but the word he used is indeed *chords*. The quote from Chandler, "Without a little bloodletting...", can be found in Dunbar & May, p. 319; the excerpt from the Reverend Henry Ward Beecher's 1865 speech at Fort Sumter, "As long as the sun endures...", is from a quotation given in Holzer, p. 199. Beecher's sister, Harriet Beecher Stowe, was the author of *Uncle Tom's Cabin*, a novel showing the evils of slavery, which was highly influential in its time. McCullough devotes a chapter to "The Unexpected Mrs. Stowe" and quotes, p. 46, the story of Lincoln greeting her with the words, "So this is the little woman who made this big war." Information about Lewis Cass is drawn primarily from Catton 1984, and Dunbar & May. Cass' speech in Detroit on April 24, 1861, is given in its entirety in Duyckinck, vol. I, p. 145; the quotation, "The veteran statesman and soldier General Cass..." is from the same source and page; see also May, p. 138. Sources for further quotes include "too powerful to be suppressed...", McPherson, p. 274 and Morison 611; "will furnish no troops for the wicked purpose..." and "Your requisition is illegal...", McPherson, p. 276; see also Catton 1961, pp. 331-332. Information about the "Battle Hymn of the Republic" is taken primarily from William McLoughlin's essay in Boorstin 1966, pp. 399-404, an excellent source for in-depth information; Weeks & Flint, p. 133; and Ravitch, pp. 147-148. McLoughlin, p. 401, notes: "It is reported that Abraham Lincoln once wept at hearing it sung and told the singer he had never heard a better song. ...and [Civil War] Chaplain Charles C. McCabe, later dubbed 'The Singing Chaplain,' 'raised thousands of dollars for the Christian Commission's war work by singing the song at rallies at which he gave his lecture on 'The Bright Side of Life in Libby Prison.'" Julia Ward Howe helped lead the American Woman's Suffrage Association for fifty-five years, and at her funeral in 1910 four thousand mourners joined in singing the "Battle Hymn of the Republic." "Thank God for Michigan!" is quoted in Dunbar & May, p. 321 and Powers, p. 105. Information about the first Battle of Bull Run is found in all Civil War histories cited, and also in Boatner. Civil War battles often have two names; First and Second Bull Run are the same as First and Second Manassas. Most battles were fought in confederate territory, and southerners tended to give a battle the name of the nearest town; northerners tended to name them for a landmark. Bull Run is a small river, located near Manassas Junction, Virginia. For estimates of losses at the first Battle of Bull Run, see McPherson, p. 347. "There is Jackson, standing like a stone wall!" appears in many sources, among them, Catton, 1961, pp. 455-456. "There is nothing in American history...", is quoted from Catton 1960, p. 45. "The Civil War Recollections of John Nies" are archived, *Nies*. Nies served under Colonel (later General) Philip Sheridan, another short man who was magnificent on a horse; Morison, p. 694, refers to "dashing...five-foot-two-inch Philip Sheridan." The quotation "There were some in Holland..." is from Van Hinte, pp. 433-434. Information about the consistory controversy over "Nomen Nescis" can be found in Van Hinte, p. 434. Sources for "*Op nu Nederandsch wakkere zonen...*," written by H. Grootemaat, are Lucas 1955b, p. 562 and Lagerwey, pp. 252-253. (The version in Lucas is correctly spelled.) The soldier pictured with the verses is Renke De Vries. For information about politics in Holland, Michigan, and Pella, Iowa, in the years leading up to and during the Civil War, see Lucas 1955b, pp. 562-565, Mulder, p. 159, Oostendorp, pp. 182-187, Swierenga 1965, Van Hinte, pp. 430-438, and Wagenaar, 1992; see Rietveld, p. 153 for Lincoln's reference to Scholte as his "good Dutch friend." Letters excerpted include ""Last week our very beloved, high esteemed friend...", Dirk to parents, February 16, 1863, CCA-ACVR; Yesterday evening I received your letter of the 20th...", Ben to ACVR, August 1, 1864, JAH-HHT; "It does my heart good that Co. I is so down on the copperheads...", Ben to ACVR, August 24, JAH-HHT; "We were also overjoyed to have Lieut. Kramer drop in...", Ben to ACVR, July 14, JAH-HHT. The quotation, "The copperhead disreputable portion of the press...", is from Grant's memoirs, pp. 562-563. See McPherson, p. 494, for a description of the attempt to avoid having the copperhead label be seen as pejorative. "P. S. You must have the greetings of B. van Raalte..." is from Frederick Van Lente to Johannes Van Lente, December 18, 1864, Catlin, p. 101. Soldiers from the colony constantly reassured their families about themselves, and about friends who were not seriously ill, with the statement that they were "heavy and fat." The Dutch language has several words for *fat*; the word which usually appears in these letters is *vet*, e.g., Ben describes Dirk by writing *"hij is goed vet,"* Ben to CVR, March 9, 1863, JAH-HHT. Both Union and confederate troops suffered greatly from illnesses and to grow thin was a cause for fear; soldiers on both sides were occasionally short of rations, though confederate troops suffered much worse privation, especially as the war continued. Most histories of the war include accounts of the lively diversity in uniforms at the start of the war. The information about the Lancer Regiment - "lances, which were made in Michigan..." - is from May, p. 140. The most famous Zouave unit was the New York Fire Zouaves; see Catton 1961, pp. 390-392. Their first colonel was twenty-four year old Elmer Ellsworth, who became a hero, to the Union side, in May, 1861, when he cut down a Confederate flag from an Alexandria, Virginia inn and was shot and killed by the innkeeper. Information about volunteerism, the Confederate conscription law, the federal Enrollment Act, and the bounty system can be found in all complete histories of the war period. See McPherson, pp. 430-436 for Confederate conscription, and 491-493 for the U.S. Enrollment Act. Riots in some places in the north were a consequence of the draft, and the New York draft riot in 1863 was particularly vicious. See McPherson, p. 493 and pp. 608-611 on the rioting, and Catton 1960, 206-210 on conscription and the bounty system. Letters excerpted are "I foster more contempt than fear...", ACVR to Phelps, August 7, 1863, JAH-HOPE; "I lost my pen in the straw", Ben to CVR, November 15, 1862, JAH-HHT; "All I write had better be kept confidential...", Ben to parents, November 11, 1862, JAH-HHT.

CHAPTER EIGHT: "**The poor Rebs who fall into my hands are going to pay for Dirk's arm.**" The title quotation is taken from Ben Van Raalte's letter to his mother, September 16, 1864, JAH-HHT. Excerpts quoted in the chapter are from Catlin and archived sources *Nies*, *Visscher* and *Vogel*. Letters from Wulf Van Appeldoorn and Ary Rot are from Catlin. Information about Civil War history is drawn primarily from Boatner, Catton (all books referenced), and McPherson. Bradford includes descriptions of the Atlanta campaign by General Oliver O. Howard, U.S.A., "The very woods seemed to moan and groan," and General John B. Hood, C.S.A., "It was painful yet strange to mark how expert grew the old men, women, and children in building their underground forts." Quotations include "The Michigan Hollanders, who flocked… ", Mulder, p. 159; "the town of Holland has been aroused…" and "the boys have organized a company…", ACVR to Phelps, August 29, 1862, JAH-HOPE; "but I am afraid…", ACVR to Giles Van de Wal, June 29, 1862, CCA-ACVR; "the company carried with them…", *Allegan Journal,* September 8, 1862; excerpts and information about the Van Lente family, from Catlin; "the music of bullets", Ben to ACVR, May 31, 1864, JAH-HHT (a longer excerpt is quoted later in this chapter); "I think that you should try to get so far…", and "it is to our happiness that I learn…", ACVR to Dirk, September 15, 1862, CCA-ACVR; "I am enjoying myself…", Ben to parents, November 11, 1862, JAH-HHT; there is much sickness…", Ben to ACVR, (date illegible), 1862, JAH-HHT. Information about "the tent d'abris" and the quotation "when boards can be ripped off our neighbors' houses" is from Fellman, p. 176-177. Further quotations include "now it is again my turn…", Dirk to parents, February 16, 1863, CCA-ACVR; "at present it is very damp here … ", Ben to CVR, November 15, 1862, JAH-HHT; "through the Lord's mercy…", Ben to CVR, July 28, 1864, JAH-HHT; "I received your letter yesterday and was overjoyed…" Ben to ACVR, March 23, 1863, JAH-HHT; Johannes Van Lente to family, February 13, 1863, Catlin, p. 30, refers to "Morgan fever: "Our second lieutenant [Jacob Otto Doesburg] has left us yesterday. He said that he could not take it any longer. I myself think that he has gotten the 'Morgan fever.'" Information about Moore's reply when Morgan called on him to surrender is given in Wichers 1964, p. 121. Further quotations include "Our boys 200 in number had a tremendous fight…", ACVR to Phelps, August 7, 1863, JAH-HOPE; and "with gratitude to God for sparing them…", Catlin, p. 66. Lincoln's statement about Grant - "He fights" - is quoted in Rhea, p. 42; for an excellent discussion of Grant's style see the chapter on "Grant and Unheroic Leadership," in Keegan. Like Van Raalte, Grant was short, and Keegan's chapter opens, "In the early light of a spring morning during the presidency of Abraham Lincoln, a small man on a large horse was galloping through the dense woodland… ." Further quotations include "one evening we were shelled very heavily…", Ben to ACVR, May 31, 1864, JAH-HHT; "much of the Rebellion has been licked…", Ben to ACVR, July 14, 1864, JAH-HHT; I am happy to be able to write…", Ben to ACVR, August 13, 1864, JAH-HHT; "in haste but with much pleasure…", Ben to ACVR, June 20, 1864, JAH-HHT; "last night I received your letter of the 15th…", Dirk to CVR, July 15, 1864, CCA-ACVR; "we are directly in front of the city…", Ben to ACVR, July 26, 1864, JAH-HHT; "in his death the army lost…", Grant, *Memoirs,* p. 385; "I have had the pleasure to see most of the generals…", "Dear sister, a few days ago I received your kind letter…" and "General Sherman looks like an old down-broken farmer," are from Ben to Christine, July 30, 1864, JAH-HHT (note that Benis writing in English, and thus there are some non-standard spellings and expressions). The description of General Howard as "the one-armed Christian general from Maine…" is from McPherson, p. 754; the first author is indebted to Herman Ridder for the explanation that looking "like a Drenthe farmer" probably meant Colonel Cooper had a rural air and dressed carelessly. "The Rebs sometimes resort to false alarms…", is Ben to ACVR, August 1, 1864, JAH-HHT; this letter contains the confederate soldier's jest, "Hood can only stand one more killing." The description of the Battle of Fair Oaks, "amid thick woods and flooded clearings…" is from McPherson, p. 462. Additional quotes: "last night I received your letter of the 13th…", Ben to ACVR, August 24, 1864, JAH-HHT; the description of Smith, from Boatner; "it is with much sorrow…", Ben to ACVR to tell about Dirk's injury, August 29, 1864, JAH-HHT; the description of Andersonville Prison is from Boatner; "Daily our prisoners come here to be exchanged…", Johannes Van Lente to family, March 3, 1865, Catlin, p. 114; "Bouman has hard time of it…", Ben to ACVR, May 2, 1865, JAH-HHT; "dear parents, I am doing well…", Dirk to parents, August 30, 1864, JAH-HHT; "today I received your letters of September 12…", Dirk to ACVR, September 23, 1864, CCA-ACVR. In Ben's letter to his mother, from which the title quotation for this chapter is taken, he also writes, "I can make myself feel so full of hate against the Rebels that I could fight them the rest of my life and shoot them down in cold blood." "Yesterday I received your letter of April 7th…" is Dirk to ACVR, April 10, 1865, CCA-ACVR. The quotation from *Ecclesiasticus,* one of the books of the Apocrypha, " There be of them that have left a name… " is used by Shelby Foote to introduce his history of the Civil War. Boatner's encyclopedia, as well as Civil War histories, provides information about Civil War generals Barnard Bee and Stonewall Jackson, who died during the war, and P. T. G. Beauregard, Ulysses S. Grant, Oliver Howard, Joseph Johnston, Robert E. Lee, Philip Sheridan, and William Tecumseh Sherman, as well as Jefferson Davis and Henry Wirz. Dunbar & May's history of Michigan gives information about Lewis Cass and Zachariah Chandler. The quotation, "I had been a light smoker…", Grant, *Memoirs;* "suffering intense pain…", Morison, p. 734. Obituaries and Catlin provide information about Johannes Van Lente, Dirk and Ben Van Raalte, Renke De Vries and John Wilterdink; information about John Huizenga, including the quotation "beloved by all who knew him," is from his obituary in *The Acts and Proceedings of the General Synod of the Reformed Church in America, Volume XXIV,* pp. 936; Catlin, and Wichers, 1964, are sources for information about the deaths of Charles Eltinge Clark, William Dowd, Jacobus Grootenhuis, Hendrikus Nyland, William Ledeboer, Ary Rot. Wulf Van Appeldoorn, and Cornelis Van Dam. Information about the death of John Douma is from *Records of the City Council of Holland,* January-February, 1939, JAH-HHT. The reminiscences of John Nies and Jan Vogel are archived: *Nies* and *Vogel.*

CHAPTER NINE: "I am glad that my children are on the west side of the ocean." The title quotation is taken from one of Albertus Van Raalte's letters. May 14, 1866, printed in *De Hope,* JAH-HOPE, written during his travels in the Netherlands. His letters about the trip recount experiences over an extended time. The legal documents giving Dirk power of attorney are exact transcriptions of archived records, CCA-ACVR. Note Kerber, in Kerber *et al.* 1995, *U.S. History as Women's History,* pp. 21-22: "The husband, by marriage, acquires an absolute title to all the personal property of the wife. …The legal system acknowledged [a woman's] dependency by the practice of holding private examinations of married women before permitting them to sign away their right to any dower property." Archived sources include *Visscher* and *Vogel.* Much of the information in the chapter is taken from letters: "I am in a position which…requires my full time…", ACVR to Giles Van de Wal, June 29, 1862, CCA-ACVR; "My plan of visiting the Netherlands was given up…" and "I am at once to work…" (note that Van Raalte's estimate of the synod meeting time in this letter is incorrect), ACVR to Phelps, and the postscripts from Margaret Phelps, "If Mrs. Van Raalte comes on I would expect to see her…" and from Philip Phelps, "Bremen fortnightly…" are all from the same letter, March 26, 1866, JAH-HOPE. "Fanie," is the way Margaret Phelps spelled her daughter's name in the letter; the name was almost certainly pronounced *Fannie*; however, families have a right to spell and pronounce family names as they choose. Schieffelin's generosity is recognized in the *Hope College Remembrancer*, and evidenced in his gift of funds for the trip, and other financial support (see endnotes for Chapter Ten). The quotation, "You asked me what my opinion was…", Ben to ACVR, November 17, 1864, JAH-HHT, (the phrase "like a man standing on ice" is from this letter). Information about the trip to New York, to England and thence to the Netherlands, and the quotations "Friday morning, at 11:00, we walked… " and "the joy on Mother's face…", are from ACVR to his children, *"Zeer Geliefde Kinderen,"* May 14, 1866, printed in *De Hope*, JAH-HOPE. Information and quotations about the inauguration and commencement ceremonies are taken from *Hope College Remembrancer*, and Jacobson. "People have asked me what name…" is from Brummelkamp, p. 37. For information about names of Michigan cities, see Dunbar & May 1995, p. 180. City names listed are eponyms; that is, they are named for people. Andrew Jackson was a famous general, then seventh U.S. president; John Marshall was Chief Justice of the U.S. Supreme Court; James Monroe was the fifth U. S. president. Ann Arbor is said to be named for two people - the wives of the city's founders, both named Ann. Ypsilanti is named for Demetrius Ypsilanti, a hero of the Greek War of Independence fought against Turkey from 1821-1827, during which time the Michigan town was settled. Henry Rowe Schoolcraft was Commissioner of Indian Affairs in Michigan, well-known for his research and writing; Jenison was named for Luman Jenison (son of Lemuel and twin of Lucius) whose portrait and biography are given in *Portrait and Biographical Record:…* pp. 370-372; Fennville is named for Elam Fenn, who owned a mill there. Sources of other quotations include "the woods encircled them too closely…", Dosker; "I know the reality of my weakness…", ACVR response to Ferris, June 30, 1858, CCA-ACVR; "when Van Raalte was given the floor to speak…", Bruins, 1996; "a person who does not put all his interests in God's hands…", "Mother and I are both well…", "in the provinces …the pest among the cattle…", "the failure of banks…" and "the tension created by the threatening attitude…", are all ACVR to Ben, June 11, 1866, JAH-HOPE; "in London we hear…", and "in the Netherlands many families…", ACVR to the colony, June 30, 1866, JAH-HOPE. Information about anthrax among the cattle is taken from Haggard, pp. 377-378 and Rapport and Wright, p. 378; information about cholera is given in Chapter Three, and sources are cited in the endnotes for that chapter.

CHAPTER TEN: "I thirst after an opportunity to free myself of these annoyances and to devote myself entirely to the Kingdom of God." The title quotation is taken from a letter written by Van Raalte to Philip Phelps, August 31, 1860, JAH-HOPE. The "Resolution of the Common Council" which opens the chapter is from Holland City Council Minutes, March 25, 1869, JAH-HHT. Two boxed diary excerpts are archived: *Visscher.* Sources of information include Peter Zuidema's recollections of the colony, JAH-HHT; and Van Hinte, pp. 527-534. Descriptions of the colony include conflicting dates and information, and undocumented assertions in an effort to determine blame. Although a definitive history has not yet been written, archived family letters and newspapers - though the colony venture preceded the Holland fire, in which years of records were destroyed - provide useful partial information. Clearly, the attempt to found a colony in Virginia failed; however, there is no conclusive evidence to support the idea that Van Raalte was permanently discouraged by it. His energy in continuing to work for Hope College and helping Holland to recover after the fire of 1871, and his notable speeches in his later years indicate that he retained his enthusiasm and zeal for good causes even as his strength waned. There is substantial though not yet definitive evidence that Albertus and Christina Van Raalte and their daughter Anna went to the colony in the spring of 1869 and returned to Holland in the fall of the same year; sources include the Resolution of the Common Council, which was passed in 1869, Zuidema's recollections, and Lucas 1955b, p. 291; and an entry in the Visscher's diary about bidding farewell to the Van Raaltes in the spring of 1869. (Note that Zuidema reports that Van Raalte left the Amelia colony, fearing "mob violence" in 1871. This date does not coincide with other 1871 letters, however.) "Whether Dominie Van Raalte had visited Virginia as an army chaplain or to visit his son Benjamin who was a soldier in the army I do not know," Zuidema comments; such rumors existed when he wrote, in 1941, and have persisted; but they are untrue. Van Raalte was never an army chaplain, and his sons did not serve in Virginia. When Albertus Van Raalte went south in 1864 to bring his wounded son Dirk home, he got only as far as Nashville Tennessee. (See Frederick Van Lente to Johannes Van Lente, December 18, 1864, Catlin, p. 100: "Rev. Van Raalte could not come to his Dirk, because he got as far as NachVille and then he could go no further and returned home having accomplished nothing.") The quotations, "We are enjoying our vacation and rest…", and "You can well imagine that I am keeping my eyes open…", are from ACVR to Ben, June 11, 1866, JAH-HOPE; family information is from genealogies, and inferred from obituaries. The source for Mayor Cappon's report, "At the close of the first year…", is the Journal of the Common Council, April 20, 1868, JAH-HHT. All Holland citizens at the time would have noted the mayor's comment, "I am happy to report that (with the exception of the Marshal and Street Commissioner) all officers of the city have worked together harmoniously, and have performed the duties required of them faithfully and well." There were not two council members contributing to disharmony; the same man was both Marshal and Street Commissioner: Teunis Keppel, later to become - to community surprise - Van Raalte's son-in-law. (See his obituary, *Holland City News,* July 4, 1896, JAH.) Information about Cappon's emigration is from Pieters, p. 39; about the founding of Hope Church, *Hope Church Historical Booklet;* about Roelof Pieters and the founding of Third Church, Bruins 1995, pp. 9-12. Quotations include "the young men from New Brunswick…", ACVR to Phelps, August 31, 1860, JAH-HOPE; "in another place he found a carpenter…", Pieters, pp. 136-137; "My spirit does not enjoy…", ACVR to Van de Wal, June 29, 1862, CCA-ACVR; "I am exceedingly anxious to devote…", ACVR to Phelps, July 15, 1869, JAH-HOPE. The well-known statement by Will Rogers is included in Bartlett, p. 954, where the source is given as "Address, Boston [June 1930]." For information about criticism of Van Raalte, see Bruins 1977, p. 90, and Bruins 1991, pp. 15-16; Pieters, p. 176; and Wagenaar 1992. The reference to himself as a "stumbling block" occurs in ACVR's reply to Chancellor Isaac Ferris, June 30, 1858, CCA-ACVR. Information about the period before Lee's surrender at Appomattox Court House, and the relation of the events to Amelia Court House, is drawn primarily from Davis; see also Catton 1956, pp. 383-393 and Morison, pp. 701-702. Information about Libby Prison is taken from, among other sources, Boatner; see also p. 322 in Stimpson 1946. Will Gilmore's address - "that foul enclosure known as Libby prison…" - is included in *Hope College Remembrancer*, JAH-HOPE. Jefferson Davis' proclamation, and Lee's request for provisions, "The Army of Northern Virginia arrived here today…", are quoted in Davis, p. 199 and pp. 190-191; the complete text of Davis' message is given in Commager, pp. 444-445. Catton 1965, pp. 447-448, describes Lincoln's visit to Richmond, noting that "the way his visit was handled would have given a modern security officer the vapors," p. 447. Grant's message to Lee, "The results of the last week…", is quoted in Bradford, p. 602, with the full exchange of messages between Generals Grant and Lee. Lincoln's assassination is described in virtually every book of American history dealing with this time period; see, for example, Butterfield, pp. 180-183, Lorant, pp. 278-282, and Morison, pp. 702-704. Woodward, pp. 177-178, is the source for the quotation, "The loss of every third horse or mule..."; Van Hinte, p. 527, asserts that Schieffelin purchased land in Amelia county prior to Van Raalte's settling there. Sherman's advice that land in the former confederacy "is not Southern but Northern - where water freezes and wheat grows...", Fellman, p. 305, is a reminder that many people besides Van Raalte saw the advantages of such land purchases. Most people attribute the saying "go west, young man" to Horace Greeley; Greeley himself tried to set the record straight: John Babsone Lane Soule first created and published the phrase in the *Terre Haute Express*; see Bartlett, p. 678. "The main argument against Virginia..." is from ACVR to Oggel, October 6, 1868, JAH-HHT. For information about Phelps' loan, see Bruins 1991, p. 16 and Wichers 1968, p. 99. Quotations include "he was, at the same time, developing into an entrepreneur", Bruins 1991, p. 14; "it does not take place, sleeping!" and "It is my conviction that the transplanting of a generation...", ACVR to J. G. Van Heulen, August 3, 1869, JAH-HHT; "I wish to express my deepest thanks...", Christine to Ben and Dirk, May 31, 1869, JAH-HOPE. Note the sisterly sarcasm in the letter's opening.(Ben and Dirk had *not* written ("Maybe you are so busy now that you do not have time to write...") and Christine was using wit to encouraging them to do so. "At first I didn't like this place..." is Christine to Ben, May 3, 1869, JAH-HHT; "Miss Annie" is the Van Raaltes' youngest daughter; "that sweet Karel" is Helena's and Albertus' youngest child (at this time); the source for "quite a few emigrants are arriving..." is Christine to Ben and Dirk, May 31, 1869, JAH-HHT. The conclusion to this letter, "Kiss Karel for me - how anxious I am to see him" suggests that Helena and her children were expected to travel to Amelia for Will and Christine's wedding. Sources for other quotations are "we are well by God's kindness...", ACVR to Phelps, July 15, 1869, JAH HOPE; "my strength is not improving...", ACVR to Ben, May 4, 1869, JAH-HHT. For the "push-pull metaphor, see tenZythoff 1987; the idea that Van Raalte was perceived as aging is supported by Zuidema: "I saw Dominie Van Raalte, a fine looking and mild mannered gentleman who appeared to be in his late fifties," and Van Raalte's own comment that "I feel like an old man and walking is becoming very difficult for me," ACVR to Ben, May 4, 1869, JAH-HHT. Sources for other quotations are "Mrs. Van Raalte's mind is bent upon Michigan...", ACVR to Phelps, August 3, 1869, JAH-HOPE; "attend to Michigan matters...", ACVR to Phelps, August 3, 1869, JAH-HOPE; "to bring the property into a secure position", ACVR to Phelps, November 20, 1869, JAH-HOPE. Information about A. C. Van Raalte Gilmore is taken from *Hope Church Historical Booklet*, and his obituary in *Holland City News*, January 27, 1955; about Huizenga's work in the colony, from *The Acts and Proceedings of the General Synod of the Reformed Church in America, Volume XXIV*, pp. 935-936; "I do not wish Dr. Van Raalte to have any responsibility or anxiety...", and information about the cost of land, are from Schieffelin to Will Gilmore, March 25, 1871, JAH-WTS.

CHAPTER ELEVEN: "The world loses its color with such a blow." The title quotation is taken from Albertus Van Raalte's letter to Hendrik Scholte, January, 1844, on learning of the death of Scholte's wife Sara, who died on January 23, 1844. The letter is part of a series of Scholte papers, which have been translated by Elisabeth Dekker at the A. C. Van Raalte Institute. An excerpt beginning, "Yesterday evening after coming home I heard...", appears after the second paragraph in this chapter. Information about Sara Maria Brandt Scholte is given in Oostendorp, pp. 42 and 132. Oostendorp, p. 132, comments, "Sara Maria ranks with the sisters De Moen as one of the faithful women who valiantly supported their husbands in the great work of the Lord." Archived recollections in this chapter are from *Cahill*, *Post*, and *Visscher*. Family information in this and other chapters is taken from genealogies and obituaries. A project of the A. C. Van Raalte Institute is the compilation of an annotated genealogy of Albertus and Christina Van Raalte and their descendants. Van Raalte's description of his wife as "the strong, loving helper, granted by God" is from Van Raalte's "Biographical sketch of Christina Van Raalte, written by A. C. Van Raalte, soon after her death", translated by Harry Boonstra, CCA-ACVR. Christina Van Raalte's funeral oration, given by the Reverend Christian Vander Veen, from which excerpts are given in the chapter, is archived JAH-HHT; Vander Veen's description of seeing Christina Van Raalte cradle her child while listening to her husband preach appears here; the incident is mentioned in Bratt, p. 27. Christian Vander Veen and Jacob Vander Meulen were the first of a long and continuing line of ministers prepared by the schools Albertus Van Raalte founded. In 1854, they left the colony to study at Rutgers College in New Jersey; letters concerning their departure are quoted in Chapter Five, and sources are cited in endnotes for that chapter. The quotation, "Every great man puts his work first,...", is from Schoolland, p. 112. Excerpts from letters include "Dear wife, I hope...", ACVR to CVR, October 2, 1837, CCA-ACVR (also cited in Reenders); "A certain gentleman did call...", ACVR to Phelps, December 26, 1859, JAH-HOPE. Pieters, p. 166, describes Christina Van Raalte's musical talent and charm as a hostess. Information about puerperal fever and the life and work of Semmelweiss is drawn from deKruif, Guthrie, and *Merriam-Webster's Medical Desk Dictionary*. Paul deKruif, who concluded the introduction to his popular book of medical essays, "written May 20, 1932, Hungry Street, Holland Michigan," described Semmelweiss' obsession with protecting women from an preventable disease whose cause his medical colleagues refused to recognize. "In the epilogue to his masterpiece, Semmelweiss told how sure he was that childbed fever almost never came from 'self-infection' of mothers. He said he could only dispel his sadness at the deaths of those thousands of mothers by looking into the happy future when no death would be brought in from outside to any woman having a baby. 'But if it is not granted to me to look upon that happy time with my own eyes,' wrote Semmelweiss, 'from which misfortune may God preserve me... the conviction that such a time must inevitably come sooner or later will cheer my dying hour',", deKruif, p. 50. In 1932, many women still died of puerperal fever. "God didn't preserve him from that misfortune," deKruif. p. 53, wrote angrily. "It's seventy years now since Semmelweiss wrote that wistful happy prophecy. Yet every year in our land seven thousand mothers are killed - there's no other word for it - by somebody's failure to practice this forgotten Hungarian's simple art of keeping out blood-poisoning death... by cleanliness. [I]n our land... childbed fever today is a medical scandal." The quotation "[he] raised a storm of hostile argument..." is from Guthrie, p. 319. Oliver Wendell Holmes, Sr. (1809-1894) was 34 when he made the speech, and 84 when he commented on "the little army of microbes" which supported his position. Sources for quotations: "I have had good days, because God gives strength...", ACVR to children, July 30, 1866, JAH-HOPE; "[She] is in reasonably good health although...", ACVR to Phelps, May 4, 1869, JAH-HOPE; "Mrs. Van Raalte is suffering...", ACVR to Phelps, March 12, 1871, JAH-HOPE. The persecution of separatist ministers and their families in the Netherlands is discussed in Chapter Two, and sources are listed in endnotes there. Van Hinte, p. 249, is a source for the complaint about too much laughter in the Van Raalte home; for information about Jacob Vander Meulen and William Visscher see *Visscher*, and Bruins 1995. William Visscher's story is admirable, but tragic; his mother's diary recounts it. "Our son went to Grand Rapids to confer with Dominie Vander Meulen and ask his advice. He came home the 13th of July and then went to consult Dr. Phelps. It had always been his intention to be a missionary and now he wanted to study medicine for a year before he went out as a missionary. Dr. Phelps was wholeheartedly in favor of this plan. He had always been a good friend of our son and the action by Classis had upset him terribly and now he was willing to help all he could. He thought it would be well for him to go to Albany to study medicine. …We regularly had a letter from Willem every week and sometimes two… Now [in January] we didn't hear from him. …We hadn't had a letter for two weeks… that afternoon Dr. Phelps and an elder came to see us. 'God, who acts according to His own good pleasure and gives no accounting of His acts, has taken your son unto Himself - you will never see him on earth again but you will see him in heaven.' He had died Sunday February 11th, 1972, a victim of smallpox. He had requested the minister with whom he was staying not to write to us for fear we might become alarmed." Quotations and sources for information include "the brunt of the hardship of pioneering…" Schoolland, p. 110; "half wolf, half man, and 'tother half saw mill", May, p 33; Cappon's emigration, Pieters, p. 39-40; "bake a good cake…", comment from CVR included in ACVR to Ben, May 4, 1869, JAH-HHT. The story about bread appears in several sources including Van Hinte, p. 224 and Bratt, p. 27. Information about Christina Van Raalte's musical ability is provided by Dosker, "she could sing so sweetly…", and Pieters. Sources for quotations include "although Mrs. Van Raalte was brought up to a life of refinement…", Pieters, p. 166; "I thank God that my wife without hesitation…", ACVR translated by Lucas 1947, p. 27; "there were very few musical instruments…", Van Hinte, p. 249. The colony's first marriage, the wedding of Lambert Floris and Jantjen Meijering on July 25, 1847, is described in Pieters, p. 107 and Van Hinte, p. 245. (Note that there are variant spellings of Meijering/Meijerink.) Van Hinte states, p. 1042, that Versteeg is incorrect in stating that the first marriage in the colony was the wedding of Hendrik Michmershuizen and Hendrika Rozendom, which was conducted in August. (Some other sources have repeated the error.) There is a minor error in Van Hinte's book: separate index entries are given to "Mrs. A. C. Van Raalte (Christina Johanna De Moen)" and "C. J. Van Raalte." The latter has a single listing, as one of the signers of the wedding certificate. The two are, however, the same; Mrs. Van Raalte often signed as a witness at the marriage services her husband performed, and her typical signature was "C. J. Van Raalte." The information that she chaired the committee to decorate Pillar Church is from *De Hollander*, January 13, 1858. Sources for information include Helena Winter, Christina Van Raalte's talent for playing the piano and singing; the Van Raalte home and its setting, *Hope Alumni Magazine*, first issue, 1948, p. 10; purchases of trees and fruit-bearing bushes, Schoolland, pp. 127-128; Scholte and his second wife, Maria Hendrika Elisabeth Krantz Scholte, Oostendorp, pp. 133-134 and 173, and Rietveld. The quotations, "Scholte and his wife have reached such disagreement…" and "to encourage his wife, the Dominie pictured…", are taken from Rietveld, p. 143, who notes that the report, though "undoubtedly exaggerated,… contained the truth of Mareah's [Maria's] unwillingness to leave." "The death of his wife was the hardest thing …" and "Oh, if only I could rest my head…" are quoted from Dosker.

CHAPTER TWELVE: "The Fire King has devastated nearly our entire City, throwing men, women and children upon the charities of the world." The title quotation is taken from the Report of the Common Council, Holland Michigan, October 27, 1871, JAH-HHT, excerpted from a series of resolutions passed by the council after the fire, shown, boxed, later in this chapter. The style of the *Holland City News*, evidenced in the editorial from the newspaper's first issue, used as an illustration at the beginning of this chapter, was not unique to Holland or the middle west. The *New-York Daily Times,* soon thereafter retitled the *New York Times*, began publication in September 18, 1851, with "an editorial, one that fittingly announced the paper's arrival in the first edition. It was rather cozily titled, 'A Word About Ourselves'", Shepard, p. 18. Two main sources for information about the fire are Bruins 1971, and Van Schelven. The chapter includes several archived excerpts from *Visscher*. Quotations used in the chapter include "resulted from a lack of concern…", Dunbar & May, p. 348; "what with wooden buildings…", Pieters, p. 156; "the importance to the settlers of this regulation is evident…", Pieters, pp. 156-157. (Note the minor error on p. 156, dating the *Volksvergadering* session as February 8, rather than February 7; Pieters gives the date correctly on p. 197.) *Volksvergadering* minutes are archived, JAH-HHT. A special election to set a 1% property tax to purchase a fire engine was held on October 28, 1867; the tax was agreed to. "The City has a very good fire apparatus…" is from Mayor Cappon's report to the Common Council; see the boxed quotation in Chapter Ten, and endnotes for that section. For descriptions of early fire engines, and the gradual switch to steam-propelled engines, see Lyons. For information about weather and the effect on crops in the summers of 1870 and 1871, see Dunbar & May, p. 349; Lucas 1955b, p. 311; and *Visscher*. Information about the Chicago and Peshtigo fires is taken from Clevely, Lyons, and encyclopedias; the quotation, "Peshtigo, White Rock, Forestville… the names read like a roll call", is from Clevely, p. 136. For a useful article describing crown fires, see *National Geographic, 190 (30)*, September 1996, especially p. 125. Quotations include "so deep and dismal…", Clevely, p. 120; "the greater part of the southwest addition…", Van Schelven. in Lucas, 1955a, p. 2; "much attendant danger…", *Visscher*; "the townspeople turned out *en masse* to fight fires…", and "barely singed", Bruins 1971, p. 292 and p. 293; "the fire got over…", *Memorials of the Grand River Valley*, p. 472, JAH-HHT, Van Schelven. Charles Post's letter is archived, JAH-HHT. Bruins 1971 gives information about the death of Sarah Ooms Tolk, p. 295, and the destruction of Third Church and the tannery. p. 292. "From thence on, the devastating fire fiend…" is from Van Schelven, in Lucas 1955a, p. 2; the quotation from Van Raalte, "With our Dutch tenacity and our American experience,…", is from the same source, p. 5. "After finishing our labors in Muskegon…", is from Van Raalte's letter to the *Christian Intelligencer,* published November 2, 1871, JAH-HOPE. Information about Van Raalte's fundraising is taken from Bruins, 1971 and 1991. The donation of blankets by William Visscher is reported in his mother's diary, *Visscher,*. Reporting his energetic generosity illustrates the problem of whether, and when, to use anglicized forms of names. The diarist always refers to her son as Willem; however, names in the younger generation became anglicized quickly. It was William Visscher who served in the Civil War, and William Visscher whose name is listed in *The Milestone* (Willard Wichers, editor), along with Gerrit John Kollen's, as a member of Hope's third graduating class. The quotation "Cappon insured…" is from "A Taste of Holland," by Larry Wagenaar, JAH-HOPE. Estimated losses and issues of insurance coverage are discussed in Van Schelven and Bruins 1971; the latter source, p. 297, gives information about the Ebenezer Society debate; information about the Ebenezer fund is from Elton Bruins. Van Raalte's letters to Phelps, "a few remarks: Today Governor Baldwin was here…", November 2, 1871, and "I must go forward, or give up…", ACVR to Phelps, October 23, 1971, are archived, JAH-HOPE.

CHAPTER THIRTEEN: "God's temporal deliverances are many; each settlement and family has a history of its own."
The title quotation is taken from Albertus Van Raalte's speech at the twenty-fifth anniversary celebration (the Ebenezer celebration) of the founding of the colony; JAH-HHT; it has been adapted; "God's temporal deliverances *were* many" is the original version. Information about the ten children of Albertus and Christina Van Raalte, given in a series of boxes and elsewhere throughout the chapter, is drawn from genealogies, obituaries, and family letters. Published information about their children and grandchildren is sparse, and some of what has been printed is incorrect. There are several reasons for the mistakes. Some are the result of typographical or clerical errors (dates are particularly subject to misstatement), typographical errors in obituaries include a headline that one of the descendants died of "heat trouble," and an oddity in Mary Kollen's obituary, where her first name is never mentioned and the headline refers to the death of "Mr. [sic] G. Kollen." In this family, names also pose a challenge. Albertus Van Raalte was the son of Albertus Van Raalte, father of Albertus Van Raalte and grandfather of Albertus Van Raalte. The statement (in Schoolland) that Van Raalte's son became a minister is incorrect; but a younger son also named his son Albertus Van Raalte and that grandchild of Albertus Van Raalte did become a minister. In all branches of the family the same names tended to be used repeatedly, and when children died in infancy, the next child of the same sex was often given the name of the child who had died, causing confusion in genealogical listings. In addition, inaccurate statements have been printed, and faulty inferences made, when information is drawn from a single letter. Marriages and resulting name changes add to the complexity, as do name similarities: for example, the wife of Dirk B. K. Van Raalte (son of Dirk B. K. Van Raalte and grandson of Albertus Van Raalte) was named Christine, thus becoming, by marriage, yet another Christine Van Raalte. Primary sources, when available are the most reliable; e.g., different birth months are given in genealogies for Mina's third child; an inscription on the back of the baby photograph shown in this chapter proves which is correct. The Chicago fire made sad havoc...", is quoted from the *Christian Intelligencer*, November 2, 1871, JAH-HOPE, part of a series of news items about the Chicago fire, published in the same issue as Van Raalte's letter about the fire in Holland. (The section about destruction of newspaper offices is preceded by an announcement that "Mayor Mason, of Chicago, has issued a proclamation appointing Sunday, October 29th, as a day of fasting, humiliation, and prayer.") Henry Dosker wrote that "the man who destroyed all his private papers before his death did not concern himself much with what people would say abut him after his death. He knew he had done what he could and he left the future to God and to the workers that would be living then. Van Raalte was concerned more for the judgment of God than that of the people." (It was not possible for him to destroy all his correspondence, a fact for which the authors are grateful.) The story about Christina Van Raalte and bread-making is told in Chapter Eleven, and sources are cited in endnotes there; the quotation, "Dirk has no desire or courage...", is used in Chapter Eight and discussed there and in endnotes for that chapter. Civil war correspondence of Ben and Dirk Van Raalte provides information from which Dirk's courage during the war can be inferred. Quotations include "The boys were very bitter against me...", Van Vleck to ACVR, July 1859, from Ulsterville NY, CCA-ACVR; "Write and let me know how the rye looks and how the horses are doing...", postscript in a letter from Ben to ACVR, February 4, 1864, JAH-HHT; "when the bridegroom was an infant, he, the dominie...", is archived, *Post*. "There is what seems to me a fascinating problem about Albertus...", a letter from the first author to her colleagues, early in the process of researching documents for this book. "Geliefde Dirk: The reminder that you have reached the age of thirty...", ACVR to Dirk, February 27, 1874, CCA-ACVR. Information about Mina Oggel's first and last children is sparse; *Visscher*, archived, is a useful source: "She had only one daughter and had lost two small sons and a girl, or rather they had preceded her to heaven" is quoted in Chapter Ten. Information about the daughter who was born and died during the Civil War and the daughter of the same name who survived is well documented in genealogies and the Civil War correspondence; the early deaths of two sons, the Oggels' first and fourth children, is inferred from *Visscher*, genealogies, and correspondence: "our Oggelje" - our little Oggel - was the first child, since that letter (referenced below) was written in 1861. Information about Pieter Oggel's career is from Wynand Wichers 1968, and correspondence, including ACVR to Giles Van de Wal, June 29, 1862, CCA-ACVR. "Here we are in that nice, cold, distant Pella..." is a letter from ACVR to Dirk, February 7, 1861, CCA-ACVR, while the Van Raaltes, with their daughter-in-law Helena and grandson Albertus IV, were visiting there. "Annatje" - Annie - was the Van Raaltes' youngest daughter, then four and half years old. Information about Dirk's legislative career - like much other state information - is limited not only because of the loss of newspaper records in the Holland fire of 1871, but also because of the destruction of state records, through arson, in this century. An employee in the records department in the Lewis Cass building, believing that a criminal record would disqualify him for service in the Korean War, set a small fire in his office, where records were kept on microfiche. The fire was started during lunch hour on a payday, so many people were out of the building long enough for the fire to become a dangerous blaze; it burned for two days, requiring the fire departments of four cities to fight it; two floors of the Cass Building were destroyed, along with most state records. (This account was given to the first author by Lee Barnett, state archivist.) The description of Dirk's oratory, "with his ringing voice and fine command of English..." is from a newspaper article quoted in Schoolland. The invitation from Dirk Van Raalte to a reception on the occasion of his sister Mary's marriage is archived, CCA-ACVR; Mary Kollen's photograph is from a composite picture of members of the Holland Women's Literary Club, JAH-HHT. The quotations about Gerrit Kollen, "Van Raalte came to the farm house...", and "Gerrit J. Kollen, LL.D., are from Pieters, p. 137, and Vennema, p. 295. Two letters from ACVR to John Garretson, "Our dear youngest child...", April 18, 1854, and "My dear wife has got a baby...", October 16, 1856, are archived RCA-BDM. Ann and John Kleinheksel's third son's name is spelled in various records as John Lewis and John Louis, with the former predominating. The quotations about Allie Van Raalte are taken from his obituary; the quotation, "the little Van Raalte sleeps with me. He is a precious talker", is from ACVR to Dirk, February 27, 1874, CCA-ACVR; information about the ordination of the Reverend Albertus C. Van Raalte, Dirk's older son, is from the *Holland City News*, June 14, 1914. The boxed excerpt about the death of Christine Van Raalte Gilmore is based on information from her obituary in the *Holland City News*, April 13, 1933 (died April 12, 1933); the headlines are exact quotations. Additional obituaries which are sources, from the *Holland City News* except as noted, include those simulated: Frank Edwin Gilmore, February 22, 1879 (died February 13, 1879), and Margaret Anna Gilmore, March 1, 1879 (died February 21, 1879); those quoted: Teunis Keppel, July 4, 1896 (died June 27, 1896), and Albertus C. Van Raalte IV, June 23, 1932 (died June 17, 1932); and those noted or used as sources for information: Will Gilmore, April 26, 1884 (died April 24, 1884), Mina Keppel, January 30, 1897 (died January 22, 1897), Mary Van Raalte Kollen, March 16, 1905 (died March 15, 1905); Vera Kleinheksel, February 3, 1910 (died February 2, 1910), Dirk Van Raalte, February 17, 1910 (died February, 12,

1910), Helena Van Raalte, September 21, 1910 (died September 19, 1910), Gerrit Kollen, September 9, 1915 (died September 5, 1915), John Kleinheksel, June 15, 1916 (died June 11, 1916), Ben Van Raalte, August 16, 1917 (died August 14, 1917), Raalte Gilmore, June 23, 1932 (died June 17, 1932). O. S. Reimold, April 19, 1962 (died April 12, 1962) and Estelle Kollen Pelgrim, from the *Holland Sentinel*, August 2, 1984 (died July 30, 1984). Of all the chapters, this has been the one hardest to part from. There are many more answers to be sought, and stories to be told. One quotation about family life which was excluded, with reluctance, is a charming statement about intergenerational family gatherings from Grace Visscher's diary. JAH-HHT: "It was a busy time for us having guests in our home and the little darling of a baby made the most work. "

CHAPTER FOURTEEN: "He was the virtuoso orator of God's word." The title quotation is taken from Dosker, quoted in Van Hinte, p. 434. The drawings used as opening illustrations for the chapter are Numbers Eight and Six in the First National Bank's Heritage series of drawings, used by permission of the bank (now First of America); notes on the Orphan House drawing are titled, "Out of Holland's first Community Chest was built an orphan house that was never used." Sources for this chapter include Classis *Holland Minutes*, Dosker, and Pieters, chapter VI, "Religious Life of the Settlers": also archived diary excerpts and reminiscences: *Frederiks*; *Langdon*, and *Visscher*. Maxine Hopkins Robberts' account appears on the first page of *Hope Church Historical Booklet: Our Time for Rededication*. The quotation beginning "un the summer of 1847, the people of Holland…" is from Pieters, pp. 114-116; "worship services were held in the open air …" is from Versteeg, p. 178. The Michmershuizen-Rozendom marriage is described in Versteeg, pp. 178-179, and mentioned in a footnote in Van Hinte, p. 1 042. The two sources give different spellings for the groom's middle name; Versteeg's spelling has been used in the text. The error made in some sources in identifying this as the colony's first wedding is discussed in the endnotes for Chapter Eleven. The boxed excerpt "This is to certify…" is a translation of the actual marriage certificate; note Christina Van Raalte's signature as witness. The story about Professor Clarisse and Van Raalte's preaching before fellow students at Leiden appears in many biographies, including Dosker and Pieters; the quotation, "preached an excellent sermon that astonished his professor…" , is from Pieters, p. 161. The text notes, "the words of the Bible were in his mind as well as in his heart"; the style of the Bible was also in Van Raalte's letter writing: note the frequent use of colons (:) as punctuation in Biblical excerpts and in his letters. The story about Van Raalte condemning those who had taken the maple sap trays is told in Pieters, p. 95 and Reenders, and the quotation, "Dominie Van Raalte so worded his sermon…" is from Reenders, p. 209. Information about Cornelius Vander Meulen is taken from his biography, written by his son Jacob, in Lucas 1955a, pp. 361-371; the quotations, "he had made a promise, after the death of his two children…" and "for the second time in his life, he lost…", are from that source, p. 370; the story of the children's burial is given in Cornelius Van Loo's biography of Jannes Van De Luyster, Lucas 1955a, pp. 388-405; the quotation, "It is enough, God will know his own" is from that source, p. 404. The sermon at the funeral of the boy who drowned in Black Lake is described in Dosker. Henry Post's letter to J. S. Bussing, "Enclosed is thirteen Dollars…", February 13, 1851, is archived, RCA-BDM; and Post's letter to ACVR, "I promised to write you on the subject of my religious feelings…", May 9, 1858, is archived CCA-ACVR. Information about founding members of Hope Church is from *Hope Church Historical Booklet*. Other quotations include the description of Dirk, "the same old scoffer and teaser", Christine to Ben, May 3, 1869, JAH-HOPE; "that you labor diligently…", ACVR to Ben, November 14, 1854, JAH-HHT, (a longer excerpt from this letter is given below: "…another matter, my child…"); "you must understand my language or you will be eternally lost…", ACVR to Ben, November 14, 1859, JAH-HHT, (longer excerpt given below: "Benjamin, I often think about you…"); "consider for a moment that you are a sinful being…", ACVR to Ben, May 4, 1869, JAH-HHT, (longer excerpt given below: "I felt the need to write a hastily composed letter…"), ACVR to Ben, JAH-HHT. The original of Van Raalte's speech to the Reunion of the 25th Michigan infantry, in English in Van Raalte's handwriting, is archived, CCA-ACVR; "it was as a pastor that Van Raalte was best loved…" is from Pieters, p. 175.

CHAPTER FIFTEEN: "Oh beautiful for patriot dream that sees beyond the years." The title quotation is taken from Katherine Lee Bates' patriotic hymn, used as the chapter's opening illustration. A Dutch version - "Schoon zijn uw heem'len uitgebreid op velden govend graan…" by B. D. Dykstra - is found in Lagerwey, pp. 256-257; readers who compare it with the first stanza of Bates will find it sing-able. Photographs in this chapter are by Lou Schakel. Boxed excerpts are archived: *Brown, Cahill,* and *Visscher*. "He lived for his people, planned conscientiously…", is from Dosker, which is also the source, with local newspapers, for the description of Albertus Van Raalte's death, including quotations. Information about Cornelius Vander Meulen is from his son Jacob's biography in Lucas 1955a, and local newspapers of the time. "It was the most beautiful of our beautiful fall days… " is from Dosker. Information about the funeral is from newspapers of the time, and the *Christian Intelligencer*, JAH-HOPE, as well as from Dosker; about the Masonic controversy, from Bruins, 1983 and 1995, Chapter III, "Troubled Days"; (for information about such controversy nationally, see Butterfield, p. 94); about the separation of Pillar Church from the American Dutch Reformed denomination, Bruins 1977, 1983, and 1995. "Van Raalte's moderating presence was gone after 1876…", is from Bruins, 1983, p. 61; the quotation from Doesburg, "a disgrace to the city and especially to that church…", is cited in Bruins, 1995, p. 33. Information about the presidency of Hope College after the resignation of Philip Phelps is taken from Stegenga and Wynand Wichers, 1968. The statement, "we need to read about heroes," was made to the first author in an early conversation about the book by a friend of Hope College. The quotation from Willa Cather, "The history of every country begins in the heart of a man or woman" is from her novel, *O Pioneers*, part II, chapter 4. The picture caption, *"De separatistenleider in de provincie Overijssel en de "Mozes en Aäron" figuur …,"* appears in Roetman, p. 187. Bruins, *Historic Hope College: A Guide for a Walking Tour of the Campus.* (Hope College), p. 9 notes, "On April 28, 1980, Van Raalte Hall was totally destroyed by fire. Fundraising for its construction began in 1897, the year the City of Holland was celebrating its 50th anniversary dedication." Information about the history of Van Raalte Hall is taken from an interview with Dr. John Hollenbach, professor emeritus at Hope College, whose first faculty office and classrooms were in the building, and who supervised efforts to salvage documents after the fire. The beautiful quotations, "After him was no one like him…", and "When people were angry at him, he smiled…", are, respectively, from Dosker and Versteeg.

Name Index

* pictured on page 194, at the beginning of Chapter Thirteen

Note: At some points in the text, people are referred to by a description or shown in a picture, but not referred to by name. Thus Captain Tully Crosby, for example, has three Index entries, although on two of those pages he is referred to only as the captain of the ship on which the Van Raaltes sailed to America; and Renke DeVries, pictured in Chapter Eight with a Dutch-American patriotic song, has an Index entry for that page. Family members are often referred to in the text by childhood nicknames; for example, "Little Chrisje #3" is Albertus III's second child (Christina Johanna Van Raalte Van Putten), seen as an older woman with daughters of her own in the family pictures on page 194. *Readers who have information to share about members of the Van Raalte family are encouraged to write to the authors.*

Topic Index

248

Afterword

The authors begin their acknowledgments by thanking each other. No one of us could have produced this book without the others as partners. The process has been an exciting, learning-filled time, and we finish with a deepened appreciation of each other as colleagues.

Heartfelt, enthusiastic thanks are due to Tom Renner, for knowledge coupled with great patience as he guided the publication process. Mark Cook's scholarship and skill in preparing maps, and Lou Schakel's artist's eye in providing photographs are greatly appreciated. Graphic artist Rich Nienhuis designed a cover to do our subject proud. We are grateful for the expertise of the talented staff at Holland Litho.

We thank also Greg Olgers, for keeping news about the book in the press while it has been in process and in press, and for his eagle eye in proofreading; Ellie Dekker, of the A. C. Van Raalte Institute, for assistance in finding and translating documents; Lori Trethewey, for providing cheerful and efficient liaison with the Joint Archives; Elizabeth McKee Williams and Jennie G. Jacobson, for historical and scientific knowledge, and research at state libraries; Alex Lignac and Toon van der Pas, for their bilingual talents; Jodie Grabill, for her expertise and diligence in obtaining and checking resources; Theresa Hansen, for willing and efficient participation in checking clerical details; Karsten Voskuil, for providing a rich compilation of documents relating to the Van Raalte family and for his search of area English language newspapers for references to Holland; and Jessica Owen and Amanda Black, for their assistance in locating archived materials.

Helena Winter, Del and Trudy Van der Haar, and John Hollenbach have been generous in sharing time, documents and knowledge. We thank them, and everyone who has encouraged our efforts.

Finally, we are grateful to our subject, Albertus C. Van Raalte, who was not only "a man mighty in words and deeds," but a person whose deeds are so admirable and whose words so beautiful that we find our lives changed for the better by coming to know him.

Once having decided upon him, the more I found out while pursuing his traces through the chronicles and genealogies, the more he offered.

Historian Barbara Tuchman, in her essay, "Biography as a prism of history," p. 82, commenting on the fourteenth century hero, Enguerrand de Coucy, subject of her book, A Distant Mirror.

Errata

for *Albertus C. Van Raalte, Dutch Leader and American Patriot*
Jeanne M. Jacobson, Elton J. Bruins, and Larry J. Wagenaar

p. v, l. 14	*for* patriot's dream *read* patriot dreams;
p. 1, l. 2	*delete* by;
p. 2, l. 16	*for* northeastern *read* northwestern;
p. 17, l. 22	*for* Afgescheiding *read* Afscheiding;
p. 17, l. 44	*for* Afgescheiding *read* afgescheiden;
p. 18, l. 5	*for* March 15 *read* March 11;
p. 18, l. 7	*for* Afscheidenen *read* afgescheiden;
p. 20, l. 5	*for* Afgescheiding *read* afgescheiden;
p. 23, l. 31	*for* longlasting *read* long lasting;
p. 24, l. 40	*for* Afgescheiding *read* Afscheiding;
p. 35, l. 23	*for* eight *read* seven;
p. 117, l. 9	*for* August 22 *read* August 14;
p. 119, l. 38	*for* dominie *read* Dominie;
p. 169, l. 23	*for* June 6 *read* June 30;
p. 179, l. 11	*for* March 15 *read* March 11;
p. 183, l. 10	*for* years *read* hours;
p. 195, l. 2	*for* four *read* five, for ten *read* eleven, for seven *read* eight;
p. 195, l. 3	*for* three *read* four;
p. 197, l. 33	*for* July 1 *read* January 15;
p. 197, l. 37	*for* 1858 *read* February 2, 1859;
p. 197, l. 40	*for* March 3, 1866 *read* June 3, 1867;
p. 199, l. 20	*for* April *read* August 18;
p. 200, l. 45	*for* June 27 *read* July 4;
p. 202, l. 14	*for* February 10 *read* February 12;
p. 202, l. 34	*for* March 31 *read* March 30;
p. 202, l. 38	*for* Gilmore, born *read* Gilmore, born September 1871;
p. 203, l. 21	*for* September 21 *read* September 14;
p. 203, photo caption	*for* Mary Van Raalte Kollen *read* Mary Diekema Kollen;
p. 204, l. 27	*for* tenth *read* eleventh and for seventh *read* eighth;
p. 204, l. 29	*for* had died *read* had died July 11, 1855;
p. 204, l. 33	*for* May 5 *read* April 5;
p. 204, l. 35	*for* February 2 *read* February 23;
p. 209, l. 27	*for* Grijpmast *read* Grijmoet;
p. 228, l. 2	*for* govend *read* golvend;
p. 232, l. 37 & 39	*for* ten Zythoff and tenZythof *read* tenZythoff;
p. 243, l. 61	*for* June 14 *read* June 19;
p. 244, l. 1	*for* September 19 *read* September 18.